D0929876

THE UNVEILING OF ARABIA

AMS PRESS
NEW YORK

THE MOSQUE OF THE TOMB OF THE PROPHET AT MEDINA
Photo E.N.A.

Fr.

THE
UNVEILING OF ARABIA

*The Story of Arabian Travel
and Discovery*

BY

R. H. KIERNAN

GEORGE G. HARRAP & CO. LTD.
LONDON   BOMBAY   SYDNEY
1937

Library of Congress Cataloging in Publication Data

Kiernan, Reginald Hugh, 1900-
    The unveiling of Arabia.

    Reprint of the 1937 ed. published by G. G. Harrap,
London.
    Bibliography: p.
    Includes index.
    1. Arabia—Discovery and exploration. 2. Arabia—
Description and travel. 3. Explorers. I. Title.
DS204.5.K5   1975   915.3'04   70-180353
ISBN 0-404-56285-X

Reprinted from an original copy in the collection of the
Wilbur L. Cross Library, University of Connecticut

From the edition of 1937, London
First AMS edition published in 1975
Manufactured in the United States of America

AMS PRESS INC.
NEW YORK, N. Y. 10003

PREFACE

ARABIA and its inhabitants were not revealed to the West by a systematic process of discovery, each explorer adding to the work of his forerunner. Information was gained, forgotten or lost, and later recovered and supplemented; it was a haphazard process, effected under conditions of danger from nature and mankind by a long series of greatly varied personalities, who seem to have had but two qualities in common—curiosity and courage. I have tried not simply to summarize their work and, as Hogarth did so ably a generation ago, attempt the solution of geographical problems. Most of the knots have now been unravelled or boldly cut. Here the attempt is to link the story of exploration to the history of the land and show something of Arabia as the great explorers saw it. To avoid repetition, where they covered the same ground I have concentrated the account on the thing each did best, as, for instance, Burckhardt showed Mecca, the Meccans, and all the great streams of pilgrimage; the precise "Ali Bey" the temple at Mecca; while Burton is given most space on his way to the Hejaz and at Medina, where Burckhardt was too ill to exercise his normal thoroughness. In this way, I hope, a varied picture has been drawn of Arabia and Arabian travel throughout the ages, with an assessment of results and their comparative value.

Lawrence wrote that all theories of Arabic transliteration were "rot," and in practice developed a fine impartiality in spelling. From a complete lack of qualification to judge the merits of any of the systems, I have spelled names simply as they are often encountered in books and on maps, and at least they are spelled consistently. In the case of quotations, however, the explorer's own rendering has been left to stand; for the look of his words, I feel, is of the savour of his style, and comes even to be a part of his personality, to the reader.

I wish to thank Major R. E. Cheesman and Mr Douglas Carruthers for the use of photographs, and Messrs G. Routledge and the author, Mr H. A. R. Gibb, for permission to quote from *The Travels of Ibn Battuta*.   I am grateful to the Reverend Father Rector and the Librarian of Stonyhurst College for giving me access to Maffei's *Historiæ indicæ* and for providing information regarding W. G. Palgrave.

R. H. K.

CONTENTS

CHAPTER   PAGE

I. INTRODUCTORY   11

II. ARABIA IN THE ANCIENT WORLD   19

III. MEDIEVAL ARABIAN TRAVEL   40

IV. A RENAISSANCE ADVENTURER   54

V. THE GREAT AFONSO D'ALBOQUERQUE   67

VI. THE FIRST ENGLISHMEN IN ARABIA   76

VII. THE FIRST ENGLISHMAN IN THE HOLY CITIES   83

VIII. A DANISH EXPEDITION   88

IX. WAHHABIS AND A SPANIARD   104

X. THE UNVEILING OF MECCA AND MEDINA   118

XI. A BRITON MAKES THE PILGRIMAGE   162

XII. EXPLORERS IN OMAN AND HADHRAMAUT   193

XIII. THE FIRST TRANS-ARABIAN JOURNEYS   224

XIV. STRANGER THAN FICTION   242

XV. DOUGHTY AND THE BLUNTS   268

XVI. TWENTIETH-CENTURY EXPLORERS   289

XVII. THE EMPTY QUARTER   312

BIBLIOGRAPHY   341

INDEX   345

ILLUSTRATIONS

PAGE

THE MOSQUE OF THE TOMB OF THE PROPHET AT MEDINA *Frontispiece*

THE MOSQUE BUILT ON THE SITE OF ABRAHA'S CHRISTIAN
    CHURCH AT SANA   38

A TOWN IN YEMEN, SHOWING CITADEL AND MOSQUE   39

BEDOUIN OF THE HEJAZ   60

A YEMENITE JEWESS WEARING BRIDAL HEADDRESS   61

PILGRIMS PASSING THROUGH THE MECCA GATE AT JIDDA   80

SANA: A GENERAL VIEW   81

BAURENFEIND'S SKETCH OF THE YEMEN COFFEE HILLS   96

THE MARKET-PLACE AT SANA   97

PART OF A PILGRIM CARAVAN ON THE WAY FROM JIDDA TO
    MECCA   112

JEWS OF SANA   113

A GENERAL VIEW OF TAIZZ   128

THE KAABA AND COURT OF THE GREAT MOSQUE AT MECCA   129

JOHANN LUDWIG BURCKHARDT   144

THOUSANDS OF PILGRIMS IN THE VALLEY OF MUNA, NEAR
    MECCA   145

PART OF THE PILGRIM CAMP AT MUNA   158

VIEW OVER RIYADH, NEAR THE ENTRANCE TO THE PALACE   159

SIR RICHARD BURTON   176

MEDINA: A GENERAL VIEW   177

A FRANKINCENSE-TREE   190

A TOWN IN THE WADI DUWAN   191

HAJAREIN   208

WADI HADHRAMAUT, LOOKING NORTH-EAST OF TERIM   209

GEORGE AUGUSTUS WALLIN   240

AN INHABITANT OF TEIMA   241

CAMEL GUARDS OF THE IMAM OF YEMEN   270

PILGRIMS BEING TRANSPORTED FROM THE STEAMER TO THE
    DOCK AT JIDDA   271

9

PAGE

Douglas Carruthers on a "Sharari" Camel 298

The Main Wadi of Hadhramaut nearing the Sea 299

Shibam 308

Major R. E. Cheesman at Bahrein on his Return from the Jabrin Expedition 309

MAPS

Arabia 13

The Roman Invasion of Arabia 27

Jourdain's Route in Yemen 79

Journeys in Northern and Western Arabia 137

Wellsted's Route in Oman 197

The Province of Hadhramaut, showing Explorers' Routes 215

Dhofar, showing Bent's Route 221

Sadlier's Route 229

Routes followed by Palgrave and Colonel Pelly 255

Doughty's Route 273

Routes of Four Modern Explorers 297

Bertram Thomas's Route in 1930 319

Bertram Thomas's and Philby's Routes across the Rub' al Khali 330

CHAPTER I
INTRODUCTORY

The Aarab, in their suffering manner of life (their cup of life is drawn very low, and easily stirred at the dregs), which eagers the blood and weakens the heart . . .

CHARLES M. DOUGHTY, *Travels in Arabia Deserta*

ARABIA lies between the great land-masses of Africa and Asia, from which it is divided only by long inlets from the Indian Ocean. Caravans have crossed the land and ships have sailed by its shores from the earliest ages, yet until modern times little was known with accuracy of the inhabitants or of the physical features of their country. To the ancient world the peninsula was a region of luxury and fabulous wealth; to the medieval traveller, like Sæwulf of Worcester, it was simply "Arabia, hostile to Christians." At the beginning of the present century, after nearly a hundred and fifty years of determined investigation, the general features and life of the country were known, but hardly a fraction had been mathematically surveyed; astronomical observations were confined to three or four points, and altitudes even on the coast were only approximate. Vast areas in the south, east, and centre were entirely unexplored.

On the outbreak of the Great War at least one-half of existing knowledge was so vague as to be almost useless for any purpose demanding exact information, such as the conduct of a military operation. The British officers concerned with the Arab Revolt were ignorant, for instance, of the precise distance from the Red Sea of the superlatively important Hejaz Railway. When Dr D. G. Hogarth, who had summarized results of Arabian exploration in 1904, attempted the same task in relation to the War, he confessed that the longitude of Medina, the southern terminus of the line, a city famed among Christians and Moslems for thirteen hundred years, was still unknown. This was in 1920. Ten years later there still remained great regions uncrossed by Europeans.

Absolute accuracy in a description of Arabia cannot be achieved within a brief space, for almost every prominent characteristic is modified by a list of exceptions. But the peninsula may be described in general as a plateau falling gently eastward from a mountain range, averaging 5000 feet in height, which runs along its western side at about ten to fifteen miles from the Red Sea. This chain of highlands, beginning in the north with the coastal granites and inland *harra* (lava and volcanic matter) of Midian and Northern Hejaz, and continuing as limestone, gradually rises to 9000 feet and more in Asir and Yemen, at its southern end. Extending round the southern shore to Hadhramaut, the range sinks, and is eventually lost in the sands. But as the coast turns inward to the Persian Gulf highlands rise again in Oman, so that on the west and part of the south and south-east the Arabian hinterland may be said to be masked from the sea.

The next general characteristic is aridity, but Oman has sufficient rain, and Yemen not only receives the moisture from heavy mists rising from the plains, but also catches the rain-bearing south-west monsoon winds before they can penetrate to the interior. Behind the coastal ranges an area equal to England, France, Germany, and Italy must be content with rains carried over the Palestine hills from the Mediterranean, the moisture left in north and east winds which have already passed over arid lands, and with dews. Arabia is thus one of the most waterless lands. It has no true perennial rivers, only *wadis*, the beds of torrents which flow irregularly and are often dry for generations. There are no forests in the land, and only three groups of permanent, spring-fed pools—in Hasa, Kharj, and Aflaj.

From its latitude Arabia is also among the hottest countries, though again exceptions must be made, for the highlands of Yemen have a warm temperate climate, and districts of the centre have a dry, pleasant, and healthy atmosphere. On the coasts of the Red Sea and the Persian Gulf, on the contrary, there is often excessive humidity and temperatures of ninety and a hundred degrees. Though higher temperatures are recorded in other parts of the world, as in Sind and Mesopotamia, the popular impression of great heat in Arabia is

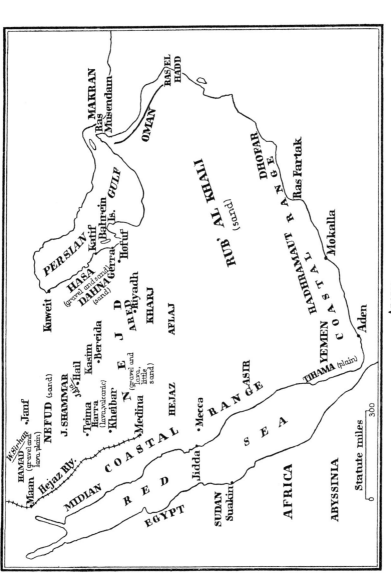

ARABIA

correct, and so, in general, is the idea that Arabia is a desert country.

The main geological formation is of limestone and sandstone. As the latter is easily denuded and disintegrated under conditions of wind, water, and sun, with marked diurnal ranges of temperature, vast sand tracts have been formed over wide areas. In the north is the sand-dune region called Nefud, extending 400 miles from west to east and 200 in breadth, waterless almost entirely, but rich in pasture after the winter rains. The most striking features of the Nefud are the extraordinarily long ridges of sand, divided by valleys sometimes ten or twelve miles wide, and the deep pits in the sands, shaped like a horseshoe, which sometimes reveal the underlying rock.

The southern sand area, the Rub' al Khali, was until the last few years entirely unexplored, and was thought to be similar to the Nefud, but probably marked by gravelly stretches and salt plains. How near conjecture approached actuality will be shown in the following pages. From the Rub' al Khali, a desert covering some 300,000 square miles, an arm of sand about thirty miles wide runs for 400 miles northward on the east of the peninsula. This tract is called the Dahna.

The Nefud, the Rub' al Khali, and the Dahna, with various minor stretches of sand on the west, form a rough border of sands round the heart of Arabia. Beyond this circle on the north is the Hamad, dry desert of gravel and flint relieved by the depression of the Wadi Sirhan and the wells and oases of Jauf and Sakaka.[1] On the east, beyond a region of steppe desert, lie the Hasa coast lands, with hot and cold springs, reservoirs of water, irrigation channels, rich vegetation, and important towns such as Hofuf (population, about 30,000) and the port of Katif. South-east, beyond the desert and the Oman mountains, is the fertile coastal plain of the Batina; south-west is Yemen, well watered and productive.

In certain areas where the sandstone has been protected by lavas, or where there are granite and limestone belts, hills

---

[1] This Hamad area of Northern Arabia is the "Arabia Deserta" of the ancient geographers. "Arabia Petræa" was to them merely the Petra region. The whole of the peninsula was "Felix." The restriction of "Felix" to South-west Arabia began in the Middle Ages.

and mountains appear, with independent precipitation, *wadis*, oases, towns, and settlements. Parts of Arabia within the sand ring are among these hard cores. The granite range of Aja, 100 miles long, in Jebel Shammar, and the lava and granite regions of Western Nejd give rise to settled conditions. The Wadi Rumma, for example, begins in the Kheibar *harra*, and has been known to flow mightily, leaving pools which last for months. The Wadis Hanifa, Sirra, and Dawasir cut this central district, which is marked by many oases and settlements, as in Kasim (Aneiza, population 15,000, and Bereida, population 20,000), Jebel Shammar (Hail, population 20,000), and Ared (Riyadh, population 30,000, the centre from which to-day Ibn Saud rules most of desert Arabia).

The settled districts produce dates and other fruit, wheat, millet, *samn* (clarified butter), indigo, leather-work, mantles, pearls, barley, large white donkeys, gums, frankincense and myrrh, the last of which come from Dhofar, a tropical enclave on the south coast, cut off from the Rub' al Khali by highlands and a region of steppe desert. The trees from which these substances are collected grow also in Hadhramaut, westward of Dhofar. Hadhramaut gives its name to the district's main *wadi*, a valley curving inland from the coast for some 400 miles, and containing the towns of Shibam, Terim, and Seyun, between which and the Arabian Sea lies a high, stony plateau cut by subsidiary *wadis*.

The amount of export in Arabian products is small, but helps to pay for the imports of rice, flour, sugar, and piece-goods, while the balance is met mainly from the money brought in by pilgrims. Outside the towns, large oases, and settlements the life of Arabia is pastoral and nomadic. It is a vast land, with about 7,000,000 people in 1,000,000 square miles. One would have to walk between London and Birmingham six times to equal roughly the distance covered in desert by Bertram Thomas on one of his expeditions. Eighteen times would approximately equal the distance travelled by Captain Shakespear on a journey through every kind of Arabian scenery—sand, gravel, and flint desert, *harra*, and mountain. In this wide territory the sands, steppe, and rocky deserts are the home of the Bedouin.

II

Who first lived in the wilderness none can tell, but Bedouin origins are aptly suggested by the saying that Yemen is the cradle and Iraq the grave of the Arab. It is certain that the Anazeh tribes of Northern Arabia came from Yemen, and south of Mecca there are numerous traces in place-names and tradition of tribes that are now in Nejd, Jebel Shammar, Hamad, Syria, and Iraq. Yemen, with rain and productive soil, was the desirable land; yet it could support only a limited population, so that successive waves of people were pushed out. They could not seek fresh homes along the highlands of the coastal range northward, for there lay Mecca across the path, a city fortified by the public opinion of all Islam. So the emigrant movement set in to the east and north-east. The last oases, springs, and soil of Yemen were held bitterly, but the increasing pressure of fresh waves forced people clinging to the peasant life out into the wilderness, where, in order to live, they adopted the nomadic life, raising flocks of sheep and herds of camels.

The nomads are organized in tribes, each tribe defending its own members and being responsible for the individual's misdeeds. The tribes have their own stretches of country, the *dira*, but are divided into clans over the scattered pastures, pools, wells, *wadis*, and water-holes. The emirs and sheikhs govern paternally, administer justice, levy tribute, and lead the men to battle. Tribal wars were until very recently a common occurrence, and blood-feuds were, and generally are still, part of the order of life. To travel through the district of another tribe the Bedouin secures a *rafik* or *rabia* of that tribe, a sponsor, who accompanies him for a fee and saves him from hostile attentions. The word itself, says Sir Percy Sykes, actually means your (camel) pillion-rider, your friend who will guide and defend you, but from this viewpoint he is "a living passport to his own tribe."

With his sheep and camels the nomad moves from pasture to pasture in the dunes, the bare yellow plain, or the desolate hills. There is no comfort or luxury in his life; he must be content to wander beneath the blazing, empty sky under the eye of God. Just enough water and pasture, brushwood, coffee, coarse tobacco, and, in the words of a post-War traveller, "several young wives, unclean but sportive, with their hair well soaked in camel urine," would be almost a full measure of happiness for the average Bedouin. But it would lack one thing—the element of sport and excitement. This necessity is provided for by the *ghrazzu*, the foray for flocks of sheep or herds of camel. The raiding party may approach the objective by camel, with led horses, on which the actual attack is made while the camels are left with boys. Women and children are spared; men may be slain or merely robbed, according to circumstances. In this way the nomads have fought since before Islam.

The Bedouin character is most difficult to define and assess. The great Arabian travellers have described the peoples of the desert in all their moods and humours and from many angles: Burckhardt with favour, Palgrave with detestation, but Doughty with clearer vision than any. A mere glance at his "Index and Glossary of Arabic Words," a book in itself, is enough to set the mind longing to establish understanding with a people who are smiling speakers, their mouths full of cursing and lies and prayers, easily cast down by derision, timid and ill at ease in the towns, phrenetic in the field, of murderous wildness towards an adversary, their meditations always of treachery; yet who are very tender of other men's opinions, have patience of evil times and of fasting, are mild and forbearing at home, and have in their tents the peace and assurance of Allah.

CHAPTER II

ARABIA IN THE ANCIENT WORLD

There is such an abundance of these aromatics that cinnamon, cassia, and other spices are used by them instead of sticks for firewood.

STRABO, *Geography*

FROM earliest times the Red Sea and the Persian Gulf have made the littoral of the Arabian peninsula easily accessible. These long narrow inlets open to the Arabian Sea, which is marked by regular winds called monsoons, blowing between East Africa and North-west India. From November to March the monsoon comes steadily from the north-east; it is strongest in January. From the end of April to the beginning of October its force is felt from the south-west. Once they were fully realized and rightly employed these winds were of the greatest importance in the opening up of the Middle East and India to Mediterranean, and general European, commercial enterprise.

The Red Sea takes its name from the Greek *erythra*, which means "red." Various explanations have been offered for the name, such as that it commemorates Erythras, a Persian king, or that it was the name applied to Phœnician traders (Red or Sunburned men) who settled in the Bahrein Islands and voyaged round the Arabian coast. Another explanation suggests that the general name Erythræan, applied to eastern seas by the Greeks, originated in Himyar the Red, a ruler in ancient Arabia. The Greeks applied the name originally to the sea between Egypt and the peninsula, and later extended it to all Arabian coastal waters.

Although in the midsummer months a useful north-west wind blew down its entire length, the Red Sea was not popular among the ancient sailors. The summer climate was hot, damp, and unpleasant, while irregular currents and rocks and reefs made progress dangerous, especially for coastal navigation, and the inlet was subject to frequent storms.

19

The earliest explorers of Arabian waters were not the Greeks, but those peoples who dwelt near or within coastwise sailing distance of the peninsula. At least 3500 years before Christ Egyptians sailed and fought in these seas, before powers in the peninsula itself raised barriers against the commercial adventurers of other races. Then Egyptian vessels, and Mesopotamians out of Abu Shahrein, had to shorten their voyages. The Egyptians, however, drove their prows as far as the land of Punt—that is, to Somaliland west of Guardafui —and possibly the Yemen coast. In the Eighteenth Dynasty Queen Hatshepsut sent a great expedition past the Straits of Bab el Mandeb to Somaliland, Socotra, Hadhramaut, and beyond to Dhofar. The Mesopotamians sailed to Oman, and occasionally as far as the African coast. The Phœnicians voyaged to Ophir, which was somewhere on the south coast of Arabia, and before 650 B.C. actually controlled the Persian Gulf trade. Indian vessels also plied in these waters, sailing across to Africa by using the monsoon directly behind them. The Arabians themselves, then as always, made coasting voyages to East Africa, Southern Asia, and the coasts of India.

Though the Greek ships were early seen against the horizons of the Mediterranean, weaving their fringe of towns and trading posts round the lands of the barbarian, none sailed Arabian seas until the end of the sixth century before Christ. Darius Hystaspis, wanting to define the estuary of the Indus, sent out Scylax, a Carian, with a number of Ionian Greeks, about 510 B.C., from somewhere near the modern Attock, in the North-west Frontier Province.

Scylax came into the Indus from the Kabul river, sailed to its mouth and coasted westward, passing the Persian Gulf, until he came to Arsinoë, near Suez. Some of the information about South Arabian trade given by Herodotus may have come from this explorer. While Persian vessels trading round Arabia from Egypt may have been commanded by Greeks, or Greek-owned ships may have sailed the Red Sea by Persian licence, no considerable exploration seems to have been carried out by Greeks; and though references in Aristophanes and Euripides suggest that the idea of Arabia was something definite to the Greek audience, little was generally known, save what had been told by Herodotus. In his pages Arabia was the land of spices, frankincense, myrrh, cassia, cinnamon, and ledanum, products gained for the most part at great peril and difficulty. The trees bearing the frankincense, for example, were guarded by small multicoloured winged serpents, which had to be driven off by the fumes of gum storax. No less difficulty attended the seeker after cassia, who, to approach the shallow lake where it was found, had to cover his entire body with hides, for protection against the winged animals on guard.

But of all the rare products of this strange land of Arabia none required such patience in the garnering as the sticks of cinnamon. These, according to Herodotus, were discovered stuck in the muddy nests of birds on high, inaccessible cliffs. The dealer in cinnamon had to slay oxen, cut up the carcasses, and leave the pieces scattered about below these heights. The birds swooped down for them, carried them up to the distant eyries, and the additional weight caused collapse in the nests, so that the cinnamon fell to the earth.

The gum called ledanum was acquired fairly simply, being gathered from the beards of goats, where it adhered from the bushes on which they browsed. This gum was used in unguents. The whole air of the Arabia of Herodotus was full of sweet odours from rich perfumes and spices. The Greek world saw no picture approaching the actuality of these far lands until the time of Alexander the Great.

The Macedonian penetrated Asia overland, and, reaching the Indus, decided to explore the possibilities of a sea route to the Euphrates. For this purpose his admiral, Nearchus, was detached, and, like Scylax, carried out an exploration from east to west. In the early autumn of 325 B.C. he set out from the Indian coast with more than 5000 men. His report, used by Arrian, writing centuries later, tells of the voyage past Baluchistan and Makran, of the loss of three ships in a great gale, of the savage and primitive inhabitants of the coast, of fish-eaters, whales, and a mermaids' island. At length the fleet saw the great Arabian headland of Ras Musendam. Here, then, Nearchus passed into the Persian Gulf, and after a meeting with Alexander at Gulashkird returned to the fleet and explored Kishm Island and other points along the coast, noting shoals, reefs, headlands, frankincense-trees, "sea hedgehogs" (turtles?), and the pearls of Bahrein. He passed six months in this exploration.

Alexander intended to extend the voyages from the Gulf round the whole coast of Arabia, but such plans were interrupted by his death in 323 B.C. However, preliminary voyages were made by Archias and Androsthenes in thirty-oared vessels, the first touching Bahrein, making measurements of distances, noting the trade of Gerra and the pearling industry, while the second reached the landward end of the Ras Musendam peninsula. A third expedition, led by Hieron, using a thirty-oared ship like his predecessors, reached the gates of the Gulf, but the long, seemingly endless line of the coast beyond Ras Musendam frightened him back. Vessels were also sent down the Red Sea from Suez, reached Yemen beyond the Straits, and learned something of the prosperous southern tribes of Arabia and their trade in aromatics.

Had Alexander lived to be the driving force behind these explorations the full benefit to navigation of the monsoon winds might have been found by Western sailors in his time instead of more than three hundred years later. His motives had arisen from the desire of conquest and knowledge rather than from the pursuit of commercial profit; but those who next came thrusting through Arabian waters were impelled only by hopes of gain.

Ptolemy I sent an expedition, under an admiral named Philo, down the Red Sea. Keeping mainly to the western shore, it brought back specimens of chrysolites and stories of elephants and ivory. The second Ptolemy began a trade between Egypt and the Arabians of Yemen, founded new ports along the western littoral, and sent ships to explore the opposite coast. Ptolemy III suppressed piracy in the Red Sea, and perhaps continued the exploration of the Arabian coast. At the death of this ruler the western seaboard of the peninsula from Akaba to Aden was well known, and much had been learned about Hadhramaut. The Egyptian Greeks had opened trade with Yemen and the opposite African coast.

Meanwhile, on the eastern side of the Arabian peninsula, the troubles following Alexander's death had ended with the rise of the Seleucid monarchs, but the rivalry displayed by Gerra and Parthia prevented their developing trade between Euphrates and Indus by sea. Yet they did contrive to study the coast of Arabia past Gerra and Oman.

So far one has regarded Arabia from the outside, for knowledge of what was happening within the peninsula in these centuries is scanty. References in Greek and Latin writers, Assyrian and South Arabian inscriptions, do not shed much light on the origins, migrations, and changes of the Arabian peoples. Yet there is archæological evidence of early and highly developed civilization. The most important known kingdoms were those of Ma'in, Katabanu, Hadhramaut, and Saba. The Minæan power, which flourished at least as early as 1200 B.C., may have extended even to the northern districts of Arabia. Its chief towns were Ma'in, Karnau, and Yathil, in the neighbourhood of Southern Jauf. It was partly contemporary with the Sabæan kingdom, one of whose queens was said to have visited Solomon about 950 B.C. The capital of Saba was first at Sirwa and then at Marib. About 115 B.C. dominion in this part of the peninsula passed to the Himyarites, a people from the extreme south-west. We know that at this time there was much fighting with Katabanu and Hadhramaut, a country which enjoyed riches from the incense trade and had an advanced civilization. But the ancient writers group all these districts and kingdoms under the title "Sabæan."

While the powers and dynasties of the Middle East were waxing or waning the might of Rome knew only increase. Europe was brought under a single rule, and the eagles were carried to the Nile, the Euphrates, and the borderlands of Arabia, where the Nabathæans of Petra, in the north-west, became vassals of the Empire. Within the dominion of Augustus there was peace, wealth, security, and increasing commercial enterprise, stimulated by the demand in the West for the luxuries of the Orient. Roman capital was placed at the disposal of Greek merchants and seamen, and Red Sea ports like Berenice and Myos Hormos began to pulse more strongly with the traffic of ships and caravans.

African, Indian, and Arabian products, spices, pearls, ivory, gums, perfumes, and precious stones, came in a rising flood to the Mediterranean lands, while Roman money flowed into Arabia and India. This increasing sea trade was subject to the depredations of the Parthians in the Persian Gulf, and on the way to and from the north of the Red Sea lay open to raids from Yemen and Hadhramaut. Where the people of these parts of Arabia, "the Sabæans," acted as middlemen for the Indian sea trade, using Aden as the mart for the Mediterranean-Indian trade, the path of commerce was smoother. But Augustus did not favour the idea of such a profitable status for the South-western Arabians, and decided to introduce them to the iron hand of Rome.

The Romans regarded the Sabæan corner of Arabia as a most prosperous and powerful district. They knew that its wealth arose from agriculture and from the export of aromatics, which were in demand for perfumes, unguents, spices, ointments, death and wedding rites, and religious ceremonies. These substances, and gold, pearls, and precious stones, were carried by sea and land to Egypt, Palestine, and Syria by the Sabæan middlemen. The main land route ran from Dhofar and Hadhramaut to Yemen, northward to Leuke Kome, near the mouth of the Wadi Hamdh, thence to Ælana, on the Gulf of Akaba, and then to Petra, where it branched to Egypt and Syria. As the caravans were open to Arab attack all the way, the local chiefs were paid to organize the routes and provide them with escorts.

The wealth of Saba was undoubtedly exaggerated by hearsay, but the aristocracy and merchants were certainly wealthy, and the remains of city walls, palaces, temples, and engineering works such as the barrage across the Wadi Dena at Marib, forming a vast reservoir for irrigation, are testimony to a rich and advanced civilization.

It seemed to Augustus that the South-western Arabs sold their own wares, and those of the East generally, to Rome at high prices and bought nothing in return. He resolved, therefore, to make their land a dependency of Egypt, control the Red Sea shore of Arabia, and promote a direct trade by sea with India, cutting out the expensive caravan transport and lowering prices in Rome. In the ensuing campaign in the south he had the support of the Nabathæans of Northern Arabia.

Command of the expedition was given to Ælius Gallus with about one-third of the garrison of Egypt, 10,000 men, legionaries and auxiliaries, including 1000 sent by the Nabathæan king and 500 supplied by Herod. From the beginning the Romans seem to have been handicapped by lack of information regarding the country over which they would march and the form of resistance likely to be met. The force was assembled at Arsinoë, near Suez, and Gallus began by wasting time and effort in constructing eighty warships before he learned that Saba had no fighting fleet. Then he built 130 transport vessels and, instead of sailing direct to the Yemen coast, made for Leuke Kome, thus leaving himself a march of 900 miles to the Sabæan capital, Mariaba (Marib). In the fortnight's voyage the shallows and reefs of the Red Sea accounted for many ships, and he was held up for some months at the port of disembarkation by the scurvy and palsy which attacked his men.

In the spring of 24 B.C. he started southward from Leuke Kome, and at once was hampered by lack of water and the roadless wastes. Even where his reception was friendly the country could provide little food. For months, with scanty supplies of water carried by camel, the Roman troops moved through the deserts. As yet they met with no active resistance; the country itself was defeating them. At length, in the valley of the Wadi Nejran, they came to the town of Negrana, which they took and destroyed. When the Romans had advanced by a further week's march the Arabians gave battle, probably on the banks of the Wadi Harid. The Romans flung themselves into the attack with such ferocity that the enemy were easily driven back, and the casualties, numbering 10,000 against only two Romans, suggest a flight in panic.

Following this victory, the Romans took Athlula, which is perhaps Barakish, and Nasca, now Baida. Leaving a garrison in the former place, Gallus moved onward to a place recorded as "Marsyaba," or "Maryama," which he besieged and attacked for six days before he was forced to retire on account of lack of water. The capital, Mariaba, was never reached.[1]

This point, which had taken six months to attain, marks the limit of the Roman effort. Retreating through Negrana and by another arduous march to the coast within Nabathæan territory, Gallus then moved his army, which was probably a considerably diminished force, by sea to Myos Hormos. He then marched to Coptos, and the army was transported down the Nile to Alexandria.

The advance to the south had taken six months; the retirement, though doubtless harassed by the enemy every yard of the way, took only sixty days. Gallus had seen enough of the peninsula to discourage the undertaking of another expedition, and especially were ideas modified regarding its fabled wealth. Actually he had reached only the edge of the richer southern districts.

Despite his failure Gallus had achieved a splendid feat of tactics and organization. The water supply alone must have presented almost insuperable problems, and the *moral* of the troops must have been of the highest order for the army to have returned at all as an organized military force.

The guide and Quartermaster-General of the expedition was Syllæus, Vizier of the Nabathæan king. Had the Roman enterprise succeeded, Petra, the Nabathæan capital, would doubtless have lost a considerable part of its caravan trade. Situated in the wilderness of Edom, a bazaar and caravanserai city, walled, and with an unassailable rock-fortress, it lay on the point of convergence of many trade routes across the Near and Middle East, and was strong enough in the fourth century before Christ to beat off an attack by about 5000 men led by a general of Alexander the Great. Through Gaza it could send the products of the East to Athens and the whole Mediterranean seaboard. The wealth of Petra came mostly by inland

---

[1] Marsyaba may have been a place south-east of Mariaba (Marib), near Harib, and in this case Gallus must have passed his objective at a considerable distance. It seems impossible to trace a correct route for this astonishing march. G. Wyman Bury, whose remarks on the ancient history of Yemen were sometimes inaccurate, was nevertheless closely in touch with local traditions and legends. He believed that Gallus followed the Medina-Mecca pagan-pilgrimage route, bore east through Nejran and the Jauf to avoid the mountain fortresses of Yemen, and was finally halted by the Ans and Madhig tribes.

routes, but the Nabathæans fully realized the value of the Red Sea passage, developed the port of Leuke Kome, and became powerful enough at sea to defeat the navy of Cleopatra. From Yemen by land and sea it traded in great loads of frankincense:

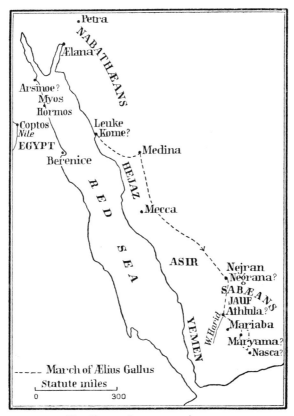

THE ROMAN INVASION OF ARABIA

1000 talents a year were used on the altar of Marduk at Babylon alone, and every prayer, public and private ceremony, required it. No doubt there was anxiety in Petra when the Roman legions marched towards Yemen. Suspicion of Syllæus is aroused when one contrasts the time taken in the advance, for which he was responsible as guide, apparently choosing an indirect route towards the country of the Sabæans, with the speed of the return journey, after the Romans had learned something of the country. But it seems unlikely that he was guilty of treason. He was executed at Rome for various misdeeds, including murder, but this was twenty years after the Arabian venture, and the ruin of the expedition was not charged against him. Treachery, and perhaps even the suspicion of treachery, to a large Roman military force would have brought a swifter retribution.

The expedition certainly increased Roman knowledge of the peninsula, if only by supplying a criterion of distance in legionary marching hours. Moreover, it seems that after this time the South-western Arabs, having experienced the long arm of Rome, may have vaguely acknowledged some form of overlordship. The caravan trade of Arabia continued, but the direct sea trade between Egypt, India, and the Somali coast also developed rapidly, and was furthered in the early years of Tiberius by the navigational discovery of a Greek merchant named Hippalus, who was engaged in the Eastern trade and had acquired a thorough knowledge of the Arabian and Indian coasts and of the direction and periods of the monsoon winds. One summer he set out with a south-west wind along the Arabian coast, and after passing Cape Fartak headed boldly into the open sea, reaching the Indian coast at the estuary of the Indus. His example was followed by other merchants, who made the direct return voyage with the north-east monsoons. At length it was discovered that by leaving the Gulf of Aden and sailing on the arc of a northward circle one could come to Southern India, the source of many luxuries, with a coast less dangerous to approach than the neighbourhood of the Indus. The journey from Italy to India via Egypt took about sixteen weeks. Leaving the coast at Aden or Guardafui in July, the merchants could return in the autumn, on a course curving southward.

From traders adventuring on the frontiers of the known world, and from soldiers like Gallus, the ancient geographers gathered much of their knowledge. Strabo, a Greek of Pontus, based his famous *Geography* on such accounts, on the work of previous Greek writers, whom he sometimes quotes, and on his own travels, which did not, however, take him as far as Arabia.

28

His account of the world of his time, just before the beginning of the Christian era, is lively and informative, and may have been intended for the use of officials in the Roman civil service. Regarding Arabia he knew roughly the length of the peninsula, the character of some of the desert lands, whose only vegetation was thorn and palm, and of the great lack of water in the whole (he was a friend of Gallus!). He described Petra, the Nabathæan capital, missing its wall but mentioning its smooth, level fortress rock, abrupt and precipitous, with abundant supply of water within, and beyond the city mostly desert. Like most of the ancient geographers, he had an eye for picturesque and wondrous detail. The people of Gerra, on the Persian Gulf, for instance,

> inhabit the district where salt is found, and have houses built of salt. As scales of salt, broken off by the burning heat of the sun, are always falling, the houses are sprinkled with water, and the walls thus kept firmly together.[1]

More important, he shows this port as a base for overland traffic across the peninsula, and remarks that merchandise was also sent by raft along the coast to the Euphrates, whence it was distributed over the country.

Of the Red Sea coast he writes that

> in the deep part of the water grow trees resembling laurel and the olive. When the tide ebbs the whole trees are visible above the water, and at high tide they are sometimes completely covered. This is the more singular in that the coast inland has no trees.

He knew of the Sabæan country, that it was a populous and most fertile district, producing myrrh, frankincense, and cinnamon, and he was aware of the chain of middlemen who passed the produce northward.

> On the coast is found balsamum and another kind of herb of a very fragrant smell, but which is soon dissipated. There are also sweet-smelling palms and the calamus. There are snakes also of a dark red colour, a span in length, which spring up as high as a man's waist, and whose bite is incurable. On account of the abundance which the soil produces the people are lazy

---

[1] The translation used is that by H. C. Hamilton and W. Falconer (London, 1854).

and indolent in their mode of life. The lower classes live on roots and sleep in the trees.

The people who live near each other receive, in succession, the loads of perfume and deliver them to others who convey them as far as Syria and Mesopotamia. When the carriers become drowsy with the odour of the aromatics, the drowsiness is removed by the fumes of asphaltus and of goat's beard.

Mariaba, the capital of the Sabæans, is situated upon a well-wooded mountain. The king lives there, and determines absolutely all disputes and other matters; but he is forbidden to leave his palace; if he does so the rabble immediately assail him with stones, according to the direction of an oracle. He himself and those about his person pass their lives in effeminate voluptuousness.

The people cultivate the soil or are dealers in aromatics, both the indigenous and those brought from Ethiopia. To procure them, they sail through the Straits in vessels covered with skins. There is such an abundance of these aromatics that cinnamon, cassia, and other spices are used by them instead of sticks for firewood. In the country of the Sabæans is found the larimnum, the most fragrant perfume.

By the trade in these aromatics the Sabæans and the inhabitants of Gerra have become the richest of all the tribes and possess many wrought articles in gold and silver, such as couches, tripods, basins, drinking vessels. There is costly splendour in their houses, for the doors, walls, and roofs are variegated with inlaid ivory, gold, silver, and precious stones.

Strabo gave some account of the Bedouin, nomads who rode and fought on camels, and lived on the animals' milk and flesh.

His work was not widely known in his own time, but it was printed, at first from faulty manuscript, in the fifteenth, sixteenth, and seventeenth centuries at Venice, Geneva, and Paris. A French translation, made at the order of Napoleon, who greatly admired Strabo, appeared between 1805 and 1819.

Knowledge of Arabia steadily increased during the first century after Christ. Pliny was able to give the names of some inland settlements and tribes of the peninsula and to draw a distinction between the nomad and the settled Arabs, but of greater value is his account of the trade with the East. The short direct voyage was being made to India, but the Arabian land routes were also still in use. Silk from China, cotton and calico from India, might come from Yemen and the Hadhramaut up the west coast of Arabia to Petra and Syria, or from Gerra, in the Gulf, to Petra, or up the Euphrates to Ctesiphon, and then across the desert to Palmyra or Damascus. From India one and a half million sesterces of produce, retailing at a value of one hundred and fifty million, came into the empire. India, China, and Arabia together took one hundred million sesterces from the empire, mostly in money. The caravan route from Southern Arabia to Gaza, Pliny tells us, was enormously expensive, and he instances how a camel-load of frankincense incurred a sum of 688 denarii for transport and safe-conduct money, exclusive of Roman Imperial customs duties. The Eastern trade, by land and sea, was almost entirely in luxury products—gold, silver, and precious stones, ivory, ostrich feathers, pearls, tortoiseshell, drugs, spices, and rare woods. The Imperial ports at the beginning of our era were fully engaged in it. "Most of the population of Gades [Cadiz]," wrote Strabo, "is constantly at sea." The Roman ships that plied to Egypt or down the Red Sea were probably large sailing vessels, carrying a large crew, passengers, and perhaps a thousand tons of cargo. It is hardly possible to assess in modern currency the imposts on the trade overland, such as the 688 denarii on the load of frankincense, but the amount must have been out of proportion to merit special notice. It is difficult, however, to believe that even in the case of a luxury trade, which is frequently ill balanced economically, the Roman Empire paid only in currency. The holds of Imperial ships probably carried eastward such things as were conveniently exported from Alexandria—glassware, cheap and expensive, coloured beads, copper ornaments, clothing, fine linen, and papyrus, which was an Egyptian monopoly.

Shortly after Pliny's time there appeared the *Periplus maris erythræi*, a mariner's guide to the coasts of Africa, Arabia, and India. It was written by an unknown Greek-Egyptian merchant who knew those seas well, for his account of the trade, harbours, and navigational difficulties of the Red Sea has been proved accurate. The *Periplus* was only one of the many guides written by Greeks, and was compiled when the coasts of Arabia had been widely explored, though the interior, where distances were largely computed from the time taken in caravan marches, was largely unknown. To the author of the *Periplus* the western shore of Arabia was dangerous not only by its rocks and shoals, but from the robbers of the hinterland, some settled and some nomadic, who would attack those sailing too close inshore, or who would make slaves of shipwrecked seamen. But Yemen he described as settled and peaceful; Mocha was crowded with ships in a busy trade, and along the south coast Aden was a good anchorage. Farther to the east he knew well the character of the frankincense country and its ports, which traded with Africa, India, Persia, and Oman.

The Red Sea, then, was the principal outlet for the great Eastern trade, and the west coast of Arabia became well known to subjects of the Empire. The east coast offered less opportunity for enterprise, because of the frequent hostility of Parthia to Rome, though Syrians travelled to the Persian Gulf.

The general accuracy of the *Periplus* may be corrected on one point, where its author states that at some time in the first century the Romans occupied Aden, in order to give Egyptian merchants a monopoly of trade in Arabian and Indian seas. He had probably heard of the expedition of Gallus to Southern Arabia, and thought that Aden was the objective. The *Periplus* is an example of the ancient geographic literature, that included also various land itineraries, and was built from the records of early discoverers, merchants, traders, or sailors like Nearchus. The more formal geographers of the ancient world dealt with the character of places and peoples at least equally with physical features of the world. Strabo's panorama of the Roman Empire, for instance, is of this descriptive order. Attempts were made, too, at mapping the world, by putting known places in a system of meridians of longitude and parallels of latitude. Of such geographies only one has survived the centuries—namely, that of Claudius Ptolemy.

For twenty or thirty years in the middle of the second century after Christ Ptolemy worked on the terraces of the temple of Serapis, at Canopus, near Alexandria. With Hipparchus he was the founder of the study of plain and spherical trigonometry, including the formation of a table of chords. In the form given to it by Ptolemy their work endured for fourteen hundred years, and during these centuries the

Alexandrian's teaching as to the movement of the heavenly bodies—the Ptolemaic system—also held sway. But his authority as a geographer was highest during the Renaissance, in the sixteenth century, and his geographical work had greater influence by reason of its scientific form.

Hipparchus conceived the idea of mapping the world by observations of the latitude and longitude of the principal places. Marinus of Tyre, immediately before Ptolemy, had attempted the task, and his results, especially in regard to Mediterranean lands, Strabo's geography, the reckoning of distances and directions in various *Itineraries* and guides like the *Periplus*, and accounts gathered from travellers, were all used when Ptolemy began his map. Using this data, and dividing the equatorial circle into 360 parts, drawing parallel circles of latitude and other meridians through the poles, he had a basis for the outline of a world map.

His map, so much of which was based on inaccurate information respecting distances, had further basic faults, for his prime meridian of longitude was a line drawn through the supposed position of "the Fortunate Isles," the Canaries and Madeira, which he placed $2\frac{1}{2}°$ west of "the Sacred Promontory," Cape St Vincent, instead of 9° 20', so that all his longitudes were about 7° in error. For some reason unknown Ptolemy also adopted a smaller reckoning of the earth's circumference than that estimated by Eratosthenes, and this made all his distances between degrees of latitude and longitude at the equator about ten miles too short. With his maps Ptolemy supplied a list of towns, estuaries, and mountain ranges, and in the case of Arabia he was accused in Bunbury's classic *History of Ancient Geography* of filling in fictitious names and claiming an exact placing for them.

Bunbury failed to understand that Ptolemy did not claim that any of these places had been fixed by astronomical observation, and he should have known also the writings of Mengin and Jomard, the historians of the Egyptian expeditions to Arabia in the early nineteenth century, which bore out the existence of places mentioned by the ancient geographer. But Sprenger's *Ancient Geography of Arabia* (1875) restored Ptolemy's credit. It showed that the Alexandrian had learned with approximate accuracy the general outline of Arabia, and that many of the places he gave the peninsula could still be identified as towns and oases, some probably and some with certainty. Ptolemy's "Thaim," for instance, was Teima, his "Iathrippa" Yathrib, now Medina, his "Egra" Hejr, now Medain Salih, and his "Iambia" Yenbo. Ptolemy's Arabian mountains cannot now be definitely compared with the actuality because his maps are missing, but it seems that he realized and indicated some of the coastal ranges. He showed also five rivers of the peninsula, and though they are *wadis*, not rivers, attempts have been made to identify them—his "Bætius" as the Wadi Hamdh, "Prion" as the Wadi Hadhramaut, "Lar" as the Dawasir, and his springs of "Omanum" and "Styx" as waters of the Yemen and Oman lands—waters which to-day, as in his time, do not reach the sea, unless subterraneously.

Ptolemy's geographical work added a comparative precision to the more descriptive writings of Strabo and Pliny. Arabia could be visualized out of the vaguer dreams of wealth, luxury, savagery, and strange beasts. But Western Europe came to know it only hundreds of years after the work was accomplished. The first Latin edition of the *Geographia*, marked by inaccuracy, appeared in the fifteenth century, and was followed by many other editions up to the middle of the sixteenth. A version edited by Erasmus appeared at Basle in 1533, three years before the great scholar's death, and in 1618 a Greek and Latin Elzevir edition appeared at Leyden. This contained as many errors as its predecessors, and it was not until the middle of the nineteenth century that valuable critical editions were undertaken.

The geographical literature of the ancient world does not really reflect the extent of discoveries. Sound information was neglected, and false was used even when it was known to be untrue. Ptolemy himself, with good information from voyagers at his disposal, made India flat instead of peninsular. A glance at the true outline of Arabia in relation to Ptolemy's reconstructed map will show how widely even one working for precision could err. Moreover, there is no doubt that early geographers were led astray by the unwillingness of merchants and traders to give information about districts where they

34

hoped to sustain a commercial monopoly, the spirit which invented strange animals and reptiles to discourage competition. Also they suffered from a lack of accurate instruments for measuring distances and taking bearings. The ordinary layman is often filled with wonder that they attained even recognizable accuracy in some of their maps.

II

The Greek and Roman geographers after Ptolemy added almost nothing to knowledge of Arabia, nor were the Western and the Byzantine worlds greatly interested. The land of the Nabathæans became a Roman province under Trajan, but Imperial authority, Roman or Byzantine, was not felt in the peninsula, except perhaps on the Red Sea coast as far south as Umm Lej. Roman arms ceased to be concerned with the Middle East. The purchasing power of the West declined, and the trade of the Arabian seas lessened, and was left to Ethiopians, Persians, and Arabs. The rise of Christianity, and later of Islam, struck heavily at the trans-Arabian land routes, by lessening the demand for incense at funerals and sacrificial offerings.

Arabia to the Romans and Byzantines was, then, a decreasingly interesting cog in the commercial system. The Nabathæans, followed by the kingdom of Ghassan, an outpost of Rome, warred with their neighbours of North-eastern Arabia and Iraq, subjects of the kingdom of Hira, which was a frontier state of Persia. In the south Abyssinians who had originally left Arabia began to return, and fought against the Himyarite "kings of Saba," who had accepted Judaism. Struggles which were at first apparently for a foothold on the peninsula later took the character of religious war, Jew against Christian.

Of Central Arabia in these centuries little is known, except that in the last years of the fifth century of our era the tribe of Kinda was supreme from Hira to the Yemama and Bahrein, and was allied to the Abyssinians who had established dominion in Yemen. Arabia contained many other independent tribes, such as the Koreish, to which Mohammed (A.D. 570–632) belonged, before all became for a time united in one thing at least—the faith of Islam. But the political history of the pre-Islamic period is vague, almost as indefinite as the history of Christianity in the land. In all the ecclesiastical histories and the writings of the Fathers there are references to Arabia, but often Ethiopia and India is meant, as well as Arabia proper. There seem, however, to have been three main centres of Christianity, in Ghassan, Hira, and the Yemen; its penetration to Nejd and Oman is very doubtful.

Among the Northern Arabs Christianity made steady progress, Christian tribes being scattered through Syria, Phœnicia, and Northern Arabia, with their own bishops and churches. From this region there was doubtless missionary effort into the peninsula, and in times of persecution the northern desert fastnesses would provide refuge from Roman or Persian. There were hermits in the Syro-Arabian desert, and the example of St Simeon Stylites probably made converts among the Arabs. Sometimes, it is known, whole tribes adopted Christianity, following the example of their rulers, as in the case of Aspebætos, a sheikh bishop who attended the Council of Ephesus (A.D. 431). Incited by the Persians, the kings of Hira frequently persecuted the Christians, but on occasion the Christians found a protector, like Numan Ibn Mundir, a convert from paganism and one of the last kings of Hira (A.D. 580–590), whose son fell leading an army of Christian Arabs against the Moslems in 633. The Christians of Hira professed the Nestorian and Monophysite heresies.

In Southern Arabia Bartholomew the Apostle is said to have preached Christianity on his way to Ethiopia, and there were other missionaries, such as Pantenæus, who preached to the Jews of Yemen, and Frumentius, a Tyrian who had been Treasurer to a Himyarite king. Frumentius may have been the missionary to Nejran, where Christians seem to have been very numerous.

In the fifth and sixth centuries the Gospel gained numerous adherents in Southern Arabia, but was faced by the hostility of many Jewish communities which exercised great religious, political, and financial influence. "Like other religious communities which preach toleration when oppressed," writes Margoliouth, "they [the Arab Jews] became persecutors when they had acquired sovereignty." About the beginning of the sixth century the kingdom of Himyar was subject to the Abyssinian king Elesbaan, and was ruled by a Jew, Dhu Nuwas, "Lord of Curls." This vassal king revolted and began a persecution of the Christians in Yemen, putting to death all who would not accept Judaism. The town of Nejran, a Christian stronghold in the north of Yemen, was captured by treachery, and Dhu Nuwas ordered a general massacre.

Large pits were dug and filled with fire. Thousands of those who refused to abjure their faith, including priests, monks, and women, were thrown into these pits. The bones of Nejran's bishop, Paul, were disinterred, burned, and their ashes scattered to the winds. Arethas, the chief man of the town, with other local leaders, was imprisoned and then beheaded. Their wives suffered the same fate, and Ruma, the wife of Arethas, after seeing her two daughters slain, was compelled to taste their blood before being herself murdered. The number of Christians killed is given variously as from 4400 to 20,000. While much of the history of Christianity in Arabia is obscure, this massacre at least is vouched for by the Koran, and by all Arab, Nestorian, Jacobite, and Occidental historians and writers subsequently.

The news of the slaughter spread throughout the Roman and Persian worlds. Elesbaan invaded Yemen with a force of 70,000 men, killed thousands of Jews, slew Dhu Nuwas and defeated his army. The churches were rebuilt, new bishops and priests took the places of the martyrs, and an Abyssinian general was appointed king. A few years later a Christian Abyssinian, Abraha, seized power, and was ultimately acknowledged as sovereign by Abyssinia. Christianity knew peace and quiet in his time; he was respected by all his subjects, and was loved by the Christians for his zeal in religion. A magnificent new cathedral was begun at Sana.

At this time the Kaaba at Mecca was a pagan shrine, visited by thousands of Arabs, who brought to it rich gifts and donations. Mecca, indeed, a small settlement in a barren valley, growing through the increasing use of an east-to-west trade route, was the centre of pagan worship, and its small rectangular building, the Kaaba, or Cube, contained images of the gods. In a wall of this building was the Black Stone, possibly of volcanic origin, a fetish which exercised a powerful fascination on the imagination of the Arabs. The settlement of Mecca grew up round a well of brackish water, later known as the famous Zemzem; an annual fair was held there, and the pagans regarded it as a place of yearly pilgrimage, for the duty of pilgrimage was apparently one of their religious ideas, as it was among the Jews. Mecca, for certain months of the year, and especially at the time of pilgrimage, was a trucial area in a country of savage warfare, where tribe fought tribe continually and blood-feuds were perpetual. Obviously the tribe controlling the holy region would attain a position of special power; the Koreish of Mecca became the richest in the Hejaz.

When the cathedral of Sana was completed the heathen shrine at Mecca was outshone, so that the pilgrims came to Yemen, and the revenues of the Koreish fell away. Therefore the Meccans hired agents to strew their excrement in the church, to profane it in the eyes of the Arabs. The desecration was accomplished, and Abraha resolved on a war of vengeance. He was determined to wipe out the Koreish and destroy the Kaaba.

As he marched north with a large army, accompanied by many elephants, courage deserted the Koreish. But their offer to surrender and hand over a third of the wealth of Hejaz in return for the sparing of the Kaaba was refused, and Abraha marched on inflexibly. Then the Meccans, it is said, in desperation, prepared an ambush in a narrow defile. Abraha entered the trap, and was suddenly assailed by stones and masses of rock hurled down the steep sides of the pass. Even the swallows, says Arab tradition, dropped small stones on the invaders; forced to retreat with heavy losses, Abraha died from wounds and disappointment shortly afterwards. It is more likely, however, that the host was dispersed by an epidemic of smallpox, from which probably Abraha died just after his return.

Under his sons the Christian Abyssinian power declined, and in the year 568 a Persian military expedition succeeded in overthrowing it. This, with the increasing disputes between

THE MOSQUE BUILT ON THE SITE OF ABRAHA'S CHRISTIAN CHURCH AT SANA

Photo E.N.A.

38

A Town in Yemen, showing Citadel and Mosque

Photo E.N.A.

Byzantium and Persia, and then the advent of Islam, led to the passing of Christianity in the south-west. But the faith died hard. The great church at Sana still flourished in the time of the Prophet, and it was not until the days of Omar (A.D. 634–644) that Nejran wilted under the pressure of Islam. Then those were expelled who refused to be proselytized.

It was, in fact, Omar's policy that practically ended Christianity in Arabia. In the time of Mohammed there were Christians in the Hejaz, and especially round Mecca. Slaves and traders were frequently Christian, and many of the Prophet's followers were renegades from the faith. To the Jews Mohammed was hostile, since he regarded them as a political danger; to the heathen Arabs he was inflexible; but for the Christians, it seems, he retained courtesy and tolerance, though Moslem tradition relates that on the point of death he ordained that none but those of Islam should dwell in the land. Again, under the Omayyad and Abbasid caliphs, Christianity was regarded with respect, and enjoyed much freedom throughout the Moslem Empire.

But the quality of Christianity in the peninsula was perhaps never high, except possibly in the south. The Arian, Nestorian, and Monophysite heresies were adopted, and Arabia by the Syrian border was from the third century regarded as "the mother of heresies." Like the Arabian Jews, the Christian Arabs in general were probably not remarkable for the practice of their religion. Christianity bowed to the storm of Islam and was destroyed.

Had Arabian Christianity survived, or become part of an ecclesiastical system centred on Rome or Byzantium, a province of an organized Church appointing its priests and prelates, and tolerated throughout by Islam, the nature of the people and the geography of the land would not have remained so long and so thoroughly hidden from the West. In the event more than a thousand years passed before Europe could receive the first satisfactory answers to its many questions.

CHAPTER III

MEDIEVAL ARABIAN TRAVEL

> The Meccan women are extraordinarily beautiful and very pious and modest. . . . They visit the mosque every Thursday night, wearing their finest apparel; and the whole sanctuary is saturated with the smell of their perfume.
>
> IBN BATTUTA, *Travels*

THE decline of the Roman Empire was followed by Arab domination of the African and Asiatic provinces. The geographical learning of the Greeks was inherited by the Arabs, but was forgotten in Europe, where, for instance, Ptolemy did not appear in Latin until early in the second half of the fifteenth century. Even then small interest was displayed in his work till a hundred years later. Nevertheless geographical speculation was not the monopoly of the Arabs during the Middle Ages.

In Christendom progress was made in navigation and cartography, while the inquiring spirit of such Catholic schoolmen as Vincent of Beauvais, Albertus Magnus, and Ristoro of Arezzo led to the development of geographical theories. They discussed the effect of water action on land formations, the influence of latitude and altitude on climate and on men, animals, and plants. They pondered on the nature of the world's surface. Was it a slowly cooling crust round a central fire? Long before the Ptolemaic revival the West saw a gathering interest in map science and in the latest explorations, as when Roger Bacon summarized the travels of William of Rubruck. The learned Alexander Neckham, an English professor at Paris in the twelfth century, knew the properties of the magnet, or magnetized iron, to indicate the north. Moreover, the Moslem conquests were not, after the first rush of victory, an absolute bar to Christian travel.

The desire and necessity for trading was but one of the influences tending to bring Christian and Arab into contact.

40

Though the Eastern commerce remained for a thousand years almost entirely in Moslem hands, Westerners passed through Mohammedan as well as Mongol territory. In the thirteenth and fourteenth centuries Christian merchants occasionally sailed the Red Sea and, with less danger from Islam, the Persian Gulf, whence they coasted South Arabia even to East Africa, and travelled the south coast of Asia towards the distant Orient.

Christian traders entered Arabia even as far as Medain Salih, where they sold provisions to the Moslem pilgrim caravans bound for Medina and Mecca ! From the eleventh century to the fourteenth Christians penetrated the Near East, and made the acquaintance of the Arabs as traders, pilgrims to the Holy Land, or Crusaders. Among such voyagers were men like Adelard of Bath, who brought back and translated Arabic texts of Euclid and astronomy. The Crusades vastly increased the Levant trade with Europe through Venice and Genoa, and while Palestine was in Christian hands the Near East, at least to the edge of the desert, was open to European travellers. Sæwulf of Worcester could reach the Jordan, but beyond that deep valley lay "Arabia, hostile to Christians." It was not only hostile to Christians. The temporary unity caused by the rise of Islam soon gave way to tribal wars and fighting in various independent districts—Nejd, Oman, Hasa, and the Yemen. Towns like Petra and Gerra, living by trans-peninsula caravans, declined and decayed. Warfare made the routes of Arabia difficult even for Arabs.

One of Sæwulf's escapes illustrates the perils and adventures faced for trade or knowledge by the medieval voyagers. Arriving at Jaffa in October 1102, he left the ship at once, fortunately for himself, as on returning from Mass next morning he heard shouting from the direction of the shore, and saw mountainous waves, wreckage, and countless drowned bodies on the beach. The ship he had travelled in and others, laden with corn and merchandise or with arriving and departing pilgrims, were still held by their anchors, but were tossed and rolled in the waves, while the terrified crews hurled cargo overboard. Other vessels had dragged their anchors and were being dashed to pieces on the rocks.

For the violence of the wind would not allow them to put out to sea, and the nature of the coast did not permit them to put into shore. Among the sailors and pilgrims who had lost all hope of safety, some remained on the ships; others laid hold of the masts or beams of wood; many, in a state of stupor, were drowned without any attempt to save themselves. Some (incredible as this may seem) before my eyes had their heads knocked off by the rafters to which they clung for safety; while others were swept out to sea on the beams which they hoped would wash them up to land. Even those who could swim had not strength to battle with the waves, and few who thus trusted to their own power reached the shore alive.[1]

Out of thirty very large ships, some of them dromonds, bireme galleys, each tier having twenty-five benches, with two rowers to each bench, only seven were saved, and a thousand men and women were drowned.

Though the East was open freely to the Moslem travellers, the voyagers from Christendom are beyond measure greater, in boldness of conception and in daring enterprise, than those out of Islam. Their discovery of the interior of Asia is balanced only by their penetration to the New World.

From the Caliphate to the end of the Middle Ages the Moslems produced many travellers and geographers, but they rarely attained any concise or ordered treatment. No original mind, no supreme intelligence, is apparent in Moslem geographical speculation or in records of travel. Their tales of sea monsters, mists, fogs, and whirlpools merely perpetuated old fears and superstitions regarding far places, and even the antithesis and rhetoric of their literary style was in contrast to the lucidity of the Greek masters, whom in other respects they followed slavishly. Of Southern and Eastern Asia, for instance, though they had a far wider and more exact knowledge than Ptolemy, they were prepared to follow his tradition, adding other mistaken fancies of their own. Yet with their manifold advantages they could hardly fail to extend geographical knowledge at least a little.

Arab trade routes ran along the Mesopotamian valleys, from the Gulf and Red Sea ports along the coasts of Arabia and East Africa, and eastward to India and China. According to

[1] Sir Raymond Beazley, *The Dawn of Modern Geography* (London, 1897–1906).

one of the more reliable Arab chroniclers there were some
10,000 Moslems in Bombay and 700 in Canton about the
year 900 of the Christian era. For hundreds of years after
Mohammed the merchandise of the Sudan, South-eastern
Asia, and the Far East came into Aden, Jidda, and Suez, and
was transported overland through Arabia as well as by sea
to Egypt, Syria, and Europe. Before rotation of crops was
introduced, and the growing of turnips for feeding cattle in
the winter, the beef for the season was killed and salted in
November. To make this 'hard tack' palatable there was a
great demand for pepper and cloves. In the absence of modern
beverages, such as tea and cocoa, beer and wine were the
common drinks of our forefathers. Medieval beer was thin;
wine priced to suit the average man's pocket was sour, and
spices were lavishly used to flavour these and other home-
made drinks. In the insanitary conditions of medieval urban
life, moreover, strong perfumes were not only a necessity, but
were considered a guard against fevers, plague, and pestilence.
Among the populace, strong-smelling jars of spices and perfume
were as beneficial to the physician's practice as are a long
string of 'letters' to his name to-day. Pepper, cloves, cinnamon,
nutmeg, cassia, aloes, incense, camphor, sandalwood, and
other products of South-eastern Asia and the Indian Ocean
islands were brought over sea and land by Arab traders of
the Red Sea and the Gulf, and were ultimately marketed at
Constantinople and, later, Venice. From the men engaged
in this far-flung trade much knowledge was available to
geographers.

Again, the pilgrimage to Mecca was in itself a duty which involved long journeys. Most of the geographers of the Moslem
world had made the journey at least once, and the fact that
the pilgrimage was an experience common to hundreds of
thousands perhaps explains why the Arab geographers say less
than one would expect of the holy cities. The Moslem scholar
could also draw upon reports made by governors of outlying
districts in the Mohammedan Empire, and could probably use
maps made by order of the administrators of distant provinces.

Moslem investigators had, in fact, a vast fund of knowledge
and information. As early as the eighth century a translation

of the Sanscrit astronomy was made. In the ninth century an observatory was built at Baghdad, a degree was measured on the plains of Mesopotamia, and the approximate size of the earth was deduced. They possessed also an Arabic version of the *Almagest* and *Geography* of Ptolemy and the works of Marinus of Tyre, Euclid, Archimedes, and Aristotle.

One of the early geographers, Abu Zeid, tells a little about the South Arabian shore and the dangers of navigation in the Red Sea. Another, Ibn Khurdadbih, a notable disciple of Ptolemy's mathematical theories, describes the coast routes from the Red Sea and the Persian Gulf to the Yellow Sea, and gives a list of Arabian ports, caravan stages, and distances in the peninsula, with incidental information of commercial interest. He notes, as almost all travellers did, the barrenness of Aden, remarking that there was no corn and no cattle, but that the port was rich in amber, aloes, and all the spices of the East. The Jews, who knew many languages, he describes as the chief middlemen of the trade routes between Asia and Europe, from France and Italy to Suez, the Red Sea, and the Far East, up the Orontes to Antioch, and down the Euphrates to the Gulf, Oman, and Southern Asia. Istakhri (*c.* 950) journeyed extensively in the Moslem world and wrote a *Book of Climates*, beginning with Arabia. Ibn Haukal wrote a very similar book, but both survived only in fragments, which were held in esteem by later Arab geographers. Masudi in the tenth century also travelled widely and visited Oman and South Arabia, yet Arab maps showed little advance.

The Jews of the medieval world made their interesting contribution to travel and exploration. The first of the Jewish geographers was Benjamin of Tudela, a rabbi or merchant who travelled widely in the twelfth century, visiting the Hebrew colonies from Spain to Baghdad. But his *Records* interested mainly the people of his own race, with whom they dealt, and of Arabia he could only give, from hearsay, some information that is vague and rather incredible. If one travelled for twenty-one days through the deserts of "Yemen or Sheba," he tells us, one came to the Jews of Southern Arabia, who were Rechabites, rigid Talmudists, and were regarded with great fear by their neighbours. They dressed in black, and kept a continuous fast except on the Sabbath and holy days. Their capital was a large city called Thema or Tehma. According to Tudela, other warlike groups of Israelites held out in the land that was then forbidden to all save those of Islam. Kheibar had 50,000, "Telmas" 100,000, and "Thanæym" 300,000 in a city fifteen square miles in extent.

If Benjamin of Tudela was unable to shed much light on the internal state of the Arabian peninsula he could at least show the part played by its seas and ports in the contemporary commercial system. In the world of this Jewish traveller the Nile Delta was commercially equal to the trade centres of Baghdad and the Bosphorus. It was a clearing-house, and a source of supply, for the trade of the Mediterranean. Thither flowed traffic from India, China, the Red Sea, Oman, and Yemen. Sometimes this Red Sea traffic was far greater than that into and from the Persian Gulf. When the Franks conquered Syria, for instance, the old trade route across Sinai to Alexandria was interrupted, and more Egyptian trade was diverted to Red Sea towns. Eastern traffic filled the Arabian ports; Jidda was fully occupied, and merchandise crossed the sea thence to Myos Hormos and Berenice, whence it proceeded by camel to the Nile and then went down the river to the delta.

Other notable Arab geographers were Abulfeda (1273–1331) and Idrisi (1099–1154). Although the latter's work in geography was developed in the West, at the Court of Roger II of Sicily, it failed to affect European thought. Idrisi used the works of Ptolemy, Masudi, and other geographers, and had travelled extensively, possibly even to Scandinavia. But he kept to a rigid climatic treatment, regarding the world under seven zones, from equatorial to polar, without considering physical and other differentiations or their effects. Abulfeda and Idrisi were informative only on the general topography of West and South-west Arabia. Elsewhere they have little to tell, and seem to have been largely ignorant of the country away from the pilgrim routes; nor apparently did they seek first-hand information from those who had travelled routes they mentioned. Idrisi had one sentence on the Hadhramaut and another on the Great Southern Desert. Abulfeda gave some account of Ared, Northern Jauf, and Jebel Shammar, but of Central Arabia in general neither writer has much to say. In any case, as will be seen, their writings did not reach Europeans in any adequate form for hundreds of years. Before that time came Europe had been given a novel introduction to the Arab of old.

The adventures of Sindbad the Sailor are as the *Odyssey* of the medieval Arab. Having their origin in the voyages of Moslem merchants and explorers, as well as in Persian and Greek sources, the adventures are the vivid reflection of ninth- and tenth-century travel, in a setting of romance, danger, resource, escape, and good fortune. The wonders, fables, and fancies enchanted the Moslem audience, but Sindbad's voyages have intrigued modern geographers rather in spite of these extravagances. Yet Sindbad's actual routes and destinations matter little compared with the brilliant and colourful kaleido-scope of Arab activity which the tales present; and the *Arabian Nights*, as Burton said, showed the medieval Arab at his best and worst: childish, astute, simple, cunning, super-stitious, ignorant, self-satisfied but of "radiant innate idealism," capable of fortitude in bad times, a man of dignity, deep religiousness, generous, and liberal.

This bright Arabic tapestry of the Middle Ages did not reach the West until the French *savant* Galland produced his brilliant paraphrase in 1704-17. It was more than a hundred years later that Europe read fragments of the writings of the most interesting of all Arab travellers, five hundred years after he had lived; and the middle of the nineteenth century had passed before a complete translation of his work was made by French scholars.

II

Ibn Battuta has been called the traveller, not of an age, but of Islam.

Born at Tangier about the year 1300, he set out at the age of twenty-five on the journeys which were to carry him across almost every tract of the known world, and on which he saw more of the Arabian peninsula than any other traveller. As the first object was to make the pilgrimage to Mecca, he moved eastward along the North African coast road until he reached the "magnificent port" of Alexandria, and thence continued to Cairo, "mistress of broad regions and fruitful lands, boundless in multitude of buildings, peerless in beauty and splendour." Next he travelled to Upper Egypt, intending to cross the Red Sea from a port opposite Jidda.

Already in the first few pages of his narrative [1] one notices some of the qualities which make him a very real person, and his book a living record of the Moslem world of his day. In Tripoli he arranges to marry a lady of Sfax, the project falls through, but soon afterwards he marries the daughter of a student of Fez, and detains his companions of the caravan by his wedding party. It is only the first of several weddings in his long years of travel. With his great uxoriousness one notices other qualities—his piety and his interest in holy and learned men, especially workers of miracles. At Alexandria, for instance, he mentions the Kadi and the Sheikh el Murshadi, "who bestowed gifts miraculously created at his desire." His superstition and belief in dreams are soon apparent, for while staying in the cell of this holy man he dreamed that a great bird flew with him to Mecca, and thence to Yemen and over the track of many of his future journeys. Though his account was dictated many years later, he did not forget the religious centres and holy relics which he saw on his way through Egypt.

Reaching the Red Sea coast, he found that a war was in progress between the local ruler and Egypt. It was impossible to embark for Arabia, so he decided to return down the Nile and make his pilgrimage from Damascus. Eight days of river travel saw him back in Cairo, where he stayed but one night before beginning the desert journey to Gaza. Time remained to travel extensively in Syria and Palestine before he set out for Mecca in the pilgrim caravan, with the new moon of the month Shawwal, in the autumn, 1326.

The pilgrim route roughly followed the line of the modern Hejaz Railway. After leaving Damascus the pilgrims rested four days at Bosra, to enable late-comers to overtake the

[1] My quotations are from the translation of H. A. R. Gibb: *The Travels of Ibn Battuta, 1325–54* (London, 1929).

47

column. Near Kerak the caravan halted again, and Ibn Battuta noticed the famous castle, "one of the most marvellous, impregnable and celebrated of fortresses." Here there was another rest before they entered the desert, of which it was said, "He who enters it is lost, and he who emerges from it is born." Next came the valley of Bazwa, and Tebuk, marked by another halt of four days for the pilgrims to lay in supplies of water and rest the camels for the desert ride to El Ula. Ibn Battuta observes:

> The custom of the water-carriers is to camp beside the spring, and they have tanks made of buffalo hides, like great cisterns, from which they water the camels and fill the water-skins. Each emir or person of rank has a special tank for the needs of his own camels and servants; other people make private arrangements with the water-carriers to tend their camels and fill their water-skins for an agreed price.

From Tebuk the caravan moved at great speed, night and day, for fear of the desert. In the middle of the waste lands they passed "the valley of Hell," a narrow pass with sides strewn with lava. One year the pilgrims suffered here from the simoon wind; the supplies of water dried up and the price of a single drink rose to fantastic heights, but buyers and sellers perished.

Five days later Medain Salih was reached. Here water was abundant, yet none touched it, for the Prophet, on an expedition to Tebuk, passed it by, enjoining that none should drink there. But eighteen miles farther lay El Ula, a place of palm gardens and springs, where another long halt enabled the pilgrims to wash their clothes and replenish provisions. Three days' journeying from this oasis brought them to the outskirts of Medina.

Here Ibn Battuta prayed, performed the ritual ceremonies, touched the remains of a palm-trunk against which Mohammed leaned when preaching, and read and recited the Koran each night in the courtyard of the mosque. Four days later the traveller set out for Mecca. At the mosque of Hulayfa, five miles from Medina, he changed into pilgrim's garb, donning the *ihram*,[1] bathed, prayed, and dedicated himself to the

[1] "The *ihram* consists of two pieces of linen, or woollen or cotton cloth, one of which is wrapped round the loins, and the other thrown over the neck and

48

pilgrimage. From this point he enumerates the halts, springs, stagnant water-holes, and indicates the character of the country, desert, hilly, or blessed with palms and water, until he reaches his bourn, "the City of Surety, Mecca—may God ennoble her."

There follows a description of the Meccans which is more favourable than those provided by many later visitors:

The inhabitants of Mecca are distinguished by many excellent and noble activities and qualities, by their beneficence to the humble and weak, and by their kindness to strangers. When any of them makes a feast he begins by giving food to the religious devotees who are poor and without resources, inviting them first with kindness and delicacy. The majority of these unfortunates are to be found by the public bakehouses, and when anyone has his bread baked and takes it away to his house they follow him, and he gives each one of them some share of it, sending away none disappointed. Even if he has but a single loaf, he gives away a third or a half of it, cheerfully and without any grudging. Another good custom of theirs is this. The orphan children sit in the bazaar, each with two baskets, one large and one small. When one of the townspeople comes to the bazaar and buys cereals, meat, and vegetables he hands them to one of these boys, who puts the cereals in one basket and the meat and vegetables in the other and takes them to the man's house, so that his meal may be prepared. Meanwhile the man goes about his devotions and his business. There is no instance of any of the boys ever having abused their trust in this matter, and they are given a fixed fee of a few coppers. The Meccans are very elegant and clean in their dress, and most of them wear white garments, which you always see fresh and snowy. They use a great deal of perfume and kohl and make free use of toothpicks of green arak-wood. The Meccan women are extraordinarily beautiful and very pious and modest. They too make great use of perfumes to such a degree that they will spend the night hungry in order to buy perfumes with the price of their food. They visit the mosque every Thursday night, wearing their finest apparel; and the whole sanctuary is saturated with the smell of their

---

shoulders, so as to leave part of the right arm uncovered. Every garment must be laid aside before this is put on. Any piece of stuff will answer the purpose, but the law ordains that there shall be no seams in it, nor any silk or ornaments; and white is considered preferable to any other colour. The head remains totally uncovered—there is no prohibition against the use of umbrellas—while the natives either brave the sun's rays or merely tie a rag to a stick and make a little shade by turning it to the sun—the law forbids any other covering even at night, but with this few *hajis* strictly comply." (Burckhardt, *Travels in Arabia*.)

perfume. When one of these women goes away the odour of the perfume clings to the place after she has gone.

Ibn Battuta's return journey is perhaps of greater interest, as it was made across country less known even to Syrians than the Hejaz route. Leaving Mecca in November, he returned to Medina, and then made for Baghdad. So great was the host of pilgrims that the earth surged with them like the sea, and any man who left the caravan for a moment and had no mark to guide him back to his place could not find it again, because of the vast company of people. Camels were specially detailed for transporting supplies for the poor, provisions were issued as alms, medicines were provided for the sick, and camels for those who could not walk. All this assistance for the poor pilgrim was from the endowment of the Sultan of Baghdad. A whole bazaar of shops accompanied the multitude, moving in front at night with torches burning, so that darkness was turned into day.

Four stages out of Medina the caravan entered the plains and pleasant air of Nejd. The route was supplied, where water was lacking, with reservoirs, provided hundreds of years before at the expense of Zobeida, the wife of Haroun al Raschid. Ibn Battuta tells us that the Bedouin traded with the pilgrims, exchanging sheep, milk, and butter for coarse cotton cloth, and that the pilgrims occasionally made a show of arms, out of nervousness of the desert men. Feid, between Mecca and Baghdad, an old capital of Nejd, was the next stage, and then Wakisa, where there were water-tanks and traders selling bread, flour, dates and other fruit. Thence to Baghdad the narrative describes desert areas alternating with welcome towns and villages.

After much travelling in the Middle East Ibn Battuta returned to Mecca in 1327, staying there three years, studying and leading a pleasant life, doubtless with the intention of gaining prestige from a long sojourn in the holy city, and thus fitting himself for advancement in Moslem countries. In 1330 he visited East Africa, and then sailed from Suakin to Asir, which was then an outlying part of Yemen. He had previously met the ruler of Yemen between Mecca and Jidda. A scholar and man of letters himself, he received Ibn Battuta gladly.

On his voyage across the Red Sea Battuta notes the dangerous navigation, the landings made at nightfall, and by day the watch constantly kept for rocks and shoals.

In Yemen Zebid, Taizz, Aden, and Sana were visited. Zebid pleased him by its running water, palm-groves, fruits, handsome men, and women who were beautiful and virtuous. He contrasted the inhabitants with those of the capital, Taizz, who were overbearing and insolent, "as is generally the case in towns where kings reside." At Sana, a former capital, there were houses of brick and plaster, a large population, a temperate climate, and good water. It was during the southwest monsoon, and the rainfall must have been welcome to one with so much desert travel in his experience. During his stay at Sana rain fell almost every afternoon in a downpour that drove the people into their houses. As the town was paved throughout the rain thoroughly cleaned the streets.

From Aden, hot and waterless, with a population of fishermen, merchants, and porters, he sailed to East Africa and then returned to Dhofar, which by the land route was a month's journey from Aden. He describes the tropical cultivation of this territory, unique in the peninsula; its great quantities of fish and fruit, beasts fed solely on fish, the bananas, betel, cocopalms, and the cultivation of millet. Then, on the way along the coast to Oman, he describes the frankincense-tree and the manner in which the gum is obtained. In places the people of the coast lived entirely on fish, and even built their houses of fish-bones, using camel hides for roofs. He landed at Sur, in Oman, and found the country rich in streams, orchards, palms, and fruit, with a population generous, warlike, and courageous. Thence he entered the Persian Gulf, visited Ormuz and noted the barrenness of the island, which was to be an important Portuguese outpost less than two hundred years later.

Now the varied contacts made with the Arabs in the Middle Ages, added to the work of Moslem and Jewish geographers and travellers, might have provided Christendom with useful knowledge of Arabia. But traders, Christian pilgrims, and Crusaders were usually neither geographers nor literary men, and so failed to make written records. As for the Moslem and Jewish writings, they were unknown, or did not affect European knowledge, until the Renaissance, and often long afterwards. Idrisi's geography was published at the Medicean Press in an abridged form in 1592, and the abridgment was printed in Latin at Paris in 1619. The work of Abulfeda, who died in 1331, was in part translated and printed in 1650, and appeared again, in an abridgment, in the early eighteenth century. Benjamin of Tudela was translated from Hebrew into Latin in 1575, into French in 1734 and English in 1840. Extracts from Ibn Battuta appeared in European languages from the eighteenth century; an incomplete English edition appeared in 1829, but the full, critical publication by M. Defrémery and Dr Sanguinetti came only in 1858. It was not until 1697 that the West learned even of the existence of most of these Arab writers, through d'Herbelot's *Bibliothèque orientale*, which indicated the character of the works and gave some extracts. Texts and full translations of their writings, trivial or important, were not printed until the nineteenth century.

The movement which was to reveal Africa, India, and Arabia to the West began in the first half of the fifteenth century. The stirrings of the movement are first perceived far from Arabia, across seas and a vast continent. In 1441 slaves and gold were brought from the Guinea Coast to Portugal; four years later Cape Verde was passed; the Congo was reached and the equator crossed; Henry the Navigator died, but the Portuguese pushed onward round the Cape of Good Hope. Then, in 1497, the sea way to India lay before them. It was the twilight of medieval Moslem domination of the Arabian and Indian seas.

Ten years before this turning-point in history John II of Portugal had dispatched Pedro da Covilham across the Mediterranean, into Moslem territory, on an extensive commercial reconnaissance to the cinnamon and spice lands. He travelled by Egypt and the Red Sea to Calicut, the Persian Gulf, and Sofala. Then, after forwarding information to Portugal regarding the cinnamon, pepper, and clove trade, with some particulars as to the ocean route to India, Covilham entered Abyssinia. He was received hospitably, but was either not allowed to leave or prospered so exceedingly that he decided to remain. Forty years after his departure a Portuguese mission discovered him, and Covilham wept for joy at the sight of men from his own land.

Covilham apparently is the first European to have visited Arabia, for, though no account of his travels survives, he is known to have touched thrice at Aden.

Shortly after Covilham's visits to Arabia an Italian adventurer travelled the whole length of the peninsula, entering on his way the holy cities of Mecca and Medina.

CHAPTER IV

A RENAISSANCE ADVENTURER

Our captain replied, "*Lami ianon ancati telethe elphi seraphi; vualla anemaiati chelp menelchelp !*" Which means, "Oh, fools, I was willing to give you three thousand ducats, by God, but I won't give you them now, you dogs, you sons of dogs!"

LUDOVICO DI VARTHEMA, *Travels*

LUDOVICO DI VARTHEMA'S account of adventures and travels in Egypt, Syria, Arabia, Persia, India, and Ethiopia was read considerably in the sixteenth century, yet little beyond what can be gathered from internal evidence is known of the author. He was an Italian of Bologna, had in all likelihood served as a soldier before he began his travels, and was evidently a person of some physical stamina and of a bold spirit. Varthema was not only stirred by a great longing to see other lands, but impelled to win fame by the honour in which travellers were held in an age that was revealing vast unknown continents. He could not by reading fulfil his desire to learn of the strange places of the world's surface, for he deemed himself "of very slender understanding" and was not given to study. Therefore he resolved to see

personally, and with his own eyes, to endeavour to ascertain the situations of places, the qualities of people, the diversities of animals, the varieties of the fruit-bearing and odoriferous trees . . . remembering well that the testimony of one eyewitness is worth more than ten thousand hearsays.

In writing himself of "slender understanding" Varthema was unduly modest. His book gave pleasure in his own time, and its charm has not diminished through the centuries. Few travellers have written with such manliness, restraint, and honesty, while the accuracy of his descriptions of Arabia has been searchingly tested, to his great credit and vindication, by the writings of such later travellers as Niebuhr and Burckhardt.

54

Early in 1503 Varthema arrived in Alexandria from Europe. On reaching Cairo by way of the Nile he impresses the reader favourably from the beginning by the common sense of his observations. He was not to be impressed by the mere strangeness of his surroundings or by preconceived ideas implanted by the wondrous tales of traders and merchants. Cairo, for example, was reputed to be a city of vast extent, but Varthema remarks that its size has been commonly exaggerated, a mistake probably arising from the inclusion of neighbouring villages with the city itself. From Egypt he went by sea to Beyrout, and thence to Aleppo and Damascus, and seems to have picked up rapidly a working knowledge of Arabic. At Damascus he began the adventure that was to lead him to the holy cities. He is the only European to have reached them by this pilgrim route, and was the first European to leave an account of Yemen.

In April 1503 the *haj* caravan was preparing in Damascus for the pilgrimage to Mecca, and Varthema formed a friendship with a Christian renegade, the captain of the Mameluke escort. After certain financial formalities, much to the captain's benefit, and possibly after professing Islam, the Italian was enrolled in the force under the name of Yunas (Jonah). He tells us that the Mamelukes in Damascus were constantly exercising themselves in arms and in letters, "in order that they may acquire excellence." In the city they went about in pairs or in threes, and had various "privileges." For instance, if an Arab met a Mameluke, though the former might be a great merchant, he was obliged "to honour and give place" to the soldier under penalty of being bastinadoed. In a seemingly artless passage Varthema shows the Mamelukes following a traditional habit of mercenaries and irregulars, for

> if they accidentally meet two or three ladies they possess this privilege, or if they do not possess it they take it: they go to lie in wait for these ladies in certain places like great inns, which are called *chanos* (khans), and as the said ladies pass before the doors each Mameluke takes his lady by the hand, draws her in, and does what he will with her.

For thirty days in the summer of 1503 the *haj* caravan moved through the desert among scenes which would have tempted earlier travellers to introduce a varied assortment of devils and strange animals into their narratives. Varthema, however, writes with sanity and acute observation. His account of the Bedouin, for instance, written four hundred years ago, would suffice as a general description to-day. To one emir, near Mezerib, he attributed property amounting to 40,000 horses, 10,000 mares, 300,000 camels, and pasture extending a two days' journey.

And this lord Zambei, when he thinks proper, wages war with the Sultan of Cairo and the Lord of Damascus and of Jerusalem, and sometimes in harvest-time, when they think that he is a hundred miles distant, he plans some morning a great incursion into the granaries of the said city, and finds the grain and the barley nicely packed up in sacks and carries it off. Sometimes he runs a whole day and a night with his said mares without stopping, and when they have arrived at the end of their journey they give them camels' milk to drink because it is very refreshing. Truly it appears to me that they do not run, but fly like falcons; for I have been with them, and you must know that they ride for the most part without saddles and in their shirts, except some of the principal men. Their arms consist of a lance of Indian cane ten or twelve cubits in length, and when they go on any expedition they keep as close together as starlings. The said Arabians are very small men, and are of a dark tawny colour, and they have a feminine voice, and long, stiff, and black hair. And truly these Arabs are in such vast numbers that they cannot be counted, and they are constantly fighting amongst themselves. They inhabit the mountain, and come down when the caravan passes through to go to Mecca, in order to lie in wait at the passes for the purpose of robbing the said caravan. They carry their wives, children, and all their furniture, and also their houses, upon camels, which houses are like the tents of soldiers, and are of black wool and of a sad appearance.

When the caravan came to water the Mamelukes had many encounters with the Bedouin. Sometimes considerable numbers harassed the escort of sixty men, but did not press their attacks closely, and "never killed more than one man and one lady."

Three days from Medina the convoy reached a mountain inhabited by four or five thousand Jews, dwarfish people, very dark-skinned and with "a feminine voice." The existence of a Jewish colony in Arabia long before Varthema's time is well authenticated, and his "Mountain of the Jews" is usually identified as Kheibar, a colony perhaps originally founded by refugees after the devastation of Judea by the armies of Nebuchadnezzar, and fed by fugitives from later disasters, such as the destruction of Jerusalem by Titus. At the foot of the mountain there was a reservoir which supplied the pilgrims with 16,000 camel-loads of water; "whereat the Jews were ill pleased; and they went about that hill madly like wild goats."

Four miles from Medina the pilgrims halted by a well, washed themselves, and put on clean linen to go into the city. Medina, Varthema wrote, contained about three hundred hearths and was surrounded by earthen walls.

> The first day we went into the city, at the entrance by the door of the mosque, and each of us, small or great, was obliged to be accompanied by some person, who took us by the hand, and led us to where Mohammed was buried.

Varthema's description of the tomb of the Prophet is in general borne out by the accounts of Burckhardt and Burton. He took pains, moreover, to correct an idea that was widely current in those days and for long afterwards—namely, that the Prophet's coffin was made of metal and was suspended in mid-air by the action of magnets.

The renegade Christian commanding the Mamelukes seems to have been, like Varthema himself, a stout, bold fellow, ready always to show his contempt for the local religious hierarchy and to try to convict it of pious fraud. For instance, a supernatural light was supposed to emanate from the sepulchre of the Prophet. It is referred to in the second part of the following extract, after the Hakluyt Society translation, which is especially interesting because it corrects the orthography and mistranslations of Varthema's romanized Arabic, preserving the barbarisms of the original:

> In order to explain the sect of Mahomet, you must know that over the said tower (in the sepulchre of the Prophet) there is a cupola, in which you can walk round the top—that is, outside. You must understand the trick they played off upon the whole caravan the first evening we arrived at the tomb of Mahomet. Our captain sent for the superior of the said mosque, to whom

57

he said that he should show him the body of Nabi—this Nabi means the Prophet Mahomet—that he would give him three thousand serafin of gold, and that he had neither father nor mother, nor brother nor sisters, nor wife nor children, neither had he come to purchase spices or jewels, but that he had come to save his soul, and to see the body of the Prophet. Then the superior answered him with great violence and rage and pride, "How do those eyes of yours which have done so much evil in the world desire to see him for whom God has created the heavens and the earth?" Then answered our captain, "*Sidi intecate el melie*" [1]—that is to say, "Sir, you say true, but do me a favour; let me see the body of the Prophet, and immediately that I have seen it I will pull out my eyes for the love of him." And Sidi answered, "O sir, I will tell you the truth. It is true that our Prophet wished to die here in order to set us a good example; for he could well have died at Mecca had he so willed, but he desired to exercise poverty for our instruction, and as soon as he was dead he was carried at once into heaven by the angels, and he says that he is equal with God." Our captain said to him, "*Eise Hebene Marian phion?*" [2]—that is, "Jesus Christ, the son of Mary, where is He?" The Sidi answered, "*Azafel al Nabi*" [3]—that is, "At the feet of Mahomet." Our captain answered, "*Bes bes hiosi*" [4]—that is, "Enough, enough. I will not know more." Then the captain came out and said to us, "See where I wanted to throw away three thousand seraphim." In the night-time at three o'clock there came into the camp about ten or twelve of these old men of that sect, for the caravan was encamped near the gate, two stones' cast off, and these old men began to cry out some in one part and some in another, "*Lei la illala; Mahometh resullala! Iam Nabi, hia la, hia resullala, stasforla!*" [5]—that is, "God pardon me." "*Leilla illala*" means "God was, God will be," and "*Mahometh resullala*" is "Mahomet the messenger of God will rise again"; "*Iam Nabi*" means "O Prophet, O God." "*Hia resullala*" means "Mahomet will rise again"; "*Stasforla*" signifies "God pardon me." Our captain and we, hearing this noise, immediately ran with our arms in our hands, thinking they were Arabs who wanted to rob the caravan, saying to them, "What is this you are crying out?"

---

[1] *Sidi anta tehki el-melieh.* ("Sir, you say well.")

[2] *Isa iben Marian fain hu?* ("Jesus, the Son of Mary, where is He?")

[3] *Asfel-en Nabi.* ("Below (or under) the Prophet.")

[4] *Bas, bas.* ("Enough, enough.") *Hiosi* equals *Mush 'awaz*—"I don't want (any more)."

[5] *La ilah illa Allah; Muhammed Rasul Allah! Ya Nabi! Hayya Allah! Hayya Rasul Allah! Ist-aghfer lana!* ("There is no god but God! Mohammed is the Prophet of God! O Prophet! Salute God! Salute the Prophet! We invoke forgiveness.")

for they made just such a noise as is heard amongst the Christians when a saint performs a miracle. These old men answered, "*Inte mar abser miri igimen elbeit el Nabi uraman el sama?*"[1] —that is, "Do you not see the brilliant light which comes out of the sepulchre of the Prophet?" Our captain said, "I do not see anything," and he asked all of us if we had seen anything and we answered, "No." One of the old men answered, "Oh, sirs, you cannot see these celestial things because you are not well confirmed in our faith." Our captain replied, "*Lami ianon ancati telethe elphi seraphi; vualla anemaiati chelp menelchelp!*"[2] Which means, "Oh, fools, I was willing to give you three thousand ducats, by God, but I won't give you them now, you dogs, you sons of dogs!" You must know that these lights were certain artificial fires which they had cunningly lighted on the top of the said tower to make us believe that they were lights which issued from the sepulchre of Mahomet; wherefore our captain ordered that none of us should on any account enter the said mosque.

Varthema proceeded with the *haj* to Mecca. He has not told us much about the fauna and flora of Arabia—his pages merely show utterly barren stretches and sandy wastes, sometimes varied by thornbush—but he has impressed the reader by his adaptiveness, quick observation, and by the ease with which he acquired enough Arabic to understand what is said around him. The chapters which follow, describing the trade, ceremonial, and city of Mecca, are remarkable, considering that he could have had scant previous knowledge of the place or of the doctrines and practices of Islam. Greater scholars and more scientific travellers have confirmed his account even in many details.

"The very noble city of Mecca" was unwalled, for the surrounding mountains were its defence. It contained some 6000 families. Eight or ten miles eastward from the city stood the mountain, Arafat, where part of the *haj* ceremony took place. Below this lay two fine reservoirs: one for the caravan from Cairo and the other for that from Damascus. The Cairo

---

[1] *Antar mar tabsar en-nûr* [*alladhi*] *yaji min beit en-Nabi wara min es-sama?* ("Do you not see the splendour proceeding from the house of the Prophet beyond the heavens?")

[2] *Ya majnun! ala 'aati thalath elf ashrafi! W'allah, ana ma 'aati. Kelb bia el-kelb!* ("You fool! I give three thousand ducats! By God, I will not give. You dog, son of a dog!")

pilgrims, with 64,000 camels and an escort of 100 Mamelukes, had arrived a week before Varthema, who reached the city on May 18.

The land round Mecca was barren and desolate, so that almost all provisions came from Jidda. The town was full of Indians, Persians, Syrians, and Ethiopians, some engaged in trade and others seeking pardon. The merchandise on sale consisted of jewels, spices from India and Ethiopia, cotton and silk stuffs from Bengal, wax, and "odoriferous substances."

Varthema's description of "the pardoning" may be recalled later, against the experiences of Burckhardt and Burton:

> In the midst of the said city there is a very beautiful temple, similar to the Colosseum at Rome, but not made of such large stones, but of burnt bricks, and it is round in the same manner; it has ninety or one hundred doors around it, and is arched . . . on entering the said temple you descend ten or twelve steps of marble, and here and there about the said entrance there stand men who sell jewels and nothing else. And when you have descended the said steps you find the said temple all around, and everything—that is, the walls—covered with gold. And under the said arches there stand about 4000 or 5000 persons, men and women, which persons sell all kinds of odoriferous things; the greater part are powders for preserving human bodies, because pagans come there from all parts of the world. Truly it would not be possible to describe the sweetness and odours which are smelt within this temple. It appears like a spicery full of musk and of other most delicious odours. On the 23rd of May the said pardon commences in the above-mentioned temple. The pardon is this; within the said temple and uncovered in the centre there is a tower, the size of which is about five or six paces on every side, around which tower there is a cloth of black silk. And there is a door of silver of the height of a man, by which you enter into the said tower. On each side of the door there is a jar which they say is full of balsam, and which is shown on the day of Pentecost.[1] And they say that that balsam is part of the treasures of the Sultan. On each side of the tower there is a large ring at the corner. On the 24th of May all the people begin, before day, to go seven

---

[1] Varthema, says the Hakluyt editor, was probably thinking of Good Friday and the Easter which follows, and connecting in his mind the Mohammedan sacrifices of Arafat with the solemnities of these Christian seasons, when he writes of "the day of Pentecost."

BEDOUIN OF THE HEJAZ
Photo E.N.A.

A Yemenite Jewess wearing Bridal Headdress
Photo E.N.A

times around the said tower, always touching and kissing each corner. And at about ten or twelve paces from the said tower there is another tower, like one of your chapels, with three or four doors. In the centre of the said tower there is a very beautiful well which is seventy fathoms deep, and the water is brackish. At this well there stand six or eight men appointed to draw water for the people. And when the said people have gone seven times around the first tower they go to this well and place themselves with their backs towards the brink of the well, saying "*Bizmilei erachman erachin stoforla aladin*," [1] which means "In the name of God pardon me my sins." And those who draw the water throw three bucketsful over each person, from the crown of their heads to their feet, and all bathe, even though their dress be made of silk. And they say in this wise that all their sins remain there after this washing. And they say that the first tower which they walked round was the first house that Abraham built. And all having thus bathed, they go by way of the valley to the said mountain of which we have before spoken, and remain there two days and one night. And when they are all at the foot of the said mountain, they make the sacrifice there. . . . Every man and woman kills at least two or three, and some four and six, sheep; so that I really believe that on the first day more than 30,000 sheep are killed by cutting their throats facing the east. Each person gives them to the poor for the love of God, for there were about 30,000 people there who made a very large hole in the earth and then put in it camels' dung, and thus they made a little fire, and warmed the flesh a little and then ate it. And truly it is my opinion that these poor men came more on account of their hunger than for the sake of pardon, and as a proof that it was so we had a great number of cucumbers which came from Arabia Felix, and we ate them all but the rind, which we afterwards threw away outside our tent. And about forty or fifty of the said poor people stood before our tent and made a great scrambling among themselves in order to pick up the said rinds, which were full of sand. By this it appeared to us that they came rather to satisfy their hunger than to wash away their sins.[2] On the second day a *cadi* of their faith like one of our preachers ascended to the top of the said mountain and made a discourse to the said people, which discourse lasted for about an hour; and he made in their language a sort of lamentation, and besought the people that they should

---

[1] *Bism-Illah er-rahman er-rahim. Istaghfir lana.* ("In the name of God, the Pitiful, the Compassionate, pardon us.")

[2] Burton says that this illustrates the poverty of the Takruri and other Africans, but attributes an unworthy motive. He gives examples of the poverty of many of the pilgrims.

weep for their sins. And he said to them in a loud voice, "Oh, Abraham, well wished for and well loved of God." And then he said, "Oh, Isaac, chosen of God, friend of God, beseech God for the people of Naby," and then were heard very great lamentations. And when he had finished his sermon the whole caravan rushed back into Mecca with the greatest haste, for at a distance of six miles there were more than 20,000 Arabs, who wanted to rob the caravan, and we arrived for the defence of Mecca.

On this occasion there may have been some fear of a Bedouin attack, but such a rush back from Arafat occurred on every *haj*. Three hundred and fifty years later Burton described it vividly. The pilgrims hastened because the prayer shortly after sunset should be said at the mosque of Muzdalifa some three hours later. About half-way back to Mecca the pilgrims threw stones at a small wall, where, Varthema writes, Isaac is said to have thrown a stone in the devil's face.

When the time came to return to Syria Varthema decided to desert from the Mamelukes. It was apparently his intention to make for India. He won the assistance of a Mohammedan confederate by aiding him to get merchandise—fifteen camels laden with spices—out of the town without paying duty, and by convincing him that he intended to manufacture large mortars for the use of Moslems in Yemen against the Portuguese. The Mohammedan concealed him in his own house, where Varthema listened with considerable trepidation to the trumpet rallying the Mamelukes, under pain of death, for the homeward journey. He was in such danger before the departure of the Mamelukes that even the presence of the merchant's niece, who was infatuated with him, could bring no consolation. But he dared not offend her. In the words of a translation in an older idiom, "in the middest of these troubles and fears, the fyre of Venus was almost extinct in me; and therefore with daliaunce of fayre woordes and promises, I styll kepte myselfe in her favour." Some days later, when the town was free of the Mamelukes, he set off for Jidda.

At that time Christians and Jews were forbidden the port, and Varthema sought safety among the crowds in a mosque which sheltered large numbers of poor people. Here he lay all day covered with a cloth, upon the ground, groaning constantly as though in great pain. In the evenings he went out to buy food. On these excursions he used his eyes and ears well, and noted correctly the name of the ruler, the barrenness of the land around, the great scarcity of fresh water, the sea beating against the houses, the bad air of the place, which induced much illness, that the population numbered 500 families, and that supplies were imported from Cairo and Arabia Felix. After nearly three weeks of this existence in Jidda he found a place on a vessel bound for Persia, and continued his journey down the Red Sea, sailing only during the daylight, and then with a man at the top of the mast to watch for reefs and rocks.

Soon he noted, as they came to the Yemen coast, the signs of a richer cultivation. At Jizan, where the ship put in for provisions, he found

> good grapes and peaches, quinces, pomegranates, very strong garlic, tolerable onions, excellent nuts, melons, roses, flowers, nectarines, figs, gourds, citrons, lemons, and sour oranges, so that it is a paradise . . . abundance of flesh, grain, barley, and white millet, which they call *dora* and which makes good bread.

The vessel at length reached Aden, walled on two sides and with mountains on the others, along which were five forts. Though it was so hot that the market was held two hours after sunset, it seemed a beautiful city to Varthema, perhaps because it was for him the gateway from Arabia. He learned that Aden was the meeting-place for all ships coming from India, Persia, and Ethiopia, and noticed that vessels entering the port were boarded by the customs officers, and that their masts, sails, rudders, and anchors were removed, so that they could not depart without paying the Sultan's dues.

At Aden Varthema experienced his first real misfortunes. Accused of being a spy of the Christians, he was thrown into prison with eighteen pounds of iron on his feet. To make his case worse there arrived some twoscore Mohammedans who had escaped from ships captured by the Portuguese. These refugees accused him of having been present at the attack, and Varthema was in considerable danger. After being kept in prison for two months he was taken, still in irons, an eight days' journey by camel to Radaa, about 160 miles north of Aden.

In the presence of the Sultan he insisted that he was not a spy of the Christians, but a good Mohammedan. By this time the Italian seems to have lost some of his self-confidence, for when he was asked to repeat the formula of Islam he "could not pronounce the words at all, whether such were the will of God, or through the fear which had seized me." He was therefore thrown into prison, and kept on very short rations of water and millet bread.

Two days later the Sultan led an expedition against Sana. His army contained 2000 Abyssinian horsemen, who were, in Varthema's opinion, worth more than all the rest of his 80,000 men together. Five thousand camels carrying tents and ropes accompanied the army.

After the departure of the troops one of the Sultan's wives, "very faire and comely, after theyr maner, and of colour inclining to blacke," showed a very definite liking for the adventurer. Varthema's mind, however, was solely occupied with thoughts of escape. He tried to gain release by feigning madness, and though he imposed upon some of the wise men the Sultan's wife was not impressed. She would spend hours of the day gazing upon him, admiring his fine figure and white skin, and bemoaning the fate that would give her only black children. Varthema seems to have resisted her admiration, for "the fyre of Venus" was again dampened by his sense of peril. As his body, he avers, was already in sufficient danger, he did not wish to imperil his soul. In the end he managed to persuade her that he was ill and in need of the attentions of a particular holy man at Aden. He had skilfully avoided offending her, and when the Sultan returned from the campaign she not only helped Varthema to gain his freedom, but gave him money and transport to the sea.

Two days at Aden wrought a complete change in the adventurer's health! He was careful to visit the holy man, and then wrote to the Sultana that he was well and intending to see something of the country. He dared not yet attempt escape, as a Mohammedan fleet was in the harbour.

In the subsequent weeks he visited many of the towns and

villages in this corner of Arabia. Comparing his account of these places with that of Niebuhr, one remarks the accuracy of this earlier, untrained traveller's observations. Lahej he describes as a populous place, with a great produce of meat, and grain from its fertile plain, but a scarcity of wood for fuel and no dates. Wool, silk, many fruits, were also produced in the district. Niebuhr's account agrees with Varthema's. His account of Zebid, in the Tihama, and his description of Sana, again tally closely with those of the later, more instructed, explorer. He notes the very strong position of Sana on its mountain, its very thick walls (of earth, where Niebuhr says earth faced with unburned brick), its vines and fine gardens. Both travellers remark the great troops of apes in Yemen. One place, however, which the Danish traveller does not enumerate in his list of towns and villages is described by Varthema. This is El Makranah, which Varthema calls "Almacarana," in a very strong position at the top of a seven-mile incline, with plentiful food supplies, fine climate, great reservoirs of water, and a population almost white in complexion.

On his return to Aden Varthema again adopted the ruse of lying by day in a mosque to avoid dangerous encounters. He again emerged only at night, and finally made arrangements with the master of a vessel bound for Persia. Soon the Arabian coast was left behind, and Varthema's later excitements and adventures are not concerned with Arabia.

His book was printed in Italian at Rome in 1510 and 1517, at Venice in 1518, 1535, and 1563. The first English translation came in 1576–77 (in Richard Eden's *History of Travayle*). An extract from Varthema appeared in Purchas's *Pilgrimage* (1625–26), and the Hakluyt Society edition by J. W. Jones and G. P. Badger was published in 1863. Varthema's picture of the pilgrimage, the holy cities, and of Yemen was known to subsequent explorers, who sometimes distrusted his facts, though Varthema in the event was often proved correct. Burckhardt particularly, of travellers up to the early nineteenth century, knew the Italian's narrative thoroughly well. Yet in the nineteenth century Varthema's story was little known except to the geographer and specialist reader. Burton in 1855 helped to make it known more widely by quoting extracts from the sixteenth-century translation in his *Pilgrimage to Al-Madinah and Meccah*.

Little material reward came to the Bolognese from his writings, but he would have been well pleased with the opinions of his great successors, for his story has a notable place in the records of Arabian travel.

CHAPTER V

THE GREAT AFONSO D'ALBOQUERQUE

The advantage of time and place in all martial actions is half a victory; which being lost is irrecoverable.

SIR FRANCIS DRAKE

THE opening of the sea route round the Cape of Good Hope brought to Arabia men of a sterner mould than Covilham and Varthema. The new road to the spice lands, representing cheaper transport than that of Arab dhow and overland caravans, was simply a commercial revolution which gave Lisbon the place of Venice as the emporium of the spice trade. But the Portuguese went mainly in search of the pepper of India and Ceylon and the cloves of the Moluccas. They were not at first interested in Arabia. Their aims, however, became eventually more complex, and included not only the pursuit of commercial monopoly, but also imperial and proselytizing objectives. Vasco da Gama and others might think chiefly in terms of economic opportunity, but resistance to traders brought the soldier, and Afonso d'Alboquerque was the first to build a fort in India. Portuguese fleets began to harry the Moslem on the high seas, so that ships set out from the East for the Red Sea and the Persian Gulf without waiting for the monsoon, and were glad to sell their wares to native merchants at Aden. The Aden ships would slip round with the monsoon to Jidda and Suez to sell the goods that had been bought. Aden gained a reputation for wealth beyond all other places on the Arabian coast.

As Varthema saw the Arabian shore fall astern, the prows of Tristão da Cunha and Alboquerque were turned towards the Arabian Sea, but some years were to elapse before "the Portuguese Mars" attacked the main centre of Arab commerce and attempted to close the Red Sea to Moslem trade. If Alboquerque was superior to many contemporaries in his sense of justice towards subject peoples he was typical of the

Portuguese of his age in his piety, cunning, cruelty, and sur-
passing courage. His countrymen had been hardened in the
wars against the Mohammedans in Spain and North Africa;
they had better ships and an artillery better served than their
foes in Indian waters. Thus for some years they pursued a way
of conquest, establishing themselves at Ormuz and Goa before
Alboquerque found time to essay his favourite but long-
delayed scheme of closing the Red Sea to Mohammedan
commerce. However, three days before the Good Friday of
1513 the semi-independent Moslem Governor of Aden received
a report that a fleet of Christian vessels was approaching. On
Good Friday Alboquerque appeared off the harbour, feeling
his way carefully, for he had no chart, to an anchorage in
fourteen fathoms. As night fell the garrison of Aden lit fires
on the shore at some distance from the harbour to mislead him.
But Alboquerque was less interested in the fires than in the
signs of approaching bad weather, and issued a general order
to the ships to anchor and strengthen their cables. A storm in
the night justified his caution.

There had been some discussion during the approach to
Aden as to whether the Portuguese should attack at once or
parley with the Mohammedans. The captains finally adopted
Alboquerque's opinion, that negotiations would give the
garrison

> time to prepare defence and for help to come if they needed it,
> for the Moors of that land would not pay tribute in consequence
> of philosophical arguments, but only after much blood had been
> spilt amongst them.[1]

When the storm died down the Governor, Mira Mirgao, sent
messengers to ask the Portuguese intentions. Alboquerque
replied that he was bound for Suez on duty for his king. The
Governor then sent presents of fowl, sheep, and fruit, and
asserted that he was the King of Portugal's servant. Alboquerque answered that in that case the gates of the city should
be opened, and that he would then allow safe conduct to such
vessels in the harbour as applied for it to him. The Governor

[1] *Commentaries of the Great Afonso d'Alboquerque,* translated by W. de Gray Birch
(London, 1877).

suggested a parley at the water's edge, but Alboquerque replied that he would meet him only in the city itself.

During the rough weather the gangways intended for the landing had been lost, and now Alboquerque began to collect barges round the harbour to be used in putting the storming parties ashore.

The *Commentaries of the Great Afonso d'Alboquerque*, published by Alboquerque's son in 1557, reprinted in 1576, and republished in 1774, describe Aden as a town of beautiful lofty stone and mortar houses, fortified by a wall, with an island bastion, and with walled hills containing forts behind the town. Water had to be brought to the city, which had only the slightest rainfall, and the town's chief product then was madder. Alboquerque judged the wall of Aden too long to be carried by a frontal attack along its whole extent, and ordered the assault to be launched in two places by parallel columns. In his plan the first and vital objective when the wall was crossed was to be the gate opening on to the high ground behind the city, so that the place should be cut off from help from the interior.

During the night the assaulting troops assembled at the flagship and pulled for the shore two hours before dawn. The barges, however, grounded farther out than was expected, the musketeers had to wade ashore, and much of their powder was spoiled. But many such mishaps could not stay the Portuguese of this heroic age. They rushed for the wall and put the scaling ladders into position. There was then such a press of men to mount them that all the ladders save one broke. Alboquerque was at the wall with his men, and rallied a party of halberdiers to support the remaining ladder with their weapons. But again too many troops swarmed up, and the ladder gave way. A few of the men had reached the top of the wall, but could do little, as they were armed only with short swords. An embrasure in the wall was then smashed in, and the Portuguese occupied it until the defenders drove them back, filling the gap with earth, stones, and burning straw. One party, led by Jorge da Silveira, fought their way from the wall and reached the street barricades before they were driven back and the leader killed. A few others held out in a turret on the wall.

69

By this time Alboquerque saw that the attack had failed, and endeavoured to withdraw this small party. Here one of his difficulties lay in the indiscipline of his officers, who now, as at other times, showed no anxiety to retire from the enemy. Some of the men slid down the wall to safety by means of ropes. But one officer, Garcia da Sousa, flatly refused to retreat, and remained on the wall with his mulatto servant, beating off a great crowd of foes, until he fell dead with an arrow through his head. Then the mulatto slipped down the rope, carrying his buckler stuck full of arrows.

Alboquerque had some difficulty in rallying his men for embarkation. Guns from the island of Sirah opened out, killing some and wounding many others. Under fire from the town also, the rank and file clamoured for the heavy guns to be taken out of the ships and brought ashore, so that they could make a breach in the walls. Alboquerque, however, had to envisage wider considerations. He saw that the troops, though full of fighting spirit, were becoming exhausted in the terrific heat, and he knew that the tidal waters left no place for batteries to be mounted against the walls. Furthermore, the end of the Eastern monsoon was approaching, and he had planned to visit the Red Sea. No more time could be spent at Aden, though he had every intention of revisiting the port. Sirah, however, was sufficiently troublesome to necessitate the dispatch of a storming party. It was captured by Alboquerque's nephew, Garcia da Noronha. Thirty-six cannon were taken, and the embarkation was then covered by a Portuguese bombardment of the city, which destroyed many houses. The ships in the harbour were stripped of shrouds and rigging, emptied of merchandise and provisions, and set on fire. Alboquerque then sailed for the Straits of Bab el Mandeb and the Red Sea.

His attack seems to have caused a general uneasiness throughout the Mohammedan world, even as far north as Cairo and Damascus. Alboquerque was of the opinion that four key positions were necessary for Portuguese dominion in the East —namely, Ormuz, Goa, Diu, and Aden—but the last of these never fell into his hands.

As a leader in battle Alboquerque would have inspired the

troops of any nation. But he was more than a soldier. His most grandiose scheme involved the establishment of a Portuguese empire in India, a dream which to his contemporaries seemed beyond attainment. On the grand scale, too, was his plan for striking a mighty blow at the Moslems in Egypt by diverting the Nile, turning it through the Abyssinian Christian empire of the mythical Prester John. So forward was this conception in his mind that he even asked for miners to be sent from Madeira, men used to working through rock. Insignificant in relation to such mighty projects seems another of his plans—to raid Yenbo and Medina with a force of 400 cavalry, seize the body of Mohammed and hold it in ransom for the Holy Temple at Jerusalem. That the project was something more than vague in his mind is shown by the fact that he had gathered some preliminary data—that the raid inland should take only one and a half days to reach the objective, as against thirty days for the news to reach Cairo and for the organization of a march across the desert to the holy city. As the guard there numbered, according to his information, only 300 Africans, who were without firearms, he considered that before help could arrive he would have embarked at Yenbo with the body!

But as yet he did not even know the Red Sea, so while he sailed along the South Arabian shore a vessel was sent ahead, captured a pilot and forcibly detained him. After two days' sailing from Aden the mouth of the Straits was reached and Alboquerque led the first Portuguese fleet into the Red Sea. To celebrate the occasion he ordered that "the ships should be dressed with all their flags, and all the artillery fired, and great rejoicing made." After a short stay at Perim he proceeded up the Red Sea, capturing ships laden with supplies for Jidda and Mecca. The *Commentaries* here describe the anchorages, winds, and some of the navigational features of those waters.

His stay in these waters led to no substantial results, though it added something to existing knowledge of both shores. Finally, before leaving the Yemen coast, Alboquerque anchored again off Aden and suggested burning the large number of ships which had congregated in the harbour. But the military officers demurred, pointing out the many guns trained on the ships to protect them from just such an operation. Alboquerque then led a hundred picked sailors in a rapid midnight raid on the harbour, killed some thirty guards, and set fire to many ships. The soldiers felt themselves put to shame and begged permission to carry out a second attack, but Alboquerque held them back, knowing that the enemy would be henceforth thoroughly alert. Like the experienced raiding officer of the Western Front, "the Portuguese Mars" possessed a highly developed instinct for the things that can be done only once.

Alboquerque's cruise in the Red Sea gained some information for his successors, but they failed to profit by it. Some years later, when Aden had suffered in fighting with the Egyptians and its fortifications were in disrepair, the Portuguese, under Lopo Soares, appeared off the port with a great armament. The ruler of Aden offered surrender, but occupation would have necessitated landing a garrison, and Soares, considering he should conserve his forces for an attack on the Mohammedans in the Red Sea, refused. It was a colossal error of judgment. When storms and insubordinate captains had ruined his expedition Soares reached Aden again, only to find the forts had been strengthened and the ruler had changed his mind. In 1541 Estavão da Gama, a son of Vasco, entered the Red Sea, but was repulsed in an attack on Suez.

Alboquerque's work was never determinedly followed up. The Portuguese founded settlements at four points on the coast of Oman, at Muscat, Sohar, Matrah, and Kiryat, but they made no effort to extend inland, and, in fact, were dominated by the Arabs. In the middle of the sixteenth century a Jesuit missionary landed at Muscat on his way to Ormuz, and tried to make the European exiles who had fled there for refuge return to the duties of their faith and do penance. From Muscat he proceeded to Ormuz, whose state was probably better than that of the wretched Christian remnants on the Arabian peninsula. Following Xavier's precepts he kept his own counsel, but by his humanity, submission, and prudence made himself "acceptable and dear" to the authorities, and through them got to know the condition of the merchants and the people in the trading stations. He found a "contempt of sacred things, ignorance of divine law, and forgetfulness of the next world." For many years the Christians had lacked religious services, parish priests, and all guidance. "The clergy lately arrived, such were the times, were hardly more anxious for gaining souls than money." The Jesuit, whose denunciation probably should not be modified on the grounds of asceticism (like the tirades of a medieval saint), found weeds in the soil of Christianity—ceremonies and errors, magical arts, superstition, communism in wives, marriages with Jews and Turks, Christian children brought up as Mohammedans and Jews. "With great force and preaching and terrible denunciation of the anger of Heaven" the Jesuit began the task of "correcting the customs adopted from other nations."[1]

II

Eight years before Alboquerque entered the Red Sea a Portuguese vessel had been wrecked off the Yemen coast. Alboquerque had, in fact, put in at Zebid and made fruitless inquiries regarding the fate of some of the survivors who had been captured. Gregorio da Quadras, who commanded the ship, managed to escape, and eventually reached Ormuz. If his strange story is true—and it is not utterly improbable—this seaman performed an astonishing Arabian journey.

After the loss of his vessel da Quadras was held prisoner by the Arabs, learned Arabic, and practised as a tailor, making principally hats, for which the Arabs gave him dates and raisins. During his captivity he earned a reputation among them for great patience and saintliness. Then there was a revolt against the local ruler, and the victorious rebel leader not only freed all captives, but proclaimed his intention of making a pilgrimage in thanksgiving to the holy cities. Da Quadras attached himself to the party, for he saw an opportunity of reaching Mecca and of going northward to Damascus with the returning pilgrim caravan. From Syria he intended to make for Basra and then Ormuz.

At Medina the Arabs with whom da Quadras had journeyed were performing their devotions round the tomb of the Prophet when the Portuguese was suddenly overcome by

[1] Maffei, *Historiæ indicæ* (Venice, 1592).

memory of the Christian faith in which he had been reared, and cried out with many tears, "Prophet of Satan, if thou art that one whom those dogs adore, manifest to them that I am a Christian, for I hope, by our Lord's mercy, that I shall yet behold this thy house of abomination become a Church for His praise, like as is that of our Lady of Conception at Lisbon."

At this outburst the Arabs were astounded, but admired his sanctity, and begged him very earnestly "to make his abode with them for some days." However, it is hard to reconcile this profession of Christianity with his next act. He told the leader of his party that he would like to visit the temple of Mohammed's grandchildren in Persia, and would not listen to those who warned him of the great deserts that existed to the north. He set off alone, and, having consumed his little store of provisions, lived on "locusts and other winged creatures, for the way lay mostly through country of desert and loose sand." He wore only a loincloth, and his body, burned by the sun, was soon covered with blisters, so that he could not lie down to rest, but dug a pit in the sand, in which he slept standing. At length he became so weak that he could go no farther, and, crawling to the foot of a hill of sand, cried out to God for mercy, saying, "Lord, seeing that I am Thy creature, redeemed with Thy precious blood, and that Thou hast permitted me to escape from a captivity in which I lay, have mercy upon me, and be not willing that I should come thus miserably to my end here in these deserts." Then he began to confess his sins to God, "begging Him to bear his soul in remembrance, having quite made up his mind to bring his journeying to a close at that spot." Suddenly he was raised by people he could not see, borne to the top of a sand-hill and left there. Down the reverse slope he saw an Arab and a camel, and as he went towards them he perceived that there was a caravan at a watering-place.

The Arabs, amazed at seeing a man in that place, thought that he must be a saint, took him with them, clothed him, and healed his wounds. He told them that he was on a pilgrimage to Persia, and went in their caravan as far as Babylon, where the caravan proceeded to Damascus, and da Quadras to Basra. Thence he made his way by sea to Ormuz, where he told his story to Garcia da Coutenho, the captain of the Portuguese post. From Ormuz he was passed on to India, and thence reached Portugal, where he became a Franciscan of the Capuchin Order, "and so ended his days with holiness."

The story of da Quadras cannot be entirely dismissed. The compiler of Alboquerque's *Commentaries*, obviously a man of high intelligence and judgment, recounts it soberly. Those who carried the wretched, almost unconscious fugitive up the dune into sight of the caravan may have been some small party of Bedouin, or of Selaib, the elusive gipsies of the desert. If the story is true da Quadras was the first recorded European to traverse the entire peninsula.

CHAPTER VI

THE FIRST ENGLISHMEN IN ARABIA

Much perill and small hope of trade may be expected at Aden,
yt being a garrison towne of souldiers rather than of merchauntes;
yet neare to Aden . . . there is a towne called Mocha, governed
with marchauntes onelie and a place of spetiall trade.

AN EAST INDIA COMPANY'S OFFICER, 1609

SOME fifty years after the Portuguese had allowed opportunity to pass them by the English ship *Ascension*,
accompanied by the pinnace *Good Hope*, arrived off Aden
after a year's adventurous voyage from the Thames. It was
April 1609, and the English East India Company was endeavouring to force a way into the Indian trade, in the face of
Portuguese and Dutch resistance. Alexander Sharpeigh was
the 'general' in charge of this venture, and with him as chief
factor was one John Jourdain, a shrewd, brave, resourceful,
and enterprising man, of Lyme Regis, in Dorset. The vessels
carried a cargo of general merchandise—iron, tin, lead, and
cloth.

Aden had been in Turkish hands for some seventy years, and
was no longer, as in ancient times, the chief mart for European,
Arabian, and Indian produce. Mocha was becoming more
generally used, as more convenient for Red Sea and Indian
shipping and for Arabian caravans. Just at this time, too, it
was in particular favour, for fighting round Jidda had made
that port unpopular.

The Governor of Aden, a Greek renegade, welcomed
Sharpeigh, entertaining him "with tabour and pipe and other
heathen musicke." But when the seaman wished to go back
to his ship he was quite courteously restrained. A message had
been sent to the Turkish Pasha at Sana, he was told, and until
instructions were received he would have to remain ashore
under guard. He was lodged in a "faire house," while the
Greek tried to persuade him to bring the *Ascension* closer inshore

and land her cargo. This he refused to do, but landed a little merchandise in order to play for time.

At length the Pasha's reply arrived from Sana, and Sharpeigh was informed that it permitted the Governor to buy some of his cloth and all the lead. But he was still kept prisoner. When certain Aden officials came aboard to examine the cloth John Jourdain judged it was time for action. Says his narrative:

> Wee tooke them into the cabbin and told them that seeing the Governor had falsified his promise soe often with the Generall and detayned him aland, doubtinge much his meaninge towards us, wee ment to keepe them as pledges untill our Generall came aboard.[1]

Sharpeigh was then surrendered, though the Greek uttered "vile wordes," demanded heavier customs duties on the goods that had been landed, and said that if the English did not pay he would send Jourdain and another factor, who had gone ashore, to the Pasha at Sana to settle the amount of duty. As Sharpeigh would not agree to the demands, and as Jourdain was quite willing to go to Sana, the journey was made, and the Yemen was traversed for the first time by Englishmen.

Meanwhile an Indian ship with a cargo of indigo was reported at Mocha, and after the report had been verified by two of Sharpeigh's officers who sailed along the coast in a native boat the *Ascension* sailed from Aden. William Revett and Philip Glascock, the two officers, were the first Englishmen to pass through the Straits of Bab el Mandeb. On the morning of May 9, 1609, says the former's story,

> wee had syght of Babarmandell, which is a necke of lande that lyeth into the sea some league or more from the mayne, and sheweth farre of as it were an iland, but is a baye. At this place begynneth the entrannce into the Read Sea, having the Coast of Abex [Abyssinia] on the larboard syde and the mayne of Arabia on the starboard, some eight leagues dystannce the one from the other. . . . Barbarmandell is a necke of a lande which ryseth lyke mountaynes here and there, as though there were passages through, and that an iland some league and haulfe into the sea; but when you come nye it, you may perceive it joyneth to the mayne. Into the entrannce of the Read Sea ther lyeth

---

[1] *The Journal of John Jourdain,* edited for the Hakluyt Society by William Foster (London, 1905).

on the starboard syde of us, not above one myle and haulf dystannce, a small ilande [Perim], which maketh the mouth of the Read Sea. . . . At the entrannce the sea cockells in such sorte that you would thinke it were showldes, but is nothinge but a currant that setteth in and out of the strayght. About eleven of the clocke wee entred, the landes bearing next hande E. and W. This is a place of some 20 or 30 cottages of Arrabbs, with a house of white stone where a proffett is intoumbed, who in his lyfe tyme was in great esteemation, as also synce his death resorted too by pylgrymmes for devotion sake; but I will let him sleepe with God or the Divell, not knowing whose servannt hee is, and goe onwardes with the Lordes helpe on my way. Here wee cam to ankor about twelve of the clocke, and stayed here, for the master of our barkes pleasure, untill mydnight, and then weyed with a fresh gale of wynde. . . . About nine of the clocke wee lannded at the city of Mocha, where wee founde many shippes rydinge, some of Dabull, some of Dieu, some of Chaull, or Surratt, Cocheen and Ormus.

The Aden which Jourdain describes was a ruinous place, but surrounded by strong stone walls vigilantly guarded, and an outpost fort on the island of Sirah afforded further protection. The Arab inhabitants were kept in awe by a small Turkish garrison, and were not allowed to carry arms of any kind or have weapons in their houses. Immediately on arrival the English were warned against selling arms, and were told that if any Arab bought arms secretly it would cost him his life. If the Arabs were allowed to buy, wrote Jourdain, "our peeces and sword blades would bee a good comoditie in those partes."

Jourdain's Aden was a dry, craggy, decayed place, visited by perhaps two or three small ships each year, sailing from India or the Persian Gulf with calico, turban cloths, and cotton-wool, and returning with gum arabic, frankincense, myrrh, and madder. In the Yemen hinterland the Turkish grip was weaker; they could hold only the main routes and the towns.

His narrative of the journey to Sana presents an alternating view of barren regions, mountains, and districts fruitful in crops of grain; water cisterns and irrigation systems; walled towns and castles on mountain-tops. He received from the Pasha permission to sell the English goods, but could get no redress in the matter of customs duty, and was warned against returning to Yemen without a special licence from Stamboul. He then set out to join the *Ascension* at Mocha, which he reached safely in a fortnight's travel.

In the castle of Sana hostages were held by the Turks, as pledges for the good behaviour of the Arab population and the

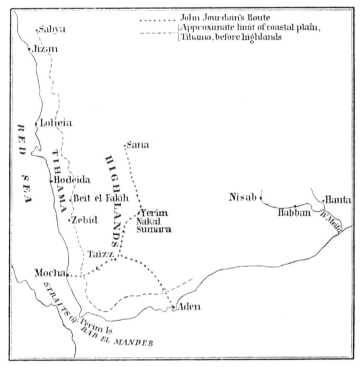

JOURDAIN'S ROUTE IN YEMEN

payment of tribute. The trade of the town was largely in the hands of Banyans, Indian merchants from Gujrat, who dealt in cotton piece-goods and turban cloths and acted as inland agents for their countrymen at Aden, Mocha, and Jidda. The climate was temperate, and the surrounding country provided ample food. Jourdain describes a hill, near the town, where cornelians and stones like emeralds could be obtained, then as now—"catts eyes, agatts and blud stones in great number,

79

with other stones amongst of better valewe." Sana had
buildings of brick, with "many faire howses and churches with
faire towres and many prettye gardens within the town, the
cittie standinge in a very plessant plaine."

In an account which is generally quite in harmony with those
of modern travellers Jourdain makes one curious error.
Remarking that "cohoo" (coffee) was "a greate merchandize
. . . carried to Grand Cairo and all other places of Turkey
and to the Indies," he seems to have thought that it would
grow only on the high and steep mountain of "Nosmarde"
(Nakal Sumara), which he passed on his way to Sana.

On the way to Mocha he stayed some days at Taizz, which
was larger than Sana. He says little of the town, but tells of
an old Portuguese renegade with whom he spent much time.
The old man seems to have been a sorcerer or dervish.
Jourdain calls him a "witch," for the term was then used of
man or woman. The people of Taizz used to come to his
house clamouring for his blessing, and when he had given it
the old man would return laughing to Jourdain, saying that

> these foolish infidel people thought him to be a saint, and hee
> was none other than a divell, and because he could doe a few of
> the Divell's miracles, which he had taught him, they thought him
> to be a saint.

At Mocha Sharpeigh tried to drive too hard a bargain for
his goods, and did little business, selling only a few sword-
blades. But Jourdain and Revett both considered there was
scope there for the sale of tin, iron, lead, cloth, and all
English commodities. Turks, Moors, and Armenians from
Constantinople, Aleppo, Damascus, Tripoli, Suez, and Jidda
traded in cloth, tin, silk, and kerseys, but principally brought
ready money to invest with merchants coming from Ethiopia
and all parts of India. The port had a great daily "bussart"
(bazaar), and food was cheap, grain sold at eighteenpence a
bushel, fish enough for a meal for ten men could be bought for
threepence, and there was an abundant supply of "apricocks,
quinces, dates, grapes, peaches, limmons and plantains."
As at Aden, the Turkish garrison was small, numbering only
forty men, but apparently adequate for holding the Arabs in
check. Revett thus described Mocha and its trade system:

PILGRIMS PASSING THROUGH THE MECCA GATE AT JIDDA

Photo E.N.A.

SANA: A GENERAL VIEW

Photo E.N.A.

The citty is sittuated in a playne, and consysts in some 6000 houses, the three parts whereof are of canes covered of straw. The reason is it rayneth very lytell there. It hath the water from wells some myle out of the citty, and brought in by poore pepell upon asses, by which meanes they get their livinge. It hath neither walles, castell, nor fort. . . . But the chiefe manntenannce of it is the trade of marchannts, which with the easterly monsoones commeth out of India with the wyndes between the east and the north-east, and there stayeth all the said monsoone, which continneweth some seven monnethes; the which tyme they have to seel their marchandize unto the marchannts . . . which commeth by bark from Swes [Suez] and Zidda [Jidda], to transporte their monnyes and goods with west and south-west wyndes which continneweth five monnethes in the yeare; at the latter ende of which wyndes the India shippes depart, which is about the fyne of Agust . . . and with that wynde is carried for India; and the small barks and shippinge with the fyrst of the east and north-east wyndes goeth for Swes and Zidda; which is an infallabell rule amongst them for their trades. Now by reason of troubles in Zidda and other places in those parts, this citty . . . serveth the marchannts of Constantinopell, Alleppo, Trippolie, Damasco and Grand Cairo of turbandes, callicoes of all sortes, pyntadoes and divers other coullored stuffes as also white of great vallew, cotton wolle and in fyne indico, which goeth by this passadge into most parts of the worlde. They bringe also and serveth this place out of India much iron, which they reape great bennefytt by and are shewer of their salles dewringe the easterly and most part of the westerly monsoone, which they stay for salles, reservinge a tyme by computation for their retourne.

When Sharpeigh found no market to meet his price he sailed for India. The renegade Governor of Aden shortly afterwards seized another commander of an East India Company expedition, Sir Henry Middleton, and murdered some of his companions. Middleton escaped and demonstrated, by raiding and plundering the shipping lanes to Yemen, that Englishmen could hit as hard as Portuguese or Dutch. Jourdain was serving with Middleton during this interruption of the South Arabian sea traffic.

The English and Dutch had combined to overthrow the Portuguese domination of the eastern trade areas, but once such small resistance as Portugal could offer to the two determined northern states was crushed quarrels began between the victors. The Dutch, who had gained the monopoly of the spice trade, that golden lure of the East, did not hesitate at murder and general ruthlessness to keep it. In 1623 occurred the torturing and death of the English trade agents at Amboyna, in the Spice Islands, a deed which remained un-avenged until the Commonwealth's Dutch War, thirty years later.

Four years before these murders John Jourdain was at Patani when the approach of a strong Dutch flotilla under Hendrik Janszoon and Coens was announced. Jourdain's force was much weaker, and he was urged to escape with it, as, indeed, he could have done easily. To retreat, however, would have been to lower English prestige in the eyes of the Asiatic shipping in the harbour, which was then an important trade centre. Apart from this consideration, Jourdain scorned the thought of an English ship flying before "a Fleming." Despite his inferiority, and the fact that he knew the fight would be something in the nature of a personal vendetta—for the Dutch leaders held him responsible for some of the reverses they had met—Jourdain stood and gave battle. During a lull in the action he was treacherously shot dead by the Dutch while standing under a flag of truce.

CHAPTER VII

THE FIRST ENGLISHMAN IN THE HOLY CITIES

In this journey many times the skulking, thievish Arabs do much mischief to some of the Hagges.

JOSEPH PITTS, *A Faithfull Account of the Religion and Manners of the Mahometans*

JOSEPH PITTS, of Exeter, was the first known Englishman to visit the Haramain, the holy territory of Arabia forbidden to Christians, and the first to describe the holy cities of Mecca and Medina. At fifteen or sixteen years of age, in 1678, he was captured at sea by a pirate out of Algiers, and was bought by a captain of cavalry, who determined "to proselyte a Christian slave" as atonement for a former career of murder and vice.

When verbal suasion failed the boy's bare feet were bastinadoed, until, he tells us, "I roared out to feel the pain of his cruel strokes, but the more I cried, the more furiously he laid on, and to stop the noise of my crying would stamp with his feet on my mouth." At last Pitts gave way and accepted Islam, but he still ate pork in private, hated the whole body of Mohammedans, and regarded the Prophet as a "bloody impostor."

For many years he remained a slave, learned Arabic and Turkish, and acquired a considerable knowledge of Moslem beliefs and practices. When his master made the pilgrimage to Mecca and Medina, travelling by Alexandria, Cairo, Suez, and Jidda, Pitts accompanied him, was freed from his bondage at Mecca, but remained with his "patroon" as a paid servant. His improved status failed to reconcile him to his fate, and for some time he had been examining plans for escape when "the Grand Turk" sent to Algiers for ships. Pitts managed to join the squadron, the British consul at Algiers gave him a letter of introduction, and this he presented to the consul at Smyrna

83

where he deserted. A Cornish merchant settled in the town paid his passage in a French ship to Leghorn, but his troubles continued, for no sooner had he reached England than he was seized by a press gang, and was kept for some time in Colchester gaol. Only the intervention of Sir William Falkener, of the Smyrna and Turkey Company, to whom he had written earlier, saved him from service in a warship.

The following extracts are taken from his little book, *A Faithfull Account of the Religion and Manners of the Mahometans,* published early in the eighteenth century:

First, as to Mecca. It is a town situated in a barren place (about one day's journey from the Red Sea) in a valley, or rather in the midst of many little hills. It is a place of no force, wanting both walls and gates. Its buildings are . . . very ordinary, insomuch that it would be a place of no tolerable entertainment, were it not for the anniversary resort of so many thousand Hagges, or pilgrims, on whose coming the whole dependance of the town (in a manner) is; for many shops are scarcely open all the year besides.

The people here, I observed, are a poor sort of people, very thin, lean, and swarthy. The town is surrounded for several miles with many thousands of little hills, which are very near one to the other. I have been on the top of some of them near Mecca, where I could see some miles about, yet was not able to see the farthest of the hills. They are all stony-rock and blackish, and pretty near of a bigness, appearing at a distance like cocks of hay, but all pointing towards Mecca. Some of them are half a mile in circumference, but all near of one height. . . .

The town hath plenty of water, and yet but few herbs, unless in some particular places. Here are several sorts of good fruits to be had—viz., grapes, melons, water-melons, cucumbers, pumpkins, and the like; but these are brought two or three days' journey off, where there is a place of very great plenty, called, if I mistake not, Habbash.[1] Likewise sheep are brought hither and sold. So that as to Mecca itself, it affords little or nothing of comfortable provisions. It lieth in a very hot country, insomuch that people run from one side of the streets to the other to get into the shadow, as the motion of the sun causes it. The inhabitants, especially men, do usually sleep on the tops of the houses for the air, or in the streets before their doors. Some lay the small bedding they have on a thin mat on the ground; others have a slight frame, made much like drink-stalls on which we

---

[1] Hejaz? Taif is meant.

place barrels, standing on four legs, corded with palm cordage, on which they put their bedding. Before they bring out their bedding they sweep the streets and water them. As for my own part, I usually lay open, without any bed-covering, on the top of the house · only I took a linen cloth, dipt in water, and after I had wrung it, covered myself with it in the night; and when I awoke I should find it dry; then I would wet it again: and thus I did two or three times in a night.

There follows an account of the temple, "the Beat-Allah," and the religious ceremonies there and at Muna and Arafat. From Mecca Pitts proceeded to Medina.

In this journey many times the skulking, thievish Arabs do much mischief to some of the Hagges; for in the night time they will steal upon them (especially such as are on the outside of the Caravan), and being taken to be some of the servants that belong to the carriers, or owners of the camels, they are not suspected. When they see an Hagge fast asleep (for it is usual for them to sleep on the road), they loose a camel before and behind, and one of the thieves leads it away with the Hagge upon its back asleep. Another of them in the meanwhile, pulls on the next camel to tie it to the camel from whence the halter of the other was cut; for if that camel be not fastened again to the leading camel, it will stop, and all that are behind will then stop of course, which might be the means of discovering the robbers. When they have gotten the stolen camel, with his rider, at a convenient distance from the Caravan, and think themselves out of danger, they awake the Hagge, and sometimes destroy him immediately; but at other times, being a little more inclined to mercy, they strip him naked, and let him return to the Caravan. . . .

Medina is but a little town, and poor, yet it is walled round, and hath in it a great Mosque, but nothing near so big as the temple at Mecca. In one corner of the Mosque is a place, built about fourteen or fifteen paces square. About this place are great windows, fenced with brass grates. In the inside it is decked with some lamps and ornaments. It is arched all overhead. (I find some relate that there are no less than 3000 lamps about Mahomet's tomb; but it is a mistake, for there are not, as I verily believe, an hundred; and I speak what I know, and have been an eyewitness of.) In the middle of this place is the tomb of Mahomet, where the corpse of that bloody impostor is laid, which hath silk curtains all around it like a bed; which curtains are not costly nor beautiful. There is nothing of his tomb to be seen by any, by reason of the curtains round it, nor are any of the Hagges permitted to enter there. None go in but the

Eunuchs, who keep watch over it, and they only light the lamps, which burn there by night, and to sweep and cleanse the place.[1] All the privilege the Hagges have, is only to thrust in their hands at the windows, between the brass grates, and to petition the dead juggler, which they do with a wonderful deal of reverence, affection, and zeal. My patroon had his silk handkerchief stolen out of his bosom, while he stood at his devotion here.

It is storied by some that the coffin of Mahomet hangs up by the attractive virtue of a loadstone to the roof of the Mosque; but, believe me, it is a false story. When I looked through the brass grates I saw as much as any of the Hagges; and the top of the curtains, which covered the tomb, were not half so high as the roof or arch; so that it is impossible his coffin should be hanging there. I never heard the Mahometans say anything like it. On the outside of this place, where Mahomet's tomb is, are some sepulchres of their reputed saints; among which is one prepared for Jesus Christ, when he shall come again personally into the world; for they hold that Christ will come again in the flesh, forty years before the end of the world, to confirm the Mahometan faith, and say likewise that our Saviour was not crucified in person, but in effigy, or one like him.

Medina is much supplied by the opposite Abyssine country, which is on the other side of the Red Sea: from thence they have corn and necessaries brought in ships: an odd sort of vessels as I ever saw, their sails being made of matting, such as they use in the houses and Mosques to tread upon. . . .

It is thirty-seven days' journey from Mecca to Cairo, and three days we tarry by the way, which together make us (as I said) forty days' journey; and in all this way there is scarce any green thing to be met with, nor beast nor fowl to be seen or heard; nothing but sand and stones, excepting the one place which we passed through by night; I suppose it was a village, where were some trees, and, we thought, gardens.

In the days when Barbary pirates could penetrate to the Irish Sea and the Bristol Channel there must have been numbers of men who reached Moslem countries, and perhaps even Mecca, with masters who made the pilgrimage, but never again reached their homelands to tell the story. Pitts mentions one such man,

who was taken very young, insomuch as he had not only lost his Christian religion, but his native language also. This man

---

[1] This account, on Burton's authority, is perfectly correct, except that the eunuchs did not go into the tomb, but only lit the lamps and swept the passage round the sepulchre.

had endured thirty years' slavery in Spain, and in the French gallies, but was afterwards redeemed and came home to Algier. He was looked upon as a very pious man, and a great zealot by the Turks, for his not turning from the Mahomedan faith, notwithstanding the great temptations he had so to do. Some of my neighbours who intended for Mecca the same year I went with my patroon thither offered this renegado that if he would serve them on this journey they would defray his charges throughout. He gladly embraced the offer, and I remember when we arrived at Mecca he passionately told me that God had delivered him out of hell upon earth (meaning his former slavery in France and Spain), and had brought him into a heaven upon earth— viz., Mecca. I admired much his zeal, but pitied his condition.

Pitts concludes his narrative of fifteen years' adventure and slavery at the reunion with his father at Exeter. His little book was not widely known, and perhaps failed to attract the attention even of scholars, for Gibbon missed it. His story was recalled, after a hundred and fifty years, in Burton's *Pilgrimage to Al-Madinah and Meccah.*

CHAPTER VIII

A DANISH EXPEDITION

If any people in the world afford in their history an instance
of high integrity, and of great simplicity of manners, the Arabs
surely do.

KARSTEN NIEBUHR, *Travels through Arabia*

ABOUT the middle of the eighteenth century it was
suggested, probably by the Hebraist Michaelis of
Göttingen, that an expedition might be sent to Arabia
for Biblical and geographical research. Frederick V of
Denmark showed interest in the idea and drew up a list of
instructions for such an expedition. There was to be no official
leader, and each member was to help the others, while pur-
suing the line of inquiry for which he was best qualified. The
work was to be completed in three years.

Six variously qualified men were chosen, and sailed for the
Mediterranean in January 1761. The party consisted of Peter
Forskal, a doctor and botanist who had worked under
Linnæus; Christian Cramer, surgeon and zoologist; Frederick
von Haven, philologist and Orientalist, who with Forskal knew
more Arabic than any of the others; George William Baurenfeind, an artist; a Swedish servant named Berggren (a stout
ex-cavalryman, who laughed at the idea of hardship in a mere
journey to Arabia); and finally Karsten Niebuhr, a farmer's
son who had learned surveying, and had spent some eighteen
months studying mathematics and Arabic before the voyage
began.

Their journey was uneventful, for none of the party was
of the type to seek adventure or take risks without a very
definite chance of a compensating gain to knowledge. There
were, of course, some inevitable dangers, due to such things
as Turkish seamanship amid the rocks and reefs of the Red
Sea, and there was the general uncertainty as to what might
happen to Christians among Moslems. Yet Forskal at least

became popular in the motley crowd of pilgrims when news of his medical knowledge reached their ears. He was constantly plagued for advice on a multitude of complaints, until at last some one remarked that he could not see in the dark. Forskal advised him to light a candle—an answer that delighted the crowded pilgrim ship.

After a drunken pilot had narrowly missed causing disaster on the reefs of Yenbo they reached Jidda, the port for Mecca. Here, with a caution that marked most of their actions, they put the bulk of their money, which was in Venetian sequins, into the bottom of their medicine chest, as they expected to be plundered by the customs officials. The medicines were not disturbed, and the expedition began happily, by retaining its funds. It was to end in tragedy.

Of the six men only Niebuhr survived. Sickness accounted for all of them, in Arabia, on the voyage to India after the expedition, or on arrival. To Niebuhr, who displayed tireless energy and great endurance throughout the exploration, it thus fell to write the story. His book was marked by such restraint and judgment that it still holds an honourable place in the bibliography of travel.

Niebuhr endeavoured, with considerable success, to record the discoveries made by the whole party, not merely his own adventures. Indeed, whenever he indulged in personal anecdote it was invariably for the purpose of illustrating some wider observation, such as the character and outlook of the Arabs or Moslems in general, or the attitude which Europeans should adopt in the East. For instance, when he writes of dancing and the "tsiganes" whom he had seen he mentions the distaste which dancing of the sexes together arouses in Mohammedans, and adds,

> the Europeans who live among Mohammedans would be more beloved and respected if they did not vilify themselves in the eyes of Orientals by amusements which they might surely spare.[1]

He avoided the pitfalls of Western conduct himself, and his calm, detached habit of mind drew no hasty conclusions from the individual bearing of Arabs whom he met, equally whether

---

[1] *Travels through Arabia*, translated by R. Heron (Edinburgh, 1792).

it happened to be harsh and ignorant or courteous and intelligent. Of peasant stock, sent out on discovery by a small nation, and living at a time before the 'imperial mind' had developed, Niebuhr never regarded himself as a being intrinsically superior to those whom he studied. To him 'native' meant the inhabitant of a country; it was not a general term denoting a lower order of mankind.

Yemen, the goal of this exploration, was already in Europe the best known of the Arab lands. Niebuhr was acquainted with the adventures of previous travellers such as Varthema and the Englishman Middleton, and knew of the journey, as far as Sana, of a French surgeon called Barbier and his companion de la Grelaudière. Moreover, the good will of the Imam had been won by the conduct of the Dutch and English, at peace now, and established in trade on the coast for a hundred and fifty years. At this time there was, in fact, little danger for Europeans generally in the south-western corner of the peninsula, and still less for men as circumspect as Niebuhr and his companions. They were able to separate in order to pursue various lines of inquiry, and thus covered much of Yemen thoroughly.

As far as Arabia is concerned the interest of the narrative begins with the arrival at Jidda, in the Hejaz, where the travellers were delayed for some two months awaiting a ship for Mocha. On landing at Yenbo they had been insulted by an Arab, and feared a repetition at Jidda, but were agreeably surprised to find no intolerance there, although they were prohibited from even approaching the gate that led to Mecca. The old defences built against the Portuguese lay in ruins; with few exceptions the houses were of wood; water had to be brought in by camel from reservoirs in the hills. The port was, indeed, no more than a mart between India and Egypt. There was an English trade in Taif almonds ("five hundred thousand hundredweight a year to India"), and balm of Mecca was brought down from the Medina district for export. The hinterland was barren and sandy, so that corn, rice, lentils, and other products were imported of necessity from Egypt.

The travellers considered the authorities at Jidda less given to fraud and chicanery than those at Suez, but the local officials had a habit of forestalling revenue by requiring merchants to pay some part of the duties expected from the next year, promising to discount these payments when they fell due. Those traders who acquiesced in this arrangement found that the advances were merely allowed to accumulate and were never repaid. One is glad to read that "the English have not yet submitted to these impositions," though "their firm refusal continually embroils them with the officers of Government."

At length a vessel bound for Hodeida appeared in the port, and the party decided to take another step towards Yemen. The appearance of the vessel was not reassuring, for it was "more like a hogshead than a ship," being some forty feet long by eighteen in the beam.

> It had no deck; its planks were extremely thin, and seemed to be only nailed together, but not pitched. The Captain wore nothing but a linen cloth upon his loins, and his sailors, nine in number, and all black slaves from Africa or Malabar, had nothing to cover their nakedness but about an hand-breadth of linen, bound upon their haunches with a cord.

The ship proved safer than it appeared, for Cramer's watch, which slipped down between some branches of trees (a mat over the goods in the vessel to keep them dry), was not retrieved until the end of the voyage, and was found to be quite undamaged by water.

They sailed along a shore with few villages, casting anchor every night from fear of the coral reefs. After sixteen days they reached the harbour of Loheia, where the Governor was found to be dignified, honest, and kind, and, as Niebuhr wrote, "we were delighted to find the Arabs more civilized the farther we proceeded from Egypt." (In Egypt Forskal had been robbed of his clothes by Arabs, who, "with a generosity very uncommon with them, left him his drawers.")

The travellers veiled their intention of exploring Yemen by telling the Governor that they were making for Mocha, where they intended to join an English ship which would carry them to India. Loheia was a place with only a few stone houses. Most of them were built of mud and dung, with grass roofs.

The nearest drinking water was at least three miles from the town. It was a barren place with a poor harbour, but had a considerable trade in coffee.

The inland depot for coffee on its way from the Yemen hills to Loheia, Hodeida, and Mocha was the town of Beit el Fakih, half a day's journey from the hills and a few days' from the sea. Hodeida was a small port only a little better than Loheia, for Mocha was the chief centre for merchants from Egypt, Syria, Barbary, and Persia engaged in the coffee trade.

When the explorers visited Beit el Fakih they again found the local governor amenable. They were allowed to go where they wished in the country, and also learned a good deal in the town itself from the more educated Arabs, who were accustomed to Europeans. From this town they made many explorations across Yemen, visiting Taizz, Sana, and the mountain villages. Again they were careful to cover their activities and lull all suspicion by explaining that they needed a great deal of exercise for their health.

In general, they noted that the coastal strip of Yemen, the Tihama, was from thirty to sixty miles wide. It was a barren, dusty, waterless area, producing some earthenware, some poor indigo, mostly for local use—blue shirts and drawers were much in evidence—and engaging in a little tannery. This district the explorers covered fairly completely. Farther inland in the more prosperous coffee areas they saw less, though Forskal, the botanist, searched the upper waters of the Tihama *wadis*, with excellent results.

On these excursions Niebuhr invariably travelled as a poor man, riding a donkey, as a discouragement to robbers.

A turban, a greatcoat wanting the sleeves, a shirt, linen drawers and a pair of slippers were all the dress I wore. It being the fashion of the country to carry arms when travelling, I had a sabre and pistols at my girdle. A piece of an old carpet was my saddle, and served me likewise for a seat at table and various other purposes. To cover me at night I had the linen cloak which the Arabs wrap about their shoulders, to shelter me from the sun and rain. A bucket of water, an article of indispensable necessity to a traveller in these arid regions, hung by my saddle. I had for some time endeavoured to suit myself to the Arabian manner of living, and now could spare many conveniences to which I had been accustomed in Europe, and could content myself with bad bread, the only article to be obtained in most of the inns.

On the higher ground of the interior, which averaged about 8000 feet, they discovered many agricultural settlements. There was more stone here for houses; basalt was made into steps on the steep ascents and into walls for the coffee plantations. Niebuhr continues:

> The coffee-trees were all in flower . . . and exhaled an exquisitely agreeable perfume. They are planted upon terraces in the form of an amphitheatre. Most of them are only watered by the rains that fall, but some, indeed, from large reservoirs upon the heights, in which spring water is collected in order to be sprinkled upon the terraces, where the trees grow so thick together that the rays of tke sun can hardly enter among their branches. We were told that those trees, thus artificially watered, yielded ripe fruit twice in the year; but the fruit comes not fully ripe the second time, and the coffee of the second crop is always inferior to that of the first.

The coffee plantations apparently failed to enrich many of the villages, which were wretched places declining into poverty. The peasants' chief food was durra, a coarse sort of millet.

In the higher parts of Yemen, still farther from the sea, the Danes passed quickly, merely as travellers, but made notes of the towns. They realized, however, that this highest belt of land sloped towards the east and passed into desert.

In all Yemen the Europeans met with unpleasantness only at Mocha. Here they fell in with the treacherous son of a merchant who "instigated the younger officers of the customs to harass and oppress us that we might be forced to throw ourselves into a blind and implicit dependence upon him." The officials opened a barrel of fish kept in spirits of wine, and were enraged by the "smell of the spirituous liquour no less than by the smell of the dead fish." Their collection of shells was tossed about, and when such things were found in their baggage the officials thought the Europeans were playing with them, by showing the customs things of no dutiable value. When some serpents in spirits of wine, preserved by Forskal, were uncovered the officials said the Franks intended to poison the Mohammedans, and that one of them was pretending to be a doctor for this purpose. The Governor, who was normally a mild old man, fell into a rage, and swore by God they should not remain a night in the city. The customs house was then closed, and the party was not allowed to remove anything. Even then their troubles were not ended. They had hired a house, but their books and papers were thrown out into the street, and for a time they could find no other lodging. At length a citizen took them in, and then a rescuer appeared in Mr Francis Scott, an English merchant, who dined them and put himself at their service.

Later the Governor was wounded in the foot, and Cramer was sent for when the wound had worsened under local treatment. After this their stay in Mocha became more pleasant, but was saddened by the death of von Haven. Again it is good to read that "the Captain of an English ship lent six of his sailors to bear the body to the European burying place. All the English in Mocha attended the funeral."

At Sana, the capital of Yemen, the travellers were received by the Imam. Niebuhr describes the large room with its arched roof, and the Prince sitting cross-legged on cushions, dressed in bright green bedecked with gold lace. After kissing his hands and the hem of his robe they explained that they were journeying to the Indies, and were visiting his country merely to describe its plenty and security to their countrymen. The Imam then gave them permission to stay as long as they pleased. They remained only ten days, but in that time contrived to learn something of the city and the surrounding country:

> The city of Sana is situated at the foot of Mount Nikkim, on which are still to be seen the ruins of a castle, which the Arabs suppose to have been built by Shem. A brick wall surrounded the city, and aqueducts built on the mountain provided a good water supply.

Niebuhr tried to make a ground-plan of Sana, but was obstructed everywhere by curious crowds pressing round him. He was able to note, however, that there were seven gates, twelve public baths, many fine palaces, and that it took an hour to walk round the walls. He realized also that the city was less populous than its appearance suggested, as much of the space was occupied by gardens. Some of the better houses were built of stone, but for the most part sun-dried brick was used, and the windows were shuttered. Wood for carpentry was scarce and was brought a three days' journey into Sana, but fruit was plentiful, and twenty varieties of grape ensured refreshment all the year round. There was a large export trade in raisins.

Much that is commonplace in modern narratives of Eastern travel was of great interest to Niebuhr's eighteenth-century readers. A good deal was known of the Eastern trade, but less of native life and manners. The writers who went about with their desks at Sana and "make brieves, copy-books, and instruct scholars in the art of writing all at the same time"; the artisans working in the open street; the character of caravanserais for travellers and merchants—all were part of a picture which possessed fresh colour for them, and was the more convincing because it came from an exact, observant, scientific mind.

Niebuhr showed particular interest in the Jewish colony, which numbered about two thousand. The Jews were not allowed to live within the city, but outside the walls they had a village to themselves. They were treated with contempt, yet the best artisans were Jews, especially the potters and goldsmiths, who worked in their little shops in Sana during the day and returned to their own district at nightfall. A little wine was made by the Jews for their own use, but the practice was disliked by the Arabs, and a Jew who conveyed wine into an Arab house was severely punished. A disgrace which had fallen upon one Jew had drawn further persecution upon the whole body.

> One of the most eminent merchants among them, named Oroeki, gained the favour of two successive Imams and was for thirteen years in the reign of El Mansor and for fifteen years under the present Imam, comptroller of the customs and of the royal buildings and gardens, one of the most honourable offices of the Court of Sana. Two years before our arrival here he . . . was not only imprisoned, but obliged to pay a fine of 50,000 crowns. Fifteen days before our arrival at Sana the Imam had set him at liberty. He was a venerable old man of great knowledge, and although he had received the Imam's

permission had never chosen to assume any other dress than that commonly worn by his countrymen.

The old Jew wanted to meet the Europeans, but these cautious travellers "durst not hold frequent intercourse with a man so newly released out of prison."

The Government, as part of the persecution, had ordered the demolition of fourteen synagogues and of all houses above "fourteen fathoms" in height. The Jews were also forbidden to build to such a height in future. Moreover, all the stone pitchers in which they had kept their wine were broken. The building restriction upon Jews was still in force when Wyman Bury journeyed through Yemen just before the Great War, and was noted again by a recent traveller, Ameen Rihani.

The Indian merchants in Sana were not persecuted like the Jews, but were mulcted of 300 crowns a month to live in the city, and the heirs of a deceased Banyan had to pay a tax of forty or fifty crowns. Further, if an Indian died without heir his property went to the Imam. The Indians told Niebuhr that recently two of their number had been cast into prison and forced to surrender 1500 crowns of an inheritance which had fallen to them in India, though they had received no part of it in Yemen.

Europeans, however, seem to have been well treated. When the party left Sana the Imam sent each of them garments as a present, and provided them with a letter to the Governor of Mocha, instructing him to give the travellers 200 crowns. Niebuhr's new clothes consisted of a shirt, wide cotton trousers, a vest with straight sleeves, a flowing gown, and a pair of "half-boots or slippers." The Imam was indeed so generous to strangers, wrote Niebuhr, that Turks would often abuse his hospitality, remaining months at Sana and then demanding their expenses, whereupon the Imam would give them an order on his ports, and was glad to be rid of them at the price.

On the way back to Mocha through Beit el Fakih Niebuhr remarked the local irrigation methods:

> After ploughing up a field they yoke a plank of wood to two oxen, lead these over the field till the plank is loaded with earth, empty it upon the line where the dyke is to be drawn, and repeat this until it is formed.

BAURENFEIND'S SKETCH OF THE YEMEN COFFEE HILLS

THE MARKET-PLACE AT SANA
Photo E.N.A.

The dykes were made round the fields, and when a *wadi* was full the water was turned off into them.

As they travelled back quickly to Mocha under the fierce August sun Niebuhr, Cramer, and Baurenfeind fell ill. Mocha stood in dry, barren country, and, like Sana, had its Jewish colony, Indian merchants, and a mixture of good stone houses and wretched hovels. Some twenty-five years before Niebuhr's time the French East India Company, by bombarding the castle, the Governor's house, and the mosque, had endeavoured to persuade the Imam to meet a debt of 82,000 crowns. The Arab populace seems to have recalled this exciting display with lasting pleasure, and to have formed a high opinion of European military talent. In official quarters, however, the reaction of this incident had proved beneficial to English and Dutch traders. English merchants and the English East India Company had gained most of the trade, which was mainly with India.

Turks, Arabs, and Indians had to meet an impost of 10 per cent. on the value of their goods at the Mocha customs, whereas Europeans, which meant mainly the English, were taxed only 3 per cent., and were privileged to have their goods inspected in their own warehouses. English ships carried Indian goods to Yemen and returned usually with specie, sometimes amounting to great sums, mostly in Venetian and German coinage, entrusted to them by Arab merchants.

At the end of August 1763 Niebuhr sailed from Mocha for Bombay. Forskal had died during the journey to Sana. Baurenfeind and Berggren died on the way to India, and at Bombay in the February of the following year Cramer passed away. Thus the hot Yemen summer had taken toll of all the party except Niebuhr, who remained fourteen months in Bombay, before returning to Europe by Muscat, in Oman, the Persian Gulf, Iraq, and Syria.

In the first part of his book he tells of observations and journeys made in Yemen, and in later chapters of Arab manners and customs and the character of those parts of the peninsula which none of the party had visited. Much of this data Niebuhr based on information gained from educated Arabs and merchants. He was thus able to name some of the provinces and chief settlements of Arabia and indicate the flora and fauna. Regarding the inhabitants, he contrasted the Turks, "an ignorant, grave, and silent nation," with the livelier Arab, who rejoiced in beauties of poetry and songs of the exploits of sheikhs. Though he probably never came into contact with the Bedouin in their own particular surroundings, he sifted his information impartially and accurately:

> The Arabs settled in cities, and especially those in the seaport towns, have lost somewhat of their distinctive national manners, by their intercourse with strangers; but the Bedouins who live in tents and in separate tribes have still retained the customs and manners of their earliest ancestors. They are the genuine Arabs, and exhibit, in the aggregate, all those characteristics which are distributed respectively among the other branches of their nation. . . . The sheikhs and their subjects are born to the life of shepherds and soldiers. The greater tribes rear many camels, which they either sell to their neighbours or employ in the carriage of goods or in military expeditions. . . . The genuine Arabs disdain husbandry, as an employment by which they would be degraded. They maintain no domestic animals but sheep and camels, except perhaps horses. . . . Those Arabs who wander in the desert will live five days without drinking and discover a pit of water by examining the soil and plants in its environs. They are said to be addicted to robbery, and the accusation is not entirely unfounded, but may be laid to the charge of all nations that lead an erratic life. The sheikhs ride continually about on their horses or dromedaries inspecting the conduct of their subjects, visiting their friends or hunting. Traversing the desert where the horizon is as wide as the ocean they perceive travellers at a distance . . . they naturally draw nigh to those whom they discover, and are tempted to pillage the strangers when they find their own party the strongest. . . . The Arabian robbers are not cruel, and do not murder those whom they rob unless when travellers stand upon the defensive and happen to kill a Bedouin, whose death the others are eager to avenge. Upon all other occasions they act in a manner consistent with their natural hospitality.

Of the constitution of Bedouin society he noted:

> The dignity of sheikh is hereditary, but is not confined to the order of primogeniture. The petty sheikhs who form the hereditary nobility choose the grand sheikh out of the reigning family without regarding whether he be more nearly or more distantly related to his predecessor.

Little or no revenue is paid to the great sheikh, and the other sheikhs are rather like equals than subjects. If dissatisfied with his government they depose him, or go away with their cattle and join another tribe. . . . The Bedouins . . . of the desert have never been subdued by any conqueror.

The account he gathered of the holy cities, places of wonder, speculation, and mystery to Europeans of his time, was marked by a characteristic simplicity and moderation. He wrote that, though Christians were not allowed to visit them, Mohammedans made no secret of what they contained, or of the religious rites practised there. He was able to acquire a drawing and a painting of the Kaaba, whose riches, he averred, even when exaggerated by his informants, were far from equal to those in some European churches. He corrected the belief, still current in his day, that the tomb of the Prophet at Medina was suspended in mid-air by enormous magnets.

Only a little need be mentioned regarding the parts of Arabia upon which Niebuhr merely reproduced hearsay evidence. Touching at Muscat, he roughly fixed its position, heard of the existence of strong towns inland (named Rastak and Nezwa), that the land in parts was mountainous down to the sea, and that somewhere inland was Jebel Akhdar, rich in vines and cultivation. As to the Hejaz, he knew that the low, flat, barren coastal area changed to a highland plateau inland, suggesting an analogy with Yemen; but he did not realize the greater rainfall of the latter. The characteristics of the Hadhramaut he gave with general accuracy, indicating its desert, barren uplands, deep *wadis*, where there was a measure of fertility, the exclusiveness of its people, the variance in type of inland and coastal inhabitants, that the largest *wadi* was called Duwan and was twenty-five days' march from Sana, and that the chief town was Shibam.

Of all Niebuhr's balanced and acute observations none perhaps deserve more credit, or show a deeper insight, than those on Wahhabism. In fact, his views on Arabian religion generally presented a new viewpoint to most contemporary Europeans, for he held that Mohammedanism was not by its nature an aggressive creed, and that it did not persecute unless from fear. Of all religions that he found in Arabia,

Indian, Jewish, and Christian, the last met with least contempt. In Islam itself he realized, with truly astonishing perception, the significance and potentialities of a movement that was dawning in his time—though knowledge of it came to him only by hearsay, from an intelligent Arab.

> Some time since a new religion sprang up in the district of El Ared. It has already produced a revolution in the government of Arabia, and will probably hereafter influence the country still farther. . . . Abd ul Wahheb taught that God is the only proper object of worship and invocation, as the creator and governor of the world. He forbade the invocation of saints and the very mentioning of Mahomet or any other prophet in prayer as practices savouring of idolatry. He considered Mahomet, Jesus Christ, Moses, and many others respected by the Sunnites in the character of prophets, as merely great men whose history might be read with improvement; denying that any book had ever been written by divine inspiration, or brought down from heaven by the Angel Gabriel. He forbade, as a crime against Providence, the making of vows, in the manner of Sunnites, to obtain deliverance from danger.

The Sunnite sect, wrote Niebuhr, had departed from Mohammed's teaching by following the authority of commentators on the Koran, who exalted their private opinions into doctrines. His tone, indeed, when dealing with the Sunnites recalls strongly the manner of the Humes and Robertsons of the eighteenth century, when they wrote of Roman Catholicism in words besprinkled liberally with "fanaticism," "enthusiasm," and "idolatry." The Sunnites, he wrote, invoked a long list of saints, credited the virtue of amulets and the efficacy of vows; they had adopted superstitions condemned in the Koran and justified only by the interpretations of the Doctors. Other sects had also corrupted Mohammedanism, but less than they.

> The new religion of Abd ul Wahheb deserves, therefore, to be regarded as a reformation of Mohammedanism, reducing it back to its original simplicity. He has gone farther, perhaps, than some other reformers; but an Arab can hardly be expected to act in such matters with a delicate hand. Experience will show whether a religion, so stripped of everything that might serve to strike the senses, can maintain its ground among so rude and ignorant a people as the Arabs.

Niebuhr's *Travels through Arabia* was published in German in 1772, in French at Amsterdam in 1774–80, and was abridged in an English translation in 1792. Forskal's important work on the flora of Yemen appeared in 1775, but Niebuhr's work alone gave not only a clear picture of one corner of Arabia, but the first modern introduction to the whole country. Many succeeding travellers, and those who read their narratives, were to feel with him that

> If any people in the world afford in their history an instance of high antiquity, and of great simplicity of manners, the Arabs surely do. Coming among them one can hardly help fancying oneself suddenly carried backward to the ages which succeeded immediately after the Flood. We are here tempted to imagine ourselves among the old patriarchs, with whose adventures we have been so much amused in our infant days. The language which has been spoken for time immemorial, and which so nearly resembles that which we have been accustomed to regard as that of the most distant antiquity, completes the illusion which the analogy of manners began.

Yemen was governed in Niebuhr's time by an independent Imam. After Alboquerque's failure at Aden the land came under Turkish suzerainty until the seventeenth century, when Stamboul decided to evacuate it, on the grounds of its remoteness and expense. But when Wahhabism flamed across Central Arabia a chief of Asir sided with the movement, and in 1804 seized several of the Yemen coast towns. Mohammed Ali of Egypt, fighting Wahhabism, recaptured several and restored them to the Imam—on tribute. Then when the Pasha of Egypt revolted against the Sultan the coast towns were again occupied by one of the Pasha's lieutenants. When the Egyptians were obliged to leave by troubles nearer home a relative of the Imam at Sana tried to seize the country and acknowledged Ottoman supremacy; he succeeded at first in holding the littoral, and later pushed his power inland up to Sana. A Turkish attempt on Sana in 1849 failed, but the opening of the Suez Canal in 1869 brought the south-western coast into immediate prominence, and in the seventies the Turks again occupied Yemen.

In these years South-western Arabia was visited by many notable travellers, scientists, and scholars. Louis Arnaud in

1843 reached Yemen, travelling with a Turkish party from Jidda, and studied in detail the Marib dam, rock inscriptions and carvings. Twenty-six years later Joseph Halévy, a French Jew born at Adrianople, commissioned by the Academy of Inscriptions, examined the Marib dam again, studied rock-cut inscriptions, visited various sites of ancient cities, including those of Ma'in and Pliny's "Nesca," and spent several weeks with a colony of Jews in the district of Nejran. Altogether he copied 600 inscriptions. His successor in 1889, E. Glaser, an Austrian, also visited Marib, secured over a thousand inscriptions, traced the course of two important *wadis*, but failed to solve the problem of the drainage of Jauf, a district farther north than Niebuhr's, or to find its connexion with the main Hadhramaut valley. On the inscriptions copied by these travellers our knowledge of pre-Islamic Arabia is based. They are in two languages, Minæan and Sabæan, and in the Katabanian dialect of Minæan, but are usually called collectively Himyaritic.[1]

Among other European visitors of far less importance, some of whom were in Ottoman service, was Renzo Manzoni, a grandson of the famous Alessandro. He lived at Sana for a time in the last years of the seventies, left an excellent description of the city, but did not venture into unexplored districts. W. B. Harris, a British traveller, described Sana again in 1892. More useful was the work of a French engineer, A. J. Beneyton, who in the early years of the present century did some mapping and survey work for a proposed railway between Hodeida and Sana.

For more than a generation, however, Niebuhr's work remained the only sound authority, not only on Yemen but on Arabia. Gibbon, writing of Islam in his famous fiftieth chapter, used Greek and Latin sources, notably Strabo, Pliny, and Ptolemy. He knew the extracts from Idrisi in Pococke's *Specimen historiæ arabum* and an abridgment published at Paris in 1619. Parts of Abulfeda, whose account of Arabia he thought "most copious and correct," he read in French and

---

[1] An inscription copied by Glaser records the destruction by a flood of the dam at Marib, and its repair by the Abyssinian ruler Abraha about 447–450. This disaster would increase the normal exodus from Yemen due to pressure of population.

Latin translations. Beyond this he supplemented his material from d'Herbelot's *Bibliothèque orientale*, learned something in addition from the reports of East India Company officials, and had d'Anville's honest but very faulty map, printed in 1775. This data helped him to portray the salient characteristics of Arabia and its people, noting the lack of water and navigable rivers, the differences of dialect, the distinction between the settled Arab and the Bedouin, the latter's love of freedom, the character of the nomadic life, the importance of the camel, the blood-feuds of the nomad and his attacks on caravans, as well as his character for hospitality. All this was the background for his account of the rise of Islam, and was constructed with that quality of smooth, infallible conviction that did so much to make the *Decline and Fall* the Bible of the fashionable Victorian agnostic.

But even Gibbon could not from such limited sources have attained that air of certainty and completeness without the assistance of the first modern traveller in Yemen. He had read Niebuhr's work in the French translation.

CHAPTER IX

WAHHABIS AND A SPANIARD

Beit Allah, or the House of God, is a quadrilateral tower, the sides and angles of which are unequal, so that its plan forms a true trapezium.

ALI BEY, *Travels*

FROM ancient times Europe's fullest information about Arabia related to Yemen, but in the middle of the eighteenth century for a thousand years, since the time of Mohammed, interest had centred rather on Mecca. The exclusiveness of the holy cities was in itself a direct challenge to Western curiosity, and something was known of the Hejaz in extracts from Idrisi and in three European accounts of the district. In 1604 an Austrian named Wild had published a book about Mecca and Medina which Niebuhr read, but which cannot have been important or interesting, as Burton missed it. There was the book published by Joseph Pitts, of Exeter; but Varthema's account of the Hejaz was much the most important, and had even indicated physical features beyond the Hejaz that were new to geographers, such as the Nefud, a great northern sandy desert which took five days to cross. Niebuhr indicated, as has been shown, some of the general physical characteristics of the region, and mentioned the Harb, one of the great Bedouin tribes.

For a generation after his time little was added to knowledge except of the coast, which was visited by James Bruce and by Eyles Irwin in 1769 and 1777 respectively. Irwin was an English agent at Mocha, sent by the East India Company to explore the overland route from the Red Sea to the Mediterranean. He was arrested at Yenbo (whose forts, he noticed, despite his anxieties, were in a ruinous state) and was released at Jidda. Bruce, on his way to Abyssinia, was entertained kindly for some months at Jidda. The port, he remarked, was very difficult of entry and exit, so that good pilots were necessary, these men being, indeed, so skilful that accidents were very rare. The region in general he described as barren and most unwholesome; but once a year a sudden influx of wealth from the Indian trade went through the port "as through a turnpike" to Mecca. Not much profit, however, remained to the inhabitants, as the customs duties went to the ruler and his band of ministers and dependents. Along the coast of Arabia Bruce took many observations, which were afterwards attacked by critics who had no local knowledge of this part of the Red Sea. Actually he deserved great credit for accuracy, especially for his longitudes, and his latitudes were remarkably near those observed on Moresby's laborious survey of the Red Sea.

Though knowledge was slight, and eighteenth-century interest in Arabia torpid, events were to attract the notice of Europe almost suddenly before the next century opened. Niebuhr's prophecy regarding Wahhabism was being fulfilled. The new religious movement in Arabia was about to stir all peoples with interests in the East, and to draw, in the first place, the attention of a Power whose ungainly body sprawled across European and Asiatic soil.

In the middle of the eighteenth century Arabia was divided into a number of independent principalities engaged with each other in a constant struggle for dominance or survival. About 1750 the principal states in Central and Eastern Arabia were those of Arair, in Hasa, Ibn Muammar, at Ayaina, and of Ibn Daas, at Manfuha. In that year Mohammed Ibn Abdul Wahhab, who was to be a new, vital force in Islam, returned to his birthplace at Ayaina. He was a man about fifty years of age, and had studied for many years at Basra and Damascus. A pilgrimage to Mecca had convinced him that Mohammedans had departed from the first principles of Islam, and he resolved to preach a return to the simple, unadorned practice and teachings of the Prophet. Veneration should be to God alone, Whose honour cannot be diverted to any inanimate or animate thing. There should be complete submission to God, and no indirect approach or intercession should be made to Him. The materialism of tombs, relics, and monuments should be avoided by their destruction. A simple, ascetic rule of life should be followed. Approach to God was to be direct, each spirit by itself, not through the intermediary of priest or prophet.

The ruler of Ayaina would not be converted, but the reformer found refuge with the unimportant but ambitious, energetic, and well-born Mohammed Ibn Saud, ruler of Dariya. Here was formed the nucleus of fanatical Bedouin, holding that they followed the original practice of the Prophet, regarding all those who differed from them as enemies of the faith, and sublimating every campaign to a holy war, or *jihad*, with a promise of paradise. Ibn Saud died in 1765, but his puritanical followers had established supremacy through Central and Eastern Arabia. His son Abdul Aziz carried the wars far beyond Nejd, and from 1780 raided the pilgrim caravans. The Ottoman Sultan sent a Turkish force into Hasa in 1798, but it was compelled to retire. Then in 1801 the Wahhabis captured and plundered Kerbela, the Shia holy city, and in the following year took Mecca, destroyed tombs and all mere objects of reverence, and departed with all the valuables they could carry. In the same year Abdul Aziz was assassinated by a Shia fanatic, and was succeeded on the throne by Saud, who captured Medina in 1804. In his reign the founder of Wahhabism died, but Wahhabi domination extended as far south as the frontiers of Yemen and Oman.

The discipline of the reformed faith lay heavily upon the Bedouin in time of peace. As Niebuhr had foreseen, a people "so rude and ignorant as the Arabs" might well fail to be satisfied with a creed which forbade mediation and all outward signs and emblems. More advanced peoples might indeed have reacted from so abstract a God. Furthermore, the limits of plundering seemed to be reached!

Meantime the Ottoman Sultan had by no means accepted the new conditions in Arabia, for they represented both a religious and a political challenge to his supremacy. Even as victorious Wahhabism showed signs of faltering he ordered Mohammed Ali, Pasha of Egypt, to stamp out the movement. Engaged in a struggle with the Mamelukes in his own province, Mohammed delayed until the Wahhabis raided across the Jordan almost to Damascus. Then, in 1811, he dispatched his son Tussun with 10,000 men to the Hejaz coast.

The expeditions sent from Egypt to Arabia were invariably poorly equipped and ill directed, but they had artillery, while the Arabs were badly armed and disunited. Tussun was defeated by the Wahhabis, but in 1812 Egyptian forces occupied Mecca and Medina. In 1813 14 the Pasha of Egypt himself came to the peninsula, but met with no success, and Tussun was defeated near Taif. Fortunately for the Egyptians, the great Saud died in 1814, and in the following year Mohammed captured Rass. Peace was made, the Egyptians evacuated Nejd, but the new Wahhabi ruler, Abdulla, failed to carry out some of his agreements, and in 1815 another Egyptian expedition arrived. This was led by Ibraham Pasha, cruel, unscrupulous, vain, a somewhat haphazard general, but brave and, above all, dogged. He began the task of driving the Wahhabis across Nejd. It was a difficult advance, 400 miles from Medina to the centre of Wahhabi power at Dariya, but, joined by the Harb and Mutair tribes, he defeated Abdulla and captured Aneiza and Bereida. The Ataiba and Beni Khalid now came to his standards, and by 1818 he was able to begin the siege of Dariya. The investment was continued for five months with great obstinacy in the face of reverses, until Abdulla surrendered. He was later beheaded at Constantinople.

After the fall of Dariya Ibrahim's columns scoured Jebel Shammar, Harek, Hasa, and the Wahhabi lands as far as Oman, razing strong points and destroying the fortifications of towns. His troops reached the Persian Gulf, and disturbed the activities of the Ras el Kheima pirates.

With all these Egyptian expeditions there were Europeans. With Ibrahim, for instance, there were four Italian medical officers and Vaissière, a French engineer. In 1815 the Agha of Mamelukes and Governor of Medina was an ex-private of the 72nd Highlanders, one Thomas Keith. These men left no direct record of their adventures, but the story of Giovanni Finati, of Ferrara, who served with Tussun, is not uninteresting.

Born at Ferrara and intended for the Church, Finati appeared in 1805 on the barrack square of Milan—a very unwilling conscript. When his regiment was ordered to the Tyrol he deserted and returned to Ferrara, where he was arrested, sent to rejoin his unit at Venice, and narrowly escaped a firing squad. His next desertion came when he was serving in Marmont's forces at Cattaro. With fifteen other Italians (including the sergeant's wife!) he crossed into Albania. Here the fugitives were at first well treated, but after refusing to accept Islam were made to work in the quarries until their aching backs persuaded them that in essentials the difference between Christianity and Mohammedanism was but slight. Finati took the name of Mohammed and became personal servant to a Turkish general. At Scutari he seduced his master's favourite wife and fled by sea to Egypt. Soon we find him a corporal in Mohammed Ali's bodyguard. With the Mamelukes, however, his part in the battles seems to have consisted chiefly in a search for plunder. In 1811 he was with Tussun's forces in Arabia, and in 1814 served again under Mohammed Ali. His account of the Wahhabi wars is graphic and first-hand, but his observations on Arabia as translated by a later employer, Mr Bankes, are not valuable. Burton reproduced and annotated his account of Mecca. Finati was shifty and shameless, and, though he had exceptional opportunities, was too ignorant and unobservant to contribute much to knowledge out of his travels.

The rise of Wahhabism, the capture of Mecca, Turkish intervention, Napoleon's Egyptian campaign, and Mohammed Ali's defeat of the Egyptian Mamelukes, all served to quicken European interest in Arabia and the East. During these years, whose events have been briefly outlined, travellers visited the Hejaz who were well qualified to profit from what they saw themselves and could otherwise learn.

The first of them was a Spaniard, Domingo Badia y Leblich, who landed at Jidda in 1807, while the Wahhabis were still dominant. He travelled under the name of Ali Bey el Abbasi, as a wealthy scholar, with scientific instruments and a train of servants. Proceeding to Mecca, he then took ship from Jidda to Yenbo and endeavoured to reach Medina, but was halted and turned back by the Wahhabis. After his return to Europe through Egypt, Syria, and Turkey he published his narrative at Paris in 1814, and two years later in London. Little is known of him personally except that he had a great knowledge of Arabic, geology, and botany. It has been suggested that he was either an agent of Napoleon, sent to observe the nature and effects of the Wahhabi movement and to judge if it could be used by the Emperor in any future design against Egypt and Syria, or a secret agent of the French Admiralty, sent to take astronomical observations in the Red Sea. Such projects may have been suggested to him, but it seems clear that when he landed in Arabia his aims were not political but scientific.

Ali Bey seems to have passed the scrutiny of the Meccans without arousing even the slightest suspicion that he was a European. As he was allowed to make notes and use his instruments, his was the first attempt to fix the positions of Jidda and Mecca by astronomical observation, and the latter was the first inland point in Arabia to be so determined.[1] In all, he attempted to fix the positions of eighteen places on the Red Sea. He was also the first of modern travellers to mention the *harras*, or lava formations, of Western Arabia and the first to describe the routes from Mecca and Medina to the Red Sea. His narrative is also the sole first-hand view of the Hejaz under Wahhabi domination.

Being in outward appearance a Moslem of great wealth and position he came into close contact with the Court of the Sherif of Mecca, an arbitrary ruler indulging in general robbery of his subjects, and, as was usual with Arabian rulers, laying considerable imposts on trade. Of European merchants and traders the English had been in closest touch with the Sherif, by reason of the Indian trade through Jidda, but the Sherifian power of protection had been greatly lessened by the Wahhabis, and the Hejaz was no place for the infidel. With the indigenous population of Mecca the Wahhabi discipline was not popular —people smoked, but did so in secret. Yet the Sherif's enmity could be as dangerous as the fanaticism of the invaders. Ali Bey relates that he made the acquaintance of his head poisoner, "the Chief of the Well." His duty was to offer water to the notables, and those who had made themselves objectionable to the Sherif sometimes failed to recover from his functionary's

[1] Ali Bey: Mecca—latitude, 21° 28′ 9″ N., longitude, 40° 15′ 0″ E., of the meridian of the observatory of Greenwich. Ali Bey's chronometer was stolen at Muna, near Mecca. The geographical co-ordinates accepted by the Royal Geographical Society and the War Office are: latitude, 21° 25′ 18″ N., longitude, 39° 49′ 41″ E.

ministrations. A charming fellow, Ali Bey thought him, but when accepting drinks from his hands was careful to have an emetic within reach. The traveller saw everything at Mecca, and future European visitors had few faults to find with his account of Islam's centre of worship—which merits some special description by its place in the Moslem world. Ali Bey provides the first exact picture of the temple:

> I shall begin by describing the temple of Mecca, as being the principal object, and afterwards the city and the country. The temple of Mecca is known by Mussulmen under the name of El Haram, or the Temple of Excellence. It is composed of the House of God, Beit Allah, or, as it is called also, Al Kaaba; of the Well of Zemzem, Bir Zemzem; of the Cobba, or Place of Abraham, Makham Ibrahim; of the places of the four orthodox rites, Makam Hhaneffi, Makam Schaffi, Makam Kaleki, and Makam Hhanbeli; of two Cobbas, or Chapels, El Cobbatain; of an arch, called Bab-es-selem (in the same style as a triumphant arch), near the place of Abraham; of El Monbar, or the Tribune for the Priest, upon Fridays; of the wooden staircase, Daureh, which leads to the saloon of the house of God; of an immense court, surrounded by a triple row of arches; of two smaller courts, surrounded with elegant piazzas; of nineteen doors; and of seven towers, or minarets, five of which adhere to the edifice, and the other two are placed between the neighbouring houses, out of the inclosure. . . .
>
> Al Kaaba, Beit Allah, or the House of God, is a quadilateral tower, the sides and angles of which are unequal, so that its plan forms a true trapezium. The size of the edifice, and the black cloth which covers it, make this irregularity disappear, and give to it the figure of a perfect square. I looked upon it as such at first sight, but soon discovered my mistake.
>
> I esteemed it as of the greatest interest to be able to measure the proportions of this building; but how to do it without shocking the prejudices of those of my religion? However, by dint of partial measurements and approximations, I obtained results which, if they have not a mathematical precision, are at least so accurate that I can venture to say there is not an error of a foot in any of my calculations.
>
> This edifice has none of its sides parallel to the four cardinal points. However, it is generally believed that the angle of the black stone is placed exactly to the east.
>
> The following are the proportions of the Kaaba. It is a species of cube, of the form of a trapezium, built with square hewn, but unpolished stones of quartz, schorl, and mica, brought

from the neighbouring mountains. The front, in which is the door, forms the side, in an angle of which stands the black stone, and faces the N.E. $10\frac{1}{2}$° E. It is thirty-seven feet two inches six lines [French measurement] long.

The front, which forms the other side of the angle, in which is the black stone, faces the S.E. 15'' S., and is thirty-one feet seven inches long.

The side opposite the door is to the S.W. $11\frac{1}{2}$° W., and is thirty-eight feet four inches six lines in length.

The fourth side, or that of the Stones of Ismail, fronts the N.W. $17\frac{1}{2}$° N., and is twenty-nine feet long.

The height is thirty-four feet four inches.

The door has an elevation of six feet upon the outside plane. It is eight feet high, four feet ten inches broad, six feet distant from the angle of the black stone, and is composed of two folding doors, of bronze gilt, and silvered, which are fastened with an enormous padlock of silver.

The basement, which surrounds the building, is of marble, twenty inches high, projecting ten inches. There are large bronze rings fixed in it, at distances all round, to which is fastened the lower border of the black cloth that covers the walls.

The black stone, Hhajera el Assouád, or Heavenly Stone, is raised forty-two inches above the surface, and is bordered all round with a large plate of silver, about a foot broad. The part of the stone that is not covered by the silver at the angle, is almost a semicircle, six inches in height, by eight inches six lines diameter at its base.

We believe that this miraculous stone was a transparent hyacinth, brought from heaven to Abraham, by the Angel Gabriel, as a pledge of his divinity; and, being touched by an impure woman, became black and opaque.

This stone is a fragment of volcanic basalts, which is sprinkled throughout its circumference with small pointed coloured crystals, and varied with red feldspath, upon a dark background like coal, except one of its protuberances, which is a little reddish.

The continual kisses and touchings of the faithful have worn the surface uneven, so that it now has a muscular appearance. It has nearly fifteen muscles and one deep hollow.

Upon comparing the borders of the stone that are covered and secured by the silver with the uncovered part, I found the latter had lost nearly twelve lines of its thickness; from whence we may infer that if the stone was smooth and even in the time of the Prophet, it has lost a line during each succeeding age.

The interior of the Kaaba consists only of a hall, which is raised above the outside place, the same height as the door.

Two columns, of less than two feet diameter, placed in the middle, support the roof of it, of which I cannot describe the form within, because it was covered with a magnificent cloth that hid it. This cloth also covered the walls and the columns, from the top to within five feet of the pavement of the hall. The cloth was of a rose-coloured silk, sprinkled with flowers embroidered in silver, and lined with white silk. Every Sultan of Constantinople is obliged to send a new one when he mounts the throne; and this is the only occasion on which it is ever changed.

As the columns were beginning to decay at the bottom, which was not covered with the rich cloth, they have covered them with bands of wood, of one or two inches in breadth, which are placed perpendicularly by the side of each other, and fastened by bronze nails gilded.

The lower part of the walls, which is left also uncovered, is inlaid with fine marbles, some plain, other with flowers, arabesque in relief, or inscriptions. The floor is paved also with the finest marble. There are bars that go from one column to the other, and from both columns to the wall, which are said to be of silver, and an infinite number of gold lamps, suspended one over the other.

At the northern angle of the hall is a staircase, by which persons ascend upon the roof: it is covered by a partition, the door of which is shut.

The roof is flat above, and has only one very large gutter upon the north-west side, by which the rain runs off into the stones of Ismail: it is said to be of gold; it appeared to me, however, to be only of gilt bronze.

It has been already remarked, that the House of God is entirely covered on the outside with a large black cloth, called Tob el Kaaba, or the Shirt of the Kaaba, suspended from the terrace and fastened below by means of strings, which answer to the bronze rings that are fixed in the base.

There is a new one brought every year from Cairo, as also a curtain to cover the door, which is truly magnificent, being entirely embroidered with gold and silver.

The Tob el Kaaba is embroidered at about two-thirds of its height with a band of gold two feet broad, with inscriptions, which are repeated on all the four sides: it is called El Hazem, or the Belt.

The new Tob is put up every year upon Easter Day; but they do not at first keep it spread out like the old one. They fasten it up in drapery; and the curtain of the door is kept in parade, and suspended above the terrace. The true cause of this custom is, to preserve the Tob from the hands of the pilgrims; and it is also for the same reason that they cut the old one at the

PART OF A PILGRIM CARAVAN ON THE WAY FROM JIDDA TO MECCA

Photo E.N.A.

JEWS OF SANA

The men have shaven heads, and wear black skull-caps, side braids, and blue smocks; the
women wear a kerchief of print or silk, and a blue robe over pyjamas, tight at the ankle.

Photo E.N.A.

113

ceremony Iaharmo, as well as not to lose the opportunity of selling it, which they do, at five francs a cubit; but the fraud of the priests has reduced this measure to fourteen inches five lines [French]. As I am persuaded that there are few pilgrims in our days who buy any of it, there is a great deal of it left every year; so that they will soon have a considerable depot of it, for they can make no other use of it, on account of its being covered with inscriptions. The belt and the curtain return to the Sultan Scherif as his right, except when the first day of Easter falls on a Friday, on which occasion they expedite it to the Sultan of Constantinople, to whom they send the water of Zemzem every year.

I am inclined to think that the Kaaba had anciently a second door exactly opposite the present, upon the other side (at least the exterior surface of the walls favours this belief), and that it was exactly similar in shape, etc.

It has been already said, that there is a parapet about five feet high and three feet wide, in front of the north-west side of the Kaaba, called El Hajar Ismail, or the Stones of Ismail. This parapet incloses an underangular or half-circular place, paved with very fine marbles, among which I discovered particularly some green squares of infinite value. Upon this side the base of the Kaaba is cut into steps, as under the door: the remainder of the circumference is an oblique surface, forming an inclined plane. Between the parapet of Ismail and the body of the Kaaba is a space of about six feet, which leaves a passage upon both sides. It is thought that Ismail, or Ismael, was buried in this place.

Although the hall and the door of the Kaaba are elevated above the plane of the court of the temple, as we have already seen, yet, if we consider the topography of the place, it will be easy to perceive that in former times they were upon a level with the earth.

The Kaaba is the only ancient edifice that exists in the temple of Mecca; all the others have been added at a later period.

El Haram, or the Temple, is situated nearly in the middle of the city, which is built in a valley, that has a considerable slope from the north to the south.

It is easy to perceive that when they formed the great court and the other parts of the temple, instead of digging upon one side, and removing the earth to the other to level the ground, they have hollowed it out on all sides; so that to go into the temple, on any side whatsoever, it is requisite to descend several steps, because its plane is several feet lower than the general level of the ground or the streets that surround it; and the oval surface, paved with marble, that immediately encompasses the

Kaaba, upon which the pilgrims make their turns round the house of God, is the lowest part of the temple.

If we suppose, then, the ground that surrounds the Kaaba raised to its original height, to the level of the streets that surround the temple, or as high as it was when this ancient edifice stood alone, and before the construction of the remainder of the temple, we shall find that the height of the hall, and the door in question, answer exactly to the general level of the earth at that period, and that consequently there was then no occasion for a staircase to enter it.

It is true that we must then imagine that the black stone was placed in another situation to that in which it is at present, since it is nearly two feet beneath the level of the door. An infidel would say perhaps that it did not exist, or that it was underground: for myself I cannot have such an idea concerning this precious pledge of divinity.

The wooden staircase that they place before the door of the Kaaba during the two days that it is open to the public is mounted upon six large rollers of bronze, and has rails upon each side. It is about eight feet wide, and consists of ten steps.

Near the door of the Kaaba, and on the side opposite the black stone, there is a small excavation, about a foot deep, paved with marble, upon which it is reckoned a particular merit to say a prayer.

El Makam Ibrahim, or the Place of Abraham, is a species of parallelogramic cradle, facing the centre of the wall, in which is the door of the Kaaba, and at thirty-four feet distance. It is twelve feet nine inches long, and seven feet eight inches wide, and is placed with its narrowest end towards the building. The roof is supported by six pilasters, a little higher than a man.

The half of the parallelogram nearest to the house of God is surrounded by a fine railing of bronze, which embraces four pilasters, the door of which is always shut, and locked with a large silver padlock.

This railing incloses a sort of covered sarcophagus, hung with a black cloth, magnificently embroidered with gold and silver, having large golden acorns attached to it. The sarcophagus is nothing else than a large stone, that served Abraham for a footstool to construct the Kaaba, and increased in height as the building advanced, to facilitate his labours, at the same time that the stones came out miraculously already squared, from the spot where the footstool now stands, and passed in to Ismael's hands, and from thence into his father's. Hence the rite commands that a prayer should be said there after having perambulated the house of God. The space surrounded by the railing is surmounted by a pretty little cupola.

El Bir Zemzem, or the Well of Zemzem, is situated fifty-one feet distant to the E. 10° N. of the black stone.

It is about seven feet eight inches in diameter, and fifty-six feet deep to the surface of the water. The brim is of fine white marble, five feet high.

It is requisite to ascend to the brim to draw the water; at the inside of which there is a railing of iron, with a plate of brass at the foot, to prevent persons falling in. As there are no steps by which to ascend, they are obliged to climb upon the stone of an adjoining window, and afterwards leap upon the top. These difficulties exist only to prevent the pilgrims from getting the water themselves, and that they may not deprive the keepers from receiving the gratifications attached to their office. Three bronze pulleys, with hempen cords, and a leather bucket to each end of the cords, serve to draw up the water, which is rather brackish and heavy, but very limpid. Notwithstanding the depth of the well, and the heat of the climate, it is hotter when first drawn up than the air. It resembles warm water, which proves that there is at the bottom a particular cause of vehement heat. It is wholesome, nevertheless, and so abundant, that at the period of the pilgrimage, though there were thousands of pitchers full drawn, its level was not sensibly diminished.

I have four bottles of this water, which I drew myself from the well, and closed up immediately, with all the precautions that chemistry requires, to be able one day or other to analyse it. In an hour after I had put them into some emery, the mouths being previously perfectly stopped with some crystal stoppers and sealed, the interior surface was completely covered with small bubbles of extremely subtile air, resembling the points of needles. When I shook the bottle they mounted to the superior surface, or united themselves into one bubble of the size of a grey pea. It was no doubt a gas, which the difference alone of the temperature sufficed to disengage.

It is known that this well was miraculously opened by the angel of the Lord for Agar, when she was nearly perishing from thirst in the desert with her son Ismael, after having been sent from Abraham's house.

There is a small house constructed round the well, consisting of the room in which is the well; another smaller, that serves as a storehouse for the pitchers; and a staircase to ascend to the roof, or terrace, which is surrounded by a railing, and divided into two parts, one of which is dedicated to prayer for the followers of the rite Schaffi, and is crowned with a pretty cupola, supported by eight pilasters; the other incloses two large horizontal marble sundials, to mark the hours of prayer.

A person charged with observing them begins by crying out

the form of the convocation from the spot Schaffi; and at the same instant seven mueddens or criers repeat it from the top of the seven minarets of the temple. This employment is called *monkis*.

There is a door to the staircase independent of the others; so that there are three in the edifice.

The room in which is the well is seventeen feet three inches square; it is entirely lined and paved with fine marble, and is lighted by three windows to the west, three to the north, and two in the door to the east: there are three niches in the wall on the southern side, which separates this room from the storehouse of the pitchers. The outside is decorated with a small façade of fine white marble.

The number of pitchers belonging to the well is immense: they occupy not only the room I have spoken of, but also the two neighbouring Cobbas, and several other magazines placed around the court of the temple. . . .

As soon as a distinguished pilgrim arrives at Mecca they inscribe his name in the book of the chief of the Zemzem, who orders one of his servants to furnish and carry water to the house of the pilgrim, which is executed with assiduity. The pitchers are marked with the name of the person upon the body in black wax; and some mystical inscriptions are usually added.[1]

Eleven years after his first visit Ali Bey set out again from Damascus for Mecca, but was poisoned or died of dysentery at Balka, 120 miles from Damascus, and, because of his supposed activities as an agent of France, perfidious Albion was sometimes accused of foul play. He was thought to have accepted Islam, but a cross found under his vest suggests that he had been a Christian throughout his travels. Some of his property and papers were recovered by Lady Hester Stanhope.

Just before Tussun's landing in the Hejaz another European began travels in Arabia more extensive than those of Ali Bey. Ulrich Jaspar Seetzen had lived many years in the East, had a profound knowledge of Arabic, and was a botanist of great reputation. He was in the Russian service, and in visiting the Hejaz was seeking experience among Moslems which might be useful in the exploration of Central Asia, a region of increasing interest to the Tsar. He performed the pilgrimage, and then visited Sana and Aden.

[1] *Travels* (London, 1816).

Subsequently he seems to have decided to cross the peninsula eastward. As Haji Musa, a physician, he entered the Yemen highlands and was murdered somewhere near Taizz. His death has remained a mystery, but it is improbable that he was killed as a result of a raid on his caravan. Already he had been under suspicion in Mecca, and had been examined by the Wahhabis. Perhaps Seetzen failed to pass a second fanatical test. Thus Western knowledge reaped no harvest from the Hejaz and Yemen travels of this bold scholar.

A crisis in the Wahhabi movement, the death of Saud, was at hand when the next great European traveller came to Arabia.

CHAPTER X

THE UNVEILING OF MECCA AND MEDINA

I . . . descended from Mount Arafat and . . . walked about
the camp, here and there entering into conversation with pilgrims;
inquiring at the Syrian camp after some of my friends; and among
the Syrian Bedouin for news from their deserts.

JOHANN LUDWIG BURCKHARDT, *Travels in Arabia*

JOHANN LUDWIG BURCKHARDT was born at Lausanne in 1784. After studying at Leipzig and Göttingen he was employed by the African Association to explore the interior of Africa. He then undertook a further period of study at London and Cambridge, and, being in everything thorough, inured himself to privation and hardship before leaving England in 1809.

From Malta in the autumn of that year he went to Aleppo, wore Eastern dress, took the name of Ibrahim Ibn Abdulla, learned Arabic, acquired an astonishing knowledge of the Koran and its commentaries, and fitted himself to pass easily as a learned doctor of their law among educated Mohammedans. While in Syria he visited Palmyra, Damascus, and the Lebanon, and on a desert journey discovered the site of ancient Petra—a discovery which brought his name to the notice of archæologists in every quarter of the world.

He was popular with the Europeans in Syria, and was introduced enthusiastically to Lady Hester Stanhope at Nazareth. The "Queen of Palmyra," however, took a dislike to him, partly because he adopted the attitude of the professional towards the amateur, and because she realized he had been accepted by the Arabs on his merits, she mainly for her baksheesh.

Burckhardt planned to start his African expedition from Egypt, joining a caravan to Fezzan, and thence exploring the sources of the Niger. While waiting for the caravan at Cairo he travelled up the Nile as far as Dar Mahass, but, finding he could make no progress westward, visited Berber, Shendi, and Suakin. From this Red Sea port he crossed, as "Sheikh Ibrahim," to Jidda, and visited Mecca, Taif, Medina, and Yenbo.

Like Niebuhr, he thus covered one restricted but important section of the peninsula. Niebuhr's area of personal exploration was of interest to Europeans mainly because of its age-long reputation for trade and fertility, but the district travelled by Burckhardt in the Hejaz was still exclusive and mysterious. It was associated far less with ideas of commerce than with those of strange religious rites and Moslem fanaticism. Burckhardt was to come out of this country with the most detailed account ever written of the Kaaba, the religious ceremonies, the trade, and the inhabitants. In these respects he worked an almost untouched lode to its slightest vein, but physical geography, dealing with such things as the elevation and direction of mountain ranges, measurement of slopes, drainage, and kindred matters, was not so important in his time as now, so that his account was less satisfying to the scientific geographer. On his travels, and during part of them only, a ship's compass was his sole scientific instrument, and as much of the territory was covered at night he could give only slight topographical information. His main interest was in the commerce, social life, characteristics, and religion of the Arabs, settled and nomadic. With these aims in view he provided Europe with a picture of a region which it had viewed with curiosity and speculation for centuries.

His stay in the land occupied only some nine months, and part of that time he was ill. Almost at the beginning, at Jidda, his financial arrangements miscarried. Prices were high, owing to the arrival of the Turkish forces and the pilgrims, and all supplies came from Egypt, so that his position was far from comfortable until he could obtain a supply of money. "A person who has money," he wrote, "has little to fear from Osmanlis except the loss of it."

His description of Jidda from the viewpoint of plain reporting is as satisfying as anything that has been written of the Arab towns. Burckhardt does not give, here or elsewhere, such a vision of light and shadow as T. E. Lawrence saw when lying off the port, where "the heat of Arabia came out like a drawn sword and struck us speechless." Burckhardt saw merely a well-built town with high stone houses, the dazzling white of the walls, which was trying to the eye, decayed fortifications, a big cannon, a few date-palms, and all around the barren desert.

Jidda had declined under the Wahhabis because of the slackening in the pilgrimage and the reluctance of merchants to send their goods into a disturbed area. There were few true Arabs of the Hejaz among the population, which consisted of merchants and traders from Yemen, Hadhramaut, Egypt, Syria, and Anatolia, with East Indians and Malays, a mixed stock, intermarried with Abyssinian slaves. Yet Jidda "the Rich" was the port for Arabia and Egypt and a mart for Indian goods and the coffee of Yemen. The latter trade, however, was already suffering from the imports of West Indian coffee into Turkey.

The trade in India goods is much safer, and equally profitable. The fleets, principally from Calcutta, Surat, and Bombay, reach Djidda in the beginning of May, when they find the merchants already prepared for them, having collected as many dollars and sequins as their circumstances admit, that they may effect bargains in wholesale at the very first arrival of the ships. Large sums are also sent hither by the Cairo merchants to purchase goods on their account; but the cargoes for the greater part are bought up by the merchants of Djidda, who afterwards send them to Cairo to be sold for their own advantage. The India fleets return in June or July, when the prices of every article brought by them immediately rise; and it commonly occurs that, on the very day when the last ships sail, ten per cent. profit may be obtained upon the first price. The merchants, however, unless pressed for money, do not sell at this time, but keep their goods in warehouses for four or five months, during which the price continues to rise; so that if they choose to wait till the January or February following they may calculate with great security upon a gain of from thirty to forty per cent., and if they transport a part of their goods to Mekka for sale to the Hadj their profits are still greater. It is the nature of this commerce that renders Djidda so crowded during the stay of the fleet. People repair hither from every port on the Red Sea, to purchase at the first hand; and the merchants of Mekka, Yembo, and Djidda, scrape together every dollar they possess, to lay them out in these purchases. Another cause of the India trade with

Djidda being more safe and profitable is the arrival of the merchant-ships but once in the year, at a stated period, and all within a few weeks: there is, therefore, nothing to spoil the market; the price of goods is settled according to the known demand and quantity of imports; and it is never known to fall till the return of the next fleet.[1]

Burckhardt saw that if Suez were to take part in the direct Indian trade Jidda would at once decline to the status of a mere Hejaz harbour. Mohammed Ali, he considered, was ignorant of his own real interests, for after concluding a treaty allowing English ships to come direct from India to Suez he violated the agreement by stopping a big Bombay ship at Jidda and exacting duties from it. The Swiss traveller thought that the British had been inept in dealing with this incident. "Forgetting that the favour of a Turkish ruler can never be bought by conciliation, but can only be obtained by an attitude of defiance," they submitted to this treatment, and even apparently failed to realize that they could easily retaliate upon Mohammedan ships trading to Malta, "which would have taught him to respect the British flag wherever he might meet it."

The prosperity of Jidda was bound up entirely with its commerce. There was no shipbuilding, because of a lack of timber, and its trades hardly extended beyond local requirements, such as tailoring and sandal-making. Typical of Burckhardt's thoroughness is his list of traders in the principal streets, among them two sellers of butter, honey, oil and vinegar, eight date-vendors, eighteen vegetable- or fruit-dealers, two sellers of sour milk, five of sweetmeats, two of roast meat for Turks, a supplier of fish fried in oil, "frequented by all the Turkish and Greek sailors," eleven corn-dealers, eighteen druggists who were all East Indians selling wax candles, paper, perfumery, sugar, and rosebuds of Taif, which ladies soaked in water and used for ablutions. To this catalogue is added a detailed knowledge of their sources of supply and of their clientele.

Although few of the inhabitants were true Hejazis, and while even in the native the true Bedouin character was corrupted,

---

[1] *Travels in Arabia* (London, 1829).

they despised all who did not speak Arabic or who differed from them in manners. The Turks they regarded as inferior, and resented their attitude of superiority, hating and despising them for their ignorance of Arabia, its language and its peculiarities.

Burckhardt concludes his description of Jidda, which must surely be the most detailed written by a pioneer in any Eastern port, with the following prophetic passage:

> Whenever the power of the Turks in the Hedjaz declines, which it will when the resources of Egypt are no longer directed to that point by so able and so undisturbed a possessor of Egypt as Mohammed Ali, the Arabs will avenge themselves for the submission, light as it is, which they now reluctantly yield to their conquerors; and the reign of the Osmanlis in the Hedjaz will probably terminate in many a scene of bloodshed.

On his journey from Jidda to Taif, where Mohammed Ali had set up his headquarters, Burckhardt gives merely a general picture of the route which took him past Mecca: a sandy plain, hills, of granite, sandstone, and quartz, small date plantations, countryside covered with rough, wild blocks of stone, and then, beyond Jebel Kora, rivulets and barrenness giving place to the cultivation of wheat, barley, onions, apples, figs, apricots, and peaches. One has a general idea of the range of hills, barren rocks, and fertile valleys. The journey was made mostly by night. Like Jidda, the town had suffered from the Wahhabi rule, and was now ruinous and almost abandoned, whereas before it had been a market for Yemen coffee, brought overland to escape the heavy harbour dues. It stood in a sandy plain surrounded by low hills at the foot of which were gardens, crops of wheat, barley, and fruit where the land was watered by *wadis* from the highlands.

Burckhardt's Arabic scholarship and profound knowledge of the prayers and rites of Islam were so complete that he was able to disarm the suspicion which he knew existed in some minds at Taif. He was able, for instance, to surprise the Kadi of Mecca, who was there, by his grasp of commentaries on the Koran. Mohammed Ali had known him at Cairo merely as a proselyte of some years' standing, and Burckhardt never knew whether or not the Pasha believed him to be a true Moslem.

Of several interviews which he had with the Egyptian the following may be reproduced as containing some points of historical and military interest and as a picture from close quarters of a famous ruler:

Q. Sheikh Ibrahim, I hope you are well.

A. Perfectly well, and most happy to have the honour of seeing you again.

Q. You have travelled much since I saw you at Cairo. How far did you advance into the negro country?

To this question I replied by giving a short account of my journey in Nubia.

Q. Tell me, how are the Mamelouks at Dongola?

I related what the reader will find in my Nubian *Travels*.

Q. I understand that you treated with two of the Mamelouk Beys at Ibrim; was it so?

The word *treated* (if the dragoman rightly translated the Turkish word) startled me very much; for the Pasha, while he was in Egypt, had heard that on my journey towards Dongola I had met two Mamelouk Beys at Derr; and as he still suspected that the English secretly favoured the Mamelouk interest, he probably thought that I had been the bearer of some message to them from Government. I therefore assured him that my meeting with the two Beys was quite accidental; that the unpleasant reception which I experienced at Mahass was on their account; and that I entertained fears of their designs against my life. With this explanation the Pasha seemed satisfied.

Q. Let us only settle matters here with the Wahhabys, and I shall soon be able to get rid of the Mamelouks. How many soldiers do you think are necessary for subduing the country as far as Senaar?

A. Five hundred men, good troops, might reach that point, but could not keep possession of the country; and the expenses would scarcely be repaid by the booty.

Q. What do those countries afford?

A. Camels and slaves; and, towards Senaar, gold, brought from Abyssinia; but all this is the property of individuals. The chiefs or kings in those countries do not possess any riches.

Q. In what state are the roads from Egypt to Senaar?

I described the road between Asouan and Shendy, and from Souakin to the same place.

Q. How did you pass your time among the Blacks?

I related some laughable stories, with which he seemed greatly amused.

Q. And now, Sheikh Ibrahim, where do you mean to go?

A. I wish to perform the Hadj, return to Cairo, and then

proceed to visit Persia. (I did not think it advisable to mention my design of returning into the interior of Africa.)

Q. May God render the way smooth before you! But I think it folly and madness to travel so much. What, let me ask, is the result of your last journey?

A. Men's lives are predestined; we all obey our fate. For myself, I enjoy great pleasure in exploring new and unknown countries, and becoming acquainted with different races of people. I am induced to undertake journeys by the private satisfaction that travelling affords, and I care little about personal fatigue.

Q. Have you heard of the news from Europe?

A. Only some vague reports at Djidda.

The Pasha then gave me an account of the events which ended in Bonaparte's banishment to Elba, after the entrance of the allies into Paris. Bonaparte, he said, behaved like a coward; he ought to have sought for death, rather than expose himself in a cage to the laughter of the universe. The Europeans, he said, are as treacherous as the Osmanlys; all Bonaparte's confidants abandoned him—all his generals, who owed to him their fortunes.

Mohammed was eager in his inquiries about the political relation between Great Britain and Russia, and whether war was likely between them, on account of hostile intentions which he had heard Russia entertained towards the Porte. He feared also that the English army lately employed in Spain and the South of France would be at liberty to invade Egypt. "The great fish swallows the small," he said, "and Egypt is necessary to England in supplying corn to Malta and Gibraltar." Burckhardt reasoned with him vainly on this matter, and noticed that the dragoman did not always interpret his answers correctly, for fear of contradicting his master's well-known opinions, which were deeply rooted, and had been fostered by the French mission in Egypt. "I am the friend of the English," said Mohammed Ali, and Burckhardt remarks that this addressed by a Turk to a Christian means only that he fears him or wants his money.

> But to tell you the truth, among great men we see many compliments and very little sincerity. My hope is that they will not fall upon Egypt during my stay in the Hedjaz; if I am there myself I shall at least have the satisfaction of fighting personally for my dominions.

Of the Sultan, he said repeatedly, he had no fear, for an army from Syria could never attack Egypt by land in very large bodies, from the want of camels, and separate corps were easily destroyed as they passed out of the desert.

Burckhardt told him that he was like a young man in possession of a beautiful girl; although sure of her affections, he would always be jealous of every stranger.

"You say well," replied Mohammed. "I certainly love Egypt with all the ardour of a lover; and if I had ten thousand souls I would willingly sacrifice them for its possession."

He asked me in what state I had found Upper Egypt; and whether his son Ibrahim Pasha (the Governor) was liked there. I replied, in the language of the truth, that all the chiefs of the villages hated him (for he had compelled them to abandon their despotic treatment of their fellow-peasants); but that the peasants themselves were much attached to him. (The fact is that instead of being oppressed, as formerly, by the Mamelouk Beys and Kashefs, as well as by their own sheikhs, they have at present only one tyrant, the Pasha himself, who keeps his governors of districts in perfect order.)

Mohammed Aly wished to know my opinion respecting the number of troops necessary for defending Egypt against a foreign army. I answered that I knew nothing of war, but from what I had read in books. "No, no," he exclaimed, "you travellers always have your eyes open, and you inquire after every thing." He persisted in his question; and, being thus forced to reply, I said that twenty-five thousand chosen troops would probably be able to resist any attack. "I have now thirty-three thousand," said he—a false assertion, for I am quite certain that he had at that time not more than sixteen thousand men, dispersed over Egypt and the Hedjaz.

He would next explain to me the *Nizam Djedyd*, or new system of discipline and military regulations. He said it was only the avidity of the chiefs, and not the dislike of the common soldiers, that obstructed the institution of a well-organised army in Turkey, and opposed the mustering necessary to prevent the officers from imposing on the public treasury. "But I shall make a regular corps of negro soldiers," he added. This his predecessor, Khurshid Pasha, had attempted, but with little success. The subject of the *Nizam Djedyd* was resumed as soon as Mohammed Aly returned to Egypt from this expedition; but the revolt of his soldiers, who plundered his own capital, obliged him to abandon the undertaking, which had been badly planned. In the defence of Egypt, he said, he should principally use his cavalry and horse-artillery; the former should destroy all the provisions in advance of the enemy, as the Russians had lately done; and the latter would harass them on all sides, without ever attempting to make a stand.

A copy of the peace treaty arrived at in Paris was brought to Mohammed Ali across the desert from Damascus, and Burckhardt examined the terms with him, forming the impression that the Egyptian looked forward impatiently to another war among the European Powers to relieve him of anxiety for his own safety—and to stimulate the demand for corn at Alexandria. He was quite sure that the English would one day seize Napoleon in Elba. "Have the English then fought for nothing these twenty years?" he asked. "They've only got Malta and a few other islands." He feared greatly that there were secret articles in the peace, assigning the English the possession of Egypt. It did not enter his mind that Britain had secured her own safety and independence and the re-establishment of the Balance of Power in Europe. "They should not leave Spain," he said, "without being handsomely repaid by the Spaniards; and why now abandon Sicily?" To Burckhardt he seemed unable to understand that the English were guided by the laws of honour and a sense of the general good of Europe. "A great king," he exclaimed warmly, "knows nothing but his sword and his purse; he draws the one to fill the other; there is no honour among conquerors!"

This, in Burckhardt's opinion, was a frank avowal of the sentiments which guided even the most petty of Turkish rulers.

Mohammed Ali had some idea of the English parliament, knew the name of Wellington, thought he was a great general, but doubted whether, with such bad soldiers as the Turkish troops were, he would have been able to achieve as much as he had done in Egypt and the Hejaz.

Burckhardt had landed at Jidda in July. He left Taif at the beginning of September, experiencing storms and inundations during his two days' journey to Mecca. On arrival he at once performed the religious rites and later attended the ceremonies at Muna and Arafat. His full and detailed account, some part of which is quoted here, fully satisfied Burton, whose knowledge of Moslem habit, custom, and ritual was peerless:

> Whoever enters Mekka, whether pilgrim or not, is enjoined by the law to visit the Temple immediately, and not to attend

to any worldly concern whatever before he has done so. We crossed the line of shops and houses, up to the gates of the mosque, where my ass-driver took his fare and set me down: here I was accosted by half a dozen *metowaf*, or guides to the holy places, who knew, from my being dressed in the *ihram*, that I intended to visit the Kaaba. I chose one of them as my guide, and, after having deposited my baggage in a neighbouring shop, entered the mosque at the gate called Bab-es'-Salam, by which the newcomer is recommended to enter. The ceremonies to be performed in visiting the mosque are the following: (1) certain religious rites to be practised in the interior of the Temple; (2) the walk between Szafa and Meroua; (3) the visit to the Omra. These ceremonies ought to be repeated by every Moslem whenever he enters Mekka from a journey farther than two days' distance, and they must again be more particularly performed at the time of the pilgrimage to Arafat. I shall here describe them as briefly as possible; a full detail and explanation of the Mohammedan law on this subject would be extremely tedious; indeed there exist many voluminous works in Arabic which treat of nothing else.

1. *Rites to be performed in the Interior of the Temple*

At the entrance, under the colonnade, some prayers are recited on first sight of the Kaaba, and then two *rikats*, or four prostrations addressed to the divinity, in thanks for having reached the holy spot, and in salutation of the mosque itself; after which the pilgrim approaches the Kaaba by one of the paved ways to it, through the open area in which it stands. In passing under the insulated arch in front of the Kaaba, called Bab-es'-Salam, certain prayers are said. Other prayers are recited in a low voice, and the visitor then places himself opposite to the black stone of the Kaaba, and prays two *rikats*; at the conclusion of which the stone is touched with the right hand, or kissed, if there is no great pressure of people. The devotee then begins the *Towaf*, or walk round the Kaaba, keeping that building on his left hand. This ceremony is to be repeated seven times; the three first are in a quick pace, in imitation of the Prophet, whose enemies having reported that he was dangerously ill, he contradicted them by running thrice round the Kaaba at full speed. Every circuit must be accompanied with prescribed prayers, which are recited in a low voice, and appropriated to the different parts of the building that are passed: the black stone is kissed or touched at the conclusion of each circuit, as well as another stone, walled in at one corner of the black stone. When the seven circuits are finished the visitor approaches the wall of the Kaaba, between the black stone and the door of the building, which space is called El Metzem. There, with widely out-stretched arms, and with his breast closely pressed against the wall, he beseeches the Lord to pardon his sins. He then retires towards the neighbouring Mekam Ibrahim, and there prays two *rikats*, called Sunnet-et-towaf, after which he repairs to the adjoining well of Zemzem; and, after a short pious address in honour of the well, drinks as much of the water as he wishes, or as he can on occasions when the crowd is very great; and this completes the ceremonies to be observed within the Temple.

I may here add that the *Towaf* is a Muselman ceremony not exclusively practised in the temple at Mekka. In the summer of 1813 I was present at the annual festival of the patron saint of Kenne, in Upper Egypt, called Seid Abderrahman el Kennawy. Many thousands of the people of the country were assembled on the plain, in which stands the saint's tomb, at a distance of one mile from the town. Each person, as he arrived, walked seven times round the small mosque which contains the tomb; and when the new covering intended to be laid over it for that year was brought in solemn procession, the whole assembly followed it seven times round the building, after which it was placed upon the tomb.

2. *Walk between Szafa and Meroua*

My guide, who, during the whole of the ceremonies above mentioned, had been close at my heels, reciting all the necessary prayers, which I repeated after him, now led me out of the mosque by the gate called Bab-es'-Szafa. About fifty yards from the S.E. side of the mosque, on a slightly ascending ground, stand three small open arches, connected by an architrave above, having below three broad stone steps leading up to them.

This is called the Hill of Szafa: here, standing on the upper step, with his face turned towards the mosque, which is hidden from view by intervening houses, the pilgrim raises his hands towards heaven, addresses a short prayer to the Deity, and implores his assistance in the holy walk, or *Say*, as it is called; he then descends, to begin the walk, along a level street about six hundred paces in length, which the Arabian historians call Wady Szafa, leading towards Meroua, which is at its farther extremity, where stands a stone platform elevated about six or eight feet above the level of the street, with several broad steps ascending to it. The visitor is enjoined to walk at a quick pace from Szafa to Meroua; and for a short space, which is marked by four stones or pilasters, called El Myleyn el Akhdereyn, built into the walls of the houses on both sides, he must run. Two of these stones seemed to be of a green colour; they exhibit numerous inscriptions; but these are so high in the walls that

A General View of Taizz
Photo E.N.A.

THE KAABA AND COURT OF THE GREAT MOSQUE AT MECCA
The new buildings in the foreground are used to house pilgrims.
Photo E.N.A.

it would be difficult to read them. Prayers are recited un-interruptedly in a loud voice during this walk. Persons who are unwell may ride, or be borne in a litter. On reaching Meroua the pilgrim ascends the steps, and, with uplifted hands, repeats a short prayer like that of Szafa, to which place he must now return. The walk between the two places is to be repeated seven times, concluding at Meroua; four times from Szafa to Meroua; and three times from Meroua to Szafa.

3. *The Visit to the Omra*

In the vicinity of Meroua are many barbers' shops; into one of these the pilgrim enters, having completed the *Say*, and the barber shaves his head, reciting a particular prayer, which the pilgrim repeats after him. The Hanefys, one of the four orthodox sects of Moslims, shave only one-fourth part of the head, the other three-fourths continuing untouched till they return from the Omra. After the ceremony of shaving is finished the visitor is at liberty to lay aside the *ihram*, and put on his ordinary dress; or, if he choose, he may go immediately from thence to the Omra, in which case he still wears the *ihram*, and says only two *rikats* on setting out. This, however, is seldom done, as the ceremonies of the *Towaf* and *Say* are sufficiently fatiguing to render repose desirable on their completion; the visitor therefore dresses in his usual clothes, but the next or any following day (the sooner the better) he resumes the *ihram*, with the same ceremonies as are observed on first assuming it, and then proceeds to the Omra, a place one hour and a half from Mekka. Here he repeats two *rikats* in a small chapel, and returns to the city, chanting all the way the pious ejaculations called *Telby*, beginning with the words, "*Lebeyk, Alla huma, Lebeyk!*" He must now again perform the *Towaf* and the *Say*, have his head completely shaved, and lay aside the *ihram*, which closes those ceremonies. A visit to the Omra is enjoined by the law as absolutely necessary; but many individuals, notwith-standing, dispense with it. I went thither on the third day after my arrival in the city, performing the walk in the night-time, which is the fashion during the hot season.

At the time of the Hadj, all these ceremonies must be repeated after returning from Wady Muna, and again on taking leave of Mekka. The *Towaf*, or walk round the Kaaba, should also be performed as often as convenient; and few foreigners live at Mekka who do not make it a point to execute it twice daily: in the evening and before daybreak.

Prior to the age of Mohammed, when idolatry prevailed in Arabia, the Kaaba was regarded as a sacred object, and visited with religious veneration by persons who performed the *Towaf* nearly in the same manner as their descendants do at present. The building, however, was in those times ornamented with three hundred and sixty idols, and there was a very important difference in the ceremony; for men and women were then obliged to appear in a state of perfect nudity, that their sins might be thrown off with their garments. The Mohammedan Hadj, or pilgrimage, and the visit to the Kaaba, are, therefore, nothing more than a continuation and confirmation of the ancient custom. In like manner, Szafa and Meroua were esteemed by the old Arabians as holy places, which contained images of the gods Motam and Nehyk; and here the idolaters used to walk from the one place to the other, after their return from the pilgrimage to Arafat. Here, if we may believe Mohammedan tradition, Hadjer, the mother of Ismayl, wandered about in the desert, after she had been driven from Abraham's house, that she might not witness the death of her infant son, whom she had laid down almost expiring from thirst; when the Angel Gabriel appearing, struck the ground with his foot, which caused the well of Zemzem immediately to spring forth. In commemoration of the wanderings of Hadjer, who in her affliction had gone seven times between Szafa and Meroua, the walk from one place to the other is said to have been instituted.

El Azraky relates that, when the idolatrous Arabs had con-cluded the ceremonies of the Hadj, at Arafat, all the different tribes that had been present, assembled, on their return to Mekka, at the holy place called Szafa, there to extol, in loud and im-passioned strains, the glory of their ancestors, their battles, and the fame of their nation. From each tribe, in its turn, arose a poet who addressed the multitude. "To our tribe," exclaimed he, "belonged such and such eminent warriors and generous Arabs; and now," he added, "we boast of others." He then recited their names, and sang their praises, concluding with a strain of heroic poetry, and an appeal to the other tribes, in words like the following: "Let him who denies the truth of what I have said, or who lays claim to as much glory, honour, and virtue as we do, prove it here!" Some rival poet then arose, and celebrated in similar language the equal or superior glory attached to his own tribe, endeavouring, at the same time, to undervalue or ridicule his rival's pretensions.

To allay the animosity and jealousies produced by this custom, or, perhaps, to break the independent spirit of his fierce Bedouins, Mohammed abolished it by a passage in the Koran, which says: "When you have completed the rites of the pilgrimage, remember God, as you formerly were wont to commemorate your fore-fathers, and with still greater fervency." Thus, probably, was removed the cause of many quarrels, but, at the same time, this stern lawgiver destroyed the influence which the songs of those rival national bards exercised over the martial virtues and literary genius of their countrymen.

The visit of the Omra was likewise an ancient custom. Mohammed retained the practice; and it is said that he frequently recited his evening prayers on that spot.

Having completed the fatiguing ceremonies of the *Towaf* and *Say*, I had a part of my head shaved, and remained sitting in the barber's shop, not knowing any other place of repose. I inquired after lodgings, but learned that the town was already full of pilgrims, and that many others, who were expected, had engaged apartments. After some time, however, I found a man who offered me a ready-furnished room: of this I took possession, and having no servant, boarded with the owner. He and his family, consisting of a wife and two children, retired into a small open courtyard, on the side of my room. The landlord was a poor man from Medina, and by profession a *metowaf*, or *cicerone*. Although his mode of living was much below that of even the second class of Mekkawys, yet it cost me fifteen piastres a day; and I found, after we parted, that several articles of dress had been pilfered from my travelling sack; but this was not all: on the feast-day he invited me to a splendid supper, in company with half a dozen of his friends, in my room, and on the following morning he presented me with a bill for the whole expense of this entertainment.

The thousands of lamps lighted during Ramadhan in the great mosque rendered it the nightly resort of all foreigners at Mekka; here they took their walk, or sat conversing till after midnight. The scene presented altogether a spectacle which (excepting the absence of women) resembled rather an European midnight assemblage than what I should have expected in the sanctuary of the Mohammedan religion. The night which closes Ramadhan did not present those brilliant displays of rejoicing that are seen in other parts of the East; and the three subsequent days of the festival are equally devoid of public amusements. A few swinging machines were placed in the streets to amuse children, and some Egyptian jugglers exhibited their feats to multitudes assembled in the streets; but little else occurred to mark the feast, except a display of gaudy dresses, in which the Arabians surpass both Syrians and Egyptians.

The inhabitants of Mecca and Jidda he described together, as having much in common in appearance, manner, and occupation. Here again one is impressed by Burckhardt's minute observation; he apparently misses nothing regarding dress, manners, appearance, habits, psychology, and trade. The key to all the commerce of both towns, but especially of Mecca, was the *haj*, by which a great proportion of the buying and selling of merchandise was regulated. The Meccans, rich and poor, saw in the *haj* the chief source of their revenue. It is a wonderful picture of the population of a unique city, but only a little can be given in the traveller's own words:

The colour of the Mekkawy and Djiddawy is a yellowish sickly brown, lighter or darker according to the origin of the mother, who is very often an Abyssinian slave. Their features approach much nearer to those of Bedouins than I have observed in any townsmen of the East; this is particularly observable in the sherifs, who are gifted with very handsome countenances; they have the eye, face, and aquiline nose of the Bedouin, but are more fleshy. The lower class of Mekkawys are generally stout, with muscular limbs, while the higher orders are distinguishable by their meagre emaciated forms, as are also all those inhabitants who draw their origin from India or Yemen. The Bedouins who surround Mekka, though poor, are much stronger-bodied than the wealthier Bedouins of the interior of the desert, probably because their habits are less roving, and because they are less exposed to the hardships of long journeys. The Mekkawy, it may be generally said, is inferior in strength and size to the Syrian or Egyptian, but far exceeds him in expressive features, and especially in the vivacity and brilliancy of the eye.

All the male natives of Mekka and Djidda are tattooed with a particular mark, which is performed by their parents when they are forty days of age. It consists of three long cuts down both cheeks, and two on the right temple, the scars of which, sometimes three or four lines in breadth, remain through life. It is called *meshale*. The Bedouins do not allow this practice; but the Mekkawys pride themselves in the distinction, which precludes the other inhabitants of the Hedjaz from claiming, in foreign countries, the honour of being born in the holy cities. This tattooing is sometimes, though very seldom, applied to female children. . . .

The Mekkawys are cleaner in their dress than any Eastern people I have seen. As white muslin, or white cambric, forms the principal part of their clothing, it requires frequent washing; and this is regularly done, so that even the poorest orders endeavour to change their linen at least once a week. With the higher and middle classes the change is, of course, more frequent. The rich wear every day a different dress; and it is no uncommon thing with many to possess thirty or forty suits. The people of

132

the Hedjaz delight in dress much more than the northern Mohammedans; and the earnings of the lower classes are mostly spent in clothes. When a Mekkawy returns home from his shop, or even after a short walk into the town, he immediately undresses, hangs up his clothes over a cord tied across his sitting-room, takes off his turban, changes his shirt, and then seats himself upon his carpet with a thin under-cap upon his head. . . .

The Mekkawys, who do not ostensibly follow commerce, are attached to the Government, or to the establishment of the mosque; but, as I have already said, they all engage, more or less, in some branch of traffic, and the whole population looks forward to the period of the Hadj as the source of their income. . . .

The idlest, most impudent, and vilest individuals of Mekka adopt the profession of guides (*metowaf* or *delyl*); and as there is no want of those qualities, and a sufficient demand for guides during the Hadj, they are very numerous. Besides the places which I have described in the town, the *metowafs* accompany the *hadjys* to all the other places of resort in the sacred district, and are ready to perform every kind of service in the city. But their utility is more than counterbalanced by their importunity and knavery. They besiege the room of the *hadjy* from sunrise to sunset, and will not allow him to do anything without obtruding their advice: they sit down with him to breakfast, dinner, and supper; lead him into all possible expenses, that they may pocket a share of them; suffer no opportunity to pass of asking him for money; and woe to the poor ignorant Turk who employs them as his interpreter in any mercantile concern. . . .

From trade, stipends, and the profits afforded by *hadjys* the riches which annually flow into Mekka are very considerable, and might have rendered it one of the richest cities in the East, were it not for the dissolute habits of its inhabitants. With the exception of the first class of merchants, who, though they keep splendid establishments, generally live below their income, and a great part of the second class, who hoard up money with the view of attaining the first rank, the generality of Mekkawys, of all descriptions and professions, are loose and disorderly spendthrifts. The great gains which they make during three or four months are squandered in good living, dress, and the grossest gratifications; and in proportion as they feel assured of the profits of the following year they care little about saving any part of those of the present.

It is typical of Burckhardt that he should record not only the practice of the rich *haji's* buying water for the poor, but also the chant of the water-carrier, as he pours it into the wooden bowl of the beggar:

Ed djene wael moyfe zataly Saheb es sa byl[1]

Burckhardt remained in Mecca until the pilgrim caravans arrived in the late autumn, and then undertook the full ceremony. In his time the Syrian caravan, which had been interrupted for a time by the Wahhabis, was the strongest in numbers. Setting out from Constantinople, it collected pilgrims on its route through Anatolia and Syria until it reached Damascus, where it remained several weeks. On this part of the journey the caravan was guarded from town to town by forces supplied by the local governors, and the way was easy, being blessed with numerous caravanserais and public fountains, while the pilgrims were welcomed everywhere with festivity and rejoicings. From Damascus the column journeyed for thirty days across the desert to Medina. The towns of Eastern Syria and the great Bedouin chiefs of the Syrian frontiers furnished camels for this part of the journey. In 1814 there were four or five thousand persons in the caravan, which was provided with fifteen thousand camels.

The Egyptian caravan started from Cairo and was smaller. Its route, however, was more dangerous, as it passed through the territory of wild and warlike Bedouin along the shore of the Red Sea. There were fewer watering-places, and those for the most part provided brackish water. The peasants of Upper and Lower Egypt, however, feared this desert route less than the sea.

The Persian *haj* also had been interrupted by the Wahhabis, but after the peace was made by Abdulla in 1815 it started again from Baghdad and travelled towards Mecca through Nejd, only to be attacked by the Shammar. The Persian caravan was escorted by Arabs of the Ageyl, but many of the pilgrims avoided the desert journey and came by sea, embarking at Basra and landing at Jidda or Mocha. Others travelled westward from Baghdad and joined the Syrian pilgrims. The

---

[1] "Paradise and forgiveness be the lot of him who gave you this water."

Persians were notorious heretics, and had sometimes been forbidden the pilgrimage, but the money they spent was sufficient
inducement to remove the ban.

The North African *haj* moved slowly from Tunis through
Tripoli to Alexandria or Cairo and then joined the common
caravan route. Even the Wahhabis could find no fault with
these pilgrims, and considered them free from the scandalous
practices which they attributed to the Syrians and Egyptians.

In earlier times there had been two pilgrim columns from
Yemen, one proceeding along the coast and the other along
the mountains by Taif, to Mecca, but the former in Burckhardt's time had been discontinued. He had heard of an
Indian caravan that started from Muscat and travelled through
Nejd to Mecca, but could obtain no information about it, and
none of his acquaintances could remember the arrival of
pilgrims by that route. He believed, however, that in normal
times Indian, Persian, and Arab beggars in small parties
sometimes reached the Hejaz from that direction.

In addition to the multitudes of pilgrims coming by regular
roads, large bodies of Bedouin came from every part of the
desert and the interior. But the majority of pilgrims, from
Anatolia, European Turkey, Syria, Persia, Tartary, and India,
arrived by sea at Jidda. They came in all manner of poor
vessels, closely packed, and Mohammed Ali acquired twelve
dollars a head on each passage from Suez to Jidda—paying
the masters of the vessel six dollars a head, and charging the
pilgrims a contract price of eighteen dollars. Furthermore, the
hajis were allowed to carry only the bare amount of provisions
necessary for consumption during the pilgrimage. Those who
went by land, and required more supplies, had to purchase
high-priced provisions at Mecca. The short sea route from
Kosseir to Jidda cost from six to eight dollars, but one is
ignorant of Mohammed's 'rake-off' on this.

To diminish the expenses of their journey most of the
pilgrims brought products of their own countries to sell at
Mecca. But among the poorest classes the Indians, some of the
Syrians and Egyptians, became beggars as soon as they landed
at Jidda. The African negroes earned a living by hard work
as porters, wood-carriers, and in various menial capacities at

Jidda and Mecca. They supplied a real need in the labour market at the pilgrim centres. During the Wahhabi occupation they continued to perform the pilgrimage, and Saud was said to have had a particular respect for them.

The poor Indians afford a complete contrast, both in appearance and character, to the negroes: more wretched countenances can hardly be imagined; they seem to have lost not only all energy, but even hope. With bodies which appear scarcely capable of withstanding a gust of wind, and voices equally feeble, they would be worthy objects of commiseration, did not daily experience prove that they delight to appear in this plight, because it secures to them the alms of the charitable, and exempts them from labour. The streets of Mekka are crowded with them; the most decrepit make their doleful appeals to the passenger, lying at full length on their backs in the middle of the street; the gates of the mosque are always beset with them; every coffee-house and water-stand is a station for some of them; and no *hadjy* can purchase provisions in the markets without being importuned by Indians soliciting a portion of them. I saw among them one of those devotees who are so common in the north of India and in Persia: one of his arms was held up straight over his head, and so fixed by long habit that it could not be placed in any other situation. From the curiosity which he excited I was led to suppose that such characters seldom find their way to the Hedjaz.

Dervishes of every sect and order in the Turkish empire are found among the pilgrims; many of them madmen, or at least assuming the appearance of insanity, which causes them to be much respected by the *hadjys*, and fills their pockets with money. The behaviour of some of them is so violent, and at the same time so cunning, that even the least charitably disposed *hadjys* give willingly something to escape from them.

Burckhardt was present at the ceremonies of the pilgrimage performed at Mount Arafat, a few hours from Mecca on the road to Taif; he passed the night by the mosque of Muzdalifa, and then attended the stone-throwing and sacrificial rite in the Wadi Muna. It was a cold, dark night before the assembly at Arafat, and a few drops of rain fell. He had made a bivouac for himself on the scene by tying a large carpet to the back of a Meccan's tent, and after walking about for the first part of the night had just lain down to rest when two guns, fired by the Syrian and Egyptian parties, announced the dawn of the

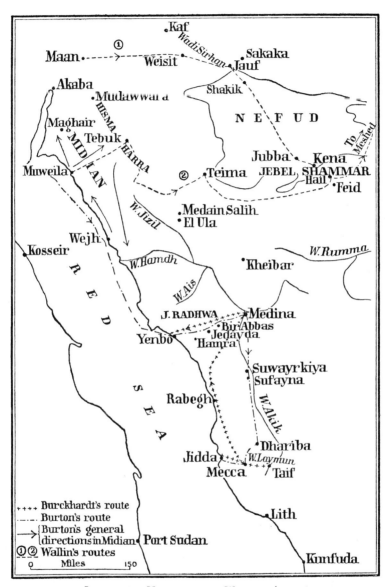

JOURNEYS IN NORTHERN AND WESTERN ARABIA

day of pilgrimage and summoned the faithful to prayer. At sunrise the pilgrims came from their tents and walked about the plain of Arafat, viewing the vast, busy crowds. Long lines of tents, like bazaars, furnished all kinds of provisions. Syrian and Egyptian cavalry were exercising, and thousands of camels were browsing on the dry shrubs of the plain all round the camps. Burckhardt walked towards Mount Arafat to view the whole scene from the summit:

> The granite hill, which is also called Djebel er' Rahme, or the Mountain of Mercy, rises on the north-east side of the plain, close to the mountains which encompass it, but separated from them by a rocky valley; it is about a mile, or a mile and a half in circuit; its sides are sloping, and its summit is nearly two hundred feet above the level of the plain. On the eastern side broad stone steps lead up to the top, and a broad unpaved path, on the western, over rude masses of granite, with which its declivity is covered. After mounting about forty steps we find a spot a little on the left called Modaa Seydna Adam, or the place of prayer of our Lord Adam, where, it is related, that the father of mankind used to stand while praying; for here it was, according to Mohammedan tradition, that the angel Gabriel first instructed Adam how to adore his Creator. A marble slab, bearing an inscription in modern characters, is fixed in the side of the mountain. On reaching about the sixtieth step we come to a small paved platform to our right, on a level spot of the hill, where the preacher stands who admonishes the pilgrims on the afternoon of this day, as I shall hereafter mention. Thus high the steps are so broad and easy that a horse or camel may ascend, but higher up they become more steep and uneven. On the summit the place is shown where Mohammed used to take his station during the Hadj; a small chapel formerly stood over it; but this was destroyed by the Wahhabys: here the pilgrims usually pray two *rikats*, in salutation of Arafat. The steps and the summit are covered with handkerchiefs to receive their pious gifts, and each family of the Mekkawys or Bedouins of the tribe of Koreysh, in whose territory Arafat lies, has its particular spot assigned to it for this purpose. The summit commands a very extensive and singular prospect. I brought my compass to take a circle of bearings; but the crowd was so great that I could not use it. . . . Several large reservoirs lined with stone are dispersed over the plain; two or three are close to the foot of Arafat, and there are some near the house of the sherifs: they are filled from the same fine aqueduct which supplies Mekka, and the head of which is about one hour and a

half distant, in the eastern mounts. The canal is left open here for the convenience of pilgrims, and is conducted round the three sides of the mountains, passing by Modaa Seydna Adam.

From the summit of Arafat across the plain he counted about three thousand tents, of which some two-thirds belonged to the two *haj* caravans and to the suite and soldiers of Mohammed Ali, and the remainder to the Sherif's Arabs, the Bedouin pilgrims, and the people of Mecca and Jidda. But most of the multitude was without tents. The two main caravans pitched their tents in rough circles, with many camels in the centre. He estimated that the plain contained in different parts twenty to twenty-five thousand camels, twelve thousand belonging to the Syrians and five or six thousand to the Egyptians. About three thousand in addition had been bought by Mohammed Ali from the Bedouin of the Syrian Desert, and after conveying the pilgrims to Mecca had been used for conveying army stores to Taif. The Syrian *haj* was encamped on the south and south-west side of the mountain, and the Egyptian on the south-east, The Hejaz people were near the Sherif and his Bedouin forces. The tents of Mohammed Ali, Suleiman Pasha of Damascus, and several of their officers were especially handsome.

During the whole morning there were repeated discharges of the artillery which both Pashas had brought with them. A few pilgrims had taken up their quarters on Djebel Arafat itself, where some small cavern, or impending block of granite, afforded them shelter from the sun. It is a belief generally entertained in the East, and strengthened by many boasting *hadjys* on their return home, that all the pilgrims, on this day, encamp upon Mount Arafat; and that the mountain possesses the miraculous power of expansion, so as to admit an indefinite number of the faithful upon its summit. The law ordains that the *wakfe*, or position of the Hadj, should be on Djebel Arafat; but it wisely provides against any impossibility, by declaring that the plain in the immediate neighbourhood of the mountain may be regarded as comprised under the term 'mountain,' or Djebel Arafat.

I estimated the number of persons assembled here at about seventy thousand. The camp was from three to four miles long, and between one and two in breadth. There is, perhaps, no spot on earth where, in so small a place, such a diversity of languages are heard; I reckoned about forty, and have no doubt that there were many more. It appeared to me as if I were here placed in a holy temple of travellers only; and never did I at any time feel a more ardent wish to be able to penetrate once into the inmost recesses of the countries of many of those persons whom I now saw before me, fondly imagining that I might have no more difficulty in reaching their homes than what they had experienced in their journey to this spot.

When the attention is engrossed by such a multitude of new objects time passes rapidly away. I had only descended from Mount Arafat, and had walked for some time about the camp, here and there entering into conversation with pilgrims, inquiring at the Syrian camp after some of my friends, and among the Syrian Bedouins, for news from their deserts, when midday had already passed. . . . After midday the pilgrims are to wash and purify the body by means of the entire ablution prescribed by the law, and called *Ghossel*, for which purpose chiefly the numerous tents in the plain have been constructed; but the weather was cloudy, and rather cold, which induced nine-tenths of the pilgrims, shivering as they were already under the thin covering of the *ihram*, to omit the rite also, and to content themselves with the ordinary ablution. The time of Aszer (or about three o'clock P.M.) approached, when that ceremony of the Hadj takes place for which the whole assembly had come hither. The pilgrims now pressed forward towards the mountain of Arafat, and covered its sides from top to bottom. At the precise time of Aszer the preacher took his stand upon the platform on the mountain, and began to address the multitude. This sermon, which lasts till sunset, constitutes the holy ceremony of the Hadj called *Khotbet el Wakfe*; and no pilgrim, although he may have visited all the holy places of Mekka, is entitled to the name of *hadjy*, unless he has been present on this occasion. As Aszer approached, therefore, all the tents were struck, every thing was packed up, the caravans began to load, and the pilgrims belonging to them mounted their camels, and crowded round the mountain, to be within sight of the preacher, which is sufficient, as the greater part of the multitude is necessarily too distant to hear him. The two Pashas, with their whole cavalry drawn up in two squadrons behind them, took their post in the rear of the deep lines of camels of the *hadjys*, to which those of the people of the Hedjaz were also joined; and here they waited in solemn and respectful silence the conclusion of the sermon. Further removed from the preacher was the Sherif Yahya, with his small body of soldiers, distinguished by several green standards carried before him. The two *mahmals*, or holy camels, which carry on their back the high structure that serves as the banner of their respective caravans, made way with difficulty through the ranks of camels that encircled the southern and eastern sides of the hill, opposite to the preacher, and took their station, surrounded by their guards, directly under the platform in front of him.

The preacher, or *khatyb*, who is usually the Kadhy of Mekka, was mounted upon a finely caparisoned camel which had been led up the steps, it being traditionally said that Mohammed was always seated when he here addressed his followers, a practice in which he was imitated by all the Khalifes who came to the Hadj, and who from hence addressed their subjects in person. The Turkish gentleman of Constantinople, however, unused to camel-riding, could not keep his seat so well as the hardy Bedouin prophet; and the camel becoming unruly, he was soon obliged to alight from it. He read his sermon from a book in Arabic, which he held in his hands. At intervals of every four or five minutes he paused, and stretched forth his arms to implore blessings from above, while the assembled multitudes around and before him waved the skirts of their *ihrams* over their heads, and rent the air with shouts of "*Lebeyk, Alla huma Lebeyk!*" (*i.e.*, "Here we are, at thy commands, O God!") During the wavings of the *ihrams* the side of the mountain, thickly crowded as it was by the people in their white garments, had the appearance of a cataract of water; while the green umbrellas, with which several thousand *hadjys*, sitting on their camels below, were provided, bore some resemblance to a verdant plain.

During his sermon, which lasted almost three hours, the Kadhy was seen constantly to wipe his eyes with a handkerchief; for the law enjoins the *khatyb*, or preacher, to be moved with feeling and compunction, and adds that whenever tears appear on his face it is a sign that the Almighty enlightens him, and is ready to listen to his prayers. The pilgrims who stood near me, upon the large blocks of granite which cover the sides of Arafat, appeared under various aspects. Some of them, mostly foreigners, were crying loudly and weeping, beating their breasts, and denouncing themselves to be great sinners before the Lord; others (but by far the smaller number) stood in silent reflexion and adoration, with tears in their eyes. Many natives of the Hedjaz, and many soldiers of the Turkish army, were meanwhile conversing and joking, and whenever the others were waving the *ihram* made violent gesticulations, as if to ridicule that ceremony. Behind, on the hill, I observed several parties of Arabs and soldiers, who were quietly smoking their nargyles; and in a cavern just by sat a common woman, who sold coffee, and whose visitors, by their loud laughter and riotous conduct, often interrupted the fervent devotions of the *hadjys* near them. Numbers of people were present in their ordinary clothes. Towards the conclusion of the sermon by far the greater part of the assembly seemed to be wearied, and many descended the mountain before the preacher had finished his discourse. It must be observed, however, that the crowds assembled on the mountain were, for the greater part, of the lower classes, the pilgrims of respectability being mounted upon their camels or horses in the plain.

At length the sun began to descend behind the western mountains, upon which the Kadhy, having shut his book, received a last greeting of *"Lebeyk,"* and the crowds rushed down the mountain in order to quit Arafat. It is thought meritorious to accelerate the pace on this occasion; and many persons make it a complete race, called by the Arabs *Ad'dafa min Arafat.* In former times, when the strength of the Syrian and Egyptian caravans happened to be nearly balanced, bloody affrays took place here almost every year between them, each party endeavouring to outrun and to carry its *mahmal* in advance of the other. The same happened when the *mahmals* approached the platform at the commencement of the sermon; and two hundred lives have on some occasions been lost in supporting what was thought the honour of the respective caravans. At present the power of Mohammed Aly preponderates, and the Syrian *hadjys* display great humility.

The whole mass of pilgrims now moved forward over the plain, and as night fell thousands of torches were lighted, twenty-four being carried before each Pasha. Their sparks flew over the plain; there were continual discharges of artillery and musketry, rockets were fired into the dark skies, the military bands of the two Pashas played, and the *haj* passed on with deafening clamour for two hours to Muzdalifa. Then at the first daybreak the Kadi appeared on a raised platform of the mosque, and began a sermon similar to the previous day's. The pilgrims surrounded the mosque on all sides with lighted torches, and accompanied the sermon again with cries of *"Lebeyk, Allah huma Lebeyk!"* This sermon formed one of the principal duties of the pilgrimage, but most of the pilgrims remained with their baggage and did not attend it. It was not a long sermon, lasting only from the first dawn till sunrise, a short time in that latitude. The *Salat el Ayd*, the prayer of the feast, was performed at the same time by the whole multitude according to its rites. When the first rays of the sun crossed a cloudy sky the pilgrims moved slowly an hour's march to Wadi Muna.

On arriving at Wady Muna each nation encamped upon the spot which custom has assigned to it, at every returning Hadj.

After disposing of the baggage the *hadjys* hastened to the ceremony of throwing stones at the devil. It is said that when Abraham, or Ibrahim, returned from the pilgrimage to Arafat and arrived at Wady Muna, the devil Eblys presented himself before him at the entrance of the valley, to obstruct his passage, when the Angel Gabriel, who accompanied the Patriarch, advised him to throw stones at him, which he did, and after pelting him seven times Eblys retired. When Abraham reached the middle of the valley he again appeared before him, and, for the last time, at its western extremity, and was both times repulsed by the same number of stones. According to Azraky, the pagan Arabs, in commemoration of this tradition, used to cast stones in this valley as they returned from the pilgrimage, and set up seven idols at Muna, of which there was one in each of the three spots where the devil appeared, at each of which they cast three stones. Mohammed, who made this ceremony one of the chief duties of the *hadjys*, increased the number of stones to seven. At the entrance of the valley, towards Mezdelfe, stands a rude stone pillar, or rather altar, between six and seven feet high, in the midst of the street, against which the first seven stones are thrown, as the place where the devil made his first stand : towards the middle of the valley is a similar pillar, and at its western end a wall of stones, which is made to serve the same purpose. The *hadjys* crowded in rapid succession round the first pillar, called "Djamrat el Awla," and every one threw seven small stones successively upon it: they then passed to the second and third spots (called "Djamrat el Oswat" and "Djamrat el Sofaly," or "el Akaba" or "el Aksa"), where the same ceremony was repeated. In throwing the stones they are to exclaim, "In the name of God; God is great (we do this) to secure ourselves from the devil and his troops." The stones used for this purpose are to be of the size of a horse-bean, or thereabouts; and the pilgrims are advised to collect them in the plain of Mezdelfe, but they may likewise take them from Muna; and many people, contrary to the law, collect those that have already been thrown.

Having performed this ceremony of casting stones, the pilgrims kill the animals which they bring with them for sacrifice; and all Mohammedans, in whatever part of the world they may be, are bound, at this time, to perform the same rite. Between six and eight thousand sheep and goats, under the care of Bedouins (who demanded high prices for them), were ready on this occasion. The act of sacrifice itself is subject to no other ceremonies than that of turning the victim's face towards the Kebly, or the Kaaba, and to say, during the act of cutting its throat, "In the name of the most merciful God! O supreme God!" ("*Bismillah! Irrahman irrahhym, Allahou akbar!*") Any place may be chosen for these sacrifices, which are performed in every corner of Wady Muna; but the favourite spot is a smooth rock on its western extremity, where several thousand sheep were killed in the space of a quarter of an hour.

As soon as the sacrifices were completed the pilgrims sent for barbers, or repaired to their shops, of which a row of thirty or forty had been set up near the favourite place of sacrifice. They had their heads shaved, except those who were of the Shafey sect, who shave only one-fourth of the head here, reserving the other three-fourths till they have visited the Kaaba after returning to Mekka. They threw off the *ihram*, and resumed their ordinary clothes, those who could afford it putting on new dresses, this being now the day of the feast. So far the Hadj was completed, and all pilgrims joined in mutual congratulations, and wishes that the performance of this Hadj might be acceptable to the Deity. " *Tekabbel Allah !* " was heard on all sides, and everybody appeared contented.

Burckhardt's description of the city of Mecca was detailed and complete, perhaps the most comprehensive view that had ever been presented. He gave a general account, and then developed it through the various quarters minutely. Only a few fleeting views of his panorama can be given here:

This town is situated in a valley, narrow and sandy, the main direction of which is from north to south; but it inclines towards the north-west near the southern extremity of the town. In breadth this valley varies from one hundred to seven hundred paces, the chief part of the city being placed where the valley is most broad. In the narrower part are single rows of houses only, or detached shops. The town itself covers a space of about fifteen hundred paces in length, from the quarter called El Shebeyka to the extremity of the Mala; but the whole extent of ground comprehended under the denomination of Mekka, from the suburbs called Djerouel (where is the entrance from Djidda) to the suburb called Moabede (on the Tayf road), amounts to three thousand five hundred paces. The mountains inclosing this valley (which before the town was built the Arabs had named Wady Mekka or Bekka) are from two to five hundred feet in height, completely barren and destitute of trees. . . .

Mekka may be styled a handsome town: its streets are in general broader than those of eastern cities; the houses lofty, and built of stone; and the numerous windows that face the streets give them a more lively and European aspect than those of Egypt or Syria, where the houses present but few windows towards the exterior. Mekka (like Djidda) contains many houses three

JOHANN LUDWIG BURCKHARDT
From a sketch made in Cairo in 1817   144

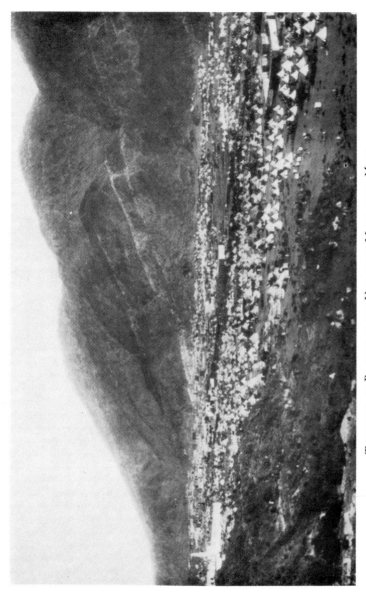

THOUSANDS OF PILGRIMS IN THE VALLEY OF MUNA, NEAR MECCA

Photo E.N.A.

stories high; few at Mekka are whitewashed; but the dark grey colour of the stone is much preferable to the glaring white that offends the eye in Djidda. In most towns of the Levant the narrowness of a street contributes to its coolness; and in countries where wheel-carriages are not used a space that allows two loaded camels to pass each other is deemed sufficient. At Mekka, however, it was necessary to leave the passages wide, for the innumerable visitors who here crowd together; and it is in the houses adapted for the reception of pilgrims and other sojourners that the windows are so contrived as to command a view of the streets.

The city is open on every side; but the neighbouring mountains, if properly defended, would form a barrier of considerable strength against an enemy. . . .

The only public place in the body of the town is the ample square of the great mosque; no trees or gardens cheer the eye; and the scene is enlivened only during the Hadj by the great number of well-stored shops which are found in every quarter.

The streets are all unpaved; and in summer-time the sand and dust in them are as great a nuisance as the mud is in the rainy season, during which they are scarcely passable after a shower; for in the interior of the town the water does not run off, but remains till it is dried up. It may be ascribed to the destructive rains, which, though of shorter duration than in other tropical countries, fall with considerable violence, that no ancient buildings are found in Mekka. The mosque itself has undergone so many repairs under different Sultans that it may be called a modern structure; and of the houses I do not think there exists one older than four centuries. . . .

Mekka is deficient in those regulations of police which are customary in Eastern cities. The streets are totally dark at night, no lamps of any kind being lighted; its different quarters are without gates, differing in this respect also from most Eastern towns, where each quarter is regularly shut up after the last evening prayers. The town may therefore be crossed at any time of the night, and the same attention is not paid here to the security of merchants, as well as of husbands (on whose account, principally, the quarters are closed), as in Syrian or Egyptian towns of equal magnitude. The dirt and sweepings of the houses are cast into the streets, where they soon become dust or mud according to the season. . . .

With respect to water, the most important of all supplies, and that which always forms the first object of inquiry among Asiatics, Mekka is not much better provided than Djidda; there are but few cisterns for collecting rain, and the well-water is so brackish that it is used only for culinary purposes, except during the time of the pilgrimage, when the lowest class of *hadjys* drink it. The famous well of Zemzem, in the great mosque, is indeed sufficiently copious to supply the whole town; but, however holy, its water is heavy to the taste and impedes digestion; the poorer classes, besides, have not permission to fill their water-skins with it at pleasure. The best water in Mekka is brought by a conduit from the vicinity of Arafat, six or seven hours distant. . . .

In proceeding along the broad street, northerly, we come to a bath, which, though by far the best of the three in Mekka, is inferior to those of other Asiatic cities, from the scarcity of water; it was built . . . by Mohammed Pasha, the Vizier of Sultan Soleyman II, and is one of the best structures in the town. It is frequented principally by foreigners, the native Arabs being little accustomed to the use of the bath, and choosing to perform the ablutions prescribed by their religion at their own dwellings.

The bath, together with several by-streets leading to the mosque, forms the quarter called Haret Bab el Omra, which is inhabited by a number of the guides called *metowaf*, and is full of pilgrims, especially of those from Turkey. The streets are narrow, and excessively dirty; but the *hadjys* prefer the quarter because it is the cheapest in the vicinity of the mosque, near which they are anxious to reside, that they may be sure of not missing the prayers; or (as they add) that, if disturbed in their sleep, they may have the temple close at hand to dispel their bad dreams. Men are seen, in the middle of the night, running to the mosque in their sleeping clothes; here they perform the walk round the Kaaba, kiss the black stone, utter a short prayer, drink of the water of Zemzem, and then return to their beds. . . .

Returning from hence . . . we descend by a slight slope into the street called Souk-es'-Sogheyr, or the little market, which terminates at the gate of the great mosque, called Bab Ibrahim. The houses on both sides of this street are low, and inhabited by the lower classes. There is a continued range of shops, in which are sold all sorts of provisions, but principally grain, butter, and dates. In some of the shops locusts are sold by measure. The Souk is frequented chiefly by Bedouins of the southern part of Arabia, who bring hither charcoal. Some poor Negro pilgrims of Africa take up their abode also in the miserable huts and ruined houses of this part of the town, and have here established a market for firewood, which they collect in the surrounding mountains. . . .

We now turn into the Mesaa, the straightest and longest street in Mekka, and one of the best built . . . it is the most noisy and most frequented part of the town. The shops are of the same description as those enumerated in the account of Djidda, with the addition of a dozen of tin-men, who make tin bottles of all sizes, in which the pilgrims, upon their return, carry the water of Zemzem to their homes. The shops are generally magazines on the ground-floor of the houses, before which a stone bench is reared. Here the merchant sits, under the shade of a slight awning of mats fastened to long poles; this custom prevails throughout the Hedjaz. All the houses of the Mesaa are rented by Turkish pilgrims. On the arrival of a party of *hadjys* from Djidda, which happens almost every morning, for four or five months of the year, their baggage is usually deposited in this street, after which they pay their visit to the mosque, and then go in quest of lodgings; and in this manner I found the street crowded almost every day with newcomers, newsmongers, and guides.

About the time of my stay at Mekka the Mesaa resembled a Constantinopolitan bazaar. Many shops were kept by Turks from Europe or Asia Minor, who sold various articles of Turkish dress, which had belonged to deceased *hadjys*, or to those who, being deficient in cash, had sold their wardrobe. Fine swords, good English watches, and beautiful copies of the Koran, the three most valuable articles in a Turkish pilgrim's baggage, were continually offered for sale. Constantinopolitan pastry-cooks sold here pies and sweetmeats in the morning; roasted mutton, or *kebabs*, in the afternoon; and in the evening a kind of jelly called *mahalabye*. Here, too, are numerous coffee-houses, crowded from three o'clock in the morning until eleven o'clock at night. The reader will be surprised to learn, that in two shops intoxicating liquors are publicly sold during the night, though not in the daytime: one liquor is prepared from fermented raisins, and although usually mixed with a good deal of water, is still so strong that a few glasses of it produce intoxication. The other is a sort of *bouza*, mixed with spices, and called *soubye*. This beverage is known (although not made so strong) at Cairo.

The Mesaa is the place of punishment: there capital offenders are put to death. During my stay a man was beheaded, by sentence of the Kadhy, for having robbed a Turkish pilgrim of about two hundred pounds sterling; this was the only instance of the kind which came to my knowledge, though thieves are said to abound in Mekka, while the Hadj continues. . . .

Eastward of the Mesaa, near its extremity at the Merowa, branches off a street called Soueyga, or the Little Market, which runs almost parallel with the east side of the mosque. Though narrow, it is the neatest street in the town, being regularly cleaned and sprinkled with water, which is not the case with any of the others. Here the rich India merchants expose their piece-goods for sale, and fine Cashmere shawls and muslins. There are upwards of twenty shops, in which are sold perfumes, sweet oils, Mekka balsam (in an adulterated state), aloe-wood, civet, etc. Few pilgrims return to their homes without carrying some presents for their families and friends; these are usually beads, perfumes, balm of Mekka, aloe-wood, which last is used throughout the East, in small pieces, placed upon the lightest tobacco in the pipe, producing an agreeable odour.

In other shops are sold strings of coral, and false pearls, rosaries made of aloe, sandal, or kalembac wood, brilliant necklaces of cut cornelians, cornelians for seal-rings, and various kinds of China ware. These shops are all kept by Indians, and their merchandise is entirely of Indian production and manufacture. Against these Indians much prejudice is entertained in Arabia, from a general opinion that they are idolaters, who comply in outward appearance only with the rites of Mohammedanism. . . . About a dozen of them reside here; the others arrive annually at the pilgrimage; they buy up old gold and silver, which they remit to Surat, from whence most of them come.

II

After the rites at Muna there followed various ceremonies, there and at Mecca, before Burckhardt proceeded to Medina. His information of the country along the coast road between Mecca and Medina, part of which he travelled at night, was only general. First there was an irregular chain of low hills with plantations of date and vegetables and a little wheat and barley. Then he passed through valleys of red and grey granite containing acacia, narrow rock-strewn passages through steep hills, until a plain of sand and clay was reached. Beyond Rabegh the earth was surfaced with black flints, some sand and brushwood, until the road ascended through low rocky hills with cultivated valleys, growing bananas, and lentils, in a granite and limestone country. His account of Medina and Yenbo is also comparatively brief, because he fell ill at Medina of the sickness from which he was to die less than two years later. But his pages have this in common with all his writings on Arabia, that they are minutely observant yet wide in outlook, revealing a calm, judicious, philosophic mind. Like Niebuhr, he gathered, extracted, and summarized clearly information from traders, pilgrims, and merchants. He was in this way able to give new important data concerning the Bedouin inhabitants of West Central Arabia and those of the northern plains, with notes and reflections on the Wahhabis which were fresh and interesting many years later when they were published.

He began by enumerating Arab tribes from the Anazeh group east of Syria to the country as far south as Mecca and Taif, indicating their numbers, manners, arms, arts, institutions, and territories. One meets many of those tribes whose names have become familiar of recent years from the writings of T. E. Lawrence—the Billi, the Juheina, the Howeitat, and others. Burckhardt endeavoured also to gather an account of weaker tribes who were unable to hold their tribal territory and became scattered in various parts of the peninsula and in Egypt. The Bedouin along the *haj* had been subdued by Mohammed Ali, all except the Omran, by Akaba, who were still a terror to the pilgrims. Of the Juheina he wrote:

> To the south of Djebel Hasany (northward of Yembo, as above described) begin the dwelling places of the great tribe Djeheyne, extending along the sea-coast as far as below Yembo, and east-ward to Hedye, a station of the Syrian Hadj road. From Yembo, in the direction of Medinah, these Djeheyne possess the ground to a distance of about twelve or fifteen hours. The cultivated valleys of Yembo el Nakhel also belong to them. Part of this tribe are cultivators, but the greater number continue Bedouins. They constitute the chief portion of the population of Yembo; and although they possess but few horses, it is said they can muster a force amounting to eight thousand matchlocks. They are constantly at war with the neighbouring tribe of Beni Harb; through whose assistance the Wahhaby chief, Saoud, was enabled to subjugate them, while all the other tribes . . . southward of Akaba had invariably refused to submit. . . . The Djeheynes nominally acknowledge the supremacy of the Sherif of Mecca . . . the Djeheyne are entitled to *surra*, or passage money, from the pilgrims of the Egyptian Hadj.

The land of the Ataiba lay between Medina and Mecca, east of the great coastal range and as far south as Taif. Their pasturing grounds were excellent; they had horses and great numbers of camels. For courage their reputation stood high, and they were constantly at war with all their neighbours, but particularly with the Harb. Burckhardt estimated their forces at six to ten thousand men. The coastal tribes he knew from personal experience, but of those inland only from reports which he attempted to check and verify. The Shammar, he wrote, were partly settled, partly nomadic, and had a force of three or four thousand men. He mentions, too, the Ageyl from the oases of Central Arabia, men who were to figure so largely in Lawrence's campaigns:

> In former ages these were a very powerful tribe, descended from the Beni Helal.
> They are now scattered about in small numbers among the villages of Nejd. But another tribe, called also Beni Ageyl, has lately sprung up. . . . All the Arabs of Nejd, whether settlers or Bedouins, who repair to Bagdad and establish themselves there, become members of the tribe of Ageyl of Bagdad, which enjoys considerable influence in that place, and is, in fact, the strongest support of the Pasha in his wars with the surrounding Bedouins and against the rebels of that city.

The chief of the Ageyl was always some native of Dariya. They were celebrated for bravery, and had frequently repulsed superior forces of the Wahhabis. They conducted caravans from Baghdad to Syria, and were usually natives of Hasa, Ared, Kasim, and Jebel Shammar.

The old tradition of Arabia's containing vast numbers of the finest horses was unmodified until Burckhardt's time. He pointed out that the breed was limited to the fertile pastures, the tribes richest in horses living in Mesopotamia and the Syrian plains. Hejaz horses were imported from the north, and horses were scarce along the whole west coast from Akaba to Yemen. From the Euphrates and Syria to Yemen and Oman, he believed, the number of horses would not exceed fifty thousand. The finest breeds of Arab horses, he judged, would be found in Syria, and especially in the Hauran. The country richest in camels was Nejd, *Om el Bel*, the "Mother of Camels," which supplied Syria, Hejaz, and Yemen. He gives the price of camels in his time, the loads they were expected to carry, speeds, types, and their endurance of thirst.

Burckhardt's information regarding the horse and the camel was gathered from townsmen and nomads, probably Syrians and Bedouin of the Anazeh, whom he knew well. The modern rifle, making horses less useful in war, and the decline of the Bombay horse-market, have both discouraged breeding in Arabia to-day. Arab princes, however, still keep their own studs. 'Arab' horses now sold in Egypt and India usually come from Trans-Jordan and Upper Mesopotamia, where original Nejdi stock improves in better conditions of pasture. The best breed of camel to-day is the Umaniya, raised by the Murra of the Rub' al Khali, which is noted even more than other good breeds for its high average speed over long distances and for its endurance of long intervals without water.

From his chapters on the social life of the Arabs one chooses his remarks on warfare, religion, matrimony, and divorce—and Burckhardt was writing largely but not exclusively from knowledge of the Anazeh tribes of North Arabia and Syria-Iraq, a people he estimated at some three hundred to three hundred and fifty thousand souls, occupying a territory of at least forty thousand square miles. They included the Rualla, who supported Lawrence against the Turks.

> The Bedouins who live in mountainous districts have fewer camels and horses than those of the plains, and therefore cannot make so many plundering expeditions into distant quarters, and are less warlike than the others. Mountain warfare is, moreover, liable to many difficulties and dangers unknown in the open country: plunder cannot be so easily carried off, and the recesses of the mountains are seldom well known to any but their own inhabitants. Still, there are very few tribes who are ever in a state of perfect peace with all their neighbours; indeed, I cannot at present recollect that this was the case with any one among the numerous tribes that I knew. The Sinai tribes were in 1816 at peace with all the Arabs in their neighbourhood except the Sowaraka, a tribe dwelling near Gaza and Hebron.
>
> I may here confirm what has been said respecting the martial spirit of the Bedouins, their cowardice when fighting for plunder only, and their bravery when they repel a public enemy. Of the last they have given repeated proofs during their wars with the Turks in Hedjaz, whom they defeated in every encounter; for the great battle of Byssel, in January 1815, was merely gained by the stratagems of Mohammed Aly Pasha. In that action whole lines of Bedouins, tied by ropes fastened to each other's legs, were found slaughtered, having sworn to their women at parting that they would never fly before a Turk. To adduce instances of personal valour among the Bedouins would be easy; but such instances are not altogether conclusive as to the character of a whole nation. Whoever has known the Bedouins in their deserts must be perfectly convinced that they are capable of acts displaying exalted courage, and of much more steadiness and cool perseverance, in cases of danger, than their enemies, the Turks.

The most renowned warrior in the southern parts of Arabia was, during my residence in Hedjaz, Shahher, of the Kahtan tribe. He alone once routed a party of thirty horsemen belonging to the Sherif Ghaleb, who had invaded the territory of his Arabs. Ghaleb, who was himself a man of considerable bravery, said on this occasion that "since the time of the Sword of God [this is one of Aly's surnames] a stronger arm than Shahher's had not been known in Arabia." At another time the Sherif Hamoud, Governor of the Yemen coast, was repulsed with his escort of eighty mounted men by Shahher alone. . . .

There is one circumstance that greatly favours the chance of a foreign general in his contests with the Bedouins. They are but little accustomed to battles in which much blood is shed. When ten or fifteen men are killed in a skirmish the circumstance is remembered as an event of great importance for many years by both parties. If, therefore, in a battle with foreign troops several hundred are killed in the first onset, and if any of their principal men should be among the slain, the Bedouins become so disheartened that they scarcely think of further resistance; while a much greater loss on the side of their enemies could not make a similar impression on mercenary soldiers. But even the Arabs would only feel this impression at the beginning of a severe contest; and they would soon, no doubt, accustom themselves to bear greater losses in support of their independence than they usually suffer in their petty warfare about wells and pasture-grounds. Of this the Asyr Arabs, who were principally opposed to Mohammed Aly in the battle of Byssel, afford a striking example. Having lost fifteen hundred men in that action (from which their chief Tamy escaped with only five men), they recovered sufficient strength to be able, about forty days after, to meet the Turkish soldiers in another battle, in their own territory, a battle less sanguinary, although better contested than the former; but it ended, after two days' fighting, in the defeat and subsequent capture of Tamy.

Whenever a tribe engages in an expedition their troops are headed by the *agyd*, of whose rank and power I had no correct knowledge, and had partly overlooked it when I composed my former account of the Bedouins. It is a remarkable circumstance in Bedouin history and policy that during a campaign in actual warfare the authority of the sheikh of the tribe is completely set aside, and the soldiers are wholly under the command of the *agyd*. Every tribe has, besides the sheikh, an *agyd*; and it rarely happens that the offices of both are united in one person—at least, no instance of such a case is known to me; although some Arabs mentioned that they had seen a sheikh acting as *agyd* among the Basrah Arabs. The office of *agyd* is hereditary in a certain family, from father to son; and the Arabs submit to the command of an *agyd*, whom they know to be deficient both in bravery and judgment, rather than yield to the orders of their sheikh during the actual expedition; for they say that expeditions headed by the sheikh are always unsuccessful.

If the sheikh join the troops he is for the time commanded by the *agyd*, whose office ceases whenever the soldiers return home: the sheikh then resumes his own authority. All Bedouin tribes, without exception, have their *agyd*. The same person acts on some occasions as *agyd* to two neighbouring tribes, if they are small and closely allied. Thus, among the Arabs of Sinai a family of Oulad Sayd is in possession of the *agyd*ship for all the tribes of the peninsula. The person of the *agyd*, and still more his office, is regarded with veneration. He is considered by the Arabs as a kind of augur or saint. He often decides the operations of war by his dreams, or visions, or forebodings: he also announces the lucky days for attack, and names other days that would be unlucky.

When the *agyd* is doubtful about the measures that should be adopted against the enemy he consults with the principal men of his army, if he think fit to do so; but the Arabs never refuse to follow him, even though he should act wholly according to his own judgment. . . .

If the *agyd* be a man of remarkable valour and sagacity he retains great influence over the affairs of his tribe, even in time of peace: his vote, however, is not equivalent to that of the sheikh; but he is consulted on intricate matters, and circumstances of difficulty, and much deference is paid to his opinion. But in this respect he has no advantage over the other Arabs of his tribe who unite the qualities of sagacity and valour.

If an Arab, accompanied by his own relations only, has been successful on many predatory excursions against the enemy, he is joined by other friends; and if his success still continue he obtains the reputation of being 'lucky'; and he thus establishes a kind of second, or inferior, *agyd*ship in the tribe. Of this advantage may be taken on partial expeditions; but whenever the whole tribe is engaged the true and regular *agyd* must be the leader.

The *agyd* possesses no more coercive power over his Arabs than the sheikh. All are at perfect liberty to join him, or to act by themselves, but if they once join him they must submit to his commands, or else expect that he will discard them, as not worthy to form a portion of his corps: in this case they forfeit all claim to any share of the booty which may be taken by the whole army. . . .

Besides the *agyd*, some tribes setting out on an expedition select one of the most respectable men of the tribe, to whom they give the title of *kefyl*. The duty of this person is to settle among them all disputes arising from the division of booty, and to watch that no part of it be secreted from the common stock by individuals. He shares in the booty always, in the same proportion with the *agyd*. The *kefyl* is not found in many tribes; there is always such an officer among the Djeheynes of Hedjaz.

Night attacks upon camps, which the Northern Anazeh regarded as disgraceful, were very common in the Hejaz. For a surprise assault the Bedouin would regulate their march so that they came upon their foe about an hour before dawn, when he was almost sure to be asleep, for the nomads had no idea of posting sentries, however necessary it seemed to their mode of life and warfare. If they apprehended an immediate danger all the men of the encampment would remain together watching by their fires during the whole night. The Wahhabi leaders, however, used to post sentinels whenever their troops were on campaign. A man who had been sent by Tussun Pasha to negotiate with Abdulla Ibn Saud told Burckhardt that he had met single outposts, covered by others and small detachments two miles distant from Abdulla's camp, and that his Wahhabi escort had to give the watchword to every sentry post. On the other hand, the Turkish camp six hours away lay quite open to sudden attack, for not even Mohammed Ali, despite his contacts with Europeans, had learned these elementary precautions against an enterprising opponent.

Whether camps are plundered by day or night the women are generally treated with respect; so far, at least, that their honour is never violated; not a single instance of the contrary has ever come to my knowledge. Sometimes, however, in case of inveterate hostility, they may be stripped of their ornaments, which the plunderers oblige them to take off themselves. This rule is invariably observed by the Wahabys whenever they obtain possession of an enemy's camp: they order the females to strip off whatever articles of clothes or valuable trinkets they may happen to wear; and during this time they stand at some distance from the women, to whom they turn their backs. . . .

When two hostile parties of Bedouin cavalry meet, and perceive from afar that they are equal in point of numbers, they halt opposite to each other out of the reach of musket-shot; and the battle begins by skirmishes between two men. A horseman leaves his party and gallops off towards the enemy, exclaiming, "O horsemen, O horsemen, let such a one meet me!" If the adversary for whom he calls be present, and not afraid to meet him in combat, he gallops forwards; if absent, his friends reply that he is not amongst them. The challenged horseman in his turn exclaims, "And you upon the grey mare, who are you?" The other answers, "I am —— the son of ——." Having thus become acquainted with each other, they begin to fight. None of the bystanders join in this combat; to do so would be reckoned a treacherous action; but if one of the combatants should turn back, and fly towards his friends, the latter hasten to his assistance, and drive back the pursuer, who is in turn protected by his friends. After several of these partial combats between the best men of both parties the whole corps join in promiscuous combat. If an Arab in battle should meet with a personal friend among the enemy's ranks he turns his mare to a different side, and cries out, "Keep away! Let not thy blood be upon me!"

Should a horseman not be inclined to accept the challenge of an adversary, but choose to remain among the ranks of his friends, the challenger laughs at him with taunts and reproaches, and makes it known as a boast during the rest of his life, that such a one —— would not venture to meet such a one —— in battle.

If the contest happen in a level country the victorious party frequently pursue the fugitives for three, four, or five hours together at full gallop; and instances are mentioned of a close pursuit for a whole day. This would not be possible with any but the Bedouin breed of horses, and it is on this account that the Bedouin praises his mare, not so much for her swiftness as for her indefatigable strength.

It is an universal law among the Arabs that if, in time of war or in suspicious districts, one party meet another in the desert, without knowing whether it be friendly or hostile, those who think themselves the stronger should attack the other; and sometimes blood is shed before they ascertain that the parties are friends; but this is not the case in the Wahaby dominions, where a strong party must pass a weak one without daring to molest it.

The Bedouin mode of fighting is most ancient. The battles described in the two best heroic romances (the history of Antar, and that of the tribe of Beni Helal) consisted principally in single combats, like those above mentioned. It is more congenial with the disposition of the Bedouins, who are always anxious to know by whom a man has been killed—a circumstance which in a promiscuous attack cannot easily be ascertained. . . .

In concluding the terms of peace an *agyd* can give but his single vote, like any other individual of the tribe. The condition 'to dig up and to bury' is common all over the desert, and is a matter of stipulation wherever the tribes entertain a sincere desire for peace. Those Arabs who are not satisfied with this condition (several of

their relations having perhaps been slain in the contests) leave
their own tribe, and settle with some other for the time, where
they are at liberty to seek revenge, which they cannot do if their
own tribe has once annulled the claims of revenge. I have found,
in general, very few tribes without some of those implacable
enemies, whose thirst for revenge exists even after a declaration
of peace, when a most friendly intercourse is at once established
between the other members. . . .

The Bedouins throughout Arabia have very just notions of the
Deity, but are little addicted to the precepts of their religion. The
Wahabys have endeavoured in vain to render them more orthodox.
The dread of punishment might induce some tribes who were
under the immediate control of the Wahabys to observe the
forms of their religion with more regularity; but it was a forced
compliance; and as soon as the Wahaby power had suffered a
diminution, in consequence of the attacks made by Mohammed
Aly Pasha, all the Bedouins relapsed into their former religious
indolence. While many Arab settlers in Nedjd and Yemen adopted
with enthusiasm the Wahaby doctrines, very few, or perhaps no
Bedouins, were ever reckoned among their favourers, although
some adhered faithfully to the system of government established
by the new sect, and were obliged to assume an appearance of
zeal and even of fanaticism, with the hope of promoting their own
political interests. Now that, in Hedjaz at least, the Wahaby
influence is for the present destroyed, the Bedouins affect still
more irregularity than before; and, to prove that they have quite
renounced the Wahaby tenets, they never pray at all. The
Bedouins are certainly the most tolerant of Eastern nations; yet
it would be erroneous to suppose that an avowed Christian going
among them would be well treated without some powerful means
of commanding their services. They class Christians with the
foreign race of Turks, whom they despise most heartily. Both
Christians and Turks are treated in a manner equally unkind,
because their skins are fair and their beards long, and because
their customs seem extraordinary; they are also reckoned
effeminate and much less hardy than the tawny Bedouin. . . .

Those Bedouin sheikhs who are connected with the government
towns in the vicinity of their tribes keep up the practice of prayer
whenever they repair to a town, in order to make themselves
respected there. But the inferior Arabs will not even take that
trouble, and very seldom pray either in or out of town. . . .

Polygamy, according to the Turkish law, is a privilege of the
Bedouins; but the greater number of Arabs content themselves
with one wife: very few have two wives, and I never met with any
person who could recollect a Bedouin that had four wives at once
in his tent. The marriage ceremony is very simple among the

Aenezes. When a man desires to marry a girl he sends some friend of the family to her father, and a negotiation commences: the girl's wishes are then consulted; if they agree with those of the father (for it is never supposed that she should be compelled to marry against her inclination), and if the match is to take place the friend, holding the father's hand, says, "You declare that you give your daughter as wife to —— ?" The father answers in the affirmative. The marriage day being appointed (usually five or six days after the betrothing, which is called *talab*, not *kheteb*), the bridegroom comes with a lamb in his arms to the tent of the girl's father, and there cuts the lamb's throat before witnesses. As soon as the blood falls upon the ground the marriage ceremony is regarded as complete. The men and girls amuse themselves with feasting and singing. Soon after sunset the bridegroom retires to a tent, pitched for him at a distance from the camp; there he shuts himself up and awaits the arrival of his bride. The bashful girl meanwhile runs from the tent of one friend to another's, till she is caught at last, and conducted in triumph by a few women to the bridegroom's tent; he receives her at the entrance, and forces her into it; the women who had accompanied her then depart. The novelty of her situation naturally induces a young virgin to exclaim; and this is considered by the friends as a sufficient evidence of maiden timidity. They do not require any of those indelicate proofs exhibited on such occasions among other Eastern nations. But if an Aeneze widow marry a second time it would be regarded as highly improper were she to utter such exclamations.

There is, in the vicinity of Nazareth, a tribe of El Ryer Arabs, among whom the two fathers negotiate the marriage of their respective children. Terms being concluded, the bridegroom's father presents to the bride's father a green leaf of some plant or vegetable just at hand, and calls on all present to witness the donation.

Among the Aenezes it would be esteemed scandalous if the bride's father were to demand money, or what is called 'the daughter's price' (*hakk el bint*); although such is the universal custom in Syria, where every Turk, Christian, and Jew pays for his wife a sum proportionate to the rank of the girl's father. Among the Ahl el Shemál a father receives for his daughter the *khomse*, or 'five articles,' which, however, become the wife's property, and remain with her, even should she be divorced. The *khomse* comprehends a carpet, a large silver nose-ring, a silver neck-chain, silver bracelets, and a camel-bag of the Baghdad carpet manufacture. An Aeneze is permitted to bestow gifts on the object of his affections; nor is it reckoned indecorous for the girl to accept them. The lover sometimes makes presents to her father, or brother, hoping thereby to influence them in his favour; but this does not often occur, the practice being reckoned as disgraceful to those who receive such presents.

I have already mentioned that the Aenezes never intermarry with the *szona*, handicraftsmen or artisans; nor do they ever marry their daughters to *fellahs*, or inhabitants of towns; but the Ahl el Shemál are less scrupulous in this respect.

If an Arab, on the consummation of his nuptials, should have reason to doubt whether he had found the bride in a state of virgin purity, he does not immediately expose her shame, being afraid of offending her family; but after a day or two he repudiates his wife, assigning as a sufficient motive that she did not please him. If an Arab has manifest evidence of his wife's infidelity he accuses her before her father and brother; and if the adultery be unequivocally proved the father himself, or the brother, cuts her throat.

Most Arabs are contented with a single wife; but for this monogamy they make amends by indulging in variety. They frequently change their wives, according to a custom founded on the Turkish law of divorce, which, however, has been much abused among the Arabs; for when one of them becomes, on any slight occasion, dissatisfied with his wife, he separates himself from her by simply saying, " *Ent tálek* " ("Thou art divorced"). He then gives her a she-camel, and sends her back to the tents of her family. He is not obliged to state any reasons, nor does this circumstance reflect any dishonour on the divorced woman or her family: every one excuses him by saying, "He did not like her." Perhaps, on the very same day, he betroths himself to another female; but his repudiated wife, on the contrary, is obliged to wait forty days before she can become the wife of another man, that it may be known whether or not she is pregnant by the former husband. Divorces are so common among the Aenezes that they even take place during the wife's pregnancy; and a woman is sometimes repudiated who has borne several children to her husband. In the former case the woman nurses her child till it is able to run about, when the father takes it to his tent. When a man discards an old mother of a family he sometimes allows her to live in his tent among her children; but she may retire to her parents. A woman who has been three or four times divorced may nevertheless be free from any stain or imputation on her character. I have seen Arabs about forty-five years of age who were known to have had about fifty different wives. Whoever will be at the expense of a camel may divorce and change his wives as often as he thinks fit.

The law allows to the wife also a kind of divorce; if not happy in her husband's tent she flies for refuge to her father or kindred.

PART OF THE PILGRIM CAMP AT MUNA, NEAR MECCA
Photo E.N.A.

VIEW OVER RIYADH, NEAR THE ENTRANCE TO THE PALACE
Photo E.N.A.

The husband may induce her, by promises of fine clothes, ear-
rings, or carpets, to return, but if she refuses he cannot take her
by force, as her family would resent the violence: all he can do is
to withhold the sentence of divorce, *ent tálek*, without which the
lady is not authorized to marry again. The husband is sometimes
bribed, by a present of many camels, to pronounce the words of
divorce; but if he persevere in refusing the wife is condemned to
a single life. A wife thus parted from her husband, but not regularly divorced, is called *tamehhe*: of this class there are great
numbers; but, on the other hand, there are not any old maids to
be found among the Arabs.

If a young man leaves a widow, his brother generally offers to
marry her; custom does not oblige either him or her to make this
match, nor can he prevent her from marrying another man. It
seldom happens, however, that she refuses; for by such an union
the family property is kept together.

A man has an exclusive right to the hand of his cousin; he is
not obliged to marry her, but she cannot, without his consent,
become the wife of any other person. If a man permits his cousin
to marry her lover, or if a husband divorces his runaway wife, he
usually says, "She was my slipper. I have cast her off."

Among the tribes of Ahl el Shemál, if it happens that an Arab
elopes with another man's wife, and takes refuge in the tent of a
third, this last kills a sheep, and thus marries the couple. In case
of such an event among the Aenezes, the wife returns safely to her
parents, and awaits the *tálek*, or word of divorce, from her husband; her lover is likewise secure from personal danger, being
dakheil of the family in whose tent he had taken refuge.

By this facility of divorce every tie is loosened that should
connect families; by the frequent change of wives all secrets of
parents and children are divulged over the whole tribe; jealousies
are excited among the relations; and we may easily conceive its
effect upon morals.

It must, however, be allowed that an Arab holds his parents in
great respect; his mother especially he loves most affectionately;
indeed, he sometimes quarrels on her account with his father,
and is often expelled from the paternal tent for vindicating his
mother's cause.

When a son attains maturity his father generally gives him
a mare or a camel, that he may try his fortune in plundering
excursions. Whatever booty falls to his lot is reckoned his own
property, and cannot be taken from him by his father. A favourite
son, on the occasion of his marriage, often receives a present of
camels or money from his father: but this is not a general rule,
and many young Arabs commence the matrimonial state with no
other property than one camel to provide for the subsistence of

his family. Sometimes the son is permitted to live with his young wife in the father's tent. As to the girl, she never receives anything from her father at the time of her marriage; the *khomse* (before mentioned), given among the Ahl el Shemál by the husband to his wife's father, is by the latter often bestowed upon his daughter.

The Bedouin generally, Burckhardt considered, were one of the noblest nations of his experience. With all their faults, they were in many respects superior to Europeans and in every way superior to the Turk. Rapacious, perhaps, and avaricious, the Bedouin made amends by his virtues, while the Turk shared the bad qualities of the Bedouin and scarcely possessed one good characteristic. The complete independence of the Bedouins of the desert gave them a character which suffered by connexion with towns and cultivated districts. Their primary love was for liberty, and that love kept them in the desert, preferring their tents to settled comfort. Despite their tribal differences, there was an attachment and a sense of national honour among all the tribes—enough, at any rate, to make them deplore the successes of Mohammed Ali and to make them lament any losses sustained by the tribes from foreign troops. In Burckhardt's estimation the finest trait in the Bedouin character, next to his good faith, was his kindness, benevolence, and charity, and his peaceful demeanour whenever his fighting spirit or wounded honour did not call him to arms. In their private quarrels the townsmen would use the meanest and foulest language; the Bedouin did not employ such expressions, which only evinced a debauched imagination:

> To call his adversary a liar, a traitor, or an inhospitable wretch, would be an insult punishable by the dagger; as sometimes has been the case. If such violent language is not used, a quarrel among Bedouins seldom lasts half an hour, and the parties become reconciled; but for insulted honour no excuse or apology can ever be accepted.

Though Burckhardt contributed little to knowledge of the broader geographical problems of the Hejaz he left nothing but minor points to be discovered regarding the trade, society, and topography of its main centres, Mecca, Taif, and Jidda, and from these bases he began a train of wider inquiry, touching upon west Central Arabia and the ethnology of the tribal system. His *Travels in Arabia* appeared in London in 1829, and his *Notes on the Bedouins and Wahabys* in 1830. Both books won the instant esteem of public and scholars, and by the latter are still held in honour.

After his Hejaz journey Burckhardt returned exhausted to Cairo, but visited Mount Sinai in the spring of 1816, reaching Cairo again in June, to make preparations for his long-delayed march to Fezzan. He died just as the caravan was ready to depart, in October 1817.

He was buried at Cairo. Burton says that when the raising of a monument over his humble grave was suggested, twenty pounds were collected—for the discoverer of Petra! Some people objected to subscribing, on the grounds that the Moslems called him a saint. The reluctant ones must have agreed with Burton in judging ridiculous a story current among the Egyptians to the effect that after his return from Arabia Burckhardt taught Koran-chanting in the Azhar Mosque, and was suspected by the learned, who examined him, and found the formula of Islam written, in token of abhorrence, on the soles of his feet. Whereupon the Principal of the mosque, in holy indignation, decapitated him with one blow of the sword.

CHAPTER XI

A BRITON MAKES THE PILGRIMAGE

I may truly say that of all the worshippers who clung weeping
to that curtain, or who pressed their beating hearts to the stone,
none felt for the moment a deeper emotion than did the Haji from
the far north.

SIR RICHARD BURTON, *A Pilgrimage to Al-Madinah and Meccah*

AMONG the great company of explorers there are some
who, for various reasons, have the power still to recall
some personal characteristics, or some incidents of their
lives, to the memory of those who know little more than their
name. Tradition clings to such pictures as that of Cook's last
desperate fight, Park's escape and first sight of the Niger, or
the meeting of Livingstone and Stanley. Few, like Scott, have
their deeds vividly imprinted on the mind of a nation. Thus,
though much of his most valuable exploration was achieved
in Africa, Richard Francis Burton survives in popular imagination almost solely by his pilgrimage to Mecca and his
translation of the *Arabian Nights*.

He was born in England, of Anglo-Irish and Scots parentage,
but childhood and youth were passed in France and Italy,
at Blois, Pau, Tours, Siena, Pisa, and Sorrento. These years of
travel and lack of restraint gave free development to traits that
were innate in the boy—a craving for adventure, love of
wandering, dislike of convention, and a passion for the acquisi-
sion of languages. This last characteristic showed itself early,
for as a boy at Pau he studied enthusiastically the dialect of
Béarn. Burton was, in fact, a Continental or cosmopolitan all
his days, and regretted in later life the lack of an English parish
to welcome, and be proud of, the explorer.

The father intended his adventurous, unconventional son
for the Church, and to Oxford he went, despite his pleadings
to enter the Army. He hated the university life, but lessened
the tedium by studying Arabic, without the assistance of the

Regius Professor, who considered that his duty did not extend to single-pupil classes. Burton was eventually rusticated for attending a steeplechase in a tandem, when both the amusement and the form of transport were forbidden. Just at this time Akbar Khan and the Khyber Pass had been making considerable gaps in the commissioned ranks of the East India Company's forces, and it was not difficult to find a place for Burton. In 1842 he sailed East to join a regiment of native infantry, and at first in India experienced further boredom, with little work to do and no society. He occupied squalid quarters, a leaking bungalow, near a burning-place whence the smell of roasted native was wafted through his windows.

However, he tried to relieve the misery and discomfort of his cadet period by a fervent application to Hindustani. Soon he was posted to the 18th Regiment at Baroda, where the mess was smart and clean, but where again there was little soldiering to be done. He was to pass seven years in India, and in this time he occupied himself mainly in travel and in the study of languages, learning Gujerati, Marathi, Persian, Hindustani, and Arabic. It amazed him that a Power with such a vast Moslem empire should take so little interest in the languages, habits, and outlook of its subjects. After his light military duties he would commonly work ten hours a day at languages, and became so fluent, and so conversant with Eastern habits and manners, that he could mix freely without detection among the natives in the bazaars, as he did when detached from his regiment for the survey of Sind. He attained an unrivalled familiarity with the mentality of the Easterner, even of the poorest and lowest orders. Such knowledge and practice gave him great confidence, but did not lessen his avidity for languages, and he found plenty of time for further study in Arabic, learning a quarter of the Koran by heart. Nor did he neglect to keep himself fit. From boyhood he loved strenuous physical activity, especially fencing. Sir Charles Napier recognized his amazing ability, linguistic and histrionic, and used him on highly dangerous secret service, but promotion came not his way. He had no 'interest' to push his claims, and India, which he left at the age of twenty-seven, almost broke his heart. Yet these years of apprenticeship fitted him supremely for the task he undertook in 1852, when he had been back in England some four years.

In that year he approached the Royal Geographical Society with suggestions for a journey across Arabia from Muscat to the Hejaz. The idea of such a journey had been born when he was mixing among the Moslems of Sind, and though there was in its inception a praiseworthy desire for exploration work, Burton was urged perhaps equally by zest for adventure. Yet he hoped to examine a great part of the peninsula which was a blank on the map—in fact, to cross the Rub' al Khali from east to west, and then to study the hydrography of the Hejaz and the ethnology of the Arab race. As he was already known for his writings on Sind and Goa, the Society agreed to his undertaking the task. Such a journey demanded a three years' absence from the Company's service, and he was allowed only one year, "to pursue his Arabic studies in lands where the language was best learned."

Burton considered that he could learn best in the Hejaz, at Medina and Mecca! Here, too, he could gather information regarding the trans-desert route. He resolved to travel throughout as a native of the East, and succeeded so completely that his origin was never questioned, in caravanserai, desert, or in the holy cities of Islam.

It was a sufficiently remarkable journey, but less notable than the book which told his adventures. *A Pilgrimage to Al-Madinah and Meccah* is marked out from all other works on Arabia by its graphic description, humour, grimness, insight into Arab and all Semitic thought, vast knowledge of Eastern manners and habits, vigorous, trenchant style, and highly individualistic opinions.

In April 1853 Burton left Southampton for Alexandria in the character of a Persian gentleman, and in the ensuing weeks steadily practised the actions and the mental attitude of an Oriental. Such things as the sitting posture, the deportment, even the manner of drinking a glass of water, all had to be recalled and made a matter of habit after some years' absence from the East. In Alexandria he had further opportunity for perfecting the *rôle*, visiting the mosques and holy places, and practising among the poor as a doctor. After a month in the port he assumed the part of a Persian dervish, wearing a short shirt and long blue pantaloons.

After a month's hard work at Alexandria, I prepared to assume the character of a wandering Darwaysh; after reforming my title from 'Mirza' to 'Shaykh' Abdullah. A reverend man, whose name I do not care to quote, some time ago initiated me into his order, the Kadiriyah, under the high-sounding name of Bismillah-Shah: and, after a due period of probation, he graciously elevated me to the proud position of a Murshid, or Master in the mystic craft. I was therefore sufficiently well acquainted with the tenets and practices of these Oriental Freemasons. No character in the Moslem world is so proper for disguise as that of the Darwaysh. It is assumed by all ranks, ages and creeds; by the noble-man who has been disgraced at court, and by the peasant who is too idle to till the ground; by Dives, who is weary of life, and by Lazarus, who begs his bread from door to door. Further, the Darwaysh is allowed to ignore ceremony and politeness, as one who ceases to appear upon the stage of life; he may pray or not, marry or remain single as he pleases, be respectable in the cloth of frieze as in cloth of gold, and no one asks him—the chartered vagabond—why he comes here? or Wherefore he goes there? He may wend his way on foot alone, or ride his Arab mare followed by a dozen servants; he is equally feared without weapons, as swaggering through the streets armed to the teeth. The more haughty and offensive he is to the people, the more they respect him: a decided advantage to the traveller of choleric tempera-ment. In the hour of imminent danger, he has only to become a maniac, and he is safe; a madman in the East, like a notably eccentric character in the West, is allowed to say or do whatever the spirit directs. Add to this character a little knowledge of medicine, a "moderate skill in magic, and a reputation for caring for nothing but study and books," together with capital sufficient to save you from the chance of starving, and you appear in the East to peculiar advantage. The only danger of the 'Mystic Path' is, that the Darwaysh's ragged coat not unfrequently covers the cut-throat, and, if seized in the society of such a 'brother,' you may reluctantly become his companion, under the stick or on the stake. For be it known, Darwayshes are of two orders, the Sharai, or those who conform to religion, and the Bi-Sharai, or Luti, whose practices are hinted at by their own tradition that 'he we daurna name' once joined them for a week, but at the end of that time left them in dismay, and returned to whence he came.

A journey of three days and nights by the Nile steamboat next brought him to Cairo, through dun country that reminded him strongly of Sind. His description of the countryside and of his fellow-travellers—noisy Greeks, solemn Moslems, silent Italians, happy Frenchmen, and two Indian officers "who naturally spoke to none but each other, drank bad tea, and smoked their cigars exclusively like Britons"—is typical of Burton, graphic, rapid, touched by a somewhat pawky humour, and full of Eastern knowledge.

He stayed some days with an Indian merchant in Cairo and then moved into a caravanserai, where a merchant of Alexandria, whom he had met on the boat, gave him some excellent advice. As a Persian, he said, Burton would be cursed in Egypt, beaten in Arabia, charged treble for everything in all places, and probably allowed to die by the roadside if he fell ill. He therefore decided to pass as a Pathan or Afghan, born in India (this to avoid discovery by any 'compatriots' he might meet), but he kept up his *rôle* of doctor and dervish. His friend also suggested that if he were questioned he should say that he was under a vow to visit all the holy places of Islam, a statement that might win him more favourable treatment.

Burton here gives an amusing picture of the Oriental physician:

> Arrived at the sick-room, you salute those present with a general "Peace be upon you!" to which they respond, "And upon thee be the peace and the mercy of Allah, and his blessing!" To the invalid you say, "There is nothing the matter, please Allah, except the health"; to which the proper answer—for here every sign of ceremony has its countersign—is, "May Allah give thee health!" Then you sit down, and acknowledge the presence of the company by raising your right hand to your lips and forehead, bowing the while circularly; each individual returns the civility by a similar gesture. Then inquiry about the state of your health ensues. Then you are asked what refreshment you will take: you studiously mention something not likely to be in the house, but at last you rough it with a pipe and a cup of coffee. Then you proceed to the patient, who extends his wrist, and asks you what his complaint is. Then you examine his tongue, you feel his pulse, you look learned, and—he is talking all the time—after hearing a detailed list of all his ailments, you gravely discover them, taking for the same as much praise to yourself as does the practising phrenologist for a similar simple exercise of the reasoning faculties.
> . . . If you would pass for a native practitioner, you must finally proceed to the most uncomfortable part of your visit, bargaining

for fees. Nothing more effectually arouses suspicion than dis-interestedness in a doctor. I once cured a rich Hazramaut merchant of rheumatism, and neglected to make him pay for treatment; he carried off one of my coffee cups and was unceas-ingly wondering where I came from. So I made him produce five piastres, a shilling, which he threw upon the carpet, cursing Indian avarice. . . . Whatever you prescribe must be solid and material, and if you accompany it with something painful, such as rubbing to scarification with a horse-brush, so much the better. Easterns, like our peasants in Europe, wish the doctor to 'give them the value of their money.' Besides which, rough measures act beneficially upon their imagination. So the Hakim of the King of Persia cured fevers by the bastinado; patients are beneficially baked in a bread-oven at Baghdad. . . . When you administer with your own hand the remedy—half-a-dozen huge bread pills dipped in a solution of aloes or cinnamon water, flavoured with assafœtida, which in the case of the dyspeptic rich often suffice, if they will but diet themselves—you are careful to say, "In the name of Allah, the Compassionate, the Merciful." And after the patient has been dosed, "Praise be to Allah, the Curer, the Healer"; then you call for pen, ink, and paper, and write some such prescription as this:

"In the name of Allah, the Compassionate, the Merciful, and blessings and peace be upon our Lord the Apostle, and his family and his companions one and all! But afterwards let him take bees-honey and cinnamon and *album græcum*, of each half a part, and of ginger a whole part, which let him pound and mix with the honey, and form boluses, each bolus the weight of a miskal, and of it let him use every day a miskal on the saliva. Verily its effects are wonderful. And let him abstain from flesh, fish, vegetables, sweetmeats, flatulent food, acids of all descriptions, as well as the major ablution, and live in perfect quiet. So shall he be cured by the help of the King, the Healer. And The Peace."

One would wish to quote his pages describing the Egyptian shop, the Ramadan which he passed in Cairo, the Persian "Consul-General's" levee, the mosque, the school of Azhar, and his wildly farcical evening with the captain of Albanian irregulars. Yet in one thing the measure of Burton's vision may be remarked. In 1853 the ratification of the Suez Canal concession was a dozen years away; the Dual Control of Egypt was not yet visualized; there is thus something prophetic in the suggestion contained in the last lines of his chapter called "The Mosque"—a suggestion of the prize awaiting:

whatever European nation secures Egypt will win a treasure. Moated on the north and south by seas, with a glacis of impassable deserts to the eastward and westward, capable of supporting an army of 180,000 men, of paying a heavy tribute, and yet able to show a considerable surplus of revenue, this country in western hands will command India, and by a ship-canal between Pelusium and Suez would open the whole of Eastern Africa. . . . Egypt is the most tempting prize which the East holds out to the ambition of Europe, not excepted even the Golden Horn.

After the Ramadan, "the month of blessings," during which stores were gathered for the desert journey, Burton set out for Suez, and on the way was joined by a Meccan boy, Mohammed el Basyuni, who became his companion and servant throughout the pilgrimage, giving occasion for a characteristic miniature:

He is a beardless youth, of about eighteen, chocolate-brown, with high features, and a bold profile; his bony and decided Meccan cast of face is lit up by the peculiar Egyptian eye, which seems to descend from generation to generation. His figure is short and broad, with a tendency to be obese, the result of a strong stomach and the power of sleeping at discretion. He can read a little, write his name, and is uncommonly clever at a bargain. Meccah had taught him to speak excellent Arabic, to understand the literary dialect, to be eloquent in abuse, and to be profound at Prayer and Pilgrimage. Constantinople had given him a taste for Anacreontic singing, and female society of the questionable kind, a love of strong waters—the hypocrite looked positively scandalised when I first suggested the subject—and an off-hand latitudinarian mode of dealing with serious subjects in general. I found him to be the youngest son of a widow, whose doting fondness had moulded his disposition; he was selfish and affectionate, as spoiled children usually are, volatile, easily offended and as easily pacified (the Oriental), coveting other men's goods, and profuse of his own (the Arab), with a matchless intrepidity of countenance (the traveller), brazen-lunged, not more than half brave, exceedingly astute, with an acute sense of honour, especially where his relations were concerned (the individual). I have seen him in a fit of fury because some one cursed his father; and he and I nearly parted because on one occasion I applied to him an epithet which, etymologically considered, might be exceedingly insulting to a high-minded brother, but which in popular *parlance* signifies nothing. This '*point d'honneur*' was the boy Mohammed's strong point.

Arriving at Suez, Burton embarked in the *Silk el Zahab* (the *Golden Wire*), a sambuk of fifty tons, undecked but with a high

poop, on which he and his party took their places. In addition
to the Meccan boy there were Omar Effendi, a Daghistani,
short, plump, and usually quiet unless roused, when he became
tigerish; Hamid, a town Arab; Salih Shakkah, a boy of
sixteen, half Arab, half Turk, from Medina; and Sa'ad the
Demon, an African negro, ex-slave, ex-soldier, ex-merchant,
and now Omar's servant.

The beach was covered with pilgrims, rushing about madly
among howling children and screaming Turkish women while
passports were examined, and some of those who had forgotten
them were promptly bastinadoed. On the ship the disorder
was worse. A party of wild, insolent pilgrims from the Maghreb
disputed the poop with Burton's companions, and were driven
off after a fierce rough-and-tumble.

> Our Maghrabis were fine-looking animals from the deserts
> about Tripoli and Tunis; so savage that, but a few weeks ago,
> they had gazed at the cockboat, and wondered how long it would
> be growing to the size of the ship that was to take them to Alex-
> andria. Most of them were sturdy young fellows, round-headed,
> broad-shouldered, tall and large-limbed, with frowning eyes, and
> voices in a perpetual roar. Their manners were rude, and their
> faces full of fierce contempt or insolent familiarity. A few old
> men were there, with countenances expressive of intense ferocity;
> women as savage and full of fight as men; and handsome boys
> with shrill voices, and hands always upon their daggers. The
> women were mere bundles of dirty white rags. The males were
> clad in 'Burnus'—brown or striped woollen cloaks with hoods;
> they had neither turband nor tarbush, trusting to their thick
> curly hair or to the prodigious hardness of their scalps as a defence
> against the sun; and there was not a slipper nor a shoe amongst
> the party. Of course all were armed; but, fortunately for us,
> none had anything more formidable than a cut-and-thrust dagger
> about ten inches long. These Maghrabis travel in hordes under
> a leader who obtains the temporary title of "Maula,"—the master.
> He has generally performed a pilgrimage or two, and has collected
> a stock of superficial information which secures for him the
> respect of his followers, and the profound contempt of the heaven-
> made *ciceroni* of Meccah and Al-Madinah. No people endure
> greater hardships when upon the pilgrimage than these Africans,
> who trust almost entirely to alms and to other such dispensations
> of Providence. It is not therefore to be wondered at that they
> rob whenever an opportunity presents itself. Several cases of theft
> occurred on board the *Golden Wire*; and as such plunderers

seldom allow themselves to be baulked by insufficient defence, they are accused, perhaps deservedly, of having committed some revolting murders. . . . We were summoned by the Maghrabis to relieve their difficulties, by taking about half a dozen of them on the poop. Sa'ad the Demon at once rose with an oath, and threw amongst us a bundle of *nabbut*—goodly ashen staves six feet long, thick as a man's wrist, well greased, and tried in many a rough bout. He shouted to us "Defend yourselves if you don't wish to be the meat of the Maghrabis!" and to the enemy—"Dogs and sons of dogs! now shall you see what the children of the Arab are." "I am Omar of Daghistan!" "I am Abdullah the son of Joseph!" "I am Sa'ad the Demon!" we exclaimed, 'renowning it' by this display of name and patronymic. To do our enemies justice, they showed no sign of flinching; they swarmed towards the poop like angry hornets, and encouraged each other with cries of "*Allaho akbar!*" But we had a vantage-ground about four feet above them, and their palm-sticks and short daggers could do nothing against our terrible quarter-staves. In vain the *Jacquerie* tried to scale the poop and to overpower us by numbers; their courage only secured them more broken heads.

At first I began to lay on load with *main morte*, really fearing to kill some one with such a weapon; but it soon became evident that the Maghrabis' heads and shoulders could bear and did require the utmost exertion of strength. Presently a thought struck me. A large earthen jar full of drinking water—in its heavy frame of wood the weight might have been 100 lbs.,—stood upon the edge of the poop, and the thick of the fray took place beneath. Seeing an opportunity, I crept up to the jar, and, without attracting attention, rolled it down by a smart push with the shoulder upon the swarm of assailants. The fall caused a shriller shriek to rise above the ordinary din, for heads, limbs, and bodies were sorely bruised by the weight, scratched by the broken potsherds, and wetted by the sudden discharge. A fear that something worse might be coming made the Maghrabis slink off towards the end of the vessel. After a few minutes, we, sitting in grave silence, received a deputation of individuals in whity-brown Burnus, spotted and striped with what Mephistopheles calls a "curious juice." They solicited peace, which we granted upon the condition that they would pledge themselves to keep it. Our heads, shoulders, and hands were penitentially kissed, and presently the fellows returned to bind up their hurts in dirty rags.

At length the ship moved slowly into the Red Sea, the first night's halt being made still within sight of Suez. Days in the "canescent heat" were followed by hours that were damp and comparatively cold. Sometimes the pilgrims landed for the night on some spit of sand, but they stopped for a longer interval at Tor (originally a Phœnician settlement) to take in fresh water and fruit, and Burton noted old Portuguese fortifications. Then they sailed on, past the mouth of Akaba, ill famed for rocks and sudden storms. At midday, wrote Burton,

> the wind reverberated by the glowing hills is like the blast of a lime-kiln. All colour melts away with the canescence from above. The sky is a dead milk-white, and the mirror-like sea so reflects the tint that you can scarcely distinguish the line of the horizon. After noon the wind sleeps upon the reeking shore; there is a deep stillness; the only sound heard is the melancholy flapping of the sail. Men are not so much sleeping as half senseless; they feel as if a few more degrees of heat would be death.

When at the anchorage of Wejh they landed "with reeling limbs," to renew provisions, Sa'ad the Demon almost destroyed their hope of repose at a large *café* near the beach by quarrelling with the proprietor, who "showed himself nowise unwilling to meet the Demon half-way."

> The two worthies, after a brief bandying of words, seized each other's throats leisurely, so as to give the spectators time and encouragement to interfere. But when friends and acquaintances were hanging on to both heroes so firmly that they could not move hand or arm, their wrath, as usual, rose, till it was terrible to see. The little village resounded with the war, and many a sturdy knave rushed in, sword or cudgel in hand, so as not to lose the sport. During the heat of the fray, a pistol which was in Omar Effendi's hand went off—accidentally of course—and the ball passed so close to the tin containing the black and muddy Mocha, that it drew the attention of all parties. As if by magic, the storm was lulled. A friend recognised Sa'ad the Demon, and swore that he was no black slave, but a soldier at Al-Madinah— "no waiter, but a Knight Templar." This caused him to be looked upon as rather a distinguished man, and he proved his right to the honour by insisting that his late enemy should feed with him, and when the other decorously hung back, by dragging him to dinner with loud cries.

On July 17, twelve days after they had left Suez, Jebel Radhwah was sighted and Yenbo reached. Yenbo al Bahr, "the fountain of the sea," was a stage on the land route to the holy cities from Cairo, and also the port for Medina, which it supplied, by import, with grain, dates, and henna. The sea journey had been arduous and exhausting. Burton need not have made it under such conditions. Sailing by other ships he could have had a cabin to himself and a degree of comfort. But he wanted to experience the pilgrim ship, like any poor Moslem.

Of his second Arabian town and its inhabitants he wrote:

The town itself is in no wise remarkable. Built on the edge of a sunburnt plain that extends between the mountains and the sea, it fronts the northern extremity of a narrow, winding creek. Viewed from the harbour, it is a long line of buildings, whose painful whiteness is set off by a sky like cobalt and a sea like indigo; behind it lies the flat, here of a bistre-brown, there of a lively tawny; whilst the background is formed by dismal Radhwah, "Barren and bare, unsightly, unadorned." Outside the walls are a few little domes and tombs, which by no means merit attention. Inside, the streets are wide; and each habitation is placed at an unsociable distance from its neighbour, except near the port and the bazars where ground is valuable. The houses are roughly built of limestone and coralline, and their walls full of fossils crumble like almond cake; they have huge hanging windows, and look mean after those in the Moslem quarters of Cairo. There is a 'Suk,' or market-street of the usual form, a long narrow lane darkened by a covering of palm leaves, with little shops let into the walls of the houses on both sides. The *cafés* . . . about here . . . are rendered dirty in the extreme by travellers, and it is impossible to sit in them without a fan to drive away the flies. The custom-house fronts the landing-place upon the harbour; it is managed by Turkish officials—men dressed in Tarbushes, who repose the live-long day upon the Diwans near the windows. In the case of us travellers they had a very simple way of doing business, charging each person of the party three piastres for each large box, but by no means troubling themselves to meddle with the contents. Yambu' also boasts of a *hammam*, or hot bath, a mere date-leaf shed, tenanted by an old Turk, who, with his surly Albanian assistant, lives by 'cleaning' pilgrims and travellers. Some white-washed mosques and minarets of exceedingly simple form, a Wakalah or two for the reception of merchants, and a saint's tomb, complete the list of public buildings. . . .

The population of Yambu'—one of the most bigoted and quarrelsome races in Al-Hijaz—strikes the eye after arriving from Egypt, as decidedly a new feature. The Shaykh or gentleman is over-armed and over-dressed, as Fashion, the Tyrant of the Desert as well as of the Court, dictates to a person of his consequence. The civilised traveller for Al-Madinah sticks in his waist-shawl a loaded pistol, garnished with crimson silk cord, but he partially conceals the butt-end under the flap of his jacket. The Irregular soldier struts down the street a small armoury of weapons: one look at the man's countenance suffices to tell you what he is. Here and there stalk grim Badawin, wild as their native wastes, and in all the dignity of pride and dirt, they also are armed to the teeth, and even the presence of the policeman's quarterstaff cannot keep their swords in their scabbards. What we should call the peaceful part of the population never leave the house without the *nabbut* over the right shoulder, and the larger, the longer, and the heavier the weapon is, the more gallantry does the bearer claim. The people of Yambu' practise the use of this implement diligently; they become expert in delivering a head-blow so violent as to break through any guard, and with it they always decide their trivial quarrels. The dress of the women differs but little from that of the Egyptians, except in the face veil, which is generally white. There is an independent bearing about the Yambu' men, strange in the East; they are proud without insolence, and they look manly without blustering. Their walk partakes somewhat of the nature of a swagger, owing, perhaps, to the shape of the sandals, not a little assisted by the self-esteem of the wearer, but there is nothing offensive in it.

At Yenbo Burton began to arrange for camels for the journey into the interior. There were rumours of Bedouin raiding in the desert, and some arrivals had been held up by them. The heat and fiery wind beating through the town from the desert made the days uncomfortable, but in the night coolness the pilgrims took their main meal of the day—boiled rice and mutton soaked with clarified butter. Here Burton adopted Arab dress and spoke only Arabic. He purchased a litter, as notes could be taken more easily in this, on camel's back. His diary book was a long thin volume which he carried concealed in a breast-pocket.

Nothing so effectually puzzles these people as the Frankish habit of putting everything on paper; their imaginations are set at work, and then the worst may be expected.

Burton found ways of hiding other equipment that would have aroused suspicion:

Pilgrims, especially those from Turkey, carry, I have said, a 'Hamail,' to denote their holy errand. This is a pocket Koran, in a handsome gold-embroidered crimson velvet or red morocco case, slung by red silk cords over the left shoulder. It must hang down by the right side, and should never depend below the waist-belt. For this I substituted a most useful article. To all appearance a 'Hamail,' it had inside three compartments; one for my watch and compass, the second for ready money, and the third contained penknife, pencils and slips of paper, which I could hold in the hollow of my hand. These were for writing and drawing: opportunities of making a 'fair copy' into the diary book are never wanting to the acute traveller.

On July 18 Burton and his party, with twelve camels, joined the caravan from Yenbo. His own camel-men were two Bedouin of the Harb, a great Hejaz tribe which, he believed, had kept its blood pure for centuries. These two members of it, however, seem to have been so corrupted by intercourse with the pilgrims that they retained none of their ancestral qualities save greed of gain, revengefulness, and a spasmodic bravery. They were small, chocolate-coloured, with "straggling beards, vicious eyes, frowning brows, screaming voices, and well-made, but attenuated limbs." They were ragged but had their pride:

> They would eat with me, and not disdain like certain self-styled Caballeros, to ask for more; but of work they would do none. No promise of 'Bakhshish,' potent as the spell of that word is, would induce them to assist in pitching my tent.

The country across which the caravan of some six hundred camels moved was stranger to Burton's generation than to ours, which has known T. E. Lawrence's brilliant word-pictures of this part of Arabia. A great iron plain of stones, where grasshoppers were the chief form of life, was dotted with a little sun-parched scrub, and then, behind it, huge hills, bare plains, and desolate valleys; granite mountains, with huge blocks and boulders, cut by dark caves and vast clefts; above, a sky "like polished blue steel, with a tremendous blaze of yellow light," without the slightest veil of mist; no bird or beast; jagged peaks ahead. So the entry to Arabia from Yenbo appeared to Burton.

With the caravan were two hundred camels laden with grain, and an escort of seven Turkish irregular cavalry. They travelled mostly by night, and by day sat and lay down almost stupefied by the heat, or slept with their boxes around them as some protection against pilferers. Half-way between Yenbo and Medina was the village of Al Hamra, which Burton remarked was out of place on Burckhardt's map. It took its name from the reddish sand near by, and was built on a hill-side next to a *wadi*, dry at that season, but a raging torrent during the rains. It was a wretched place, with hovels of unbaked brick and mud, but possessed extensive palm planta-tions. The surly villagers had also large flocks of sheep and goats, but refused to supply the travellers with milk even in exchange for bread and meat. The place had suffered, Burton conjectured, in the Wahhabi wars earlier in the century. Part of it was in ruins, and in Arabia the depopulation of a village or district could not be cured by immigration, for the land still belonged to the survivors of the tribe, and trespass would lead to revenge and fighting. At Al Hamra the caravan was detained in such inhospitable surroundings, as Saad, a famous robber with a following of five thousand men, was said to be raiding in the mountains.

At length a caravan from Mecca arrived, and the Yenbo travellers continued towards Medina in this company, with an escort of two hundred cavalry. That night little progress had been made when the column was suddenly halted. Bedouin were occupying a gorge on the route, and finally allowed them to proceed only when the cavalry had agreed to go back. Then the way led past Jedayda, where Tussun was defeated by the Harb and Wahhabis in 1811, to Bir Abbas, a place similar to Al Hamra. This point was reached on June 22. The simoon filled the air, a fiery wind swung sand from the ground, the sun burned through the tents, and tempers were sulky.

But some diversion was caused in the evening by the passing of certain Harb sheikhs on their way to draw their salaries from the Turks at Bir Abbas. The pilgrims turned out to see these "old men in the picturesque Arab costume, with erect forms, fierce thin features, and white beards, well armed, and mounted upon high-bred and handsomely equipped dromedaries."

Later there was the sound of firing in the hills, suggestive of skirmishing between Turkish troops and Bedouin. But the caravan was glad to be away after the halt at Bir Abbas in sand and the furious hot wind. It was soon to meet with further trouble. At a notorious place known as "the Pilgrimage Pass" Bedouin lined the hilltops and the precipitous sides of a gorge. Blue puffs of smoke arose, followed by the sharp crack of matchlocks echoing among the rocks. Along the heights the Bedouin swarmed like hornets and fired down on the long column, "with perfect convenience to themselves." Many of them were under cover behind sangars along the cliffs, so that they would have been difficult to hit by returned fire, and, in any case, had one of them been killed the whole countryside would have risen to a man, whereupon, wrote Burton, with a strength of three or four thousand they might have gained courage to overpower the caravan. The old Harb sheikhs, who had joined the column, were now appealed to, and after holding a council among themselves came to the conclusion "that as the robbers would probably turn a deaf ear to their words, they had better spare themselves the trouble of speaking."

The travellers could only push forward, firing back at random and endeavouring to veil their course in smoke. At this place, in addition to camels and other beasts of burden, twelve men were lost.

On July 25, after passing through stony defiles of basalt and lava, they came within sight of Medina, and Burton understood the phrase of Moslem ritual—"And when the pilgrim's eyes shall fall upon the trees of Al-Madinah let him raise his voice and bless the Apostle with the choicest of blessings." To eyes accustomed to the barren rock and narrow gorges of the coastal range it was a pleasing sight. A great plain bounded by the higher ground of Nejd lay before them, rocky Mount Ohod prominent with verdure, and a few white domes resting at its foot. To the right, under a lilac mist, were the date-groves and greenery of Kuba, emerald-green on the tawny plain, and down a winding road from the ridge lay Medina itself, two miles away, with its domes and minarets standing out brightly against the dun of houses. Particularly arresting to the eye were the four towers and flashing green dome of the Prophet's mosque.

Burton lodged in Medina at the house of one of his companions, Hamid. His days were uneventful. He rose at dawn, washed, prayed, ate a little stale bread, smoked a pipe, and

SIR RICHARD BURTON
Lord Leighton
National Portrait Gallery

176

MEDINA: A GENERAL VIEW
Photo E.N.A.

drank coffee. Then he would visit one of the holy places, and as the morning heat grew unbearable would sit with his host, passing the time until dinner. This was at eleven in the morning, and consisted of meat, unleavened bread, vegetable stews, plain boiled rice, dates, grapes, and pomegranates. During the greatest heat he lay dozing and smoking on a rug spread in a dark passage of the house, and at sunset rose to pay calls or receive visitors. Prayers followed, a supper similar to dinner, a visit to some *café*, and then to his bed—a mattress outside the front door, where all the men slept. Burton's first visit, on the day of his arrival, was to the Prophet's mosque.

The approach to the mosque was disappointing, for it lay through narrow muddy lanes, and was so crowded in with wretched hovels that the building displayed no real frontage, and so lacked outward beauty or dignity. Entering by the Gate of Pity, Burton was still further surprised by the tawdry and mean appearance of a shrine so venerated throughout Islam. It was like a museum of second-rate art, both an old curiosity shop and a place of cheap finery.

Reciting a preliminary prayer, he walked with Hamid along "the Illustrious Fronting," which ran parallel with the southern boundary of the mosque. On the left was a wall the height of a man, painted with arabesques, and within was the Mambar, or pulpit, a thing of slender columns and good carving and tracery. Passing through a door in this wall, they entered El Rauzah, or the Garden, and recited the afternoon prayers—Burton intoning two chapters of the Koran and prostrating himself in thanks and gratitude to Allah for allowing him to visit so holy a place.

El Rauzah was about eighty feet long and decorated to resemble a garden, for, according to the Apostle, "Between my tomb and my pulpit is a Garden of the Gardens of Paradise." The pediments were in green tiles, the carpets were flowered, and the columns were adorned with gaudy arabesques representing vegetation. Burton noticed that a branched candelabra was "by a London firm." However, among much which he found distasteful there was one pleasing feature, in the light cast through a stained-glass window in the southern wall.

After walking round the outer courts Burton was led to

the Hajrah, or chamber reputed to contain the remains of the Prophet and his two immediate successors. Space was left there for a single grave, destined in popular superstition for Isa, bin Maryam—that is, Jesus, the son of Mary—after a second coming in the flesh. The chamber was about fifty to fifty-five feet square, and was separated on all sides from the walls of the mosque by a corridor some six to eight yards wide. The green dome was above the chamber, and was surmounted by a gilt crescent resting on a number of globes.

Here Burton prayed again, and was allowed to look through the small windows of the chamber, where, with some difficulty, he could see a curtain, or hangings, with three inscriptions in long, gold letters, to the effect that behind them lay the Apostle and the first two successors.

At the tomb of the Prophet Burton had achieved part of his object—not that he believed the tomb actually contained Mohammed's remains. There was considerable doubt, he thought, regarding the true site of the Prophet's grave. After various prayers in other parts of the mosque and a final supplication in El Rauzah he finished his devotions for the day.

Subsequently he visited the mosque of Kuba, where prayer was held to be particularly efficacious, and other holy places, including the burial-ground of El Bakia, amid palm plantations, where so many holy men were buried that tradition said, "a hundred thousand saints, all with faces like full moons, shall cleave on the last day the yawning bosom of El Bakia."

The city of Medina he described as built on a gently sloping plateau of white chalk, salt sand, and loamy clay that was easily made into bricks. There was a plentiful supply of water (too much on occasion, after rain, when torrents swept down from the western and eastern highlands). He described the sources of supply and the underground conduit to the city. The climate was cool or even cold for most of the year, and in the rainy season, which lasts from October for six months, parts of the city and its neighbourhood were flooded. The town was about half the size of Mecca, held a population of some 16,000, and was surrounded by a wall of granite and lava blocks cemented with lime. The streets were "what they should always be in these torrid lands"—dark, deep, and narrow, paved occasionally, but for the most part covered with black earth, well watered and trodden hard. The houses were, for the East, well built of palm-wood and burned brick, flat-roofed and double-storied. The city's sanctity attracted many strangers, who came for religious purposes and then settled there, so that the population contained North Africans, negroes, Syrians, Kurds, Afghans, Daghistanis, and even a few Malays, though the Indian element was not so large as at Mecca. Although Medina was not a meeting-place of all Islam, like Mecca, the inhabitants had some privileges and perquisites. For instance, they were not taxed, and if a Medani wanted to travel he could be granted a draft on Constantinople, a sum of money regulated by his rank in the city, paid from bequests, endowments, and alms. Endowments of the shrine existed in all parts of the Moslem world. The Medani of the upper class was engaged usually in managing his landed estate or as a servant of the mosque, payment for which service was partly from endowment and partly from the Sultan. In Medina most of the artisans were either slaves or foreigners and were mostly Egyptians. Apart from the activities of a few grain, cloth, and provision merchants, there was not much business done in the city.

The true Medani was taught from childhood that he was a favoured being, that he was to be respected always, however vile, and that Allah's vengeance would fall upon anyone who struck or even abused him. The very shopkeepers met the stranger "with the haughtiness of Pashas," and went out of their way to show him by word and look that they were as "good gentlemen as the king, only not so rich." They were fair-complexioned, and the Meccans said of them that their hearts were as black as their skins were white.

Burton was surprised that so mongrel a stock should have approximated even superficially in appearance, as it did, to a pure Bedouin type, with high cheek-bones, small, deep-set, fiery eyes, small head, oval, long face, high and slightly retreating forehead, and scanty hair on the face. However, the only Arab characteristics which they impressed him as possessing were pride, pugnacity, and a patient vindictiveness.

The manners of the Madani are graver and somewhat more pompous than those of any Arabs with whom I ever mixed. This they appear to have borrowed from their rulers, the Turks. But their austerity and ceremoniousness are skin-deep. In intimacy or in anger the garb of politeness is thrown off, and the screaming Arab voice, the voluble, copious and emphatic abuse, and the mania for gesticulation, return in all their deformity. They are great talkers, as the following little trait shows. When a man is opposed to more than his match in disputing or bargaining, instead of patiently saying to himself "*S'il crache il est mort*," he interrupts the adversary with a "*Sall' ala Mohammed*"—"Bless the Prophet." Every good Moslem is obliged to obey such requisition by responding, "*Allah-umma salli alayh*"—"O Allah bless him." But the Madani curtails the phrase to "*A'n*," supposing it to be an equivalent, and proceeds in his loquacity. Then perhaps the baffled opponent will shout out "*Wahhid*," i.e., "Attest the unity of the Deity"; when, instead of employing the usual religious phrases to assert that dogma, he will briefly ejaculate "*Al*" and hurry on with the course of conversation.

Burton breaks the narrative of his journey from Medina to Mecca by a chapter on the Bedouin of Hejaz. It has little essential to add to Burckhardt's account, which was based on the Anazeh tribes, though it is more colourful and vivid. Burckhardt contrasted the Arab with the Turk; Burton notes points of resemblance to the North American Indian.

The almost complete independence of the Arabs, and of the North American Indians of a former generation, he considered noteworthy as a warning to anthropologists to avoid detecting in coincidence of custom identity of origin. Both had the same chivalry, the sense of honour and hospitality, the vendetta, and the blood-feud; both were grave, formal, and cautious in manner, "princes in rags or paint." Both loved forays and raids, both were alternately brave to desperation and shy of danger.

Both are remarkable for nervous and powerful eloquence; dry humour, satire, whimsical tales, frequent tropes; boasts and ruffling style; pithy proverbs, extempore songs, and languages wondrous in their complexity. Both, recognising no other occupation but war and the chase, despise artificers and the effeminate people of cities, as the game-cock spurns the vulgar rooster of the poultry yard. . . . Of these two chivalrous races of barbarians, the Badawi claims our preference on account of his treatment of women, his superior development of intellect, and the glorious page of history he has filled.

At the beginning of September Burton resumed his journey towards Mecca, in the company of the Damascus caravan. He had come through the first dangers safely, and knew now that in case of discovery at Mecca he was near the coast, and in a few hours might reach Jidda, where there was a British consul, perhaps even a cruiser, and at any rate protection in the Turkish authorities. At Medina escape would have been more difficult. On the road to Mecca, however, risk yet remained, for here any local official could quietly be rid of a suspected person by merely giving a dollar to a Bedouin.

Burckhardt had travelled the Darb el Sultani, the coast road between Mecca and Medina. Burton was to follow the Darb el Sharki, the eastern road, where water was scarce, despite the wells sunk at the order of Zobeida, the wife of Haroun al Raschid. No European had previously travelled by this road.

Some seven thousand men, women, and children formed the caravan, a striking sight as Burton first saw it in the morning sun on the line of march. The rich were carried in scarlet-and-gilt litters; the middle-class pilgrim rode on horseback or on splendid Syrian camels; and poor travellers went afoot, many of them almost naked and hobbling along with heavy staves—bearded Persians, shaven Turks, and negroes in the long motley column.

The simoon wind, hot and parching the skin, beat upon them, and, to add to discomfort, alternated with chilly down-blasts from the hills. The route generally passed through difficult country of narrow passes, stony ground, and thorny acacias, where the weaker beasts of burden fell by the way, so that the earth was strewn with the carcasses of dead camels, asses, and ponies. If the throats of these animals had been cut with due religious rites the poor negroes of the pilgrimage would cut them into steaks, which they carried over their shoulders to be cooked at the first opportunity. Throughout the journey to Mecca the caravan invariably halted about two miles from wells, and in the quarrelling, shouting crowd of pilgrims and servants it was always necessary to pay out an excessive amount of hard cash to the troops guarding the water supply. A day journey was exceptional; usually the pilgrims moved at night, a practice that made it difficult for Burton to observe the country. In the darkness the camels felt their way carefully from one basalt block to another, and sometimes an unseen acacia would almost tear the *shugduf* from a camel's back. But the caravan was obeying the Prophet's injunction, to "Choose early darkness for your wayfarings, as the calamities of the earth (serpents and wild animals) appear not at night." In daylight marches Burton noted the mirage and great pillars of sand, remarked by Bruce in 1769—huge yellow shafts that scudded over the plain, and were supposed by the Arabs to be the Djinns of the waste land.

Such large parties moving over desert and rocky highlands had to submit to a rough march discipline. A signal gun gave the order to strike tents after a halt, and a second denoted the command to move off speedily. The discharge of three guns meant a station on the journey. At night a single cannon sounded three or four halts at irregular intervals.

There were four principal officers in the caravan—namely, the Emir Haj, a *wakil* (his lieutenant and executive officer), the Emir el Surrah, or Treasurer, who had charge of the caravan funds and remittances to the holy cities, and an officer of the escort—in this case with command of about a thousand irregular cavalry, half soldiers, half bandits.

As between Medina and Suwayrkiya, Burton wrote, nowhere else had he seen the earth's anatomy so barren, or so rich in volcanic and primary formations. There were low plains, rolling hills cut by *wadis*, ridges, and flats of basalt and greenstone, and abrupt, vertical hills, fissured, with formidable precipices and castellated summits.

At Sufayna the Baghdad caravan joined the Darb el Sharki, and from this point marched with the Damascus pilgrims, though the two bodies camped separately. In this body of pilgrims there were Persians, Kurds, Arabs from the north-east of the peninsula, Wahhabis, and an escort of Shammar mountaineers and Ageyl. They numbered but two thousand in all, yet showed at once that they were ready to fight rather than give the Damascus body any precedence. "I never saw," Burton wrote, "a more pugnacious assembly; a look sufficed for a quarrel." One day's march he specially noted as "peculiarly Arabia."

It was a desert peopled only with echoes—a place of death for what little there is to die in it,—a wilderness, where . . . there is nothing but He. ("*La Siwa Hu*"—*i.e.*, where there is none but Allah.) Nature, scalped, flayed, discovered all her skeleton to the gazer's eye. The horizon was a sea of mirage; gigantic sand-columns whirled over the plain; and on both sides of our road were huge piles of bare rock, standing detached upon the surface of sand and clay. Here they appeared in oval lumps, heaped up with a semblance of symmetry; there a single boulder stood, with its narrow foundation based upon a pedestal of low, dome-shapen rock. . . . I remarked one block which could not measure fewer than thirty feet in height.

One night they set off at half-past ten, and as the moon was young they prepared for a hard night's work, moving south-west over what is called a *wa'ar*, rough ground covered with thicket.

Darkness fell upon us like a pall. The camels tripped and stumbled, tossing their litters like cockboats in a short sea; at times the *shugdufs* were well nigh torn off their backs. . . . It was a strange, wild scene. The black basaltic field was dotted with the huge and doubtful forms of spongy-footed camels with silent tread, looming like phantoms in the midnight air; the hot wind moaned, and whirled from the torches flakes and sheets of flame and fiery smoke, whilst ever and anon a swift-travelling *takht-rawan*, drawn by mules, and surrounded by runners bearing gigantic *nashals* or cressets, threw a passing glow of red light upon the dark road and the dusky multitude.

On September 5 the caravan began its second main stage from Suwayrkiya, crossing a basalt ridge and descending into a valley for five hours, with the simoon blowing hard and rousing tempers. A Turk and an Arab quarrelled, the former wanting to add a few sticks of wood, gathered for cooking purposes, to a camel's load. The Arab owner threw them off as often as the Turk put them in place. They screamed with rage, hustled one another, and at last the Turk dealt the Arab a heavy blow. That night the Turk was mortally wounded, the Arab ripping open his stomach with a dagger, and was left to die, wrapped in his shroud, in a half-dug grave.

At Dhariba, less than fifty miles from Mecca, the pilgrims

assumed the *ihram*. In the early evening of that day, while the sun still touched the hilltops but the valleys were in dark shadow, the caravans entered a pass between a precipice and a steep buttress of rock. A silence fell on the column, the voices of women and children were stilled, and there were no more shouts of "*Labbeyk!*" An attack was expected from the Bedouin, and suddenly a small curl of smoke appeared on the steep flank of the pass, and then came the crack of a matchlock. A camel rolled over dead, throwing its rider five or six yards in a somersault.

At once there was a scene of wild confusion, and the air rang with the screams of women and children as all pushed forward to get the danger behind them. Soon everything was jammed into an immovable mass. The irregular cavalry were quite useless, merely galloping about over the stony ground and shouting orders to each other.

But the Wahhabis of the Baghdad caravan galloped up on their camels, "their elf-locks tossing in the wind, and their flaming matches casting a strange lurid light over their features." One section took up position and began firing on the Bedouin, while others swarmed up the slope, led by a valiant sherif. The column was able to move on, and soon the noise of firing died away in the rear as the enemy fled. They had probably hoped for plunder, but in Burton's opinion their main object in attacking was to be able later to brag of the exploit.

The morning following this brush with the hillmen the pilgrims reached the Wadi Laymun, the Valley of Limes, where there was water in a bubbling stream, and the verdure of trees and gardens. On the march that evening they strained their eyes for a view of Mecca, but the town lay in a winding valley and was invisible. Darkness fell, and Burton dozed until about one o'clock in the morning, when he was awakened by cries of "Mecca, Mecca!" "The Sanctuary! Oh, the Sanctuary!" calls of "*Labbeyk!*" and the sound of sobs. He looked out from his litter, and saw by the light of the southern stars the dim outline of a large city, a shade darker than the surrounding plain.

Passing the watch-towers along the northern road, he made

his way through dark streets to the house of his young Meccan servant, and at sunrise on that same day he visited the sanctuary, the Kaaba.

> There at last it lay, the bourn of my long and weary pilgrimage, realising the fears and hopes of many a year. . . . I may truly say that of all the worshippers who clung weeping to that curtain or who pressed their beating hearts to the stone, none felt for the moment a deeper emotion than did the Haji from the far north. It was as if the poetical legends of the Arab spoke truth, and that the waving wings of angels, not the sweet breeze of the morning, were agitating and swelling the black covering of the shrine. But to confess humble truth, theirs was the feeling of religious enthusiasm, mine was the ecstasy of gratified pride.

Burton gave a very complete picture of the religious ceremonies and the city of Mecca, adding some details concerning places in the neighbourhood which Burckhardt had not visited. But, as he knew, there was really very little to add to the Swiss traveller's account, and he not only paid tribute to his great predecessor's accuracy, but was content merely to quote him freely. With all Arabian explorers he shared the common admiration for Burckhardt.

From Mecca he reached the sea at Jidda, and it was not until he was on board the steamer and about to sail for Suez, when perhaps his vigilance was relaxed, that suspicion seems to have dawned in the mind of his Meccan servant, astute as he was.

"Now I understand," said the youth, "a Sahib from India, he hath laughed at our beards."

Burton's book, *Personal Narrative of a Pilgrimage to Al-Madinah and Meccah* (1855), created a sensation, and Burton is still often credited in popular tradition with being the first European to accomplish the feat. Burton, of course, knew that many had preceded him, that Ali Bey and Burckhardt had covered the holy cities adequately, and that the journey in itself was of small value to science. But he desired, as Seetzen and Burckhardt had done, to gain the status of *haji*, as a lasting benefit in future explorations in Arab lands. Yet the object which he had originally conceived had to be abandoned, for in the Hejaz he learned that the trans-desert journey between Mecca and Muscat was never attempted, even by the Bedouin.

The pilgrimage, however, was not devoid of geographical

results. In addition to the reports of places not touched by Burckhardt, and the account of Medina (where Burckhardt was ill, and therefore less thorough in observation), which showed the city's growth in the years since the last European description, his route by the easternmost pilgrim route from Damascus enabled him to provide an account of two *harra* regions, and of their drainage towards the Red Sea.

II

Thirty years later a Dutch Arabist, J. Snouck Hurgronje, visited Mecca in the character of a physician, stayed five months, and made a careful study of the city's life "out of season," in the interval between the departure and arrival of pilgrim caravans. His book, which gives an accurate picture of such features as the holy places and slave-markets, the good qualities, bigotry, and vices of the inhabitants, was published in German, and has never been widely read in England.

We cannot follow Burton's career in the twenty-five years following his famous pilgrimage. During that time he made his expedition with Speke into Somaliland as far as Harrar and the journey into Equatorial Africa in the same company, which resulted in the unhappy Burton-Speke controversy and the vivid book *Lake Regions of Central Africa*. Burton's explorations in the Dark Continent inspired many of those who followed, including Livingstone and Stanley. In these years, too, his love of new places was provided with an outlet in the consular service, but his official career was unfortunate; he could not keep narrowly to the duties of a minor position, was tactless, and naïvely ignorant of the right and sensible mode of approach to the official mind; he was not a certain quantity which the Foreign Office could assess and rely upon implicitly. Burton is to be blamed more than officialdom that advancement again avoided him.

Now to trace the origin of Burton's next Arabian exploration one must go back to that merchant who a quarter of a century before had advised him to travel to Mecca as an Afghan. A caravan in which the merchant was travelling had one night rested near the Gulf of Akaba, where a hopeful discovery was made. Strolling along the dry bed of a small *wadi*, the merchant noticed sand of a curious colour, gathered some, had it assayed at Alexandria, and found that it contained gold. He mentioned this incident to Burton, who thought nothing more likely than that Midian, the district on the north of the Hejaz, should possess gold-bearing regions. The area had been extensively mined in ancient times, but probably superficially, on account of the lack of tools and scientific methods.

It was this casual information that led to Burton's expedition to Midian more than twenty years later. Ismail Pasha, Khedive of Egypt, stood on the verge of that chronic insolvency which was to lead to European intervention in his country. He knew of Burton's ideas regarding gold in Midian, summoned him to an interview, and commissioned him to lead a survey party. The merchant, now eighty-two years old, was traced and prevailed upon to join the search. But as he accompanied the party only part of the way, and provides little but comic relief in Burton's narrative, he may be omitted from subsequent events.

Midian was virgin territory to Burton, so he resolved to make a short personal reconnaissance of the country before the actual expedition started. This he carried out successfully in April 1877, brought back samples of metalliferous quartz, porphyry, greenstone, and basalt, and discovered the presence of iron, silver, turquoise, and gold. Then the hot season arrived and there was a delay of six months, during which time his mind ran impatiently on the Midian of the past, its many cities, its Greek, Roman, and Nabathæan miners, and the ruin which had fallen on the land. He dreamed of a new Midian, enriched and prosperous, from a rediscovery of mineral wealth.

In December 1877 the expedition set off, by train and gunboat, at Ismail's expense, to Fort Muweila, on the Midian coast. There were five Europeans, including Burton, thirty miners and quarrymen, an escort of thirty-eight Sudanese and Egyptian soldiers, and a small party of servants. On arrival Burton engaged several Bedouin guides and hired about a hundred camels.

In the first fifty-four days the main expedition covered 107 miles, carefully surveying the ground, while a further 200 miles were travelled by small parties detached from the main body. They found, as Burton expected, that the territory had been extensively but superficially worked. The sites of eighteen ruined cities were visited, including Maghair (the "Madiama" of Ptolemy), whereof there remained only the foundations of walls, a bastion on the face of a gorge, traces of furnaces, and some catacombs. A few ancient coins were found. The mineralogical discovery included deposits of copper ore, which sometimes showed 40 per cent. metal, silver, iron, and gold.

It was out of curiosity rather than from hope of a valuable find that Burton now searched for the *wadi* which had led to the journey. The place was found, but it contained no gold-bearing sand. Local gossip, however, persuaded him that there was gold in the district, and he heard that it was sometimes carried off in quills for sale at Suez. Yet he failed to influence even the poorest Arabs to give him any definite information. This first excursion from Muweila ended with a search for quartz along the Gulf of Akaba.

On this region, north of Muweila to about half-way along the Gulf, Burton could make little additional comment. The country here had been accurately mapped in 1826 by Edward Rüppell, the African explorer, and the *Palinurus*, commanded by Moresby, had in 1831 made a survey of the coast. Wallin also, in 1848, had crossed the region from Muweila to Tebuk.

After ten days' rest Burton set out again, this time to seek gold, which he expected to find unworked, farther from the coast, in the eastern districts of the *harra* and Hisma. His Arabs of the littoral were far from anxious to enter this area inhabited by wild Bedouin, but Burton had apparently disciplined them, so that they not only obeyed orders but loaded up in twenty minutes instead of the five hours taken at the beginning of the earlier journeys.

Much of the country they entered first was wild and rocky, though occasionally marked by thin woods and clumps of trees, but as they entered the highlands they found plentiful water, sheep, goats, hare, and partridge. Then they passed through the Wadis Najil, Dama, and Sharma, where the water and green vistas were reminiscent even of Damascus. On the second day through East Midian the column crossed a broad plain of golden sand, dotted with trees and bordered with an emerald ribbon of mimosas, with greenstone hills on the right and red hills on the left. From the high ground lovely views extended, and Sinai could be seen, purple and blue in the distance.

The splendid scenery was the only interest for several days, until Burton and a few of his men, riding ahead, sighted about a dozen Arabs clambering up the side of a pass, where they began to yell and threatened to fire. Burton tried to parley with them, but met with little success until the Sudanese came up. Their gleaming Remingtons then persuaded the Bedouin, who were of the Maazeh tribe, to come forward and kiss Burton's hands.

The next day one of them went off to ask the sheikh's permission for the party to pass through his territory, and soon there arrived five leading men of the tribe accompanied by thirty horsemen. The newcomers, however, showed small inclination to friendliness. Most of them were seeing European clothes for the first time, and did not like Burton's hat or the Egyptian headgear. Bertram Thomas, referring to the saying that unbelievers hide their faces from God, suspects that it originated in the modern sun-helmet, worn down over the eyes. Moreover, in Islamic prayer the brow must touch the earth; a hat with a brim or peak does not allow this, and such a consideration has led conservatives in Moslem countries to oppose the use in their armies of helmets copied from European types.

However, despite their obvious unfriendliness, the Bedouin agreed to guide the expedition forward the next day. That night was bitterly cold, and this, added to his anxiety for the future, robbed Burton of sleep. Nor did the next day's journey, through a long gorge where ambush was a simple matter, reassure him. When they came through this pass he saw, far behind, the great heights of the coastal range, and ahead the plateau of Central Arabia. He was standing on the borders of the Hisma uplands, on sandstone of red, pink, and dull white, and ahead lay a region of *harra*, volcanic, black, porous lava and basalt. It was a wild and striking scene, sufficient to banish the anxieties of the moment. But he knew that he could make no journey across that region.

He was recalled to the present by the actions of the Bedouin, who were sending off messengers in various directions, saying they would have no Nazarenes in their district, and discussing among themselves the summoning of a force to exterminate the intruders. Burton missed none of this, and realized that his only course was to retreat. When on February 25, 1878, he ordered his Arabs to strike tents and load up for the return he was obeyed with the greatest alacrity. The Maazeh seemed inclined to resist, but the efficient weapons of the Sudanese probably dissuaded them.

Burton left their territory behind, and made a leisurely return through South Midian, or the Northern Hejaz, roughly in a semicircle with Wejh as its centre, surveying, collecting specimens, noting ruins and old mines, and then marched towards the base at Muweila. A final examination of South Midian near the coast and his work was finished. The southern country was not so well watered as the north and centre, but the Bedouin of the Huteym were more tractable than the Howeitat groups previously met.

Burton had now thoroughly explored the coastal area, the *wadis* of the coastal range, including part of the Wadi Hamdh, and various areas of mountain, while his Egyptian officers had roughly mapped the country. He considered that gold might profitably be sought in Midian, and actually found vast outcrops of quartz. Ismail had given him special instructions to look for coal, but after a scrupulous search none was found.

Burton landed at Suez on April 20, 1878, with twenty-five tons of specimens in the Egyptian gunboat's hold. An exhibition of the finds was opened by Ismail himself, but neither his gold samples nor his report greatly impressed experts. Ismail, however, was so pleased that he promised Burton either a concession or a royalty of 5 per cent. on the produce of the mines. When the Khedive fell Burton visited his successor, Tewfik, but was told that there was no money in Egypt even for the most promising schemes—including mining in Midian.

In this same year John F. Keane was visiting the holy cities as Mohammed Amin, in the train of an Indian Moslem. His narrative, marked by the breezy adventurousness of a Marryat story, begins with the landing at Jidda, where he first sees the

A FRANKINCENSE-TREE
Photo E.N.A.

190

A Town in the Wadi Duwan

From "The Southern Gates of Arabia," by Freya Stark, by permission of the author

true Bedouin camel-men, dislikes their shrill voices, haggling, and "wretched appearance at first sight," but in the long run believes they have their good points. He has some qualms of conscience about conforming to Islam, but tells the lie so often that he comes to believe it himself. From Jidda he goes to Mecca, and thence by the coast road to Medina. His description of the coast from the interior is, indeed, the most valuable part of his books geographically. His story, *Six Months in the Hejaz*, aroused considerable incredulity when it appeared in print, especially that part which dealt with the Englishwoman in Mecca, but it was swift-moving, had much graphic description (the face of an old woman in charge of a harem is like "three kicks in a mud wall"), and was a best-seller in the later eighties. Keane fully shared Burton's zest for adventure.

Burton's many travels and adventures seem each to have called for literary expression. In his book *The Land of Midian (Revisited)* (1879) he described his last Arabian journeys and summarized their results, giving further topographical detail in *Itineraries* offered to the Royal Geographical Society. The expedition covered, by sea and land, some 2500 miles, of which 600, not including subsidiary reconnaissances, were mapped and planned. Detail concerning the ancient civilization of the district was collected; in the north eighteen ruined cities, including an old Nabathæan port, and in the south thirteen, were examined and surveyed. For mining purposes Burton saw the country in two divisions: rich silicates and carbonates of copper in the north, and auriferous veins, already worked but not exhausted, in the south. Three deposits of sulphur, potentialities in turquoise, salt, and gypsum were also reported. Many of Burton's books were merely of passing interest; few had the success of the *Pilgrimage*; but from the viewpoint of geography his account of Midian was immeasurably more important than his story of travel in the Haramain.

A claim might reasonably be made for Burton as the greatest explorer of the nineteenth century. Yet it is in literature, rather than from attainment in the field, that his memory is likely to survive. For many years he projected a translation of the *Arabian Nights*, and as at length he began the task Arabia was vividly present in his mind:

Again I stood under the diaphanous skies, in air glorious as æther, whose every breath causes men's spirits to bubble like sparkling wine. Once more I saw the evening star hanging like a golden lamp from the pure front of the Western firmament, and the afterglow transfiguring and transforming, as by magic, the homely and rugged features of the scene into a fairy-land lit with a light which never shines on other soils or seas. Then would appear the woollen tents, long, low and black, of the true Badawin, mere dots in the boundless waste of lion-tawny clays and gazelle-brown gravels, and the camp-fire dotting like a glow-worm the village centre. Presently, sweetened by distance, would be heard the wild, weird song of lads and lasses, driving, or rather pelting, through the gloaming their sheep and goats; and the measured chant of the spearsmen gravely stalking behind their charge, the camels; mingled with the bleating of the flocks, and the bellowing of the humpy herds; while the rere-mouse flitted overhead with his tiny shriek, and the rave of the jackal resounded through deepening glooms, and—most musical of music—the palm-trees answered the whispers of the night-breeze with the softest tones of falling water.

And then a shift of scene. The Shayks and 'white-beards' of the tribe gravely take their places sitting with outspread skirts like hillocks on the plain, as the Arabs say, around the camp-fire whilst I reward their hospitality and secure its continuance by reading or reciting a few pages of their favourite tales.

The Thousand Nights and a Night was published privately in sixteen volumes in 1885–88, and has been criticized by scholars on the grounds that it is not as true to its text as was expected from one of Burton's reputation. But to the ordinary reader, as to all Orientalists, it is an exhibition of colossal learning, complete acquaintance with Moslem qualities, customs, and habits, and catholic knowledge of Eastern life.

CHAPTER XII

EXPLORERS IN OMAN AND HADHRAMAUT

As soon as I had arrived among the crowd they all at once fell
upon me, dragged me from my camel, and disarmed me; using
me very roughly, they tied my hands behind my back and carried
me, with my face covered with blood and dust, before the reigning
Sultan.

ADOLF VON WREDE, *Journal of the Royal Geographical Society*, 1844

THE Egyptian occupation of the Hejaz and the central
districts of Arabia led to an increase in knowledge of the
territory within a triangle having its base from Wejh
to Jizan and its apex at Katif. Of the great areas north and
south of this region, which remained unexplored, much was
reported as desert by the medievals and by Niebuhr and
Burckhardt. The west coast and the southern shore were now
surveyed by Captains Moresby and Haines in the *Palinurus*.
At various times since the third quarter of the eighteenth
century the coast of Oman had been surveyed, but the charts
were far from accurate.

By reason of its rich trade in the Persian Gulf this south-
east corner of Arabia was of special interest to the English
East India Company, which established and sustained friendly
relations with the Persian rulers who succeeded the Portuguese
after 1650. Oman was invaded by the Wahhabis, but became
independent again in 1818, since which time, by supporting
and subsidizing various rulers, important and minor, like
those on the Trucial coast, and by insisting on a policy of no
territorial cessions to foreign Powers, Britain has retained
predominant influence. Treaties with Kuweit, Bahrein, and
Mokalla made the Persian Gulf "a British lake." Only on the
Hasa coastal territory of Ibn Saud is there any real measure of
independence of Britain.

But in the early nineteenth century this favoured position
was distant. Piracy on the coast had led to British expeditions,
one of which entered the country to punish the Beni Abu Ali

Bedouin for alleged depredations. The force, under a Captain Thompson, had been cut to pieces, but was revenged by a column commanded by General Sir Lionel Smith. When the Company wished to learn how far the power of the ruler at Muscat extended through the interior of Oman it dispatched Lieutenant James Wellsted in 1835 on an extensive reconnaissance. His report was communicated to the Royal Geographical Society two years later. It begins with Muscat, which Niebuhr had visited, a port in constant touch with the English in India:

> In its principal features Maskat differs little from the other eastern towns. Arriving from seaward, its forts, erected on dark-coloured hills, which almost encircle the town, the level roofs of its houses, the domes of the mosques, and their lofty minarets, have an extraordinary and romantic appearance; but as soon as we land the illusion disappears. Narrow, crowded streets, and filthy bazars, nearly blocked up with porters bearing burdens of dates, grain, etc.; wretched huts, intermingled with low and paltry houses, meet the eye in every direction. There are, nevertheless, within the town some good and substantial houses—the palace of the Imam, that of the Governor, and those of some other public officers, are of this description. Maskat is not only of importance as the emporium of a very considerable trade between Arabia, Persia, and India, but also as the principal seaport of Oman. Its imports are chiefly cloth and corn, the annual value of which is estimated at 3,300,000 dollars, which, if we except Jiddah, is greater than that of the imports into any other seaport in Arabia. The customs are fixed at 5 per cent. on all imported goods, but no duties of any kind are levied on exports. These principally consist of dates, *ruivas*, or red dye, much valued in India; sharks' fins shipped off for China, where they are used for making soup, and a variety of other purposes, and salt fish. The returns are made principally in bullion and coffee.

He estimated the population at 60,000, a mixed race of Arabs, Persians, Indians, Kurds, Afghans, and others. The ruler, who seems to have been enlightened and generous, gave Wellsted every facility for travelling into the interior. From Muscat, therefore, he proceeded along the coast to Sur, and then journeyed into the desert, south-west past the Wadi Falij, into the country of the Beni Abu Ali. These Arabs seem to have thoroughly learned their lesson from Lionel Smith, for, writes Wellsted, "they pitched my tent, slaughtered sheep, and presented me with milk by gallons." Travelling farther to the south-west for some days, he crossed more desert country, cut by the dry beds of torrents and marked by sandy mounds. After reaching a Bedouin encampment near wells in the desert he returned north-north-eastward through the Abu Ali. This expedition noted little but the featureless character of the land and the nomadic life of the people, who were both shepherds and fishermen.[1]

Wellsted now turned north, following a line of settlements and oases along the Wadi Betha, and after four days' journey came to Bedia, where there were several small villages whose territory was watered by subterranean rivulets and artificial irrigation.

> Thus abundantly irrigated, these isolated spots possess a soil so fertile, that nearly every grain, fruit, and vegetable common to India, Persia, or Arabia, is produced almost spontaneously, and the tales of the oases will no longer be regarded as an exaggeration, since a single step conveys the traveller from the glare and sand of the desert to the richest soil, moistened by a hundred rills, teeming with the most luxuriant vegetation, and embowered by noble and stately trees, whose umbrageous foliage the fiercest rays of a noon-tide sun cannot penetrate. The almond, fig, and walnut-trees grow to an enormous size, and the fruit appears clustered so thickly on the orange and lime, that I do not believe a tenth part of what they afford is ever gathered. Above all towers the date-palm, and lends its grateful shade to protect the jaded traveller. Some idea may be formed of the density of this mass of foliage by the effect it produces in lessening the terrestrial radiation. Fahrenheit's thermometer, which within the house stood at 55°, at six inches from the ground fell to 42°.

From Bedia the next town was Ibra, a day's journey. Of this place he remarked only the character of the houses:

> To avoid the damp, and to catch an occasional beam of the sun above the trees, they are usually very lofty. A parapet leading around the upper part is turreted, and on some of the largest turrets guns are mounted. The windows and doors have the Saracenic arch; every part of the building is profusely decorated

---

[1] Two generations later Sir Percy Cox visited this district with a geologist, prospecting for coal. A bag of quite good coal was collected, but the pair were shot at continually during the collecting process, and decided it was not a healthy spot for 'geologizing'!

with ornaments of stucco in bas-relief, some of them in very good taste. The doors are also cased with brass, and have rings and other massive ornaments of the same metal.

Still following the Wadi Betha, he passed through plains dotted with grassy knolls, and four days later arrived at the extensive oasis of Semmed, garrisoned by troops of the ruler of Muscat. Reaching Minna, after a further four days, he was struck by the rich cultivation in the open fields.

As we crossed these, with lofty almond, citron, and orange-trees, yielding a delicious fragrance on either hand, exclamations of astonishment and admiration burst from us. "Is this Arabia," we said, "this the country we have looked on heretofore as a desert?" Verdant fields of corn and sugar-cane, stretching along for miles, were before us; streams of water, flowing in all directions, intersected our path, and the happy and contented appearance of the peasants agreeably helped to fill up the smiling picture. The atmosphere was delig! .fully clear and pure; and as we trotted joyously along, giving or returning the salutation of peace or welcome, I could almost fancy we had at length reached that "Araby the blest," which we had hitherto regarded as existing only in the fictions of our poets.

Wellsted had set out from Sur on December 2. He reached Nezwa, the most populous of the oases, on the 23rd, and then continued his journey, skirting Jebel Akhdar, the "green mountains," cut by deep valleys from the torrents of the rainy season. The range seemed to him unworthy of its appellation "green," for much of it was bare limestone rock, barren except in some of its valleys and hollows. He took several observations on the temperature of boiling water, and estimated the highest points of the range to be 6000 feet above sea-level. Returning to Nezwa on December 31, he made some short journeys into the desert, studying particularly the social conditions of the inhabitants. In the middle of January his work was interrupted by a violent attack of fever, and when the worst part of his illness had passed he travelled by easy stages to Sib, on the coast, remaining there, to regain his strength, until the end of February.

He intended to advance from this base into Northern Oman, making his goal the town of Bireima, despite strong discouragement from the ruler of Muscat, who warned him that the

Wahhabis had recently raided the north, and that there was a local war in progress near the town of Obri, on the road to Bireima. Wellsted nevertheless moved west along the coast to

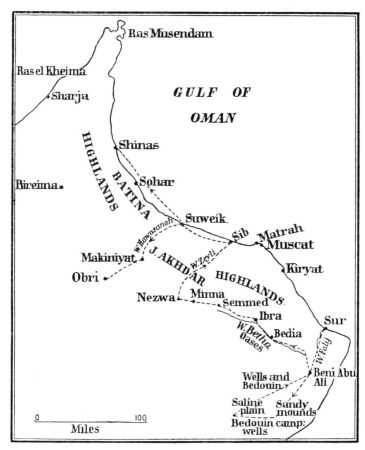

WELLSTED'S ROUTE IN OMAN

Suweik, and then entered the interior on March 4, passing through Wadi Hawasanah to Makiniyat, which was reached on March 11. The next day Obri came in sight over a succession of sandy barren plains.

The warnings which Wellsted had received were quickly justified, for the Wahhabis were met with sooner than he expected. A raiding force numbering two thousand was in the town. "The Wahhabis," he wrote, "were in general small, and had no other clothes than a cloth round their waist. Their complexion was very dark, and they wore their hair long." As the Wahhabis were making for Bedia, which was in Muscat's territory, and Wellsted was travelling under the ruler's protection, the situation was dangerous. A box which the exploring party carried aroused considerable excitement, among both the raiders and the townsfolk of Obri (who seemed to cultivate savage manners in order to impress the Bedouin among whom they lived), for the rumour grew that it contained dollars. Actually it was filled with clothes.

To prevent 'incidents' Wellsted had disarmed his escort, although there would have been little fear of a clash had all his men been in the mood of his interpreter, a giant Persian, who was so unmanned by the excitement that he went into fits. The leader of the Wahhabi party seemed to have little control over his followers, so Wellsted ordered the tents and equipment to be packed on the camels quickly and quietly. As he turned his back on the town there was a moment of tension, for the crowd around him was growing, but only hisses and a few stones followed the party as it headed for the desert again.

Returning to Suweik, Wellsted continued by sea to Shinas, hoping thence to reach Bireima and join some caravan bound for Dariya. But when no reply came to letters which he sent to the Wahhabi commander at Bireima he passed some time collecting information regarding the mountainous peninsula of Musendam, and then returned to India.

Wellsted has been described as a *tête exaltée*, and as one who borrowed from every one he met, yet did not know how to digest the material gathered. Haines, of the *Palinurus*, said that he was a poor surveyor, and he seems to have been not unwilling to forestall the credit for explorations carried out at least equally by others. On this expedition, however, full credit for the results achieved must be awarded to him, although he travelled in the territory between Semmed and Nezwa, and at Obri, with another Englishman.

It seems that Wellsted came to Oman again, in the spring following this journey, landed at Muscat in a high fever, and in his delirium shot himself in the mouth with a double-barrelled gun, inflicting hideous wounds in his upper jaws. He was sent back to India, and then on leave to England. He died some three years later, at the age of thirty-eight.

In 1876 Colonel S. B. Miles continued the exploration, crossing the mountains from Sohar into Dahira. He was the first to visit Bireima, which he found to be the centre of a fertile and populous district, and learned that the country for two hundred miles westward consisted of gravelly steppe, sloping to the salt marshes along the Persian Gulf. Wellsted's map and notes were not greatly modified by later exploration, and his general picture of the land remained authoritative.

Wellsted saw Oman in general as a narrow territory, of irregular width, but never exceeding a hundred and fifty miles. A range of mountains almost parallel to the shore traversed the country from Muscat to Sur. Jebel Akhdar ran nearly transverse to this range, and low parallel ridges extended from the two mountain formations. From Jebel Akhdar he described mountains running to Ras Musendam, with a branch to Ras el Kheima. Between the line of oases which he followed from the country of the Abu Ali, arid plains stretched to the sea, but to the northward of Sib lay the maritime plain of Batina, supporting a very large population and rich in indigo, sugar, and date-trees, which he described as extending in one district for a hundred and fifty miles continuously along the coast. Westward of the mountain ranges there were few settlements or oases. From Jebel Akhdar he saw to the west only vast plains of loose sand, across which even the Bedouin dare hardly venture. On the whole the quantity of cultivated country throughout Oman bore but a small proportion to the incorrigibly barren. He saw, in the ruins of houses and the remains of old embankments, the signs of a former extensive cultivation, "but wherever irrigation ceases the course of a few seasons converts the land, however fertile it has previously been, into a desert."

Wellsted was attached to the survey brig *Palinurus*, whose commander, Captain S. B. Haines, of the Indian Navy, carried out in the years 1834–36 a thorough survey of the South Arabian shore. His first observations dealt with the coast from the Red

Sea to Misenat; the second continued the survey to Ras el Hadd. These reports gave detailed information as to capes, shoals, rocks, bays, soundings, anchorages, currents, winds, and general navigational conditions. Moreover, brief expeditions were made on the mainland and islands of the coast, and data were collected regarding the inhabitants, vegetation, cattle, tribal territories, topography, history, and inscriptions. Here only a little can be given from these first modern accounts of the South Arabian coasts. Of Mokalla, then, as now, the principal port, the captain of the *Palinurus* wrote:

> Three-quarters of a mile W.N.W. of the cape is Ras Marbat, with a ruined fort; and 2 miles to the N.W., and within the bay, lies the town of Makallah, the principal commercial depot of the S. coast of Arabia, partly built on a narrow rocky point, projecting about ¼ of a mile to the S., and partly at the foot of a range of reddish limestone cliffs, rising about 300 feet, immediately at the back of the town, and on which are 6 square towers for the protection of the place. Almost directly above this remarkably level range of cliffs the flat-topped summit of Jebel Garrah, composed of beautiful white limestone, rises 1300 feet above the sea, and may be seen at a distance of 42 miles. The northern portion of the town is built on ground sloping from the base of the hills to the bay, and enclosed on the W. side by a dilapidated wall extending to the shore, with only one entrance gate, constantly guarded by a few Bedowins. The *nakib*, or Governor's house, [is] a large square building . . . the other buildings are chiefly cajan huts, intermingled with a few stone houses and two mosques. The population of the town may be about 4500, being a motley collection of the Beni Hasan and Yafai tribes, Karachies, and Banians, with foreigners from nearly every part of the globe. On either side of the projecting point on which the town is built is a small bay; that on the W. side is sheltered from the W. by a rocky reef, nearly dry at low-water spring-tides, and forms a haven much frequented by Arab boats and coasting vessels. I have observed 20 of these arrive in the course of a day, and some from 100 to 300 tons burden. The custom duties are 5 per cent. on goods from India. The exports consist in gums, hides, large quantities of senna, and a small quantity of coffee; the imports, chiefly of cotton cloths, lead, iron, crockery, and rice, from Bombay; dates and dried fruit from Maskat; jowari, bajeri, and honey from Aden; coffee from Mokha; sheep, honey, aloes, frankincense, and slaves, from Berberah, Bander Kosair, and other African ports. Much coasting trade is also carried on. Traffic in slaves exists to a frightful extent; I have seen 700

Nubian girls exposed at once in the slave-market here for sale, and subject to the brutal and disgusting inspection of the purchasers; the price varies from £7 to £25 a head. The duties here in 1834 amounted to about £800, but in 1836 to upwards of £1200; the chief part of the trade is carried on by the Banian merchants. The present *nakib*, or chief, Mohammed ben Abdu el Abid, is a young man of firm and upright character, and is much respected; commerce has greatly revived since his reign. A ship in want of supplies will find Makallah the best port on the coast for procuring them: the water is good, but it requires watchfulness here as well as elsewhere on this coast to obtain it pure; there is none in the town; it is brought from a distance of 1½ miles, and furnishes a means of subsistence for many of the poorer class.

The anchorage in the bay is good, from 8 to 10 fathoms, sandy bottom, with the flag-staff on the Governor's house bearing N.N.E., from ¼ to ½ mile offshore. A rock with only 1½ fathom water lies 700 yards due W. of the extreme S.W. point of the town, and must be carefully avoided.

Ras Fartak, that point from which coasting vessels had turned for nearly two thousand years, the monsoon filling sails as their prows pointed to India, Captain Haines describes as a lofty mountain, about 2500 feet high, forming a very prominent cape, visible to the navigators sixty miles off on a clear day.

At a distance it has the appearance of a dark-looking island, but on a near approach is found to be connected, by hills of much less elevation, with the range of high mountains surrounding the extensive bay of Fartak. I had no opportunity of going up to the summit of this promontory, or of permitting those under my command to do so, which I regret, as many fabulous tales are told of its productions. We saw with our glasses, however, on the western side, nearly as high as the summit, a very large grove of trees growing in a circle, the centre of which was apparently barren. The trees were tempting indeed to an observer accustomed to nothing but barren and naked ranges of hills and hillocks of sand, mile after mile; and this mountain, like an oasis in the desert, was doubly pleasing from its being the only green spot visible. What it could have been we were unable to conjecture, but the natives say that there are ruins in its vicinity; and this may be another relic yet remaining to point out the power of the Himyari kings when trade, under their rule, flourished in these seas.

Passing Ras Risut, the *Palinurus* reached the coast of Dhofar and landed an officer to examine the inland range. The report here briefly describes a district so different from the rest of the peninsula that it has given rise to enthusiastic records and legends from the most ancient times.

The soil of the district or province of Dhafar . . . is abundantly luxuriant, well irrigated by mountain streams, enabling the inhabitants to employ their industry in cultivation if they choose, and abundantly repaying the farmer for his labour. Still, though nature has been thus bountiful, the people are extremely indolent, generally contenting themselves with what the soil yields spontaneously, in preference to improving the crops by tillage. In some parts which I shall hereafter mention the little labour they have bestowed on cultivating the ground has amply repaid them, and has, in fact, been one means of making them more industrious.

On the lofty mountain range of Subhan, 4000 feet high, which runs parallel with the coast at a distance of about 16 miles, and has a luxuriant *tehamah*, or belt of low land between it and the sea, the soil is good, wild clover growing in abundance and affording pasture for cows and immense flocks of sheep and goats, while in many places the trees are so thick that they offer a welcome shade impervious to the scorching rays of the sun. Mr Smith, an officer of the vessel which I commanded, was deputed by me to examine the whole of the Subhan range. He traversed it entirely in perfect safety, and, under the name of Ahmed, became a great favourite with the mountaineers. He was everywhere hospitably entertained by them, and they would not even permit him to drink water from the numerous clear mountain streams that were meandering in every direction. "No," they said, "do not return, Ahmed, and say we gave you water while our children drank nothing but milk." In every instance they gave him the warmest place at the fire, and invariably appointed some one to attend to his wants. They even extended their generosity so far as to offer him a wife, and some sheep, if he would only stay and reside among them. On Mr Smith's expressing a wish to see some of the numerous wild animals whose footsteps were everywhere visible over their park-like mountains they immediately dispatched a party, who returned with a splendid specimen of an ibex, a civet-cat, and a very fine ounce. He himself saw plenty of smaller game such as antelopes, hares, foxes, guinea-fowl, and partridges.

These hospitable mountaineers are handsome, well made, active men, and always well armed, their weapons being the same as those used by the Mahrahs. They are of the Gharrah tribe. Their women are handsome, and much fairer than any seen on the coast. I have seen as many as 200 at a time, who came down to barter their cattle, butter, and gums for dates, at Morbat. Curiosity induced me to ask them how they accounted for being so fair; and their reply was that it was owing to their drinking nothing but milk from their childhood; little dreaming that they were indebted to the renovating breezes and temperate climate of their native hills, on the summit of which in February the thermometer ranged from 49° to 72° Fahrenheit. . . . The plants found by Mr Smith in the Subhan mountains were the same as those in the more elevated parts of Sokotrah; dragon's blood, frankincense, and aloes were seen in abundance.

Haines gave the first modern account of the district where the Wadi Hadhramaut, the main *wadi* of the whole vast district, reaches the sea. He learned that the valley was large and extensive, and formed at that time the main communication between the seaport towns and the interior. Saihut, on the sea, was a dilapidated town in the territory of the Mahra Bedouin, with a population that varied from three and four hundred to two thousand according to the trade and season. Its thirty large and small vessels were engaged in the grain trade along the coast, and smaller boats were occupied in shark-fishing. Fins and tails were dried, sold at Mokalla or Muscat, and were exported to Bombay for China. The interior trade was by camel to Terim (eight days), Shibam (eight days), Duwan (twelve days), and Kasim (eight days). His information was not gained by personal exploration, and much of it was faulty. For instance, Kabr Hud was much farther from the sea than he thought, and the valley was less well watered by running streams and contained fewer settlements.

Ten years later the *Palinurus* was again off Dhofar, under the command of Captain J. P. Saunders. The Bedouin of the interior were now apparently much less friendly. Parties landed for survey work were either fired on or warned off by a bristling array of matchlocks pointing from behind every rock. On one occasion the Bedouin allowed a landing only when Saunders threatened to sink every craft belonging to their tribe along the coast. Assistant-Surgeon H. T. Carter went ashore to inspect ruins, including the ancient harbour of Khor Rori, later inspected by Bent, and once visited a Bedouin sheikh, by whom he was hospitably received, despite the forebodings of the coast villagers. The settled people of Dhofar were terrorized by the nomads, and Carter thought that if peace could be but established the incense trade might be revived and some prosperity regained. This doctor of the *Palinurus* was one of the first to be interested in the frankincense-trees of Southern Arabia.

Such men broke the trails for more famous travellers, but their reports are neglected to-day and their names forgotten. Few, like Wellsted, ever achieved even a passing fame.

Wellsted was a pioneer of exploration, not only in Oman, but in this more mysterious land of Hadhramaut. In the company of Lieutenant Cruttenden, of the *Palinurus*, he had made a short journey of about forty miles from the south coast near Ras el Aseida to the ruins of Nakab el Hajar. The two Englishmen were rewarded by the view of an ancient city with high walls, ten feet thick, constructed of grey marble and flanked by tall square towers. They saw, too, an oblong temple in ruins and discovered one of the first Himyaritic inscriptions. Although this incursion was but brief, and undertaken in the face of local exclusiveness and suspicion, it inspired Wellsted with the ambition to explore South Arabia more widely. He resolved to reach the reputedly populous main valley of the Wadi Hadhramaut. He began the exploration of Oman only when an Egyptian defeat closed the route which he had decided to follow from Asir. After his expedition to Nakab Wellsted could never again prevail upon the coastal chiefs to open the way inland.

The name of Hadhramaut is found in Genesis as Hazarmaveth, and among the Greeks as Adramytta. Its ruins, such as those found in the Wadi Duwan, indicate a very ancient, rich, and advanced civilization. There is something analogous between this district and the north-west corner of Africa, which was called by the Arabs, by reason of its surrounding deserts and mountains, "the Isle of the West." Hadhramaut merited its similar appellation in reference to the Arabian peninsula, for it is enclosed on the north by the sand desert of the Rub' al Khali, to the east by the Mahra Desert, and on the west, towards Yemen, but only in part, by sterile tracts and barren mountains. Its position therefore encouraged exclusiveness, and the xenophobia, easily aroused by foreigners, was intensified by the fact that from the most ancient times the inhabitants considered their country well worth the conquering, for it produced frankincense and myrrh, transported even greater quantities of those products from Dhofar to Yemen and the north, and traded in all the goods of the East through its ocean shore.

Niebuhr had learned some of the characteristics of this land, and Fulgence Fresnel, the French consul at Jidda, a learned Arabist and one of the first students of Himyaritic inscriptions, had ascertained some particulars regarding the Wadi Duwan and the distances between the coast and the inland settlements. When explorers first began to enter Hadhramaut in the nineteenth century the chief elements of the population were, firstly, the Bedouin, who engaged in the carrying trade, reared camels, and roamed very large tracts of the land. The richer among them had houses; the poorer often dwelled in caves. The Arabs proper, as distinct from the ancient indigenous population, lived mostly in and round the towns and villages, and some were wealthy from the trade with India and the Straits Settlements. The third constituent, and the most hostile to explorers where all were exclusive, was provided by the Seyyids, descendants of the Prophet by his grandson Hussein, and the Sherifs, who together formed an aristocratic hierarchy with great influence based on the possession of large estates and numerous slaves, but mainly on religious fanaticism. The Seyyids of Hadhramaut claimed the purest pedigree of all, were regarded with devoted respect, and settled disputes over such matters as property and water rights. Though their influence was against foreign intrusion, they represented a force making for law and order in a dangerous land. The lowest elements in the population consisted of the slaves, some of whom had been freed and were settled on the land.

The most powerful dynasty of Hadhramaut in the nineteenth century was that of the Kaiti, a wealthy family with commercial interests reaching to India, where they owned considerable property. Mokalla and Shibam lay within their rule. In Eastern Hadhramaut power was exercised by the Kathiri, with their cities of Terim and Seyun, and this dynasty was more rapacious and more hostile to foreigners. In both territories, however, the early explorers faced considerable risks, for, despite the country's open seaboard, facing the ocean between two great continents, the outsider remained wholly unwelcome.

The main valley of the region, termed in general the Wadi Hadhramaut, runs northward and then westward for about four hundred miles, curving through the interior, and is separated from the Arabian Sea by a high plateau cut by many *wadis*, some tributary, and others running to the ocean. These valleys have numerous springs and wells which supply water in the dry season, and the fertile districts produce millet, wheat, dates, indigo, and tobacco. Frankincense and myrrh grow still in the *wadis* and on the mountain slopes, even in the desert regions of Mahra, but the trade now has not even a dim shadow of its ancient greatness, nor had it in the nineteenth century. When Aden was annexed to British India in 1839 the Indian-Red Sea trade revived to the benefit of Southern as well as Western Arabia. The arrival of the British, however, while opening improved trade relations, only served to increase the fear of foreign conquest among the Hadhramaut coastal chiefs. Further suspicion was aroused by the advent of the persistently curious *Palinurus*, and it was no simple matter for a stranger to make his way into the old incense country.

Yet in 1843 Adolf von Wrede, a Bavarian soldier who had lived for some time in Egypt, carried out a truly courageous exploration, penetrating from the sea to the edge of the Great Southern Desert.

II

Leaving Aden on June 22, he sailed for Osuram, and then proceeded by land to Mokalla. To avoid the ready suspicions of the coast he set out for the interior without delay, disguised as a Moslem on pilgrimage to the shrine of Nabi Hud, near Terim. With an escort of fifteen Bedouin he travelled in a general north-west direction, crossing steep slopes and deep narrow passes, through granitic hills about 2000 feet high, on whose sides he noted many hot springs. Though the country was largely uncultivated there was a fair amount of vegetation, plants, and trees. The last were most welcome in the narrow windless valleys where the temperature from 10 A.M. to 4 P.M.

touched 150°–160° Fahrenheit. After the first two or three days the route passed through many villages, and on the fourth day von Wrede ascended Mount Sidara, about 4000 feet. This height was clothed with aromatic plants, and from its summit he saw two other peaks, Khareibe and Farjalat, like colossal pillars rising a further 800 feet. Iron-sandstone now seemed to cover the granite of the higher country over which the party were marching. The thermometer fell and the nights were cold. On the fifth day out the party skirted Jebel Zahura. They were now at 8000 feet, travelling over a fine, hard, yellow sandstone, with a view to the west and north-west of a vast yellowish plain dotted with conical hills and ridges, while to the south a tangle of dark granitic cones stretched to the misty edge of the ocean. Then the plateau levelled out, and to right and left many *wadis* cut their way through narrow defiles carrying rain-water to the lower levels. There were a few stunted acacias, food for the camels, and cisterns every few miles, but there were no villages on this high plateau, and the temperature in the daytime never rose above 80° Fahrenheit. At night the thermometer sank to 50°. After a nine days' journey von Wrede came suddenly upon the Wadi Duwan :

> The sudden appearance of the Wadi Doan took me by surprise and impressed me much with the grandeur of the scene. The ravine, 500 feet wide and 600 feet in depth, is enclosed between perpendicular rocks, the *débris* of which forms in one part a slope reaching to half their height. On this slope towns and villages rise contiguously in the form of an amphitheatre; while below the date-grounds, covered with a forest of trees, the river, about 20 feet broad, and enclosed by high and walled embankments, is seen first winding through fields laid out in terraces, then pursuing its course in the open plain, irrigated by small canals branching from it. From the description you will, I trust, form a correct idea of the Wadi Doan, of the extent, situation, and character of which travellers have given such contradictory statements.
> My first view of the valley disclosed to me four towns and four villages within the space of an hour's distance. The road that leads down into the *wadi* is a very dangerous one, particularly in its upper part; on the right, in some places, are precipices from 300 to 400 feet in depth, while a rocky wall on the left nearly stops up the road, leaving it scarcely 4 feet in breadth; and to add to the difficulty it is paved with pebblestones, which, having been

constantly trodden by men and animals, have become as smooth as a looking-glass. No kind of parapet or railing whatever has been constructed to prevent accidents.

At Khuraiba he was well received by the sheikh of the district, and was able to make an expedition to the south-west, copied a Himyaritic inscription in the Wadi Ubne, and endeavoured to reach Nakab el Hajar. He was stopped six miles from that place by a band of Bedouin, and was forced to return to the Wadi Duwan. However, he noted the Wadi Hajar, containing immense forests of date-trees, and returned to Khuraiba after an absence of twenty days.

His next excursion was to the north-west, where he reached the Wadi Amd after two days of difficult travel, and found it similar to the Wadi Duwan in its form and settlements. He followed it to the junction with Wadi Duwan, at Haura, and then bore to the west again across a high tableland beyond which in four days he reached Shabwa, on the Wadi Rasha. This valley was not so populous as the two others and was partly filled with sand. Here he ascertained that he was but a day's journey from the desert of El Ahkaf, really the South-western Rub' al Khali, where of old an entire army, lost on the march, was said to have perished.

Von Wrede reached the borders of the desert in a six-hour journey from Shabwa, and found it to be about 1000 feet below the level of the high land. He had been told that the desert was full of "white spots," in which anything which happened to fall would sink and perish. The view over the great unknown Southern Desert struck him with melancholy and astonishment:

> Conceive an immense sandy plain strewn with numberless undulating hills, which gave it the appearance of a moving sea. Not a single bird interrupts with its note the calm of death, which rests upon this tomb of the Sabæan army. I clearly perceived three spots of dazzling whiteness, the position and distance of which I measured geometrically. "That is Bahr es Saffi," said my guide to me; "ghosts inhabit those precipices, and have covered with treacherous sand the treasures which are committed to their care; every one who approaches near them is carried down; therefore do not go." I, of course, paid no attention to their warnings, but requested to be led to those spots in accord-

HAJAREIN

Reservoirs for water may be seen in the foreground.

From "The Southern Gates of Arabia," by Freya Stark, by permission of the author

WADI HADHRAMAUT, LOOKING NORTH-EAST OF TERIM

ance with the agreement I had made with my Bedouins. It took my camels full 2 hours' walk before we reached the foot of the high plateau, where we halted at sunset in the vicinity of two enormous rocky blocks. On the following morning I summoned the Bedouins to accompany me to the places alluded to above, but they were not to be induced; and the dread of ghosts had obtained such complete mastery over them that they scarcely ventured to speak; I was therefore determined to go alone, and, taking with me a plummet of $\frac{1}{2}$ a kilo's weight and a cord of 60 fathoms, I started on my perilous march. In 36 minutes I reached, during a complete lull of the wind, the northern and nearest spot, which is about 30 minutes long and 26 minutes broad, and which towards the middle takes by degrees a sloping form of 6 feet in depth, probably from the action of the wind. With the greatest caution I approached the border to examine the sand, which I found almost an impalpable powder; I then threw the plumb-line as far as possible; it sank instantly, the velocity diminishing, and in 5 minutes the end of the cord had disappeared in the all-devouring tomb. I will not hazard an opinion of my own, but refer the phenomenon to the learned, who may be able to explain it, and restrict myself to having related the facts.

A four days' march from Shabwa saw him back at Khuraiba, whence after a short rest among friends he resolved to set out for Kabr Hud, the shrine of the Prophet Hud, a place which he believed to be of historical and geological interest. Two of the Khuraiban chief's sons and another companion travelled with him, and in two days they arrived at Sif, where a great crowd was assembled to celebrate the feast of a revered sheikh who was buried in the neighbourhood. Sif marked the end of von Wrede's exploration.

As soon as I had arrived among the crowd they all at once fell upon me, dragged me from my camel, and disarmed me; using me very roughly, they tied my hands behind my back and carried me, with my face covered with blood and dust, before the reigning Sultan, Mohammed Abdalla ibn ben Issa Achmudi. The whole of my captors raised a horrible cry and declared me to be an English spy exploring the country, and demanded my instantly being put to death. The Sultan being afraid of the Bedouins, on whom he, like all Sultans of the *wadi*, is dependent, was about to give orders for my execution, when my guides and protectors came in haste and quieted the Bedouins' minds by means of the moral influence they had over them. In the meantime I remained confined to my room with my feet in fetters. I was imprisoned for 3 days, but provided with every necessary; on the evening of the third day my protectors came to me with the news that they had pacified the Bedouins under the condition that I was to return to Makalla, and that I should give up all my writings. At night I concealed as many of my papers as I could, and delivered only those which were written in pencil, with which they were contented. After my notes were given up the Sultan wished to see my luggage, from which he selected for himself whatever pleased him. The next morning I set out on my return to Makalla, which town I reached on the 8th of September, after a journey of 12 days, and thence took a boat for Aden.

Von Wrede gave a brief report of his journey to Captain Haines, of the *Palinurus*, who communicated it to the Royal Geographical Society in 1844. But the exploit was soon called in question by Humboldt, who met von Wrede in Westphalia and doubted his account of the Bahr es Safi. Von Wrede was accused of sensationalism, and many people were inclined to treat the story of the whole expedition as more or less fictitious. Fresnel and Arnaud (the latter had travelled in Yemen, studying Sabæan ruins, inscriptions and the dam at Marib) supported him, while the great Prussian geographer Karl Ritter estimated the results of the expedition as a great addition to knowledge. The Royal Geographical Society report was, in fact, enough in itself to determine the character of east Central Hadhramaut, although von Wrede had not reached the lower, eastern waters of the Wadi Hadhramaut proper, containing the larger towns of Shibam, Terim, and Seyun. In 1870 Baron von Maltzan issued von Wrede's full journal, with a map, notes, and a copy of the inscription from the Wadi Ubne. In addition to the material of the earlier report there was added in this publication much new data relating to various adventures during the expedition, recent history, and Bedouin customs. In von Maltzan's editing the passage concerning the Bahr es Safi remained unaltered. Minor evidence existed in support of von Wrede's report; and this full account left no doubt as to the authenticity or the value of his expedition in the unveiling of Arabia. Almost fifty years were to pass before his bold feat was rivalled, though in the meantime there was one more visit to the secret land.

In 1870 Captain S. B. Miles, who had cultivated good relations with inland sheikhs at Aden, travelled from the coast up the Wadi Meifa, and reached a divide leading towards the Wadi Nisab. He was not enthusiastically received in the larger settlements such as Habban and Hauta, but learned that a practicable route existed from Nisab and Harib to the Jauf of Yemen.

III

Twenty years later the growth of British influence on the coast, due to the command of the seas between Arabia, India, and Java, enabled two further expeditions to be undertaken. Pressure could be applied to the Kaiti governors of Mokalla, but not too strongly, for behind them lay the resistance of the Seyyids, who were still highly sensitive to the introduction of external influence into their country. Despite the resistance of this class, with all its financial and religious influence, the British at Aden in 1892 supported an expedition led by Leo Hirsch, a profound Arabist and Himyarite scholar. Landing at Sheher, Hirsch marched for the interior along the line previously followed by von Wrede, up the Wadi Duwan to Sif and Haura. He found numerous ruins, though not always those described by von Wrede, and passed through rich groves and good pasture. Allowed to proceed farther, to Shibam, he was thus the first European to reach the main Hadhramaut valley. Travelling eastward, he next saw the mosques and great gardens of Seyun, the many-storied castles of the rulers, and the market of Terim. At this point, however, the jealousy of the Seyyids became pronounced, there was a moment of danger from the fanatical inhabitants, and he was forced to turn back to the coast, which he reached by the Wadis Bir Ali and Adim.

Later in the same year James Theodore Bent, much against the wishes of the British at Aden, entered the interior from Mokalla. Hirsch the British could support because of his Arabic learning and the absolute certainty that he could be relied upon to behave with tact. To them, despite his splendid work as a traveller and archæologist in other fields, Bent in Arabia was a less certain quantity. For one thing, he was not an experienced Arabist, and even one so well equipped as Hirsch had failed to leave the waters of fanaticism unruffled.

But Aden could at least find consolation in the fact that Bent was accompanied by Imam Sherif, Khan Bahadur, an Indian surveyor provided with adequate instruments, who might be expected to bring back some useful knowledge. The Indian did in fact produce a valuable survey of the country.

Hirsch had been mainly concerned with collecting inscriptions and archæological evidence of ancient life. Bent's purpose was more general, and he produced the first information of the southern interior to be read keenly by a public not principally interested in ancient history or geography. Whereas most Arabian explorers had adopted some form of disguise, Bent travelled quite openly as a foreigner, and considered that this frankness gave him greater freedom to remain longer, and to see more, than his predecessors. He was accompanied by a considerable party, including his wife, who was the expedition's photographer, and Mr William Lunt, a botanist.

Their first excursion led along the coast from Mokalla almost to Saihut. The most prominent feature of the coast was the numerous hot springs. Some of these fertilized a large tobacco-growing area, and much land that would have been waste was brought into cultivation by the conducting of the hot streams by underground channels in various directions. The fishing villages of the coast sold their catch to the Bedouin of the mountains, as food for themselves and their camels. Fish oil was also produced in these villages, and trade was carried on by native craft with Aden, Muscat, Bombay, and the Somali coast. The Bents searched for ruins of ancient civilization, but found none along the coast. "There are no Addite ruins here but in the Hadhramaut," said the Bedouin guide.

The Bents next travelled the high plateau separating the coast from the main Hadhramaut valley. Ascending the Wadi Huwera by a fatiguing four days' march, they passed over a high rocky slope until they reached the vast flat tableland, dry and lifeless, the only water being rain preserved in tanks along the paths. The first halt on this plateau was at Haibalgabrain, at an elevation of 4150 feet. There was no vegetation, but only a sandy soil, sandstone, and limestone scattered over with small black basaltic stones. In the gullies they found a certain amount of vegetation, forms of mimosa- and frankincense- and myrrh-trees. The Bedouin of this plateau did not themselves gather the produce of the trees, but rented districts to Somalis who collected it. It seemed to Bent that the decline of the trade in frankincense and myrrh had done much to ruin the country, and had contributed to the gradual silting up of the Hadhramaut and collateral *wadis*.

Although Hadhramaut was engaged in the frankincense trade, the Qara country of Dhofar was probably always the main source of supply from the peninsula, and to-day only in that region is frankincense a commercial crop in South Arabia. The tribes of Dhofar, Bertram Thomas tells us, do not even remember the Hadhramaut and Yemen as a great source of incense. To-day there are along the coast ten frankincense ports, including Risut, Salala, Taka, Mirbat, and Rakiyut.

The frankincense-tree has a very short trunk, the branches beginning near the ground; the leaves are small, and the bark is ash-coloured. The collectors make incisions in the branches, and a green, transparent, sweet-smelling gum exudes, and hardens into the resinous drops known as frank-incense, or *leban*. In some days these drops are large enough to be collected, and the cuts can be deepened. This process can be repeated for five months, and the tree is then given a rest for a period varying from six months to two years. As the craft of Dhofar do not put to sea during the south-west monsoon, the *leban*, collected in the summer or late spring, has until winter to dry well.

Marching northward, Bent's party next crossed the heads of many of the collateral *wadis* of the main Hadhramaut valley, and noticed a curious feature of most of them—a rapid descent that made it appear as if they had been taken out of the high plateau "like slices out of a cake." There was little slope in these valleys, the heads being nearly of uniform height, with the main gully between walls of rock approaching 1000 feet in height. Bent suggested that these valleys were formed originally by sea action, and that the Hadhramaut had once been a large fiord, or arm of the sea. Water was always found by sinking wells in the sand which had silted up the valleys. The steep, reddish sandstone cliffs which formed the walls of the *wadi* he described as divided almost always into three distinct stratifications, of which the uppermost was very abrupt, the second slightly projecting and more broken, and the third formed by the deposit from above. The entry into a *wadi* was made by paths along which camels could only just make their way.

To look down into a highly cultivated *wadi* was like seeing a new world, after the arid coastline and barren plateau. In the Wadi Aisa, for instance, were palm-groves and lines of villages, and before descending into it by a difficult path the travellers looked back in farewell to the austere country they had crossed. In the *wadi* Bent was astonished to see four-storied houses and fortresses, with antlers of antelope stuck on the four corners, for they had come to regard the Hadrami Arabs they had met previously as little better than naked savages. These men of the *wadi* were, of course, the more prosperous of the inhabitants.

The Bedouin of the Hadhramaut he describes as small, thin, and wiry, naked save for a loincloth, and with long matted hair tied up behind the head with a leathern band. They were armed with old matchlocks and daggers, and decorated their arms and legs with ornaments of brass and iron. Their conversion to Islam was nominal, and the pious Arabs regarded them as heathen, for they rarely said prayers, performed ablutions, or fasted; yet they had their own religious secrets which they were reluctant to communicate to strangers. The richer Bedouin possessed houses, but the poorer lived in caves or any kind of temporary shelter from the burning sun, and the black tent of Northern Arabia was not seen. Their subsistence was based mainly on a carrying trade, for which they reared camels.

At Katan Bent was well received by the Governor of Shibam, who envied him the possession of a wife who could do other things than paint herself with turmeric and antimony and live listlessly among the squabbles of the harem. Katan was a pleasant place, surrounded by acres of palm-groves. Many of the houses in Hadhramaut towns, he wrote, were exceedingly high, reaching sometimes to eleven stories. Built of sun-dried brick, decorated with chevrons, zigzag patterns, turrets,

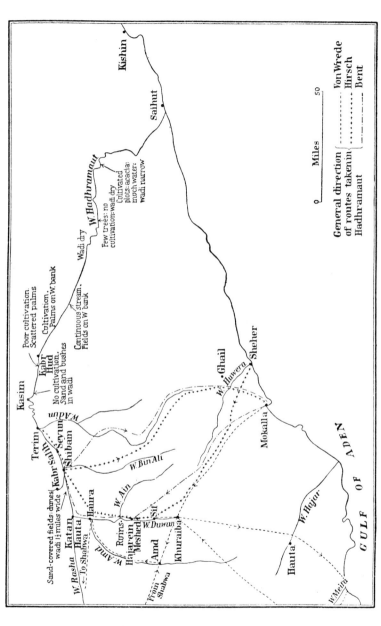

THE PROVINCE OF HADHRAMAUT, SHOWING EXPLORERS' ROUTES

Notes on the character of the main *wadi* were made by R.A.F. reconnaissance in 1929. The above map is based on this and on "Asia," Sheet 44, Geographical Section, General Staff, No. 2957.

machicolations, and buttresses, they had quite a medieval appearance. Flocks and herds were kept in courtyards and stabled at night. The first floor was used for storage, the second by servants, the third by guests, and the others by the harem and the family. Bent noticed particularly the excellence of the wood-carvings on beams, cupboards, round the unglazed windows, on domestic utensils, and on the walls. Each story had its *mussack*, or skin of water, hung in a draught for coolness, and each its bathroom, with a large jar of water and a smaller receptacle for throwing the water over the body. Drainage was by long wooden pipes into the yard below; and only the dry climate and sandy soil provided some security against disease. The greater houses, of sultans and leading men, were very imposing and, seen through the palm-groves which surrounded them, formed a delightful picture.

The accounts of travellers who followed more than a generation later will show how little changed were these Hadhramaut towns in essentials. Among the archæological features observed by the Bents in this district were the ruins of an extensive Himyaritic town in the Wadi Aisa; Hajarein, built on a hill in the centre of a continuation of the Wadi Duwan; and the remains of a very considerable Himyaritic town near Meshed. Here the ruins could be traced for two miles, and plainly showed the destruction which had occurred amid the old settlements of the frankincense country. Lofty square buildings stood up here and there, but the town around them was engulfed in sand. Bent believed that this site was the "Toani" mentioned by Pliny, a town from which the adjacent Wadi Duwan, or Doan, had taken its name. On an excursion up the Wadi Ser he found a few small Arab villages, and beyond that only a Bedouin population. The valley showed increasing masses of sand along its course. The Bedouin informed him that until quite recently a caravan route across the desert had started from the mouth of this *wadi*, but had been abandoned owing to lack of water. A Himyaritic inscription in the neighbourhood contained a central word "Masabam," or caravan station. It was obviously a landmark, and Bent considered that the spot probably indicated one long stage from Shibam towards the desert, on the old frankincense road or on a branch of it.

Bent's party also visited the shrine of Kabr Salih, which was venerated in Hadhramaut equally with the Kabr Hud, which von Wrede had failed to reach. The Bedouin were reluctant to guide them, and when eventually they did so, under threat of being reported to the Governor at Katan, there was little to see except a long pile of stones with a collection of fossils from the neighbouring mountains arranged along the top. The tomb was situated under a cliff in a desolate wilderness. The buried saint, said the Bedouin guides, was the father of Hud; he was a huge giant and created camels out of the rock; he still worked miracles, for if one even unwittingly removed a stone from the grave it caused the possessor much discomfort until it was returned. The Bents were allowed to approach within a few yards of the tomb, and when they attempted to go closer the Bedouin in charge of the shrine became so angry and ferocious that they feared arousing more fanaticism, and left the place at once. The shrine is in the Wadi Ser.

The Bents had hoped to travel east of Terim, to the shrine of Hud, but the Kathiri Seyyids east of Shibam showed clearly that they would not admit the infidel. The party therefore returned to the coast, by the Wadis Bir Ali and Adim, a long and tedious journey which revealed other Himyaritic ruins and more fertile land rich in palm-groves.

The Wadi Adim straggled tortuously to the south, and left little plateau to be crossed before the sea came in sight. Moreover, it differed from the other *wadis* of Hadhramaut in that it sloped gradually to the head, and did not end suddenly with steep precipices. Bent noted the famed honey of this region, made from palm-flowers, and possessing a delicious scented taste, and recalled that centuries before Pliny had remarked upon the flocks, herds, and honey of the district.

In the Wadi Adim a small tribal war was being waged. The expedition was fired at several times, but came out of the mountains and reached the coast safely in March.

Bent intended to make his next venture into Hadhramaut overland from Muscat, but was prevented by disturbed conditions beyond Oman, and journeyed instead by pilgrim steamer to the coast of Dhofar. This district was nominally under Muscat, but was actually ruled by the efficient Wali

Suleiman, who had been sent at the request of the inhabitants to protect them against the Bedouin tribes of Qara. With a handful of Arabs Suleiman defeated the Bedouin, built a castle at Hafa, and when Bent visited Dhofar was planning to make himself independent under British protection.

The seaboard of Dhofar from Mirbat to Ras Risut, which Bent travelled, consisted of an alluvial coastal plain never more than nine miles wide, with plenty of water and crops of tobacco, Indian corn, various grains, plantain, mulberries, papya, melons, and many fruits and vegetables. In fact, Bent regarded the coast and the highlands rising to 3000 feet behind it as forming one large oasis closed on the north and east by desert, and on the west by arid hills and sand-choked valleys, typical of the Hadhramaut. The Qara mountains were full of water, forming here and there small lakes, and were covered to the summits with rich vegetation. The whole district was in marked contrast to the rest of Arabia. There were, however, no ports for large modern vessels along this rich coast, though dhows could run for shelter in the north-east monsoon at Mirbat and in the south-west monsoon at Risut. The rest of the coastline was open to the rolling breakers of the Indian Ocean, as Bent discovered when he landed his party at Hafa, in small hide-covered boats specially constructed for riding the surf. He was later to find evidence of more secure anchorage in ancient times. At Balad, near Hafa, there were signs of a former tiny harbour and the remains of a town, encircled by a moat still full of water. There were also the ruins of old Sabæan temples, the architecture of which definitely identified them with similar ruins in Yemen and Abyssinia.

Wali Suleiman called in various Qara sheikhs to act as guides on Bent's expedition into the mountains. They were the wildest men the explorer had ever had to deal with, friendly for the most part, but of very independent spirit. Once away from the coast they ignored the orders of the soldier escort provided by Suleiman, and responded only to the lure of Bent's medicine chest, developing a great passion for quinine and pills. They were ready at the slightest provocation to fly into wild, incoherent rages. Small, active men, like the Hadhramaut Bedouin, they lived chiefly in caves and under trees. Their camels were ill trained and as wild as their masters.

At the end of December 1894 Bent set out from Hafa and ended his first day's march near Ras Risut. Here a large tract of country was covered with frankincense-trees, with bright green leaves like the ash, small green flowers and insignificant fruit. Bent was interested as an archæologist and historian in the old staple trade of the district, and found that the best qualities of incense came from this area and from two places on the inner slopes of the Qara range. West of Dhofar it was too inferior to be marketable and was not collected. The best quality was called *leban lakt*, the second *leban resimi*, and the annual export of about 9000 hundredweight was sent to Bombay. Collection was in March, April, and May, for during the rains the Qara mountain tracks were impassable. The stem of the tree was cut and the gum collected after seven days; thus gum could be brought in three or four times a month. The trees belonged to the families of the Qara tribe, and each was marked and known to its owner. The Indian merchants came for it to Dhofar just before the monsoon.

After several days spent among small gorges which ran from the sea towards abrupt walls of rock inland, and which were occupied by Bedouin living in caves among a rich vegetation of trees, ferns, and reeds, they entered the mountains by the Wadi Ghersid, a contrast to the Hadhramaut valleys in its tropical vegetation, fig-trees, limes, cactus, aloe, and mimosa. Ghersid contained a beautiful lake, well stocked with duck and other water-birds. "Such a scene as this," Bent wrote, "we never expected to witness in Arabia." He recalled passages in the ancient writings of Greece and Rome where Arabia was called "sweet-smelling," and considered that accounts of such happy lands were probably borne westward by merchants who came to Dhofar in search of frankincense.

Passing up the Wadi Ghersid they travelled through dense woods where sweet-scented white jessamine hung in garlands from the trees and the air was fragrant with flowers. The grey rocks and the hillsides were clad with trees. After passing through the narrow head of a valley they reached the highest point of the range and marched for two days along the crest.

At one point a tremendous hurricane fell upon them, blowing out of the north for two days and nights, with such force that they could hardly stand erect. It was accompanied by cold which especially attacked the Bedouin, who were completely dispirited and lay inertly round wood fires. From this point, however, Bent could take good observations. To the north the range gradually sloped downward, vegetation became sparser and thinned out to yellow desert, which stretched as far as vision could reach, and ended in a straight blue line, like a sea horizon. To the east and west, beyond this small enclave of fertile coastal territory, there was nothing but desert.

Bent descended to the lowlands by the Wadi Nahiz, and then followed the plain from Rizat to Taka, where he rediscovered a place visited fifty years before by Carter, Assistant Surgeon of the *Palinurus*. This was the estuary of a *wadi* forming quite a large lake, called Khor Rori, which was divided from the sea by a narrow sand bar. Around the lake were ruins of ancient buildings, and on what appeared to be a headland connected to the shore by a neck of sand were an ancient wall and fortifications, called Khatiya. Inland the lake dwindled to a stream which lost itself in the rocky bed of a torrent coming down the valley. Four or five miles up this valley Bent reached higher ground, and pitched his camp "at the foot of one of the most stupendous natural phenomena" he had ever seen. The valley leading down to the sea had been filled up throughout the course of ages by a calcareous deposit which had collected on either side of an isolated hill about 1000 feet in height, in the middle of the valley. The deposit had taken the form of a straight precipitous wall, 550 feet high and three-quarters of a mile long on the eastern side of the hill, and 300 feet high and a quarter of a mile long on the western side. Although it was the dry season, feathery waterfalls slid over these steep walls. Long white stalactites hung over the white and grey precipices, Huge plantains, daturas, and enormous castor-oil plants flourished below.

In the next few days Bent climbed the hill and reached the top of the abyss, where he found a grassy plain, perfectly flat and used for grazing by the Qara. Walking farther inland for a mile in the shade of large trees, he discovered a long narrow lake which fed the channels of water running over the abysses. The banks of this lake were covered with fig-trees, mimosa, and a fine convolvulus with large pink flowers. Wild duck, heron, and water-hens lived in the bulrushes. Beyond the lake, which extended about two miles, the feeder stream issued from a narrow gorge, and could be traced for about two days' journey inland. The abysses, the lake, and the flat valley impressed the Bents as the most weird and fascinating spot

DHOFAR, SHOWING BENT'S ROUTE

they had visited in any of their wanderings. Bent believed that the ancient town and harbour was the old frankincense port known to the Greeks as "Abyssapolis" or "Moscha." Bertram Thomas, who followed Bent in this district a generation later, was in agreement on this point, and appreciated with his forerunner the beauty of the abysses.

From Dhofar the Bents hoped to travel through the Mahra country westward of the Wadi Hadhramaut, but passage was forbidden, and they sailed instead, by Arab dhow, along the precipitous coast to Fartak, and then past a lower coast to Kishin, where Bent asked the Mahra ruler to provide escort up the Hadhramaut valley.

"No one goes up that way," was the reply; "it is full of robbers." The ruler himself, Bent considered, was only the head of a gang of thieves, and his people were probably regretful at seeing likely plunder allowed to depart. At Sheher Bent again met with refusal when he asked for safe conduct into the Eastern Hadhramaut. Here he wanted to visit the tomb of the prophet Hud, extensive ruins which were said to exist in the Wadi Museila, and a volcano which was alleged to emit large columns of smoke from a mountain-side in Wadi Barahut.

Hundreds of botanical specimens were brought back from these two expeditions, the most notable being those of frankincense, myrrh, and wild cotton, though none of them were novel. Forskal's botanical work in Yemen had been carried on a hundred years later by Deflers, a French resident of Egypt, and in the nineties Schweinfurth estimated the known plants of that corner of the peninsula as numbering fifteen hundred, three-quarters of them being also common to Abyssinia. Schweinfurth collected in Eritrea too half the specimens met previously in Arabia. By the middle nineties the British had garnered some two hundred specimens in the Aden district. Bent, however, was the first to return from the main Hadhramaut valley with flora that showed identity or similarity with the vegetation of Abyssinia and Somaliland.

He is less famed than some other explorers and archæologists, perhaps because he was less specialized. The Levant, South Arabia, and Abyssinia, where he was a pioneer of Ethiopian studies, did not mark the limits of his field, for in Mashonaland he was the first to make a detailed examination of the great Zimbabwe ruins, and though his theory as to their Semitic origin was not accepted, the value of his work was unquestioned.

After so many years of varied travel it was during another expedition to Southern Arabia that he contracted the malaria which led to his death in 1897, at the age of forty-five. The story of these Arabian expeditions, and others in Socotra and the Sudan, were published by his wife, the able helpmate of his journeys.

Bent did not fail to notice the influence of India upon Hadhramaut life, and instanced, among many common objects of Indian origin, furniture, arms, and jewellery. In the Hadhramaut valley, he wrote, there was absolutely no source of wealth, yet there were many fine palaces; the money which built them was not made in the Hadhramaut, but came from the widespread property in the commercial centres of India owned by the Kaiti rulers and other rich families. He found it peculiar that with such overseas interests they should so resent the appearance of foreigners in their land. He apparently did not realize that just this experience of India, where foreign rule predominated, explained at least in part their xenophobia.

This desire to keep Hadhramaut for the Hadrami was shared by the lower classes. The country could not support a large population, but emigrants to other lands sent home money to sustain their families, and sooner or later returned themselves. The main emigrant stream in the nineteenth century flowed to the Dutch East Indies, and it is curious that the best treatise on Hadhramaut, a minute and accurate description, was published in 1885 by one who had never personally visited the country—namely, L. W. C. van den Berg, an Arabic scholar living four thousand miles away, in Java. The accuracy of his account, based almost entirely on the results of questioning Hadrami emigrants, was proved by Bent and every subsequent traveller. The native of Hadhramaut evidently developed expansiveness in ratio to his distance from home.

CHAPTER XIII

THE FIRST TRANS-ARABIAN JOURNEYS

The soil of Negd suits various modes of life, and though properly a pasture-land, it is spotted over with oases which admit of cultivation and fixed abodes; it was therefore here, in the centre of the peninsula, that the two elements of Arab life, the agricultural and the pastoral, most naturally blended together and modified each other.

GEORGE AUGUSTUS WALLIN, *Journal of the Royal Geographical Society*, 1854

IN Burckhardt's time European geographers knew little of the northern inland area of Arabia, which had given birth to Wahhabism. The medieval Moslem writers, on the whole, provided little information, but the *Jihan Numa* of Hajji Khalfah, a seventeenth-century Turkish work, which was not issued in Latin until 1818, and was probably unknown to Niebuhr, gave more information. In this book Nejd was divided into four sections, proceeding from south to north. The first was a desert area, bounded by a line of oases, such as Jabrin, Dawasir, and Nejran. This was called "Nejd al Yemen." The next was "Nejd al Ared," marked by frequent *wadis*, and the third consisted of Lower Kasim. The fourth was the hill district of Shammar. The Turkish geographer mentions Dariya and Riyadh, and had an accurate idea of all the principal villages and their products. Burckhardt knew the *Jihan Numa*, and had questioned many pilgrims and merchants, so that he was able to give a good description of Northern Nejd, Kasim, Sedeir, Hasa, Dariya, and a near estimate of the width of the Nefud. He could learn less of Central and Southern Nejd because the Wahhabis in his time were a barrier to Hejazi travellers. From the Gulf coast, however, a Frenchman named Reinaud, living at Kuweit, had been sent on a mission to the Wahhabi Emir by the British Resident at Basra in 1799. Travelling by Katif and Hofuf, he reached Dariya in fifteen days, but returned with only slight information, mostly concerning the character of the Wahhabis and the scenery on his route.

Thus for the first two decades of the nineteenth century there was little knowledge of the physical geography of Central Arabia. Burckhardt believed that the region afforded a splendid field for exploration, and hoped that the Egyptian advance inland would help to reveal new facts. It was some years before his hope was realized, and even then the Egyptian advance was only indirectly responsible for the first exploration of this area. Ibrahim Pasha had overrun Central Arabia by 1819, but was already evacuating the land, leaving it once more to Bedouin tribal war and feud.

Now for many years the British administration in India had desired to establish a more efficient influence in the Persian Gulf, and especially to suppress the piracy which constantly interfered with pearling and general commerce. A beginning had been made, for the East India Company had been, since the end of the eighteenth century, in alliance with the rulers of Oman, and in 1810 a British-Indian expedition had crushed the Jawasimi pirates. In Ibrahim the British now saw a useful ally, one who already had proved his will for law and order by harrying the pirates of Ras el Kheima in the Gulf. British India considered it most probable that Mohammed Ali would make Ibrahim's conquests in Nejd and Hasa into Egyptian dependencies, and that under Egyptian rule there would be co-operation for the safety of trade.

It was such views that in the summer of 1819 sent a British warship from Bombay, carrying a special envoy, Captain George Forster Sadlier, of the 47th Regiment, with instructions to congratulate Ibrahim on the reduction of Dariya, and "to concert the necessary arrangements with his Excellency with a view to the complete reduction of the Wahhabee power." Sadlier was, moreover, instructed that if his Excellency so desired, he could have the co-operation of a military and naval force for the capture of Ras el Kheima, but he was not to promise Ibrahim the possession of such conquests as should be made. He was merely to sound his Excellency as to his intentions, and was also to question the ruler of Muscat as to the assistance he would be prepared to give.

At Muscat Sadlier discovered that there was no intention of giving any assistance whatever, and when he proceeded northward to Katif he learned that Ibrahim's evacuation of Central Arabia was beginning. Nobody knew his Excellency's whereabouts; he was on the move—out of Nejd!

If Sadlier had definitely known that Ibrahim was already on his way to the Hejaz there is little doubt that he would have returned to India at once, but he did not know what was happening in Nejd with any certainty, and considered that at least he should deliver the sword of honour that was to accompany the message of congratulation. He might even be able to obey that part of his orders which pertained to sounding his Excellency as to his intentions. Sadlier did not look forward to the journey inland; he knew nothing of Arabia or of the Arabs, and was not even mildly interested in them. Arabs to him were 'natives,' like the Indians to whom he was accustomed, not very pleasant people and of no consequence.

Yet, despite his distaste, and disadvantages in equipment for such a journey, he went into Arabia, recorded with diligence and honesty the things he saw or could learn, and attained two measures of fame. Sadlier was the first Englishman to explore Arabia and the first European to cross the peninsula from one side to the other.

Starting at the end of June 1819, he reached Hofuf in a fortnight, experiencing on the way considerable trouble from his Arab companions, "turbulent barbarians," who did not act as natives should towards a *sahib*. He has little to say regarding Hofuf, and of the Hasa merely notes that it had pools and springs but no river. He then joined an Egyptian force which was on the point of marching to Sedeir, and, though new to the situation, he could see at once that the Egyptians might still be in the field, but that the Bedouin were regaining control of the country, locally at least.

On July 21 the column with six hundred camels moved off to the wells of Rema, and the English soldier's eye noted that the destruction of these wells and others could close Nejd on the east. Through Yemama they marched to Manfuha, where he saw cotton, durra, wheat, and barley in the fields and large date-groves. Some of the contemporary maps placed a river in this area, but Sadlier reported that there was no perennial river, but merely torrents swollen by winter rains. He remarked the general direction of the Ared mountain ranges, took a careful compass course of his routes, and endeavoured to estimate the distances between places.

Passing Riyadh, he came to the ruins of Dariya, and everywhere saw the devastation wrought by Ibrahim—the wastes, the dejection of the people, and the lowered morality. It was no wonder that Ibrahim's Bedouin allies had become enemies, and that some had even abandoned all show of allegiance. On his journey Sadlier conscientiously noted the crops, commodities, water, and the general state of the districts encountered. Proceeding down the Wadi Hanifa for four days, he next came to Shakra, in Weshm, an oasis with plentiful good water and rich date plantations. Hence, after seizing the beasts of the Bedouin camel-men who had accompanied them, the Egyptians moved on to Aneiza, and Sadlier had penetrated to the centre of Arabia. He was an explorer against his will, but he considered it mere duty to garner what knowledge he could, so that now he made inquiries, and recorded what he could discover, about the distribution of Bedouin tribes in the area, before hastening on to Rass, where he expected to find the Pasha. When he arrived there he found the main body of the Egyptian army—but his Excellency had moved on to Medina!

At this Sadlier's patience gave out. He had suffered all the friction arising from his ignorance of the language and of Arabic ideas and customs; he had borne inconvenience and the hardships of Arabian travel (save perhaps lack of water, for in that summer heavy rains fell), and had forced his way almost across a continent. He now resolved to abandon the pursuit of Ibrahim and tried to arrange for transport to Basra. But the Egyptian commander in Rass would not take the responsibility of sending him through unsettled, angry, and hostile country. Perforce he had to continue his journey, with a large detachment of the retiring Egyptian garrison. Medina was reached in nine days, but he was not allowed to enter the city. He was sent instead to Bir Ali, where he met Scoto, an Italian doctor who had served in the campaign.

At last, after two long months, Sadlier met Ibrahim, at the beginning of September. The Egyptian took the attitude of "one soldier to another," said that he was merely acting under his father, and that his father was likewise simply the agent of Stamboul. In short, he could not discuss affairs with the representative of the Government of Bombay. Sadlier learned nothing of any Egyptian plans that may have existed, and was 'passed on' to Yenbo, with his Excellency's harem. In this last stage of his journey he saw the Damascus pilgrim caravan arrive; but the revered city of Medina he saw only from the outside. On September 20 he reached the Red Sea, having traversed the entire peninsula from east to west.

Unfortunately, the land which he had entered so unwillingly insisted on holding him yet longer within its grasp. He went by boat to Jidda, met Ibrahim again, quarrelled with him, and was held up for four months at the port, before finally escaping from his unpleasant surroundings in January 1820.

In 1821 a report of his journey was read to the Literary Society of Bombay—but not by Sadlier, who had been sent on another mission, to Sind! His full story was not produced from the Bombay Government records until 1866, when Palgrave had revived interest in Nejd.

It may be added that after Sadlier had disappeared into Arabia for some two months the East India Company most optimistically sent their military expedition to Katif. It was then discovered that his Excellency and his army had taken their departure, with Sadlier on their trail, and after the troops had suffered terribly from dysentery they were re-embarked for India.

Other Europeans, a Frenchman and a Pole, seem to have made short journeys into Nejd, but hardly anything was known of the first, and nothing of the second. Sadlier had carried a good compass, took frequent readings, registered the names of settlements, and listed the times occupied on the march, allowing for varying speeds. From his data it was possible to make a rough map of his itinerary. At least longitudinal distances between points in Central Arabia could be approximately fixed.

Three years after Sadlier's journey Félix Mengin published his *Histoire de l'Égypte sous le gouvernement de Mohammed-Aly*, to which was appended an essay on Nejd by the notable geographer Jomard. The facts discovered by Sadlier had proved of more use to this writer than all that he had been able to discover from other sources, for Jomard, like other geographers and explorers, found it easier to gain knowledge of a people's social life than to get an accurate picture of physical features. He described what he had been able to learn of peasant and Bedouin life in Southern Nejd, cultivation, trade, and the condition of society in the period of the Egyptian

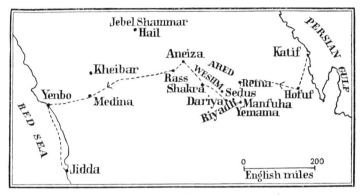

SADLIER'S ROUTE

invasion. Faulty as it was, especially in its latitudinal estimates of positions, Jomard's essay was the only generally accessible source of information for many years. Like Sadlier's travels, however, it dealt solely with Southern Nejd.

The Egyptians returned to Central Arabia, when Dariya was reborn in Riyadh. Troops entered the country in 1824 and 1836, but any Westerners who accompanied them have left no accounts.

II

Captain Sadlier, who may have been an unwilling martyr to duty, but was not lacking in soldierly and political common sense, had realized in 1819 that the Egyptian mastery of the situation in Nejd was essentially impermanent, and in the event, five years after the execution of Abdulla at Constantinople, the Wahhabi state was restored by his son Turki, who acknowledged the suzerainty of Egypt and paid tribute. A dozen years later Abdulla's son Feisal refused this payment, whereupon Egyptian forces again entered Nejd and took him prisoner to Cairo. Then, when the land after six years was once more free of Egyptian garrisons, Feisal succeeded in returning and in establishing himself as ruler in much of Eastern and Southern Arabia, excluding Oman, Yemen, and Bahrein. Until 1867 he continued to strengthen his position and consolidate the territory.

Meanwhile Abdulla Ibn Rashid, Governor of Hail, a town which had taken the place of Feid or Kafar as the principal Shammar centre, and was situated on the main trade route across Arabia, made himself independent and secure in this territory, mainly by his understanding and tactful administration of the great Shammar tribe of Bedouin. He was intrepid, manly, just, benevolent to the poor, and adhered closely to his promises. In 1843 his son Talal fortified Hail and extended his dominions over Taima, Jauf, and Kheibar. At the same time he avoided quarrels with his southern neighbour at Riyadh and kept in touch with the Turks and Egyptians, lest at some future date he might require assistance. He was succeeded by a brother, who was murdered by his nephews, one of whom, Bandar, became Emir. The new ruler intended to slay Mohammed, a younger son of Abdulla Ibn Rashid; but he was forestalled and was himself murdered, together with other members of the family, and Mohammed established himself as Emir of Hail.

To return to Riyadh, quarrels had broken out between Saud and Abdulla, the sons of Feisal. Their struggles left Hail the supreme power in Nejd. In the inevitable war between the older and the rising power Riyadh was joined by Zamil, Emir of Aneiza, the Ataiba and Mutair, but was defeated by Mohammed Ibn Rashid, who was supported by the Shammar and Harb, in 1891 at the battle of Mulaida. Zamil was killed; Aneiza, Bereida, and Riyadh were conquered, and until his death in 1897 Mohammed was supreme in the land. During these disturbances the Turks in 1875 occupied Hasa.

This brief outline of events in the north of the peninsula may serve as a background to the next group of explorations, which deal with the exploration of north Central Arabia.

The pioneer in this area was George Augustus Wallin, a Finno-Swede, who gained a travelling scholarship at Helsingfors University, and at once planned a visit to the Wahhabi country, intending to make Southern Nejd and then Yemen, with its Himyaritic inscriptions his main objectives. But he was a poor man, existing solely on his scholarship, the grants from his university, and money sent him by friends, and this was never sufficient to prevent the limitation of his travels.[1] He lived for seven years in the East, in Persia, Iraq, Syria, and Egypt; he made far voyages on Arab vessels; in Cairo he undertook long and profound studies in order to pass as a Mohammedan in Arabia; and he lived entirely as a native among the middle- and lower-class Arabs, meeting no Europeans except occasionally officials of the Russian consulate, from whom he drew his remittances.

Of this time in the East some eighteen months were spent in Arabia, which he entered from the north on the advice of Fulgence Fresnel, who thought that a traveller entering direct from Egypt would be at once suspect. Wallin was one of the most efficient European observers who ever travelled in the peninsula, could pass as a native of the East without raising suspicion, and seems to have been able to make notes of everything he saw, either at the time or immediately afterwards. His only instruments, however (though they were not inadequate by contemporary standards), were a watch, a compass, and a thermometer.

Although no European had penetrated the territory, the name of Shammar was known as that of brave and hardy Bedouin who inhabited the country of "the Two Mountains." Niebuhr had heard of some of their settlements. Seetzen had sent a scout towards their land. Burckhardt ascertained that the Shammar formed an independent group, which escorted the Mesopotamian pilgrims but raided the Syrians. Sprenger identified Ptolemy's "Aine" with Hail or Feid, and "Salma" with Selma. In the eighteenth century, however, tribal wars

---

[1] Hogarth, without stating his authority, wrote that Wallin travelled as an emissary of Mohammed Ali of Egypt. There is probably no sound basis for this idea. Hogarth had not read the Swedish sources for Wallin's career, which to-day are still untranslated. The suggestion is resented by Wallin's compatriots, who are intensely proud of him.

had frequently closed the Central Arabian routes, where in ancient times caravans had passed between Gerra, Petra, Saba, and Babylon. The Shammar were perhaps best known from their acceptance of the Wahhabi creed in the time of Saud.

Leaving Cairo on April 12, 1845, Wallin marched by Suez across the desert to the Wadis Gurandel and Araba, reaching Maan on the 30th. Thence he traversed the stony Hamad to the Wadi Sirhan, which he touched on the south at Weisit (May 22), and two days later came to Jauf. Here he stayed some weeks before proceeding across the Nefud to Jubba (September 5) and Kena (19th), to arrive at Hail on September 20.

During this itinerary he gives much information regarding the Arab tribes of the Howeitat, Sherarat, and others, the relations between the settled townsfolk and the Bedouin at Maan, conjecture and hearsay evidence regarding the character and extent of the Sirhan, and an exhaustive account of Jauf—its situation in a circular rocky valley, its sooks, cultivation, relations with the Bedouin, its origin and history. Though lacking scientific instruments he was careful to give the exact marching time between wells and settlements and noted the general direction of *wadis* and highland districts.

The second stage of his journey led from Jauf to Shakik, where there were wells in a hard, saline soil, the only water between Jauf and Nejd. Of the Nefud, across which he travelled mostly by night, he remarked only briefly the rolling hills and valleys of loose sand. Here he travelled generally south-south-east on a track that was sometimes obliterated entirely with sand. At Shakik there was adequate pasturage for camel herds of the Rualla, Shammar, and Sherarat, but they had left the district two days before Wallin's arrival, because of decreasing water in the wells. The Nefud land, on the whole, he considered one of the richest pasture grounds in Arabia, but for want of wells and sources it could be visited by the Bedouin only in the spring, when the rain gathered in ponds and pools. The centre of the Nefud, however, was so dry that it was seldom used by the nomads. A similar dry area he passed between Shakik and Jubba. To illustrate Wallin's manner one might quote his account of Jubba, only a small settlement, but thoroughly described. Moreover, it illustrates the fluid relationship between settled and nomad which he later stressed as characteristic of the Shammar region. At Jubba he stayed a fortnight before making the last short stage to Hail.

Gubbe is situated on an extensive open plain of an elliptical form, and that hard stony soil, which generally in this land distinguishes a place where water is to be found. This plain is surrounded by a ridge of very low sandstone hills, above which rises to the W.N.W. the higher mountain of Musliman, and to the E.S.E., right opposite, another somewhat lower peak, called Alghawta. The distance between these two peaks is about 10 English miles; but the length of the plain in the other direction from N. to S. is a little more. The hills, which border the plain on the southern side, are very low, and, covered with sand as they partly are, they can hardly be distinguished from the sand-hills of the contiguous Nufood; but those on the northern side are higher. Near to Musliman northward there rises another smaller peak, called 'Eneize. The village is built on the northern part of the plain, at a distance of about one mile from Musliman, and consists of five divisions or sooks—*viz.*, Altureif, Alselal, Alhamale, Alkilab, and Almug'a'alat, of which the last-mentioned is separated from the others, and extends to the S. on the plain. The four others are placed in a row from E. to W. The houses are constructed of sun-burnt clay bricks, almost the only building materials used in the desert, but they are generally larger and more comfortable than those of Algawf [Jauf], also of a somewhat different architecture, the larger of them presenting a front somewhat resembling in form the propylæa of the old Egyptian temples. Almost every house has its orchard joined to it, or it is sometimes erected in the centre of it, not as in Algawf, where the plantations are all separated from the town. Each orchard has its own well, from which the water is raised for irrigation by aid of camels; they are cultivated with great care and laid out with taste, and both the well and the roofed path which the animal takes when drawing up the skin-bucket with its contents, are overhung with vines. Besides palms (which, however, do not produce here such excellent dates as those of Algawf and Teima), and the other fruit-trees common to these countries, we now meet with a new tree, a species of pine, called athal, which more rarely occurs in the northern parts of Arabia, and then only wild, but which is frequently cultivated by the inhabitants of Negd on account of its wood, which they exclusively use in building. There is no spring of running water in the whole place, but a great abundance of wells, though all of them are very deep and contain a hard and somewhat brackish water. The number of families

233

amounts to about 170, all belonging to the tribe of Armál, regarded as one of the noblest and greatest of the Shammar race. Their character differs somewhat from that of the people in the parts whence I came, and their features present another type than the Syrian. They are of a sicklier complexion and of a weaker constitution, and diseases of various kinds are common in their village. This may in part be ascribed to the inferior quality of the dates, which constitute the principal food of the people here, as in all Negd, and the brackishness of the water. Their mode of living is quite the same as that of the nomadic Bedawies, excepting that they dwell in fixed abodes and houses. Most of them possess great herds of camels, which they either give in charge to their Bedawy brothers, or send out with their own herdsmen on the pasture grounds in the neighbourhood of their own village. The situation of their village and their own numbers protect them not only from attacks of enemies, but also from almost all dissensions with the nomad sheikhs; and they themselves make continual predatory expeditions against Sherarat and other tribes in the northern part of the Nufood land. Upon pretext of a holy war against infidels, who neither pay the Zaka tax, nor observe other precepts commanded in Alkur'an, they regard it as their duty as true Unitarians to harass and persecute with incessant plunder and pilfering all tribes who do not profess the Wahhaby creed, until they have forced them to enter in alliance with Shammar, by consenting to pay their chief the Zaka, and to pledge him their allegiance. During this summer parties of about 100 men had five different times made predatory excursions from this village against Sherarat, and collected a booty of upwards of 2000 camels. The village is seldom visited by pedlars and those wayfaring traders who so often are met with in the villages along the pilgrim routes and in larger towns of the desert. During my sojourn here there was, however, one trader from Almedina, who complained of doing but slight business. The inhabitants get their clothes and other necessaries generally from Hail, and the small supplies of rice which they want are brought to them from Irak, by their Bedawy allies. Wheat, millet, and oats they cultivate themselves, and the produce is generally more than sufficient for their wants.[1]

Wallin visited Mount Musliman, and found many inscriptions on its sides and on the huge stones which lay around its foot. Some of them were evidently made by Bedouin children, to pass the time while tending herds, but others dated from a remoter period. The most common figures were those of camels, horses, sometimes mounted by a warrior armed with

[1] In the *Journal of the Royal Geographical Society*, 1854.

a javelin, dogs, sheep, and wild animals. One represented a small cart on four very low wheels, drawn by two camels. The north-east side of Musliman contained a wall showing many characters worked in the brittle sandstone and difficult to make out.

On the way to Hail, shortly after he had passed through the Nefud again, and left the small village of Kena behind, the sand quite suddenly ended, giving way to a "hard, perfectly flat ground, covered with a slender substratum of coarse, granitic gravel." He now entered the real centre of Jebel Shammar, marked by the ranges Aga and Selma, abounding in wells and springs, palms and cornfields. Wallin was the first to give an account of these mountains, of their character, general situation, waters, wells, irrigation methods, and cultivation. He came at a happy time, for Abdulla's reign had brought peace to the land, so that the inhabitants said that one could go through their territory from one end to the other, bearing gold on one's head, without being troubled with any questions. Feisal in the south was respected, but Abdulla had greater prestige throughout Nejd, and through him and his family the Shammar were held superior by all the Bedouin and settled peoples in the neighbourhood. The house of Rashid had become wealthy by the tax imposed on conquered tribes and villages, but Abdulla ruled the land more by his virtues, the finest attributes of the Bedouin, bravery and unblemished honour. Talal was widely respected, but it was Abdulla who had established order out of anarchy.

The Shammar are . . . a very enterprising people, and show a greater propensity for trade and warlike expeditions. Contrary to the inhabitants of other desert villages, the townspeople of Shammar are regarded as superior to their Bedawy brothers in courage and in the art of using arms; and it is doubtlessly more to them than to the nomads that the sheikh family of Ibnu Alrashid owe the victories they have gained over all their neighbours. When the chief intends making an expedition against another tribe, the people of the villages are first individually summoned, and often more or less forced to engage in the enterprise, every one on his own camel or horse, and with provisions and ammunition of his own for so long a time as the expedition is reckoned to last; and these always constitute the main force of the army. A general summons is then issued to the nomads to assemble at a certain place and a fixed time, in order to partake in the expedition; and, although they generally come in great numbers, their time not being taken up by other occupations, they are regarded only as auxiliaries, and but little depended upon in the action. When the expedition is finished, every partaker in it is paid according to the decision of the chief, either in money or by a share of the booty . . . the inhabitants, however, complain that their chiefs, in this, as in many other cases, set aside both the prescripts of the Kuran and the old customs of the nation. . . . But even in peaceful enterprises the townspeople take the preference over the Bedawies. In the yearly *karawan*, which takes the Mesopotamian, and, to a certain extent, also the Persian, pilgrims from Mesh-hed Aly to Mekka, and, after performance of their religious duties, brings them back the same way, the leader himself is a member of the sheikh family, and most of the conductors belong to the townspeople of Shammar, whereas the number of Bedawies, following the *karawan*, is very small. On the other hand, it is in many respects the interest of the townspeople to keep friends with their nomadic kinsmen. For the various enterprises in which they continually engage they want a great quantity of camels; and as it is nearly impossible to keep these animals in villages so poor as those in the desert, they are obliged to give them in charge to the nomads during the time they can dispense with them. As, however, the camel is the only animal they use for the irrigation of their fields, they must always, according to the extent of their plantations, keep one or more of them at home; but after every three months, which is the term the animal can stand that wearisome labour, they exchange it for a fresh one. The poorer of the villagers, who cannot afford to buy on their own account the camels they stand in need of for irrigation, hire them for the term of three months from the Bedawies, who are paid for this, and for the charge they take of other animals delivered to them in order to be pastured with their own herds, either with ready money or (and which is more usual) with dates and corn, when harvest-time comes. Thus continual intercourse and the most intimate relations, grounded upon mutual interests and reciprocal assistance, are kept alive betwixt the two classes of Shammar, which has greatly contributed to the increasing power of that tribe. I regard the Shammar as unquestionably one of the most vigorous and youthful tribes at present in Arabia, and their power and influence extend yearly more and more over their neighbours. . . .

The soil of Negd suits various modes of life, and though properly a pasture-land, it is spotted over with oases which admit of cultivation and fixed abodes; it was therefore here, in the centre of the peninsula, that the two elements of Arab life, the agricultural and the pastoral, most naturally blended together and modified each other. . . .

In consequence of the close and intimate relations, before adverted to, which connect the two classes of the Shammar, we find the villagers, to a certain degree, still clinging to the customs and manners of nomadic life, while the Bedawies, on the other hand, apply themselves to avocations, which are generally regarded as not becoming. A great many of the former wander during the spring with their horses and their herds of camel and sheep to the desert, where they live, for a longer or shorter time, under tents as nomads, and most of the Bedawy families possess palm plantations and cornfields in the mountains of Aga and Selma, which they cultivate on their own account. . . .

Hail is probably one of the latest founded villages in the land, owing its origin principally to its being the birthplace of the present and preceding sheikh family. . . . It is situated in a flat low valley . . . at the eastern end of which there runs a spring of tepid and brackish water, the only one in the whole village. Around this spring the first clay huts seem to have been built, and there are still extensive ruins of houses of a later date to be seen; but at present this spring has been deserted, and the inhabitants have by degrees moved higher up towards the West, where, on the vast plain of Albatin, the subterranean water-rills offer a greater number of wells. The first and principal thing a new settler must think of is obviously water for irrigation, and as soon as this is found and the well is dug there rises around it an orchard of palms and other fruit-trees, in the centre of which the houses are gradually built with the same materials as those commonly used in the desert—*viz.*, sun-baked bricks of smaller size, and not so bulky as those moulded by the Syrians; and trunks of palms or the pine-tree, athal, for the doors and the ridges of the roof, which is always flat. Most of the houses consist of two stories, with large and commodious, though but very few, rooms, in which the light is admitted only through the door and small apertures made in the walls immediately below the ceiling. Every house, without exception, has a coffee-room, which stands separated from the other buildings, facing the orchard or in the centre of it, and it is here that guests are received and the men assemble for conversation and business. The whole piece of ground belonging to a house is enclosed by a wall; but the extensive area which the villages generally occupy makes such an enclosure impossible for most of them. The residence of Ibnu Alrashid is distinguished from other houses by nothing but its largeness and extent, which the accommodation of his own ample household and the numerous guests which the chief entertains throughout the year make necessary. Every stranger arriving here without relations or friends to put up with dismounts at the palace of the chief, where he may be sure of being received and entertained as long a space of time as he chooses to stop. The travellers make their camels kneel down in an open, large courtyard, called Manakh, which is surrounded by small buildings and rooms, or rather pens, not unlike those in a Persian *karawanserai*. In these rooms, the larger coffee-hall, and in the mosque, the strangers are lodged for the night, whilst the meaner guests make shift with the ground of the open courtyard to sleep upon, in company with the camels. Around the walls of the buildings encircling the courtyard sofas or benches, made of clay, are placed, upon which the chief holds his court of justice twice every day, in the morning and in the afternoon. The village contains a great many open places and markets, where meat, vegetables, and other victuals are sold, contrary to the rule in Algawf and the villages of the northern desert, where to expose food publicly for sale is regarded as ignominious. The streets are broad and commodious, though never paved, and in the principal one of them, called Lubde, there is a score of open shops kept chiefly by wandering tradesmen from Irak, Almedina, or Alkasim. Hail is now considered to contain about 210 houses and as many families; but if it continue to extend in the same manner as it does at present, it will soon join another small village with a population of 10 families called Alwuseita, which stands at a distance of about three-quarters of an hour from Hail, on the plain nearer to the foot of Aga.

At Hail Wallin remained quietly for two months, unnoticed, as he desired to be. His lack of money and the unrest in the country to the south prevented his visiting Riyadh. He came out of Arabia after making the pilgrimage to Medina and Mecca from Hail, a hurried march in the company of Persian pilgrims. Eighty-five hours' fast camel journey brought them to Medina, mostly over plain, until the chain of Aga disappeared on the right after one and a half days. Then he reached limestone ridges and the granite passes of Hejaz. In the records which he published in English he tells us little of the rites and ceremonies of Medina and Mecca, except for a full description of the excursion to Arafat, for he was ill, rather an unwilling passenger on the pilgrimage, and was anxious to leave the country.

Wallin's account of his visit to the Shammar did not reach English readers until nearly a decade after the journey was made, and even then it was brief and overweighted with learning. Helsingfors was more fortunate than the Royal Geographical Society, to which he communicated two papers, for he had forwarded his journal in parts to the university and wrote many descriptive letters to his friends.

Although Wallin was wrong in judging the general declivity of Arabia as southerly or south-easterly, he did at least add that in his view Iraq, and especially Basra, were the lowest parts of all Asia. He said little of the Nefud, though he proved its practicability for travellers. His work, especially the part which revealed the organization and the rising power of Hail, would have been welcomed by a wide public, but it was known almost solely to geographers.

He was to place geographical knowledge further in his debt by a journey which he undertook, again to Hail, in 1848, for on this occasion his first approach lay from Muweila, in Midian, to Tebuk, a region upon which geographers had no certain information. He crossed the great granitic chains a day's journey from the Red Sea coast, and found them to form a range separate from the plateau which lay behind them running from the Hejaz to the north. Strangely enough, he did not recognize that the "level tracts of a dark stony soil broken here and there by conical or pyramidal masses of rock . . . thickly strewn with black porous stones of peculiar lightness," and those "small fragments become externally quite black," which, "from the action upon their surface, have very much the appearance of cinders," were of recent volcanic origin. Wallin's profound knowledge lay in Arabic literature, history, and manners. He knew little or nothing of geology or astronomy.

After two months' travelling from the coast on this second journey he reached Shammar land at Teima, an ancient settlement known to Europeans at that time only by name. Wallin was the first to visit the place. A month later he was at Hail, but again failed to reach Riyadh. By a series of unfortunate chances his Christianity had become known at the Wahhabi capital, perhaps through the interference of official Egypt, for whom it has been suggested by Hogarth, quite baselessly, that he was acting as political agent in the Hail territory. However, he was warned to avoid the country of Ibn Saud, and finally left Arabia, travelling north to Meshed Ali, taking a line west of the Persian-pilgrim route, as less open to raids and plundering. In his paper to the Royal Geographical Society he gives a brief description, which contains no hint of the great privations suffered, of this final journey through the north-eastern corner of the peninsula. He marched again through Nefud sands, then over harder calcareous soil and sand ridges, until he reached the northern plain, a district without a "single hill or other prominent object above the undulating level to relieve to the eye the dreary monotony of the desert scene, or serve as a landmark to the traveller on his way." He passed over lower ranges of limestone or sandstone, across a low sandy plain where travel was hastened because of empty cisterns, and reached Meshed on June 15.

Of Teima this first modern eyewitness wrote:

Teima is allowed by all the Arabs of the present day to belong to Negd, and may be regarded as one of the frontier towns on the western side of that region. . . . The population may be estimated at one hundred families, all of the tribe of Shammar. They are of two clans, the one called Aly [Ali], the other Hamde [Hamdeh]. . . . Teima stands on a mass of crystalline limestone, very slightly raised above the surrounding level. Patches of sand, which have encroached upon the rock, are the only spots which can be cultivated. The inhabitants, however, have considerable date plantations, which yield a great variety of the fruit, of which one kind, called al hulwah ("the sweet"), is esteemed the best flavoured in all Arabia. Grain is also cultivated, especially oats of a remarkably good quality, but the produce is never sufficient for the wants of the inhabitants. The greater portion of the gardens are watered from a copious well, called bit-al-haddag, in the middle of the village; but more distant plantations are irrigated from wells near them. The hydraulic contrivance by which water is raised for distribution through channels among the plantations is the same as is used throughout Mesopotamia as well as in Negd—viz., a bucket of camel-skin hung to the end of a long lever, moving upon an upright pole fixed to the ground. The revolving . . . water-wheel of Egypt, seen occasionally in the towns of the coast, is never found here. This, as well as the style of the houses, and the cultivation of the gardens, and many other peculiarities, reminded me that I had now entered Negd. In the villages on the coast the influence of Egyptian customs is very manifest . . . in the interior of the desert, as far as al-Gawf [Jauf], Syrian usages predominate. Teima shows the first indications of a different sort of civilisation, brought, as it appears

GEORGE AUGUSTUS WALLIN
From a picture in the possession of the University of Helsingfors

AN INHABITANT OF TEIMA

From "Arabian Adventure," by Douglas Carruthers, by permission of the author

to me, from Mesopotamia into the adjacent part of Arabia, and gradually adopted throughout Negd.

Wallin was well aware of the existence in this district of the rock-cut houses of Medain Salih, but was never able to visit them. It remained with him only a project, which was never accomplished.

Wallin left no other record by which English readers could judge his status as an explorer than the two papers communicated to the Royal Geographical Society, and these gave no real impression of the man and his travels. They formed simply a condensed account of geographical and historical interest, and failed even barely to indicate his profound understanding of desert and nomad life, which was greater than Burton's and incomparably more sympathetic than Palgrave's. In this understanding of the Bedouin he may, in fact, be compared rather with Doughty. In his journal and letters he gave many particulars of Arabian life, customs of travel, hospitality, desert law, the education of children, music (some of which he transcribed and published); and he revealed, to the surprise of many, such things as the Bedouin ignorance of religion and the extent of their tolerance. "I think that even a professing Christian who knew the language and was familiar with Bedouin virtues, such as hospitality and manliness, could live among them."

Wallin died in 1854, before the story even of his first journey was widely known in England and elsewhere. His narrative came too late to modify the Northern Nejd section of the best contemporary map of Arabia, compiled by Karl Ritter and printed in 1852, but in Finland Wallin is rightly appreciated as one of the world's great travellers. The geographical value of his work was undeniable, and he was almost the last man to break virgin territory in the peninsula in the nineteenth century. Two biographies reveal the real Wallin and his work, one by S. G. Elmgren, published at Helsingfors in 1865, and the other by Knut Tallqvist, which appeared in 1905. It is strange that neither has been translated into the language of the nation pre-eminent for its love of travel and adventure.

CHAPTER XIV

STRANGER THAN FICTION

Palgrave, the Impressionist, gets his effect of the daisy chain
without even attempting to show each separate flower.
R. E. CHEESMAN, *In Unknown Arabia*

ALL the readable Arabian books are in English, but Jews,
Swiss, Irishmen, and others, said T. E. Lawrence, have
conspired to help Englishmen to write them. William
Gifford Palgrave, an Englishman of Hebrew descent on his
father's side, is perhaps the most obvious illustration of this
saying, but his book was more than readable; it was the most
sensational book to come out of Arabia until Lawrence's own
Seven Pillars of Wisdom.

At the end of July 1862 there arrived at Hail two strangers
representing themselves to be Syrian doctors. They were
known as Salim Abu Mahmud al-Ays and Barakat ash-Shami,
but were, in fact, Palgrave and a Syrian native teacher named
Jurayjuray from the Jesuit college at Zahleh.

The aims which impelled Palgrave to cross Arabia, as he
did, from Syria to the Persian Gulf, are not clear. Already his
career had been varied (he had served as an officer in the
Indian Army, and had then been received into the Jesuit
Order) before he entered the field of exploration—if, indeed,
he turned explorer from any preconceived plan. It is not
wholly unlikely that when he entered Arabia he had no
intention of publishing an account of his journey. According
to himself, the object of his travels resided in

> the hope of doing something towards the permanent social good
> of these wide regions; the desire of bringing the stagnant waters
> of Eastern life into contact with the quickening stream of European
> progress; perhaps a natural curiosity to know the yet unknown;
> and the restlessness of enterprise not rare in Englishmen.

He adds, however, that the necessary funds were provided by
the Emperor of the French. It is possible that, in view of the

certainty which at that time began to mark the plans for the projected Suez Canal, Napoleon III may have desired some knowledge of the strongest Power among the people in the territory east of the Red Sea. This Jesuit of the French Syrian mission, a man deeply learned in Arabic, was an obvious choice for agent on such a reconnaissance.

The two 'doctors' set out from Syria early in 1862, and travelled by Gaza to Maan. Here Palgrave begins his book, *Narrative of a Year's Journey through Central and Eastern Arabia* (1865):

> We found ourselves at fall of night without the eastern gate of Maan, while the Arabs, our guides and fellow-travellers, filled their water-skins from a gushing source hard by the town walls, and adjusted the saddles and the burdens of their camels, in preparation for the long journey that lay before us and them. It was the evening of the 16th June, 1862; the largest stars were already visible in the deep blue depths of a cloudless sky, while the crescent moon, high to the west, shone as she shines in those heavens, and promised us assistance for some hours of our night march. We were soon mounted on our meagre long-necked beasts, "as if," according to the expression of an Arab poet, "we and our men were at mast-heads," and now we set our faces to the east. Behind us lay, in a mass of dark outline, the walls and castle of Maan, its houses and gardens, and farther back in the distance the high and barren range of the Sheraa mountains, merging into the coast-chain of Hejaz. Before and around us extended a wide and level plain, blackened over with countless pebbles of basalt and flint, except where the moonbeams gleamed white on little intervening patches of clear sand, or on yellowish streaks of withered grass, the scanty product of the winter rains, and now dried into hay. Over all a deep silence, which even our Arab companions seemed fearful of breaking; when they spoke it was in a half-whisper and in few words, while the noiseless tread of our camels sped stealthily but rapidly through the gloom, without disturbing its stillness.
>
> Some precaution was not indeed wholly out of place, for that stage of the journey on which we were now entering was anything but safe. We were bound for the Djowf, the nearest inhabited district of Central Arabia, its outlying station, in fact. Now the intervening tract offered for the most part the double danger of robbers and of thirst, of marauding bands and of the summer season.

There is no better beginning to any book on Arabia, and it may be said that Palgrave sustained the vivid style throughout his two long volumes. Burton could mention and dismiss the discomfort of the simoon wind, "the lion with flaming breath," from which, however, he was never greatly inconvenienced, though travelling in high summer. But Palgrave introduces it with drama; first the unclouded Arabian sky, the scorched desert between Maan and the Wadi Sirhan, the first abrupt, burning gusts of wind; then the increasing oppressiveness of the air, the Bedouin wrapping cloaks round their faces, and a rush for cover under a small black tent. The horizon darkens to the colour of deep violet, there comes a stifling blast like the opening of an enormous oven, and the simoon is upon them. They lie in the tent, heads wrapped and almost suffocating, while the camels are outside, prostrate on the sand like dead beasts.

> We remained thus for about ten minutes, during which a still heat like that of red-hot iron slowly passing over us was alone to be felt. Then the tent walls began again to flap in the returning gusts, and announced that the worst of the semoom had gone by. We got up, half dead with exhaustion, and unmuffled our faces. My comrades appeared more like corpses than living men, and so, I suppose, did I. However, I could not forbear, in spite of warnings, to step out and look at the camels; they were still lying flat as though they had been shot. The air was yet darkish, but before long it brightened up to its usual dazzling clearness. During the whole time that the semoom lasted the atmosphere was entirely free from sand or dust; so that I hardly know how to account for its singular obscurity.

Palgrave has been treated roughly by some writers on Arabia. The general reader, however, charmed by the easy brilliance of his style, may be tempted to suspect that judgment has perhaps been prejudiced by the somewhat bombastic and Levantine personality revealed in his writings. Such prejudice may have been intensified by the old English distrust, faintly or strongly defined, of the testimony of any Jesuit, and especially, for we are not very logical in these matters, of a Jesuit who later attacked his Order and his Church. Burton was convinced of his personal insincerity and hypocrisy.

There is, however, more in the assaults on Palgrave than dislike or prejudice. Dr G. P. Badger attacked him on geographical grounds, and so did Philby, who was infinitely better equipped for the offensive. There are, in fact, so many inaccuracies, exaggerations, and incongruities in his story that it became doubtful in the minds of some that the journey was ever made. When Palgrave narrated his adventures to the Royal Geographical Society the Fellows were "gratified and excited" (though his long paper was a much more subdued performance than his later book), and the Council showed some appreciation of his labours by conferring a testimonial; yet one has an uneasy sense of the exercise of Chinese politeness when the President described his narrative as "The Thousand and Second Arabian Night's Tale." Nobody really believed his account of an "Ideal State," sheltered behind the deserts in the heart of Arabia, rich in towns and villages, cultivation, and prosperous activity. It was too unreal and romantic, set against the sterile background of the peninsula. Was Palgrave's book a piece of marvellous imaginative writing?

Doughty, Blunt, Nolde, and others accepted his account of travel in Nejd as fully genuine, though recognizing its omissions, inaccuracy, and exaggeration, while of recent years Cheesman has definitely supported belief in his visit to the Hasa. Blunt never went south of Hail, and Nolde touched Palgrave's route but slightly, so that their testimony must be qualified, but Doughty, who did not believe that Palgrave travelled in Napoleon's interests, and who knew that he was regarded during his stay with the Lebanon Jesuits as a prig and a liar, held that he described the Nejd town-dweller to the life. Hogarth too, who had read widely on Arabia in every European language, obviously disliked the man's personality, but defended him in his *Penetration of Arabia* (1904) and at the Royal Geographical Society in 1920 and 1925, at least to the extent that his journey had been made. By the last date, however, much of the judgment and conjecture in Hogarth's splendid book had been modified by further exploration: one of the main Arabian *wadis*, for instance, had been shown to drain at right angles to the direction described by him. But it seems that at least part of his first opinion of Palgrave's journey, that it was of value in its dealing with social life in Arabia, may be sustained. Credence in the second part of his travels, through Wahhabi country, the Hasa, and Aflaj, has been rudely shocked, after sixty years, by the writings of H. St John Philby.

In reading Palgrave one may keep in mind that he was essentially a dramatic writer, intent on making a colourful story, not a work of scientific geography. On the way from Maan, for instance, he shows correctly the character of the Wadi Sirhan, a long depression running roughly from the north-west to the south-east, as a "ladder," with wells and water conveniently spaced, like steps, for merchants travelling between Syria and Jauf. His account of this section of his route, though much fuller, adds nothing of value to Wallin's, but Palgrave's Jauf is larger and more luxuriant, as though the writer were remembering it only in contrast to the wearying scenes he had passed in the hard, stony, monotonous desert. Again, after Wallin's sober relation of the facts concerning Jubba, Palgrave's account seems merely impressionistic. He remembers wild, fantastic cliffs, black, red-streaked rocks of granite (actually they were of sandstone) soaring about 700 feet into the air, an irregular village, poor soil and numerous salt and freshwater springs, sometimes only a few yards from each other. One may recall Wallin's testimony that there were no springs anywhere, but that the water from the numerous wells was hard and sometimes brackish. Then of the Nefud he gives a picture from which later travellers could hardly recognize the original. It is, to Palgrave,

> an immense ocean of loose reddish sand . . . heaped up in enormous ridges . . . undulation after undulation, each swell two or three hundred feet in average height . . . in the depths between the traveller finds himself as it were imprisoned in a suffocating sand-pit, hemmed in by burning walls on every side.

The Nefud is like a vast sea of fire, swelling under a heavy monsoon wind, ruffled by a cross-blast of little red-hot waves. Palgrave was journeying in summer. Later travellers, like the Blunts, experienced the Nefud in the cooler season, but found his description of phsyical features greatly exaggerated, especially in relation to the barrenness of the area, which Palgrave stresses. But, even allowing for his too vivid descriptions, his account of the Nefud had at least one point of value, for he was the first European to note the horseshoe pits in the sands, the origin of which intrigued later explorers and geographers. Others reached a more probable explanation of this phenomenon, but Palgrave's first view of it merits quotation:

> We paced on all day; at nightfall we found ourselves on the edge of a vast funnel-like depression, where the sand recedes on all sides to leave bare the chalky bottom strata below; here lights glimmering amid Bedouin tents in the depths of the valley invited us to try our chance of a preliminary supper before the repose of the night. We had, however, much ado to descend the cavity, so steep was the sandy slope; while its circular form and spiral marking would have reminded me of Edgar Poe's "Maelstroom," had I then been acquainted with that most authentic narrative. The Arabs to whom the watch-fires belonged were shepherds of the numerous Shomer tribe, whence the district, plain and mountain takes its name. They welcomed us to a share of their supper; and a good dish of rice, instead of insipid *samh*, or pasty *Djereeshah*, augured a certain approach to civilisation. The limestone rock, at whose edge the tents were pitched, furnishes through its clefts a copious supply of water, and hence this hollow is a common resort for Bedouins and their beasts. . . .
>
> Such cavities are not uncommon amidst the sands, and occur in a very arbitrary manner, independent, it would seem, of the general laws of the desert; nor could I hit on any passable hypothesis to explain their formation. Their great size secures them against filling up; the pit in which we passed that night could not have measured much less than a quarter of a mile at its upper diameter, from rim to rim, and its depth was certainly about eight hundred feet. The huge undulations of sand, rolling apparently from west to east, and never failing in the Nefood of Arabia, may, if a hypothesis be permitted, find their cause in the diurnal rotation of the globe, and the imperfect communication of its rapid surface movement to the loose material here strewn over it. But this affords no clue to the capricious pits dug out by nature from time to time in these very wastes, and hollowed with an exactness of circular form truly surprising. I met them alike in the Nefood and Dahna, in the northern and southern desert; the phenomenon belongs to the vast aggregation of sand, not to any particular wind, or meteorological phase of a local nature.

When Palgrave passed the Nefud and reached settled territory his villages were invariably larger than the same places in the reports of others, and to Hail he gives almost three times its probable population at that time. But this lack of true

objective vision leads sometimes to a sort of inverted judgment
—he can mention an Arab 'hamlet' of 2000 souls.

His book was intended to enthral at all costs, and, since the
surprising and unexpected are, in part, the essence of a good
story, his views of the Bedouin must have helped to this object,
for his realistic attitude towards them was in complete con-
tradiction to the commonly accepted ideas of his time. These
dated perhaps from the tradition of Saladin or from Sir Walter's
presentation, and marked the nomads with such qualities as
bravery, hospitality, and good faith. In Palgrave's view,
however, they were capable of cold-blooded treachery, and
were usually remarkable for ignorance, coarseness, extreme
licence in morals, aimlessness, and degradation, occasionally
marked by considerable innate tact and shrewdness. They
were hardly touched with Mohammedanism, and were an
example of the depths to which the nomad life could help
to bring "one of the noblest races of earth," for as such
he considered the Arabs of developed lands and organized
governments.

Lack of sympathy with the Bedouin and attraction to the
townsman were natural with Palgrave, himself very definitely
an urban type, and such bias suggests a reason for his enthusiasm
in description of settled people and social life. He tells us that
the notes he made on his journey were lost in a wreck off the
shores of Oman—and his memory for topography served him
ill. Yet he needed no notes to recall the life of Hail, and his
fluent Arabic speech enabled him to mix easily with high and
low. Here is a description of a walk through Hail, a picture
of the city centre of Palgrave's ideal state. In his character of
doctor he has been called to a patient and sets forth with a
companion, Doheym:

> As we go on to the Sook he nods and smiles to some fifty
> acquaintances, or stops a moment to interchange a few words with
> those of his own land. The market-place is more crowded from
> end to end; townsmen, villagers, Bedouins, some seated at the
> doors of the warehouses and driving a bargain with the owners
> inside, some gathered in idle groups, gossiping over the news of
> the hour. For the tongue is here what printed paper is in Europe,
> and I doubt whether an Arab loses more time in hearing and
> retailing the occurrences of the day than an Englishman every

morning over his *Times*, although the latter has at least the advantage of looking the more studious. . . .

Groups of lading and unlading camels block up the path; I look right and left; there within the shops I see one merchant laboriously summing up his accounts (I know not whether the Arabs were ever good mathematicians; certainly at present a simple reckoning of addition poses nine out of the ten); another, for want of customers, is reading in some old dog-eared manuscript of prayers, or of natural history, or of geography—such geography, where almost all the world except Arabia is filled up with "Anthropophagi and men whose heads do grow beneath their shoulders. . . ."

Mixed with the city crowd, swordsmen and gaily dressed negroes, for the negro is always a dandy when he can afford it, belonging mostly to the palace, are now going about their affairs, and claim a certain amount of deference from the vulgar cits, though we see nothing here of the Agha and Basha style of the overbearing and despotic Turk. Nor do these Government men ever dream of taking aught without purchase, or of compelling those they can lay hold of to gratuitous labour, Ottoman fashion; such proceedings, also, being repugnant to that independent highmindedness which stamps the genuine Arab caste. The welldressed chieftain and noble jostles on amid the plebeian crowd on terms of astounding familiarity, and elbows or is elbowed by the artisan and the porter; while the Court officers themselves meet with that degree of respect alone which indicates deference rather than inferiority in those who pay it. A gay and busy scene; the morning air in the streets yet retains just sufficient coolness to render tolerable the bright rays of the sun, and everywhere is that atmosphere of peace, security, and thriving unknown to the visitors of Inner Arabia, and almost or wholly unknown to the Syrian or Anatolian traveller. Should you listen to the hum of discourse around, you will never hear a curse, an imprecation, or a quarrel, but much business, repartee, and laughter. . . .

Thus we beguile a quarter of an hour's leisurely walk (it were superfluous to say that no one hurries his pace in these semitropical regions, especially in the month of August), till we reach an open space behind the palace garden, where a large and deep excavation announces the Maslakhah, or slaughter-house (literally 'skinning place') of the town butchers. In any other climate such an establishment would be an intolerable nuisance to all neighbours if thus placed within the city limits, and right in the centre of gardens and habitations. But here the dryness of the atmosphere is such that no ill-consequence follows; putrefaction being effectually anticipated by the parching influence of the air, which renders a carcass of three or four days' standing as inoffensive to the nose as a leather drum; and one may pass leisurely by a recently deceased camel on the roadside, and almost take it for a specimen prepared with arsenic and spirits for an anatomical museum. . . .

We take a very narrow and winding lane on the right, by which Doheym leads me awhile through a labyrinth of gardens, wells, and old irregular houses, till we reach a cluster of buildings and a covered gallery, conducting us through its darkness to the sunglare of a broad road, bordered by houses on either side, though a low court wall and outer door generally intervenes between them and the street itself. The arch is here unknown, and the portals are all of timber-work enclosed in brick, and equally rough and solid in construction. My guide stops before one such and knocks. "*Samm*" ("Come in") is heard from withinside, and immediately afterwards some one comes up and draws back the inner bolt. We now stand in a courtyard, where two or three small furnaces, old metal pots, and pans of various sizes, some enormously big—for the Arabs pique themselves now, like their ancestors of two thousand years since, in having cauldrons large enough to boil an entire sheep—sheets of copper, bars of iron, and similar objects, proclaim an Arab smithy. Some brawny half-naked youths covered with soot and grime come up to present a shake of their unwashed hands, while they exchange Nejdean jokes with Doheym. His elder brother So'eyd, whose gravity as head of the family has been a little ruffled by the sportiveness of his younger relatives, rebukes the juveniles, hastens to purify his own face and hands, and then introduces me to the interior of the house, where in a darkened room lies another brother, the sick man on whose behalf I have been summoned.

The *rôle* of doctor brought Palgrave into contact with several of the Court and town notables. The Emir Tallal sent his two boys to be examined. They were perfectly well, and the visit was merely a gesture intended to convey a mark of confidence, and, according to Palgrave, to establish their medical status among the townsfolk. Yet his 'practice' was evidently not wholly among the opulent. A peasant comes for advice—

a stout clown from Mogah, scantily dressed in working wear, and who has been occupied for the last half-hour in tracing sundry diagrams on the ground before him with a thick peach-tree switch, thus to pass his time till his betters shall have been served. He now edges forward, and, taking his seat in front of the door, calls my attention with an "I say, doctor." Whereon I suggest to him that, his bulky corporation not being formed of glass or any other transparent material, he has by his position entirely intercepted whatever little light my recess might enjoy. He apologizes, and shuffles an inch or two sideways. Next I enquire what ails him, not without some curiosity to hear the answer, so little does the Herculean frame before me announce disease. Whereto Do'eymis, or whatever may be his name, replies, "I say, I am all made up of pain." This statement, like many others, appears to me rather too general to be literally true. So I proceed in my interrogatory: "Does your head pain you?" "No." (I might have guessed that; these fellows never feel what our cross-Channel friends entitle *"le mal des beaux esprits."*) "Does your back ache?" "No." "Your arms?" "No." "Your legs?" "No." "Your body?" "No." "But," I conclude, "if neither your head nor your body, back, arms, or legs pain you, how can you possibly be such a composition of suffering?" "I am all made up of pain, doctor," replies he, manfully intrenching himself within his first position. The fact is that there is really something wrong with him, but he does not know how to localize his sensations. So I push forward my enquiries, till it appears that our man of Mogah has a chronic rheumatism; and on ulterior investigation, conducted with all the skill that Barakat and I can jointly muster, it comes out that three or four months before he had an attack of the disease in its acute form, accompanied by high fever, since which he has never been himself again.

This might suffice for the diagnosis, but I wish to see how he will find his way out of more intricate questions; besides, the townsmen sitting by, and equally alive to the joke with myself, whisper, "Try him again." In consequence I proceed with "What was the cause of your first illness?" "I say, doctor, its cause was God," replies the patient. "No doubt of that," say I; "all things are caused by God: but what was the particular and immediate occasion?" "Doctor, its cause was God, and, secondly, that I ate camel's flesh when I was cold," rejoins my scientific friend. "But was there nothing else?" I suggested, not quite satisfied with the lucid explanation just given. "Then, too, I drank camel's milk; but it was all, I say, from God, doctor," answers he.

Well, I consider the case, and make up my mind regarding the treatment. Next comes the grand question of payment, which must be agreed on beforehand, and rendered conditional on success, as my readers know. I enquire what he will give me on recovery. "Doctor," answers the peasant, "I will give you, do you hear? I say, I will give you a camel." But I reply that I do not want one. "I say, remember God," which being interpreted here means, "Do not be unreasonable; I will give you a fat camel; every one knows my camel; if you choose I will bring witnesses, I say." And while I persist in refusing the proffered camel he talks of butter, meal, dates, and suchlike equivalents.

There is a patient and a paymaster for you. However, all ends by his behaving reasonably enough; he follows my prescriptions with the ordinary docility, gets well, and gives me for my pains an eighteenpenny fee.

The Emir of Hail, though vaguely suspicious, was reasonable and friendly enough to grant the traveller three interviews. But in view of certain elements potentially embarrassing to Tallal, and dangerous to himself, Palgrave decided to leave the town. He departed reluctantly from a place that had pleased him; Tallal's "recommendation to set out," after the third conversation, was, however, in his position, equivalent to a command.

The Emir provided him with a safe-conduct through his territory, but this would not count greatly in the true Wahhabi country to the south. Palgrave merits the tribute of "marked courage" which Sir Percy Sykes grants him for his decision to continue his journey to the Wahhabi capital at Riyadh. He faced dangers from fanaticism and raiding war to reach the main objective of his travels.

His course to Riyadh was indirect, first to Bereida, in Kasim, eastward past Aneiza, north-east through Sedeir, and then due south by Ared, passing ruined Dariya to the capital.

Palgrave's was the first full account at first-hand of Riyadh and the Wahhabi faith, practice, and ritual. Of Wahhabism he wrote:

> How stern, yet how childish a tyranny, how fatal a kindling of burnt-out fanaticism; a new well-head to the bitter waters of Islam; how much misdirected zeal; what concentrated though ill-applied courage and perseverance!

The Puritanism which forbade with all the force of the Government such offences as absence from public prayers, or from the regular attendance five times in the mosques, smoking or chewing tobacco, wearing silk or gold, conversation, or even lights, in a house after night prayers, singing or playing on musical instruments, street games for children, and strolling in the streets after nightfall completely repelled him. Insisting on Wahhabism's unfruitful fatalism, he would admit no spirituality in it. On this point Hogarth observes:

STRANGER THAN FICTION

He would not, or could not, see that fatalism is not of the essence of a system which has prescribed prayer as the first duty of man, and formulated a code of conduct making for justification; and that the gloomy rigidity of Nejdean practice in his day was largely an accident, the outcome of grievous trials which the faithful had latterly undergone by war and pestilence, especially in the cholera visitation of 1852. All spiritual communities begin with an ascetic phase and recur to it in periods of sore temporal distress; and there is more hope of stability, religious and political, for an Arabian society at any rate, in such a zealous temper as Palgrave found in Riad than in the liberal indifferentism of Jabal Shammar. Theocracy, not the pastoral patriarchate, is the durable and dominant form of Semitic government.[1]

Palgrave's sojourn of seven weeks in Riyadh became increasingly exciting. He was watched closely by the guardians of the State religion, and was suspected of espionage by the civil Government. The Emir Feisal was near the end of his reign, and plays but a small part in the story, but Palgrave became involved in the rivalry of the heir-apparent, Abdulla, and his half-brother Saud. The latter frequently sent for Palgrave, and showed him much goodwill, possibly from the impression that he was an agent of Egypt, on which country he might be able to rely in the event of a struggle with his brother. Of Abdulla, the villain of the piece, we read that

were it not for a haughty, almost an insolent expression on his features, and a marked tendency to corpulency, 'Abd-Allah would not be an ill-looking man. As he is, he resembles in a degree certain portraits of Henry VIII, nor are the two characters wholly dissimilar.

However, the Prince sent for him, on a pretext of medical advice, and received him with "a sort of rough politeness." For some weeks Abdulla remained friendly, and the two men met daily, to talk of politics, war, and medicine. At length the Prince demanded a supply of strychnine, with which, in 'the doctor's' opinion, he intended to poison Saud. Three times he asked and was refused, until at last Palgrave, after looking round to ensure not being overheard,

lifted up the edge of his headdress, and said in his ear, "'Abd-Allah, I know well what you want the poison for, and I have no

---

[1] *The Penetration of Arabia* (London, 1904).

mind to be an accomplice to your crimes, nor to answer before God's judgement-seat for what you will have to answer for. You shall *never* have it."

Shortly afterwards Palgrave was summoned at night to Abdulla's palace. For the bold sentences whispered into the Prince's ear, as for the ensuing interview, we have only Palgrave's word. Something of the kind may possibly have happened, but it is surprising that the traveller did not attempt the more tactful attitude of saying that his supplies of strychnine were exhausted. However, it is a good story, and Palgrave makes the most of it:

The room was dark; there was no other light than that afforded by the flickering gleams of the firewood burning on the hearth. At the further end sat 'Abd-Allah, silent and gloomy; opposite to him on the other side was 'Abd-el-Lateef, the successor of the Wahhabee, and a few others, Zelators, or belonging to their party. Mahboob was seated by 'Abd-el-Lateef, and his presence was the only favourable circumstance discernible at a first glance. But he too looked unusually serious. At the other end of the long hall were a dozen armed attendants, Nejdeans or negroes.

When I entered all remained without movement or return of greeting. I saluted 'Abd-Allah, who replied in an undertone, and gave me signal to sit down at a little distance from him but on the same side of the divan. My readers may suppose that I was not at the moment ambitious of too intimate a vicinity.

After an interval of silence 'Abd-Allah turned half round towards me, and with his blackest look and a deep voice said, "I now know perfectly well what you are; you are no doctors, you are Christians, spies, and revolutionists (*mufsideen*) come hither to ruin our religion and state in behalf of those who sent you. The penalty of such as you is death, that you know, and I am determined to inflict it without delay."

"Threatened folks live long," thought I, and had no difficulty in showing the calm which I really felt. So, looking him coolly in the face, I replied, "*Istaghfir Allah*" (literally, "Ask pardon of God"). This is the phrase commonly addressed to one who has said something extremely out of place.

The answer was unexpected; he started, and said, "Why so?"

"Because," I rejoined, "you have just now uttered a sheer absurdity. 'Christians,' be it so; but 'spies,' 'revolutionists,'— as if we were not known by everybody in your town for quiet doctors, neither more nor less! And then to talk about putting me to death! You cannot, and you dare not."

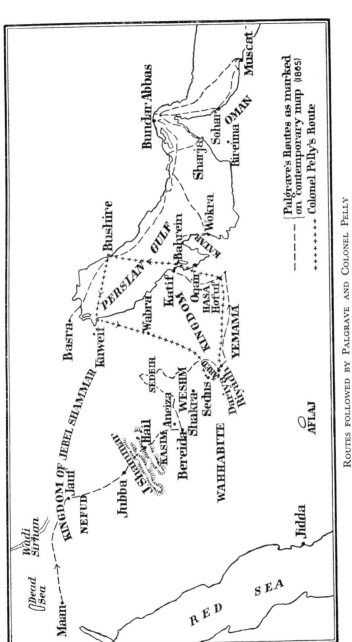

ROUTES FOLLOWED BY PALGRAVE AND COLONEL PELLY

"But I can and dare," answered 'Abd-Allah; "and who shall prevent me? You shall soon learn that to your cost."

"Neither can nor dare," repeated I. "We are here your father's guests and yours for a month and more, known as such, received as such. What have we done to justify a breach of the laws of hospitality in Nejed? It is impossible for you to do what you say," continued I, thinking the while that it was a great deal too possible after all; "the obloquy of the deed would be too much for you."

He remained a moment thoughtful, then said, "As if any one need know who did it. I have the means, and can dispose of you without talk or rumour. Those who are at my bidding can take a suitable time and place for that, without my name being ever mentioned in the affair."

The advantage was now evidently on my side. I followed it up, and said with a quiet laugh, "Neither is that within your power. Am I not known to your father, to all in his palace? To your own brother Sa'ood among the rest? Is not the fact of this my actual visit to you known without your gates? Or is there no one here?" added I, with a glance at Mahboob, "who can report elsewhere what you have just now said? Better for you to leave off this nonsense; do you take me for a child of four days old?"

He muttered a repetition of his threat. "Bear witness, all here present," said I, raising my voice so as to be heard from one end of the room to the other, "that if any mishap befalls my companion or myself from Riad to the shores of the Persian Gulf it is all 'Abd-Allah's doing. And the consequences shall be on his head, worse consequences than he expects or dreams."

The Prince made no reply. All were silent; Mahboob kept his eyes steadily fixed on the fireplace; 'Abd-el-Lateef looked much and said nothing.

"Bring coffee," called out 'Abd-Allah to the servants. Before a minute had elapsed a black slave approached with one and only one coffee-cup in his hand. At a second sign from his master he came before me and presented it.

Of course the worst might be conjectured of so unusual and solitary a draught. But I thought it highly improbable that matters should have been so accurately prepared; besides, his main cause of anger was precisely the refusal of poisons, a fact which implied that he had none by him ready for use. So I said "*Bismillah*," took the cup, looked very hard at 'Abd-Allah, drank it off, and then said to the slave, "Pour me out a second." This he did. I swallowed it, and said, "Now you may take the cup away."

The desired effect was fully attained. 'Abd-Allah's face announced defeat, while the rest of the assembly whispered together.

256

After this climax Palgrave and his companion escaped by night from Riyadh and travelled through the Yemama and Hasa to Katif, where the Persian Gulf was sighted eight months after their leaving the Mediterranean at Gaza.

Though Palgrave's account of his journey was received by English contemporaries with doubt, it certainly exercised a considerable influence on ideas of Arabia in Europe. In the maps before his time there was marked in Aflaj (to which district, far south-west of Riyadh, Palgrave claimed to have made an excursion) a lake of considerable dimensions. As Palgrave did not confirm the existence of this lake geographers ceased to include it. Yet such a lake, though far smaller than the old map-makers knew, does exist, and it is amazing that a traveller should omit so unusual an Arabian feature from his account of a district. There is, also, in Aflaj a wonderful system of irrigation channels fed from deep reservoirs, but Palgrave does not remark it. Such omissions led Philby, who had travelled all the country covered by Palgrave's later journeys, to the conclusion that Aflaj had in fact never been visited. He points out, too, that while Kharfa, in Aflaj, is 170 miles from Riyadh, Palgrave wrote that he reached it in two days' ordinary travel. Moreover, he shows that Palgrave actually invented two villages, or misquoted their names from hearsay, or found them marked on some old map in which places and distances were conventionally sited. Finally Philby proves that Palgrave failed to notice any of the true features of the Aflaj region.

Without detailing Philby's brilliantly constructed analysis, which corrected Hogarth's view that this excursion was Palgrave's best service to pure geography in Southern Nejd, one may add that it has partly succeeded, on a wider front than that of Aflaj, in undermining credence, not in Palgrave's accuracy, for that was long under grave doubt and suspicion, but in that the journey was ever made, either from Hail to Riyadh or thence to the Gulf. It is, indeed, difficult to explain much of Palgrave's description, such as that of a coastal range in the Hasa, with a long winding descent down difficult sides, where such physical features never existed! The hot springs, which in Palgrave's time scalded the hands of the unwary, are now, says Philby, lukewarm or cold! "Gone, too, are most of the many and various products of the province," he continues, "but not in vain, for barley grows profusely where papay and sugar-cane and indigo grow no more . . . but, saddest of all, the buffalo no longer wallows in the miry pools, for the buffalo is extinct."

At present one may say that while Palgrave may not have visited Aflaj, the evidence against his claim to have crossed Hasa is much weaker. Cheesman, reading Palgrave and Philby while travelling in the Hasa, has pointed out that the former might easily have mistaken papay for the castor-oil plant and the sugar-cane, which he saw on sale, for the succulent underground stem of a desert plant called tarthuth. He adds that Palgrave was in error in most of his agricultural and horticultural observations simply because he was not equipped with the necessary knowledge. Furthermore, says Cheesman, barley does not grow as profusely as Philby avers. Finally he is quite convinced that Palgrave's description of Hofuf could be based only on personal experience, despite the fact that his map of the town was so bad that he could not even orient it.

From Katif Palgrave's story moves on to Bahrein, Bundar Abbas, and Oman, where he described territory previously visited by Wellsted, and travelled a short way inland from Sharja towards Bireima. For one section at least of his travels in the Gulf there is adverse witness. Colonel S. B. Miles, British Resident and Consul-General at Muscat, who knew his own district thoroughly well, is reported to have said that there was not a word of truth in Palgrave's account of it, that he introduced, for instance, villages and palm-groves that did not exist, and a purely imaginary road down a precipice at Muscat harbour. On the other hand, Bertram Thomas holds that while Palgrave's account abounds in inaccurate detail, it is true artistically as far as Oman is concerned—"Palgrave's medium is the brush and palette, so to speak, not the camera."

If Palgrave did indeed journey beyond Hail, as seems likely, his feat merits praise on grounds of courage, however inaccurate, fruitless, or even false his subsequent story. No doubt on his return he was asked questions upon matters which had passed unobserved because he was not interested in the subject, and one of his egotistic character and overwhelming imagination neither would nor could be 'stumped' for an answer. Whatever one may think of his truthfulness, his story will always find readers, for, despite its too frequent discursiveness and the air of *habile homme* which repelled Doughty, it has qualities of rich colour, movement, lively dramatic interest, and unfailing fascination.[1]

II

Shortly after Palgrave's journey it was suggested to Colonel Lewis Pelly, British Resident at Bushire, that the Royal Geographical Society would be interested to know something of the country between the Persian Gulf and Riyadh and the exact position of the latter place and Hofuf. Pelly resolved to go to Riyadh, as there was also political business which he wished to arrange with Feisal, the Wahhabi Emir.

The Gulf coast, particularly that of Trucial Oman, was the resort of many pirates and slave-traders, who were backed by the slave-owning upper classes of Riyadh. In the time of Ibrahim Pasha the Egyptian invasion of Wahhabi territory had been welcomed by the Indian Government, who had sent Captain Sadlier to meet Ibrahim with a view to arranging a better ordering of the Gulf coast. When the Egyptians evacuated Nejd it became clear that Britain would have to continue her solitary task against the slave-raiders and those who robbed the pearlers of Bahrein. British action was vigorous enough to annoy Feisal, so that he broke off relations with the Indian Government. Pelly, however, believed that the able ruler of

---

[1] The *Dictionary of National Biography* states that Palgrave was born in London, and was received into the Society of Jesus in Madras. Sommervogel (*Bibliothèque S.J.*) says that Guillaume Cohen was born in the Indies on January 24, 1826, entered the Society of Jesus on April 22, 1849, in the Toulouse Province (the Madras Mission was run by this province), under the name of Palgrave. He was attached to the Syrian Mission, and ordained priest. He left the Society in 1865, and apostatized. His brother was *The Golden Treasury* anthologist, his father a notable historian. Had Palgrave any connexion with the Ratisbonne brothers, the Jewish converts? There is no mention of him in any of the books about them one has consulted, but it certainly looks like Palgraviana.
While in the Society Palgrave wrote *Translation of the Devotion of the Seven Dolours of Our Blessed Lady*, by the Rev. Antonio Pereira, S.J. (Bombay, 1856); *Lettre de Beyrouth, Avril 1857* (this was printed in *Lettres du scholasticat de Vals*, November 1857, and April and May 1858); *Lettre de Beyrouth*, July 1861, in *Lettres du Fourviere*, September 1861; *Lettre de Beyrouth*, July 1861, in *Lettres des scholastiques de Laval*, May 1862.

Nejd could be brought to accept the British view regarding his coastal allies. His first letters to Feisal evoked no friendly response, but at length he received a brief invitation to visit Riyadh.

Though he was offered neither guide nor escort Pelly set off from Kuweit on February 18, 1865, accompanied by Lieutenant Colville and Dr Dawes, of the Indian Navy, an interpreter named Lucas, a Portuguese cook, and some native servants. To avoid notice on the journey they wore native cloaks and headdress. They were not encumbered with heavy baggage, and the expedition lasted but twenty-nine days, including a three-day halt at Riyadh. For two days out from Kuweit a pebbly, stony belt was traversed, and then for two days longer the sandy waves of the Dahna. Shortly after this the country rose towards the plateau of Nejd. For the first ten days the land was barren, only one tree was sighted in the plains and gravelly ridges, and the camels drank but once. Then they reached the walls of Wabra,

> a great Wahhabee camping ground. It contains upward of a hundred wells within a space of 400 yards. Only a few of them were in good repair, and with one exception they were all brackish. When the Bedouins assemble there they clear the adjacent wells, which are dug some three or four fathoms through the solid rock. It is said that they are of very ancient date, and that this Wabra was a point of convergence in ancient days for caravans from Kuweit crossing Arabia.[1]

Five waterless days followed, before they reached wells at Orma; then, instead of going south to Riyadh, the party turned towards Sedus and the Wadi Hanifa, where Pelly intended to examine a reputed "monolith of great altitude," which he thought might bear Himyaritic inscriptions. Sedus proved to be an oasis town, "embosomed in date-groves," and the column merely a thing of stones and mud mortar with two Greek crosses cut upon it—possibly a relic of some early Mohammedan mosque. Wadi Hanifa he described as a ravine two to three hundred yards wide with walls two hundred feet high; it was usually dry, but became a torrent after heavy rain. Passing the old Wahhabi capital, Dariya, they were received outside Riyadh by the Wazir, Mahhub.

[1] In the *Journal of the Royal Geographical Society*, 1865.

Mahhub, as Palgrave relates, was an Afghan who knew something of the restraining effect of British influence, and was therefore averse from any dealings with the Indian Government. Feisal and Pelly, however, soon reached a footing of friendliness and mutual respect. Then Mahhub, in order to raise controversy, brought forward the suggestion of a treaty of immunity for the slave-traders. At this point Pelly judged that his further presence at Riyadh might lead merely to trouble being started by those hostile to the British. In establishing friendlier relations with the Emir he had achieved all that could be expected at the time, and he returned by a route north of Hofuf, by an arid tract, descending seven ridges from the plateau to the coast.

Although his political mission had apparently failed, an important contact had been made. Feisal died shortly afterwards, but the British were remembered at Riyadh, and when his son Abdulla had difficulties over the succession he appealed for help to Bushire. Pelly had formed no high opinion of him, and supported instead his brother Saud.

The party had carried instruments, but had had to use them with great circumspection. As their tents were pitched to northward for coolness, good opportunities for stellar observation occurred nightly. The longitude of Riyadh was taken from their housetop in the city, by means of five solar observations, and was fixed as 46° 41′ 48″ E. The latitude they found with more difficulty—24° 38′ 34″ N. The latitude of Hofuf was fixed by stellar observation at 25° 20′ 56″ N. and the longitude at 49° 40′ 50″ E.[1] Many other places were fixed on Pelly's map, and much political knowledge and useful information regarding the country between Riyadh and the Gulf was brought back.

Pelly made some interesting notes on the Selaib nomads, based on information collected among them, which may be quoted as an early account of a non-Bedouin people whose origins have given rise to much conjecture:

---

[1] The co-ordinates accepted by the Royal Geographical Society and the War Office are: Riyadh—latitude, 24° 37′ 52″ N., longitude, 46° 43′ 22″ E.; Hofuf—latitude, 25° 22′ 15″ N., longitude, 49° 34′ 24″ E.

On certain festivals, and particularly on occasions of marriage and circumcision, they fix a wooden cross, dressed in red cloth and adorned at the top with feathers, at the door of the person married or circumcised. At this signal the people collect and dance round the cross. They have a particular dance. The young men stand opposite their female partners, each advances, and the youth slightly kisses the shoulder of the maiden: anything like touch of the hand or waist is out of etiquette.

The word 'Seleeb' means a cross. But some of the caste derive their name from As-Solb-Al-Arab—i.e., from the back of the Arabs—meaning to assert that they are pure descendants of aboriginal Arabs. The Mohammedans, on the other hand, stigmatize them as outcasts. . . .

The Selaib who have emigrated into Nejd and other Mohammedan settlements conform outwardly to the religious rites and ceremonies of the dominant creed. But in their own tents, or when alone, they do not so conform.

No intermarriage takes place between the Selaib and the Arabs. Even a Bedouin will not stop to plunder a Selaib, nor to revenge a blood-feud against him. The Selaib are capital sportsmen. They live largely on deer's flesh, and wear a long shirt of deerskin coming down to the feet. Their common diet is locusts and dates when procurable; but they will eat anything. They tend their sheep and camels, wander for pasturage during eight months of the year, and for the remainder seek some town or village where to exchange their produce for necessaries of life. Their tents are black, of goat's hair, and are pitched separate from those of the Arabs. The Selaib are filthy in appearance; but the Arabs confess that, in point of features, the Selaib women are the most beautiful among them.

Forty days after birth a child must be washed, being dipped seven times in water.

Marriage is contracted by mutual consent of the parties. The assent of the father, or failing him, of the nearest of kin, must also be obtained. The father of the girl receives some sort of payment according to the ability of the bridegroom. The parties go before a mollah, or an elder of the tribe, who asks them three several times if they freely consent to the union. The parties replying in the affirmative, the mollah takes his fee, and they cohabit. The neighbours then collect at the tent, sheep are killed for them, and they dance. The only invitation is the sign of the cross fixed outside the tent.

The Selaib wash their dead, cover the body with a white shroud, and inter it with a prayer. Failing a white shroud, they use a new shirt of deerskin.

They profess to reverence Mecca, but state that their own

proper place of pilgrimage is Haran, in Irak or Mesopotamia. They say also that their principal people have some psalms and other books written in Chaldean or Assyrian. They respect the Polar star, which they call Jah, as the one immovable point which directs all travellers by sea and land. They reverence also a star in the constellation, called Jeddy, corresponding with Aries. In adoring either of these heavenly bodies the Selaib stands with his face towards it, and stretches out his arms so as to represent a cross with his own body. They believe in one God. Some of them pretend to believe in Mohammed. Others deny the prophet, but trust in certain intermediate beings, who are called the confidants of God. They pray three times a day: first, as the sun rises, so as to finish the prayer just when the entire disc is above the horizon; secondly, before the sun begins to decline from the meridian; and thirdly, so as to finish the prayer as the sun sets. It is asserted, however, that the Selaib of Haran have pure forms of prayer, in the Assyrian or Chaldean. They fast three times a year: for thirty days in Ramadan; for four or seven days in Shaban, and for five or nine days in a summer month. They are peaceful, and are undisturbed by the Arabs, who hold them below injury. They are markedly hospitable, like all people who have nothing to give. They assert themselves to be a tribe of the Sabians emigrated to Nejd. The Mohammedans deny this. The Selaib eat carrion, and profess themselves to be the chosen people of God, who pay no tribute or tax, since no one will deign to receive it from them.

Captain G. E. Leachman, writing shortly before the Great War, called them "the gipsies of the desert." One theory is that they are descendants of the Crusaders, and the Bedouin often say that they are related to the "Angles." They do not appear to visit the south, but are found in the Northern Arabian Desert, between the Persian Gulf and Nejd, and west of Nejd. Leachman found their camps to consist usually of about twenty tents of a smaller size than those of the Bedouin, and they were generally pitched some distance from a watering-place known only to the Selaib. Their transport was mainly by donkey, and they possessed goats and sheep. Their poverty-stricken appearance was perhaps assumed to avoid exciting the greed of the Bedouin, for they generally had plenty to eat. They were skilled hunters, but had to crawl within a few yards of a herd of gazelle to be sure of a hit with their ancient muzzle-loaders, which were often six feet long. Leachman once saw a trail in the sand where a hunter had crawled for nearly a mile in his approach to a herd. When asked by Arabs if they were Christians they made "a not very indignant denial." Because they avoid known watering-places as much as possible they have become famous among Arabs for their knowledge of the country. Leachman noticed their high-pitched voices and wonderful similarity of feature; like Pelly, he found that the women were spoken of among the Bedouin for their beauty. H. St J. Philby described these mysterious nomads as

a race apart, assimilated to the environment of the Arabs, but not of them. . . . They are not ashamed of the current myth, which regards them as the surviving relic of some Christian tribe of the past. They are the tinkers and smiths of the nomad community, and as such indispensable.[1]

III

Some of Palgrave's remarks concerning the Nejd horse are believed to have led to Napoleon III's commissioning Carlo Guarmani, an Italian Levantine, to buy Arab stallions for the Imperial stables. A dozen years previously Guarmani had made an expedition to Jauf, and was known to be willing to travel through Arab lands in disguise. To the grief of his family he again set out for the interior in January 1864, and seems to have been supported and sustained against the dangers ahead by hopes of making a name for himself as an explorer. In Hail he saw the body of a Persian Jew who had entered Arabia to buy horses, and feigning Islam was set upon by a mob and lynched. Guarmani might be uplifted by visions of fame, but was fully determined to avoid such an end.

Being on good terms with the Rualla and all the Anazeh, he was passed on quickly to Teima (February 11), along a line of wells east of the Syrian-pilgrim route. He then posed as Khalil Agha, a Turkish Moslem and Master of Horse to the Governor of Damascus, and freely ranged the steppe and basalt *harra* south of Teima, reaching Kheibar on February 29. He found no horses there, but only a negro population, an influx to Arabia from Africa, governed by an Abyssinian for the Shammar. The territory of the Ataiba tribe was next

[1] *The Heart of Arabia*, vol. ii (London, 1922).

visited. Its steppe and good pasture were found to be full of warriors at war with Abdulla and Riyadh.

Guarmani was arrested in Kasim and sent by Abdulla to Aneiza, where the young Emir Zamil helped him to escape to Hail. Tallal of Hail gave him liberty to go anywhere he pleased, and Guarmani took full advantage of it to visit the country round the capital, Kheibar, Aneiza, Teima, and all the oases of Jebel Shammar. He returned across the Nefud by Wallin's route with his string of horses. The Franciscans at Jerusalem issued his maps, which supplemented the information of Wallin and Palgrave. But Guarmani saw more of Central Arabia than either. Travel in Hail at that time, he wrote, was safer than in Italy. He indicated the westward and southward extent of Shammar wells and settlements, gave an account of the population and character of the villages, and reported that Wahhabism was not strong in the Shammar. But, in contrast to Palgrave's, his work was of more importance from the topographical than from the social viewpoint. Doughty, who visited Kheibar and Aneiza later, believed in his own priority, and never fully credited Guarmani's claims. He heard no mention of him in those places, yet this may have been due to the excellence of the Italian's disguise. Doughty was not impressed by one of Guarmani's maps that came his way, but he suspended judgment, as he had never given the matter his full attention. Actually Guarmani took many compass bearings and measurements of distance, and his results were, in fact, of considerable value to later scientific cartographers.

In this respect the material gathered on his journey resembled that of Charles Huber, an Alsatian, resident in Syria, who travelled across the desert from Jauf to Hail in 1878, and saw inscriptions which resulted in his being accompanied on a second exploration, in 1883, by a German archæologist, Julius Euting, on a venture commissioned by the French Ministry of Public Instruction. From Damascus the two men went by Jauf to Hail, and from the first seem to have disagreed. However, they proceeded to Teima. Euting copied the inscription on the famous Teima stone, and Huber concluded negotiations for its purchase. It was dispatched to Hail, and shortly afterwards they parted company.

Euting was later attacked by Bedouin of the Juheina tribe, killed two of them, fled to Wejh, and thence reached Jerusalem. Huber returned to Hail, and then travelled to Mecca and Jidda. On the return journey to Hail he was murdered by his Bedouin guides near Rabegh, at the end of July 1884. There was some dispute as to whether the Teima stone should go to Paris or Berlin, but finally it was handed over to an agent of the French consul at Jidda and was sent to the Louvre. This inscribed stele is one of the most valuable Semitic monuments.

Euting wrote an account of this Arabian adventure, and some of Huber's papers were recovered, at considerable peril, by an exiled Algerian sheikh, on the French Government's promise of repatriation. Among Huber's information were much useful data for the mapping of Northern Arabia, which were used by the skilled and patient Alois Musil, a Czech explorer and cartographer of the northern districts, whose work, beginning about 1908, has of recent years been printed in several large volumes by the American Geographical Society. In one volume of his great compilation of facts Musil states that no data regarding the region south of the Nefud was of any use to him, save those of Huber. He did not use the sketch maps, which Lady Anne Blunt found confusing (and which were, in fact, not Huber's, but maps made in Paris from his notes); he went to the Frenchman's original notes. Musil seems almost to have ignored the work of previous explorers, except in this case. Yet he could have saved himself the labour of building from Huber's sources, for in the years 1915–17 the Royal Geographical Society had plotted all Huber's last journey, on which he covered some three thousand miles by camel.

Almost a decade passed before the next European, Baron E. Nolde, visited Hail. Crossing the Nefud to Hayanya, Shakra, and Hail, he returned by the Persian-pilgrim route. The journey contributed nothing of topographical value, but produced some news of political changes in the Shammar and at Riyadh, and interesting information regarding horses and camels. Nolde was the last of the nineteenth-century pioneers in the north.

When the century closed, the northern half of the peninsula, above a line drawn from Mecca to Hofuf, had been well covered by explorers. South of that line the districts of Asir, Southern Nejd, and the Rub' al Khali were quite unexplored, while elsewhere no European had penetrated more than a hundred miles from the coast, except in Jauf and Nejran.

CHAPTER XV

DOUGHTY AND THE BLUNTS

The nomads' camels are strong and frolic in these fat weeks
of the spring pasture. Now it is they lay up flesh and grease in
their humps for the languor of the desert summer and the long
year. Driven home full-bellied at sunset, they come hugely
bouncing in before their herdsmen; the householders, going
forth from the booths, lure to them as they run lurching by, with
loud *Wolloo-wolloo-wolloo.*

CHARLES M. DOUGHTY, *Travels in Arabia Deserta*

IN the long list of travellers in Arabia some names, like
Wallin and Sadlier, have always been unknown except to
the specialized; the writings of others, like Burckhardt,
Palgrave, and even Burton, have long been neglected by the
average reader. While the last two made their sensations and
were then read only by the few, an inverse process evolved in
the case of Doughty and *Arabia Deserta.*

Charles Montagu Doughty, a gentleman of Suffolk, had been
intended for the Navy, but was excluded from that service
by a slight impediment of speech. He went eventually to
Cambridge, studied geology, and after graduating in 1865
read for some ten years at Oxford, Leyden, Copenhagen, and
Louvain, and wandered, generally alone and on foot, in
Southern Europe, Egypt, Palestine, and Sinai. While in the
neighbourhood of Jordan he visited Petra and Maan, where in
an Arab coffee-house he heard of the inscribed cliffs at Medain
Salih. He resolved to visit them, partly out of archæological
curiosity, partly to experience the wild Arab life, but mostly
to gain material for a narrative which should "redeem English
from the slough into which it had fallen since the days of
Elizabeth." In his later years, indeed, he was to deny vigor-
ously that he had entered the peninsula for any scientific
purpose whatever, but as a young man his interests must have
been wider or he would not have garnered with such endless
patience, and striving for accuracy, the mass of information
on the physical features, geology, hydrography, antiquities,

268

Bedouin organization, and social life of Arabia, which fills two long volumes.

At Maan Doughty knew that he could not enter Arabia alone. So he returned to Damascus, lived there for a while, and at length decided to attach himself to the pilgrim caravan of 1876, go with it as far as the frontier of forbidden Hejaz, and await its return at Medain Salih. So much concerning Doughty has very recently appeared from distinguished pens that it is hardly necessary here to indicate more than the extent and character of his journey, the geographical results, the nature of his great book, and his place among explorers of the peninsula.

With the Damascus caravan he reached Medain Salih and made a record of the inscriptions while the pilgrims proceeded to Mecca. On their return, instead of journeying back to Damascus, he began a series of wanderings in the desert, visiting Teima, Jebel Shammar, and Hail. Kheibar, where he had heard there were Jewish elements surviving since the days of the Prophet, drew him from the Shammar capital, but he returned, and thence reached Bereida and Aneiza, finally travelling with the butter caravan almost to Mecca before diverging to Taif. He came to Jidda in August 1878, after twenty-one months in Arabia.

This journey falls, physically and dramatically, into two sections, the first of which has the lesser interest for exploration, and archæological value only when Medain Salih is reached. The story unfolds with the brilliant carnival tapestry of the *haj*, the gay litters, the jingling bells, the lively, gesticulating people, the barking dogs, the rocking camels, and later the column moving slowly over the desert, southward inexorably. None can look aside to the poor dervish, fallen by the way and imploring pity with outstretched hands, out of all the six thousand people with twice that number of beasts, save only the last of seven hundred Persians travelling in the rear. Doughty followed the multitude with these unpopular schismatic *hajis*.

At Medain Salih he stayed some months in the Well Tower, while the *haj* was absent, made his study of the cliff inscriptions, and experienced no danger except from sudden gusts of Arab temper. Then, in the second part of his journey, he is suddenly alone. The Damascus caravan has departed, and Zeyd, a sheikh of the Fukara Bedouin, in whose tents he is to sojourn, gestures towards the waste land and says, "This is the land of the Beduw." Doughty is from this point the confessed infidel in the wilderness, and in the ensuing months of pastoral life learned the difficulties, quarrels, discomfort, heat, hunger, and thirst of the desert, and all its insecurities, for later he rides with the Moahib, who are raided by the Bishr, lose all their small cattle, and are left almost destitute. The traveller himself has only a few Turkish lira, an old camel, and a little practice in medicine, which is more valuable, because it sometimes wins him friends.

Doughty went openly as a Christian, which to the Arabs meant British and Western, accepting the contemptuous term *Nasrany*; yet he suffered little annoyance until the later stages of his wandering. He was a striking figure, tall, with a saffron beard, and soft, low, courteous voice. The Bedouin respected him, and, for all their wildness, sometimes took an almost possessive interest in his welfare. For instance, he once returned to Teima, where he had found inscriptions and had viewed, but not copied, the famous Teima Stone. During his absence the walls of the great well-pit had fallen in, and the townsmen attributed the disaster to the Christian's evil eye. On his arrival the nomads anxiously endeavoured to make him escape before the hasty people of Teima should murder him. The scene is described with all Doughty's dramatic construction; one actually sees and hears his desert friends, excited, urgent, then pleading, and finally exasperated by his inaction. Then at last, women, men, and children relax in wonder and despair, leaving his fate to Allah.

Across the deserts he marched to Hail, ruled at that time by Mohammed Ibn Rashid. This is one of the climaxes in his story, and by previous scattered references the reader's interest has been stimulated to curiosity about the Prince of Nejd and his power. The Emir tested his reading, and Doughty, opening a book, read out a passage indicated at chance: "the King slew all his brethren and kindred." It was an appropriately bloody text, and Ibn Rashid knew that the *Nasrany* regarded

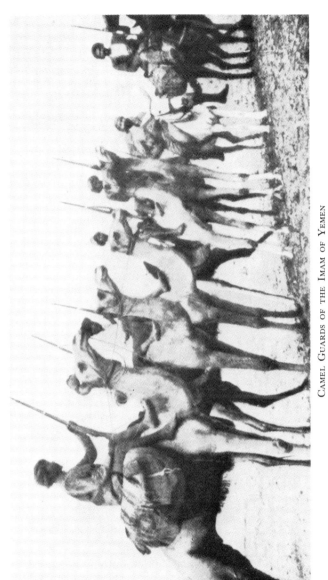

CAMEL GUARDS OF THE IMAM OF YEMEN

The guards are shown escorting a negotiator (on white donkey) on behalf of Saudi Arabia.

Photo E.N.A.

PILGRIMS BEING TRANSPORTED FROM THE STEAMER TO THE DOCK AT JIDDA

Photo E.N.A.

him as a murderer. But reasons of policy, apart from any personal feeling, made him further Doughty to Kheibar, for the infidel was wholly unwelcome at the Court and among the Hail townsfolk. At Hail some of Doughty's most interesting pages describe a meeting with Kahtan Bedouin, driven from Yemen and offering themselves to Ibn Rashid, who refused to accept the allegiance of this "dire and treacherous tribe." They told Doughty, who pleased them by praising their ancient lineage in the presence of the Nejdeans, something of the character of Aflaj and the Wadi Dawasir, and distances by camel march between various places.

No Jews were found at Kheibar, but Doughty was held for some weeks by the black governor of the town, until permission for his release was received from Medina. Returning to Hail, his first heavy misfortune began. In the Emir's absence he was cast out with ignominy. At Bereida, his next town, he was treated roughly and turned away at once, though women tried to protect him. He was thus in the heart of Arabia without a *rafik*, but his personality rarely failed to draw some measure of friendship. At Aneiza friends were found to hide him from the attentions of the rabble, provide him with a camel, and introduce him to the *samn* caravan, which would take him on towards the coast. They even tried to arrange for his safe-conduct to Jidda, and gave him a *rafik*, but this man forsook him outside the town, and Doughty knew well that it was unlikely that any Arab, after two weeks of desert travel, would postpone entering Mecca in order to see him safely to the coast.

In the journey from the neighbourhood of Aneiza towards Mecca Doughty experienced his greatest sufferings. It was the hottest part of the year, 42° Centigrade in the shade at noon, tempers were ferocious or sullen, and none would willingly give him food or water. So for four hundred miles he rode a weak camel, following wearily behind the caravan. Then, as Mecca was neared, it became quite clear that his judgment at Aneiza had been correct, for no Arab could, indeed, be found to guide him in security to Jidda. The most dangerous moment of all his months in Arabia occurred when a fanatical sherif named Salim rushed at him again and again with an uplifted knife, full of lust for murder. An old negro, who was in the service of the Grand Sherif, saved him by ordering that the Christian should be taken to his master at Taif. In a Meccan caravan Doughty then endured a short period of insults and threats and at least one attempt at murder.

His troubles ended on arrival at Taif, for the Grand Sherif was a man educated in Stamboul, politic, and anxious to seek friends, especially among the English. Doughty was ill, suffering from boils, with scorched skin and eyes bloodshot and half blinded; his hair was long, his beard unkempt, and his clothes were torn and ragged. Curiously, though he had been robbed of most of the things he carried on his person, the contents of his baggage remained intact.

This part of *Arabia Deserta* has a transcendental quality. The *Nasrany* is on trial, and comes through with soul and spirit unbroken, immeasurably superior to the Moslems who have held him physically defenceless in their hands. The Sherif fed and clothed him, provided him with an escort of a Bedouin sherif and two negroes, to conduct him easily and pleasantly to Jidda, and deferred sentence on those who had assaulted him until the traveller should be clear of their kinsfolk. From Jidda Doughty sailed for India.

On entering Arabia proper from Syria Doughty described the country ahead as a dead land, from which, if he died not, a traveller should bring back nothing but a perpetual weariness in his bones, and added further, "As for me who write, I pray that nothing be looked for in this book but the seeing of an hungry man and the telling of a most weary man." His suffering from hardship was great, and greater from cruelty and fanaticism; but there were many days of peace and tranquillity, as when he lived among the Fukara and the Moahib. The Arabs of the Hejaz frontiers, said T. E. Lawrence, still remembered "Khalil" for his courtesy, gentleness, and truthfulness. Never once did he deny his Christian status, and only on one occasion resisted proclaiming it for a time, though, in Hogarth's view, Doughty's religion was rather that of "an agnostic Humanitarian of heart-felt piety and deep reverence for any *credo* based on Reason." He would never have deigned to pass as a Mohammedan; he despised the teachings and

practice of Islam, and thought little of those, like Palgrave and
Burton, who had assumed conformity.

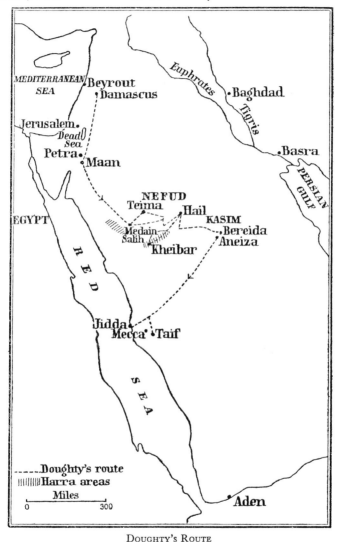

DOUGHTY'S ROUTE

Mr R. Ellis Roberts has shown well the contrast between
Doughty and Burton in their attitude towards religion and
nationality in the East:

The instinct to imitate, to cloak your own convictions and follow alien and perhaps disliked conventions, is based on a deep distrust of human brotherhood. The man who really believes that the distinctions of race, colour, language, and creed are ultimately less important than the fact of our common humanity is never afraid to admit the reality and significance of those distinctions: the man who minimizes the reality of the distinctions in the human family is the man who, at bottom, suspects them of having a terribly potent force, a force stronger than that of the brotherhood which is human nature's indefeasible privilege. . . . Doughty never leaves us with the impression that he is investigating some strange, half-human society: his contact is direct, sincere, instinctive, just because his point of view is remote and separate. He is painting a picture not of a different creature, not even of a different civilization, or order of society. He is painting a picture of people like himself who happen to have different habits and a different creed.[1]

The geographical results of Doughty's travels, which first appeared in Kiepert's *Globus*, established the nature and courses of the main channels of drainage in Northern Arabia, particularly of the Wadi Hamdh and Wadi Rumma; they showed the scenery, relief, and geology of Kheibar, the character of two great *harra* tracts, and the nature and extent of the volcanic areas between Kheibar and Tebuk. Much of the topographical work in these spheres was necessarily imperfect, in common with that of most of the old explorers, being based on little more than compass directions and rough route-distances. In the contemporary stage of exploration in Arabia Doughty, in fact, believed that exact cartography was of minor importance.

After leaving Arabia Doughty worked for nine years on his book *Travels in Arabia Deserta*, which in its first form ran to 600,000 words. Such length was not inordinate, for the story was like a great many-coloured weave, with endless figures and patterns stretching out from the central design, which was his route of travel. The descriptions of Bedouin life, of towns like Hail, and of geographical features, are mingled with pictures of men, animals, birds, reptiles, and with anecdotes, history, and even disquisitions on dogs—their names, number, use, and treatment by the Arabs. Doughty was in no hurry, and missed

---

[1] Obituary notice quoted in A. Treneer's fascinating *Charles M. Doughty: a Study of his Prose and Verse* (London, 1935).

nothing that the eye and mind could record as he moved under the vast, empty, burning sky, through his great arc across Arabia. The high plateau, rocky defile, sandstone and lava, the barren lands, and the green, the heat, the light that fell like rain through the leaking black tents, are revealed as clearly as are the men and beasts of the land. Of the Bedouin he writes as he knew them under varying conditions and reactions—factious, quick, fickle, slippery, or magnanimous. One does not easily forget their sheikhs, "of bird-like ruffling urbanity," nor yet Mohammed Ibn Rashid, who spoke "with the light impatient gestures of the Arab not well pleased," and had a way of sharply extending his head from the neck, typical of nomadic Nejd. Very appropriately to one with such a past, he "walked loftily and with somewhat unquiet glancing looks." Among the Bedouin herders Doughty notes a constant doglike grinning, caused by the constant beating sun, which makes their brows "frounced out" (wrinkled or folded), their lips drawn up, and the muscles set in that position. The swarthy or black camels of the Harb, Mutair, and Ataiba he described fully, and in all manner of situations:

> The great brutes fall stiffly, with a sob, upon one or both their knees, and under-doubling their crooked hind legs, they sit ponderously down upon their haunches. Then shuffling forward one and the other fore-knee, with a grating of the harsh gravel under their vast carcase-weight, they settle themselves, and with these pains are at rest: the fore bulk-weight is sustained upon the zora [1]; so they lie still and chaw their cud, till the morning sun.

Nothing that Doughty wrote about the desert and its people can be spared, and that is why from the merely utilitarian viewpoint he stands supreme among Arabian explorers. This position was early recognized by the few who felt a special interest in Arab things. The approbation of the many towards the book as a work of art came later; for the literary object which Doughty averred was foremost in his adventures resulted rather in delaying popular interest. His effort to invigorate English style by a return to the vocabulary and syntax of the

---

[1] The pillar-like stay under the chest of the camel which (when the beast is couched) bears up the weight of his long neck; it is soled with horny skin (Doughty's glossary).

Elizabethan and earlier language was based mainly on various translations of the Bible, Tyndale, Wyclif, Chaucer, Shakespeare, and Spenser, with a blending of "fresh-minted Anglo-Arabisms." Thus was evolved a stately, archaistic manner, rich with old, forgotten words and strange cadences, which, strange as it seems now, was not generally welcomed. Although its failure with the multitude was perhaps due to the book's high price, rather than to lack of right taste, the fact remains that Doughty's material reward for nine years' literary work was negligible. *Arabia Deserta* was a *succès d'estime*, hailed with delight by Wilfrid Scawen Blunt, William Morris, Burne-Jones —and Robert Bridges, then but slightly known. The Press generally saw nothing but affectation in the style, but praised the explorer's hardihood and courage. *The Times*, however, judged it "the most original narrative of travel since the days of Elizabeth," and the reviewer in *The Spectator* said that, "After two long volumes," Doughty, "though he had been his own single hero, leaves us neither weary nor suspicious." Among the leading critics Burton's, in *The Academy*, was the only discordant voice. He was annoyed at not being mentioned, jealous of an exploit more brilliant than his own, and, as one who had assumed Islam, was irritated by Doughty's contempt for that faith. The authority of Doughty himself, and that of the experts who had revised his book, did not prevent Burton from carping at many points of language, history, custom, and orthography. It may be added, in extenuation, that Burton was ill, a disappointed man, and near the end of his days.

Doughty had no better financial reward in the marketing of his inscriptions. But in 1904 *Arabia Deserta* began to reach a wider public. In 1908 an abridgment appeared, and copies of the original edition became *desiderata*. The Great War, which roused interest in Arabia among all classes in Britain and the United States, gave further impetus, and several reprints were issued, largely through Doughty's ardent disciple, T. E. Lawrence, who even in the Carchemish days knew the text very nearly by heart, and came to regard it as "a book not like other books but something particular, a bible of its kind."

II

A copy of Lady Anne Blunt's *A Pilgrimage to Nejd*, picked up in a Midland library, a first edition and a little over half a century old, was found to have the pages still uncut throughout. As Doughty's classic fell completely flat, perhaps one should not have expected any popular interest in this unpretentious, but charming and wholly valuable work.

The Blunts, Lady Anne, a granddaughter of Byron, and Wilfred Scawen Blunt, a diplomatist and poet, were among those travellers who visited Arabia for Arabia's sake, and for the sympathy they felt with the Bedouin, rather than for any geographical purpose. Yet the journal written by Lady Anne and the notes compiled by her husband gave a fair and accurate picture of north Central Arabia and its people. These travellers were not handicapped, as Wallin and Palgrave were, by disguise or the necessity for secrecy, and their use of Arab dress was merely to avoid attracting unnecessary attention. They were the first to visit Hail as Europeans openly, at leisure, carried compass and barometer, and were free to take notes.

Their companion on the journey was one Mohammed Abdulla, the son of a Palmyran sheikh, who had helped them previously to visit the Anazeh tribes, and was now seeking a wife from his own tribe in Nejd. He knew nothing of these relations of his, save that when his father was killed one of them had come north as avenger, and had "stayed no longer than duty required him." Their party, mounted on camels and horses, was composed of town Arabs and Bedouin, and included two of the Ageyl. Travelling south from Damascus by the pilgrim route in the second week of December 1878, they were crossing the *harra* a week later, reached Wadi Sirham at the end of the month, and entered the Nefud on January 13. Ten days afterwards they arrived at Hail, where they were entertained by the Emir, Mohammed Ibn Rashid.

Lady Anne's journal is a simple, straightforward record of scenes and events, written down day by day. Of the *harra*, for instance, she writes:

As soon as it was light we climbed to the top of the crater and looked over the plain. It was a wonderful sight, with its broken

277

tells and strange chaotic *wadys*, all black with volcanic boulders, looking blacker still against the yellow morning sky. There is always something mysterious about a great plain, and especially such a plain as this, where Europeans, one may say, have never been, and which even the people of the Hauran know little of. . . .

We have been stumbling about all day among the boulders of the *harra*, following little tracks just wide enough for the camels to get along, and making a great circuit in order to find ourselves at last barely twelve miles from where we began. . . .

Going straight was out of the question, for the *harra* is an impracticable country, not only for camels but for horses, on account of the boulders, except just where the paths lead. We had a bleak, desolate ride, for a cold wind had sprung up in our faces with a decided touch of winter. This country must be a furnace, however, in summer, with its polished black stones. I noticed that these were very regularly weathered; one side, that towards the north, being grey with a sort of lichen, so that as we rode past they seemed to change colour continually. There was very little sign of life in this region, only a few small birds, and no trace of inhabitants or of any recent passers-by. The tracks followed generally the beds of *wadys*, and wandered on without any particular aim or direction. They looked like the paths made by sheep or camels, only that the stones were so big it seemed impossible that the mere passage of animals could have ever made them. On the whole I think they must be artificial, made by shepherds in very ancient times for their flocks. In the spring, we are told, the whole of this *harra* is excellent grazing ground. It is a curious thing that every here and there in the hollows there is a space free from stones where water lies after rain, forming a pool. Why are there no stones there? The soil is a dry clay with a highly glazed surface cracked into very regular squares, so glazed, indeed, that even close by it has the appearance of water, reflecting the light of the sky. This, no doubt, is the way some of the curious mirage effects are produced in the desert, for it is to be noticed that the most perfect delusions are found just in places where one would naturally expect to find water—that is, where water has been.

Their journey contained little excitement, and a sand-storm they found more picturesque than dangerous, though once they had to turn backs to the wind, covering eyes and heads with their cloaks. Actually they made a good deal of progress during the storm, with the camels driven at speed, huddled together for protection, their long necks stretched out, heads low, ropes flying, and the men's cloaks streaming in the wind. On the 3rd of January, however, the monotony was broken by one exciting incident. The Blunts were resting and the remainder of the party had gone a little ahead, when suddenly came the thudding sound of galloping on the sands:

Wilfrid jumped to his feet, looked round and called out, "Get on your mare. This is a *ghazu*." As I scrambled round the bush to my mare I saw a troop of horsemen charging down at full gallop with their lances, not two hundred yards off. Wilfrid was up as he spoke, and so should I have been but for my sprained knee and the deep sand, both of which gave way as I was rising. I fell back. There was no time to think, and I had hardly struggled to my feet when the enemy was upon us, and I was knocked down by a spear. Then they all turned on Wilfrid, who had waited for me, some of them jumping down on foot to get hold of his mare's halter. He had my gun with him, which I had just before handed to him, but unloaded; his own gun and his sword being on his *delul*. He fortunately had on very thick clothes, two *abbas* one over the other, and English clothes underneath, so the lances did him no harm. At last his assailants managed to get his gun from him and broke it over his head, hitting him three times and smashing the stock. Resistance seemed to me useless, and I shouted to the nearest horseman, "*Ana dahilak*" ("I am under your protection"), the usual form of surrender. Wilfrid, hearing this, and thinking he had had enough of this unequal contest, one against twelve, threw himself off his mare. The *khayal* (horsemen), having seized both the mares, paused, and as soon as they had gathered breath began to ask us who we were and where we came from. "English, and we have come from Damascus," we replied, "and our camels are close by. Come with us, and you shall hear about it." Our caravan, while all this had happened, and it only lasted about five minutes, had formed itself into a square, and the camels were kneeling down, as we could plainly see from where we were. I hardly expected the horsemen to do as we asked, but the man who seemed to be their leader at once let us walk on (a process causing me acute pain), and followed with the others to the caravan. We found Mohammed and the rest of our party entrenched behind the camels with their guns pointed, and as we approached, Mohammed stepped out and came forward. "*Min entum?*" ("Who are you?") was the first question. "*Roala min Ibn Debaa.*" "Wallah? Will you swear by God?" "Wallah! We swear." "And you?" "Mohammed Ibn Aruk of Tudmur." "Wallah?" "Wallah!" "And these are Franjis travelling with you?" "Wallah! Franjis, friends of Ibn Shaalan."

It was all right, we had fallen into the hands of friends. Ibn

Shaalan, our host of last year, was bound to protect us, even so far away in the desert, and none of his people dared meddle with us, knowing this. . . . So, as soon as the circumstances were made clear, orders were given by the chief of the party to bring back our mares, and the gun, and everything which had been dropped in the scuffle. Even to Wilfrid's tobacco-bag, all was restored. The young fellows who had taken the mares made rather wry faces, bitterly lamenting their bad fortune in finding us friends. "Ah, the beautiful mares," they said, "and the beautiful gun." But Arabs are always good-humoured, whatever else their faults, and presently we were all on very good terms, sitting in a circle on the sand, eating dates, and passing round the pipe of peace. They were now our guests.

The Wadi Sirhan she described as a curious chaotic depression, probably the bed of some ancient sea like the Dead Sea, about twelve miles broad in places, with numerous wide, shallow wells at Kaf and elsewhere, for the water was only eight feet below the surface of the ground. Outside the *wadi* there were other wells at the same level. The water was drinkable, but not good. Along the edge of the *wadi* vegetation showed nothing bigger than shrubs, except some ghada-trees in a ravine. The Blunts suffered a good deal from cold and from a fierce south-east wind that stayed speech and almost prevented thought.

At Jauf the matrimonial objective of the journey was attained, and on January 13 the Blunts entered the Nefud. They had just crossed the Hamad, a black level plain bare of vegetation, covered with gravelly soil, and surfaced with small round pebbles, when

At half-past three o'clock we saw a red streak on the horizon before us, which rose and gathered as we approached it, stretching out east and west in an unbroken line. It might at first have been taken for an effect of mirage, but on coming nearer we found it broken into billows, and, but for its red colour, not unlike a stormy sea seen from the shore, for it rose up, as the sea seems to rise, when the waves are high, above the level of the land. Somebody called out "the Nefud," and though for a while we were incredulous, we were soon convinced. What surprised us was its colour, that of rhubarb and magnesia, nothing at all like the sand we had hitherto seen, and nothing at all like what we had expected. Yet the Nefud it was, the great red desert of Central Arabia. In a few minutes we had cantered up to it, and our mares were standing with their feet in its first waves. . . .

We have been all day in the Nefud, which is interesting beyond our hopes, and charming into the bargain. It is, moreover, quite unlike the description I remember to have read of it by Mr Palgrave, which affects one as a nightmare of impossible horror. It is true he passed it in summer, and we are now in mid-winter, but the physical features cannot be much changed by the change of seasons, and I cannot understand how he overlooked its main characteristics. The thing that strikes one first about the Nefud is its colour. It is not white like the sand-dunes we passed yesterday, nor yellow, as the sand is in parts of the Egyptian desert, but a really bright red, almost crimson in the morning when it is wet with the dew. The sand is rather coarse, but absolutely pure, without admixture of any foreign substance, pebble, grit, or earth, and exactly the same in tint and texture everywhere. It is, however, a great mistake to suppose it barren. The Nefud, on the contrary, is better wooded and richer in pasture than any part of the desert we have passed since leaving Damascus. It is tufted all over with ghada-bushes, and bushes of another kind called *yerta*, which at this time of the year, when there are no leaves, is exactly like a thickly matted vine. Its long, knotted stems and fibrous trunk give it so much that appearance that there is a story about its having originally been a vine. . . . There are, besides, several kinds of camel pasture, especially one new to us called *adr*, on which they say sheep can feed for a month without wanting water, and more than one kind of grass. Both camels and mares are therefore pleased with the place, and we are delighted with the abundance of firewood for our camps. Wilfrid says that the Nefud has solved for him at last the mystery of horse-breeding in Central Arabia. In the hard desert there is nothing a horse can eat, but here there is plenty. The Nefud accounts for everything. Instead of being the terrible place it has been described by the few travellers who have seen it, it is in reality the home of the Bedouins during a great part of the year. Its only want is water, for it contains but few wells; all along the edge it is thickly inhabited, and Radi tells us that in the spring, when the grass is green after rain, the Bedouins care nothing for water, as their camels are in milk, and they go for weeks without it, wandering far into the interior of the sand desert. . . .

At first sight it seemed to us an absolute chaos, and heaped up here and hollowed out there, ridges and cross-ridges, and knots of hillocks all in utter confusion, but after some hours' marching we began to detect a uniformity in the disorder, which we are occupied in trying to account for. The most striking features of the Nefud are the great horse-hoof hollows which are scattered all over it (Radi calls them *fulj*). These, though varying in size from an acre to a couple of hundred acres, are all precisely alike in shape and direction. They resemble very exactly the track of an unshod horse, that is to say, the toe is sharply cut and perpendicular, while the rim of the hoof tapers gradually to nothing at the heel, the frog even being roughly but fairly represented by broken ground in the centre, made up of converging watercourses. The diameter of some of these *fuljes* must be at least a quarter of a mile, and the depth of the deepest of them, which we measured to-day, proved to be 230 feet, bringing it down very nearly exactly to the level of the gravelly plain which we crossed yesterday, and which, there can be little doubt, is continued underneath the sand. This is all the more probable as we found at the bottom of this deepest *fulj*, and nowhere else, a bit of hard ground. The next deepest *fulj* we measured was only a hundred and forty feet, and was still sandy at the lowest point, that is to say, just below the point of the frog. Though the soil composing the sides and every part of the *fuljes* is of pure sand, and the immediate surface must be constantly shifting, it is quite evident that the general outline of each has remained unchanged for years, possibly for centuries. The vegetation proves this; for it is not a growth of yesterday, and it clothes the *fuljes* like all the rest. Moreover, our guide, who has travelled backwards and forwards over the Nefud for forty years, asserts that it never changes. No sandstorm ever fills up the hollows, or carries away the ridges. He knows them all, and has known them ever since he was a boy. "They were made so by God."

Blunt, in common with other travellers, exercised his mind to solve the problem of the *fulj*. Huber and Euting were told by the Bedouin that these formations were permanent, though the former attached little importance to this information, as he saw pits that had been filled up and others in the process of filling. D. G. Hogarth, whose summing up in the problems of Arabian geography was always masterly, supports strongly the conjecture which Blunt arrived at first—namely, that the wind causes these sand formations. At first, he wrote, westerly winds scooped up sand, which, when checked by an obstacle such as a large bush, formed a mound with a long slope on the windward side and an abrupt fall to the lee.

Beyond it the scooping process began afresh, and if a new obstacle was met with and a second dune formed, a horseshoe pit half excavated, and further deepened in appearance by its comparative relation to the two dunes on each hand of it, came into being. The dune thereafter tended to diminish or move forward, according to a well-known law of sand-drift; but the scour of the wind round its sides may long have kept the hollow clear, and even deepened it.[1]

Hogarth does not mention one fact that would have supported his argument—namely, that in the south of this area, where the prevailing winds are in that direction, the pits are turned south. The Blunts remarked that the red sand of the Nefud was coarser in texture, less volatile, and less easily moved by the wind than the ordinary white sand of the desert. Ordinary winds, Hogarth considered, could not have piled up, or scoured out, this heavier sand, so that it was probable that the pits in the red sand had been made by violent storms; they would not be affected by the usual wind, and might be changeless long enough to appear permanent to the Bedouin. The lighter white sands, blowing thinly over the surface of the red, would cover the dunes on the windward side, and thus explain a point noticed by the Blunts, that a white mound often accompanied a red *fulj*.

As for the origin of this enormous sand mass of the Nefud, mainly of heavy, red, and motionless particles, through which jutting crags of sandstone occasionally appear, Hogarth pointed out a natural inference—that the sand was the perished remnant of a bed of sandstone that overlay the limestone in this region. West of the Nefud, also, there is a tract of sandstone by the hills of Jebel Shera. As the prevailing winds are from west and south-west, this region also may have fed the Nefud. The yellowish-white grains may have drifted from far greater distances than the heavier red ones.

Lady Anne Blunt had looked forward to seeing Jebel Shammar ever since she had read Palgrave's romantic account, "which nobody believed, of an 'Ideal State' in the heart of Arabia, and a happy land which nobody but he had seen." When at length the Jebel came in sight Wilfred Blunt declared that he could die happy even if they had their heads cut off at Hail—though it was one of his maxims that every place was like every other place. Palm-groves, green fields of barley, trees of the acacia type, alternated with occasional solitary boulders of red granite rising out of the crisp firm soil, all in pleasant contrast to the desert behind them. An even plain

[1] *The Penetration of Arabia.*

gradually sloped upward towards violet-coloured mountains, and they saw the outline of Jebel Shammar, fantastic, in spires, domes, and pinnacles. Then the ground rose abruptly from the sloping surface of the plain, and little *wadis* issued from clefts in the hills. On a bright morning, after a thunderstorm in the night, with birds singing sweetly in the bushes, they began the last short stage to Hail.

They were well received by a chamberlain, who conducted them into the presence of Mohammed Ibn Rashid.

> The Emir's face is a strange one. It may be mere fancy, prompted by our knowledge of Ibn Rashid's past life, but his countenance recalled to us the portraits of Richard the Third, lean, sallow cheeks, much sunken, thin lips, with an expression of pain, except when smiling, a thin black beard, well-defined black knitted eyebrows, and remarkable eyes — eyes deep-sunk and piercing, like the eyes of a hawk, but ever turning restlessly from one of our faces to the other, and then to those beside him. It was the very type of a conscience-stricken face, or of one which fears an assassin. His hands, too, were long and claw-like, and never quiet for an instant, incessantly playing, while he talked, with his beads, or with the hem of his *abba*. With all this, the Emir is very distinguished in appearance, with a tall figure, and, clothed as he was in purple and fine linen, he looked every inch a king. . . .
>
> Of his ability I judge by his extremely interesting remarks on serious subjects, as well as by the position he has been able to seize and to keep. Of his energy no one can doubt, for he has shown it, alas! by his crimes; but he is so eaten up with petty personal jealousies that I sometimes wonder whether these would influence his conduct at an important political crisis. I think, however, that at such a moment all little vanities would be forgotten, for he is above all things ambitious, and his vanity is, as it were, a part and parcel of his ambition. He is personally jealous of all other renowned chiefs, because here in Arabia personal heroism is, perhaps more than anywhere else in the world since the age of chivalry, an engine of political power.

They attended his daily court of justice, saw his palm-groves and gardens, which contained a number of tame gazelle, including three "wild cows" from the Nefud, about which they had previously heard. They proved to be oryx, standing about as high as an Alderney calf six months old, with humps on their shoulders like Indian cattle. They were yellowish white in colour, the reddish legs turning to black towards the feet, the face parti-coloured; and the black horns, straight and slanting backward, were a yard long, with spiral markings. They were wilder than the other animals, and the slaves rather feared them, for they seemed quite ready to use their horns, which were as sharp as needles.

Then they were shown the place which interested them most, a stable-yard full of mares, tethered in rows each to a manger. Ibn Rashid's stud was one of the most famous in Arabia, and had taken the place in popular esteem of Feisal Ibn Saud's, which had been described by Palgrave. Lady Anne wrote of the stud at Hail in detail, comparing the Nejd horses with those of the Anazeh and giving the proper points of an Arabian horse. There were a hundred animals in the Hail stables, about forty greys—or, rather, whites—twenty chestnuts, thirty bays, and the rest brown. Black, roan, piebald, and dun were not Arab colours. The Emir agreed with the English taste for a bay or chestnut. In general the Blunts were not greatly impressed by Ibn Rashid's mares, and noticed that horses of any kind were rare in Nejd. What horses there were in the country were bred in the Nefuds. There is much of general and technical interest in Lady Anne's chapter on the Arab horse, but here one may quote only an old Arab direction for rearing a colt.

If you would make a colt run faster than his fellows, remember the following rules. . . .

During the first month of his life let him be content with his mother's milk; it will be sufficient for him. Then during five months add to this natural supply goat's milk, as much as he will drink. For six months more give him the milk of camels, and besides a measure of wheat steeped in water for a quarter of an hour and served in a nose-bag.

At a year old the colt will have done with milk; he must be fed on wheat and grass, the wheat dry from a nose-bag, the grass green if there is any.

At two years old he must work, or he will be worthless. Feed him now, like a full-grown horse, on barley; but in summer let him also have gruel daily at midday. Make the gruel thus: Take a double handful of flour, and mix it in water well with your hands till the water seems like milk; then strain it, leaving the dregs of the flour, and give what is liquid to the colt to drink.

Be careful from the hour he is born to let him stand in the sun;

285

shade hurts horses, but let him have water in plenty when the day is hot.

The colt must now be mounted, and taken by his owner everywhere with him, so that he shall see everything and learn courage. He must be kept constantly in exercise, and never remain long at his manger. He should be taken on a journey, for work will fortify his limbs.

At three years old he should be trained to gallop. Then, if he be of true blood, he will not be left behind. Yalla!

The Blunts came out of Nejd with the Persian pilgrims, returning to Kerbela and Baghdad. They were the first Europeans to travel by this route, and made corrections in previous maps of the country to the Euphrates. Other results of the journey included new altitude measurements of the plateau of Hail and Jebel Shammar, information on rock formations, proof of the existence of the oryx in the Nefud, and a revision of the map of Northern Arabia from the *harra* to Hail. On the outward march they took with them the nucleus of the famous Crabbet Park stud of Arab horses. In the appendices to Lady Anne Blunt's book there were included chapters on Wahhabi history and an examination of the then projected "Euphrates Railway," which was to join the Mediterranean with the Persian Gulf. Wilfrid Blunt was of the opinion that India stood in no need, politically or strategically, of such a line, and that as a commercial speculation the scheme was a delusion. These pages, even to-day, are intensely interesting, especially in the light of State documents recently published, which rather suggest that in all the diplomatic manœuvring round the Baghdad Railway in pre-War days, nobody seemed to examine the question as to whether or not the line could pay its way, or, at any rate, be a profitable investment. Blunt doubted it considerably.

Finally, one of the most interesting chapters in Lady Anne Blunt's record of the journey deals with the rise of the house of Rashid, beginning with Abdulla of the Shammar, who conquered or conciliated the other Nejd tribes, and established his supremacy over the northern towns, making his residence at Hail. Any Bedouin chief of Abdulla's ability, she considered, might have done this, but Abdulla's merit consisted in the system of rule which he founded. He realized that he had to appeal to Arab ideas and prejudices. Tribute collected from the towns he spent in the desert, in gifts and boundless hospitality. Smaller sheikhs were sent back to their territory dazzled with his riches and magnificence, and came to his assistance against the more obstinate. His hand was, whenever possible, light on the conquered, and he would even restore their property. Yet with all his generosity he took care to live within his income, and his reputed wealth brought him more power and prestige in a poor country. In these matters of policy, thrift allied to well-placed generosity, he was followed by subsequent Shammar rulers, who shared also his habit of caution, for they embarked on no enterprise in a hurry—even Mohammed's violence to his nephews was planned for many months. Similarly, the Ibn Rashids were tactful in their relations with their nominal overlords, the Ibn Sauds, and in dealings with the Turks. The liberality and conciliation which went so far with the Bedouin were equally successful with the townsmen, so that in Lady Anne Blunt's time the Rashid dominion was everywhere acknowledged enthusiastically. But the Emir did not allow the habit of town life to develop too far, and in the early spring until high summer lived in the desert with the Bedouin, abandoning fine clothes and luxury for the nomad life in the Nefud. Unlike Wallin, who stressed the power of the townsmen in the Shammar system, Lady Anne judged that the Rashid rulers were well aware of the true source of their power, which was in the hands that alone could wield it, the hands of the Bedouin. "The town cannot coerce the desert; therefore, if they are to live at peace, the desert must coerce the town." There was peace and security in the Shammar, by the will of the Rashid, when the Blunts journeyed there, yet neither town nor desert knew tyranny. Both would have abandoned a sheikh who broke unwritten laws or who ceased to be popular.

> The citizens of Jebel Shammar have not what we should call constitutional rights; there is no machinery among them for the assertion of their power; but there is probably no community in the old world where popular feeling exercises a more powerful influence on government than it does at Hail.

Lady Anne Blunt realized that the flaw in the system lay

in the uncertainty of the succession, which in the case of a young or incapable heir might be settled by force of arms. In describing the Shammar political system she gave more than might be expected of an explorer, for she saw below the outward practices of a strange land and recorded the traditional political habit of a people.

The formation of her views was doubtless influenced by her husband's broad political vision. Blunt was one of the first, in the eighties, to draw attention to the early signs of growth in Pan-Islamism and Mahdism, and prophesied the downfall of British rule in the Sudan before it was announced to the world by the death of Gordon. In Egypt and in Ireland, by word and deed, he supported the Nationalist parties, and suffered for his Irish sympathies by passing two months in Kilmainham Gaol. He died in 1922 at the age of eighty-two. T. E. Lawrence used to visit him, as one of the two surviving veterans of Arabian exploration (the other was Doughty), on each return from the East. He wrote:

> An Arab mare drew Blunt's visitors deep within a Sussex wood to his quarried house, stone-flagged and hung with Morris tapestries. There in a great chair he sat, prepared for me like a careless work of art in well-worn Arab robes, his chiselled face framed in silvered, curling hair. . . . Blunt was a fire yet flickering over the ashes of old fury.[1]

---

[1] In the introduction to Bertram Thomas's *Arabia Felix* (London, 1932).

CHAPTER XVI

TWENTIETH-CENTURY EXPLORERS

While the morning is still grey you may hear the rapping shots
of some tribal *fracas* from the foot-hills, a cheery sound, denoting
that the world is once more astir and taking an intelligent interest
in its affairs.   G. WYMAN BURY, *Arabia Infelix*

WHEN Doughty visited Hail, Mohammed Ibn Rashid
had still some twenty years of life remaining, and did
not achieve the pinnacle of power in Arabia until his
victory at Mulaida in 1891, after which the Ibn Saud family
was scattered in various places about the Persian Gulf.
Mohammed was succeeded in 1897 by a nephew, who, lacking
his political touch, roused the hostility of the Wahhabi districts.

Meanwhile Abdul Aziz Ibn Saud, a grandson of Feisal, was
living at Kuweit and learning the game of politics from Sheikh
Mubarak, an ally of Great Britain, whose backing Kuweit
needed against Hail and its Turkish allies. In 1901 the Saudi
prince, then only twenty years of age, achieved an astonishing
coup de main. While Hail was quarrelling with Kuweit he
entered the desert with a few followers, seized Riyadh by surprise, slew its Rashid governor, and assumed the Emirate. In
1904, after recovering the outlying districts of Weshm and
Sedeir, while in alliance with Mubarak and the Iraqi Muntafik,
he twice defeated the Shammar forces and drove their Turkish
allies out of Kasim. Two years later the Ibn Rashid was
defeated and killed in a fight at Muhanna; years of anarchy
followed at Hail, and though Riyadh suffered defeat in the
years of the Great War its power rose again, and Hail was
merged in the Wahhabi State in 1921.

Before this occurred Riyadh had clearly won the dominion
of Central Arabia, and in 1914, when the Turks were showing
undue interest in the Hasa and in Kuweit, owing to the
prospective completion of the Baghdad Railway, a surprise
attack was made on Hofuf, the Turkish garrison was escorted

to the coast, and Oqair and Katif were likewise cleared of Ottoman troops.

To hold his mainly tribal empire together Ibn Saud instituted in 1912 a new revival of the old puritanical Wahhabism, and created colonies on the land, hoping to lead the Bedouin to an agricultural rather than a pastoral organization. This movement, briefly visualized in the phrase "Back to the Koran and the land," is called *Ikhwan*, or "Brotherhood." More than fifty agricultural settlements have been founded, containing some 50,000 souls. The turbulent Bedouin element in the Saudi empire has been to some extent converted by the *Ikhwan* movement into a fighting force harnessed to the State through the local sheikhs, who are representatives of the central Government. No fighting between tribes is allowed before the Government has had the chance to settle a dispute without bloodshed, and there is peace such as Arabia has never known. *Ikhwan* demands more rigorous religious standards than Wahhabism, and greater self-denial: tobacco and alcohol are, of course, forbidden, and incense seems to be the only slight luxury allowed. There is no material reward for those who belong to the sect, enlistment is voluntary, a whole tribe or only individuals may join, and the *Ikhwan* forces really represent a national army that costs practically nothing.

During the Great War the Indian Government sent Captain W. H. I. Shakespear to instruct Ibn Saud to move up at once towards the British left flank in Mesopotamia, where the campaign was just opening. Ibn Saud was already mobilized for a campaign against Ibn Rashid, but in a battle shortly after the English officer's arrival his forces were so badly crippled that no help from them could be expected for a considerable time. In this action Captain Shakespear was killed. A treaty of friendship was made with Ibn Saud through Sir Percy Cox at Oqair, but British activities in Arabia thereafter were based on the Hejaz, and the support of Hussein, Sherif of Mecca. Hussein's unfortunately exaggerated notions of his position in the Arab countries roused the hostility of Ibn Saud, and though Britain managed to keep the peace for a time between the two Arab princes, the Hejaz was invaded victoriously by Ibn Saud after the Great War. The coastal districts of Asir, the country between the Hejaz and Yemen, which were on the British side, though somewhat ineffectively, during the Great War, acknowledged the supremacy of Ibn Saud in 1926. Yemen, which had sided with the Turks, remained independent.

Throughout these years, with rigid Mohammedanism in the ascendant, the general policy in most of Arabia became exclusive; the Jew, *Babu*, Greek, and Armenian financiers and traders found one field of Eastern endeavour closed to them. But in the case of exploration Ibn Saud's friendship for Great Britain and for certain individuals enabled striking work to be accomplished.

Although Arabia was of special interest to Britain, as forming the overland link between Egypt and India, exploration was largely left to chance and the initiative and courage of individuals. Yet when the twentieth century opened no part of Northern Arabia could be truly called *terra incognita*; thousands of square miles had never been visited by Europeans, but the nature of the land was known from the many lines of march which had crossed it. Still farther north, Arabia beyond the peninsula proper was revealed in detail during the next two decades by the scientific work of Alois Musil, the contacts established in the War years by the armies of Allenby and Maude, and later by the Nairn and other motor-transport companies, the Royal Air Force, and by the laying of the Palestine-Iraq pipe-line.

The general character of other districts, such as the Hejaz, Oman, Hasa, and Hadhramaut, was well known in the year 1900, but hardly a fraction of the peninsula had been mathematically surveyed; altitudes, even on the coast, were not exactly fixed, and certainly the only astronomical observations of latitude and longitude, except in Yemen, were those made by Ali Bey in the Hejaz, and Colonel Pelly at Riyadh. Precise knowledge of mountain contours and the courses of the *wadis* of the interior did not exist, and there was little knowledge of great areas by the Persian Gulf beyond a few miles from the coast. The interior of Dhofar, the district between Medina-Mecca, and Asir afforded further fields of discovery. Even in 1922 Douglas Carruthers could write, "We have better maps of the heart of the peninsula than of the region adjacent to

Medina and Mecca." The Rub' al Khali was still a blank on the map. The greater part of the geological and zoological work, the scientific mapping and surveying, remained for the twentieth-century explorer. Whereas the equipment of the older travellers consisted largely of hardihood, courage, a fine eye for country, and keen observation of manners and social life, the modern had to be ready to undertake arduous preparatory training in scientific subjects, in order to accomplish useful work.

Their labours have reaped more detailed and accurate results than those of the older explorers, and if they are less romantic characters than the Burtons and Doughtys they are not less in courage, and most of them seem to have inherited in their English style a certain colourful quality, pulsing and quick, from the great 'Arabians.' Lawrence is the great disciple of Doughty's *Arabia Deserta*, but others have achieved, with less poetic vision, the living scene of land and people.

II

Something more than a priority of courtesy should be ceded to Miss Gertrude Bell, who began her Arabian activities in 1899, when she visited Jerusalem and travelled widely in Palestine and Syria. In the next ten years she became an acknowledged expert on Asia Minor and Arabia, and eventually undertook a journey into the peninsula in 1913. From Damascus she turned to the western edge of the Nefud and reached Hail, where she was coldly received, and thence proceeded to Najaf and Lauka. She used scientific instruments throughout her journey, taking some half-dozen observations of latitude, kept her marching times, and took daily readings of thermometer and barometer. Her early wanderings gave rise to notable books, like *The Desert and the Sown*, but the story of this journey was not told for many years, and then by another, D. G. Hogarth. The years following had caught Gertrude Bell in the maelstrom of war. She became, a thing unique for a woman of the West, the chief sustainer of an Eastern dynasty, and died at Baghdad in a country she had made peculiarly her own.

Another pre-War explorer of Arabia, who, like Gertrude Bell, was later to serve nobly in Iraq, was Captain G. E. Leachman, of the Royal Sussex Regiment, whose truly amazing adventures have only recently been revealed. His first expedition came in 1909–10, when he slipped the watchful eye of the Turks at Baghdad, joined a party of raiding Shammar, and marched south with them. His subsequent experiences included an attack by the Rualla and captivity for some weeks among the Shammar. He was not allowed to go to their capital at Hail, but gave an interesting account of the raid discipline of their forces. The geographical merit of his enterprise lay in his notes on the Wadi Khar, the great length of which he was the first to record. He showed it to be the dry bed of an old river, running for 400 miles, rising near Jauf, and originally flowing, through banks in some places four or five miles wide, to the Shatt el Arab, and forming a relatively easy path, with water on or near the surface, across Northern Arabia. Leachman was also the first European to visit the wells of Leina.

All Leachman's adventures could not even be summarized here, but on one enterprise he again avoided the vigilance of the Turks and travelled for 2500 miles, on foot, horse, and camel, through Kurdistan, Anatolia, and Syria. His second Arabian journey began at Damascus, and was made at first in the company of some Ageyl and later with Anazeh and Shammar *rafiks*. Across 800 miles of desert, Hamad and Nefud, he came again to the wells of Leina, to Kasim, Aneiza, and Bereida (the only place in Arabia where he met with discourtesy, thus sharing the experience of previous explorers), managed to go farther by claiming to have a confidential message for Ibn Saud, and finally met the Wahhabi Emir at Riyadh, where he was courteously received and lodged in the palace. His original intention had been to proceed farther south, to Jabrin and the Rub' al Khali, but when the Emir refused to agree to this plan he left Arabia through the Hasa, Oqair, and Bahrein. On this journey nearly fourteen hundred miles were covered in fifty-two days, including halts. In the latter part of his route he travelled with Southern Bedouin of the Ajman, Dawasir, Hajar, and Murra, of whom he wrote:

Naturally of an entirely different character to the fine northern tribes, these tribes of the south were not improved by the fact that they were returning from Mecca after performing the pilgrimage.

Bigoted and fanatical to a degree, miserable in appearance, and capable of lying in a manner unknown elsewhere in Arabia, they did not prove the best of travelling companions.[1]

The journey resulted in interesting notes on the towns and general information of the country, but there was little opportunity for any surveying or mapping. Its importance was rather political, for it brought this British officer into touch, two years before the War, with the ruler of the Wahhabis, as his previous journey had made contact with the powerful sheikhs of the Amarat and Muntafik. Leachman was a wonderful actor, spoke the language fluently, and could pass anywhere as an Arab. At the end of his second journey into Arabia he crossed to Bahrein in a native craft, herded with a crowd of dirty Arab divers, and appeared at the British Consulate as a tall, cadaverous, and altogether filthy-looking Bedouin. He once passed among the riverain Arabs of Iraq undetected until a mistake of his servant betrayed him. Later he stayed with marauding Arabs, who would have killed him even on suspicion.

During the Great War Leachman was put in control of the Bedouin of the left flank of the British in Iraq, kept the Amarat quiet in the face of German overtures to them, and carried out effective propaganda among the tribes. No name was better known among the Arabs of the East. To them he was more than the model of courage, endurance, and foresight; to great numbers of tribesmen Leachman was the only Englishman who mattered. But his brusqueness made him some enemies. When he was treacherously murdered after the War the Arabs lost a good friend.

Another soldier and Political Officer performed work more important geographically than Leachman's in the pre-War years. This was Captain W. H. I. Shakespear, who, after service at Bundar Abbas and Muscat, was appointed Political Agent at Kuweit in 1909. From this base he made several journeys into the interior, discovering the first Sabæan inscriptions in Northern Arabia, filling in blanks on the map, and making friends with the neighbouring sheikhs. These expeditions trained him for his great exploration across Arabia from sea to sea, which began in February 1914. Setting out from

[1] Quoted in N. N. E. Bray, *A Paladin of Arabia* (London, 1936).

Kuweit with a well-equipped caravan, he marched south-west to the wells of Hafar, traversed the Nefud, and crossed the north end of the Tuwaik escarpment to Zilfi. At Riyadh he visited his friend Ibn Saud, and after accompanying him on an expedition to the north made for Shakra, the capital of Weshm, where he struck Sadlier's old route. From Aneiza (where he found that every one spoke well of "Khalil") he went on to Bereida, and then by a new route to Jauf, seeing no villages for twenty-nine days. From Jauf he was worried by the demands of the local chiefs all the way. The Howeitat lived up to their reputation for treachery: *rafiks* offered him for ten pounds safe-conduct to Akaba, and then escorted him only to the next section of the tribe. Auda, Lawrence's ally in later years, was the worst blackmailer of all, screwing the Englishman to the last farthing, but carried out his obligations. On one section of his journey eastward a smooth black basalt expanse was crossed for fourteen hours. A Turkish patrol was avoided and the Hejaz Railway crossed near Mudawwara, and at length Shakespear saw through his glasses three white objects in the distance. They proved to be the Egyptian police force at Kuntilla, on the Gulf of Akaba.

This bold trans-Arabian journey was the most notable and successful feat of the pre-War years.

Leachman's and Gertrude Bell's exploits have been noted. Raunkiaer, a Dane, had also made a praiseworthy journey by a new route from Kuweit to Bereida, and then through Sedeir to Riyadh and out by Hofuf to Oqair—a journey of seven to eight hundred miles. Shakespear's route covered eighteen hundred miles, two-thirds of it through unknown country. A hundred years had passed since Sadlier's crossing the peninsula, and about fifty since Palgrave's Gaza-Katif and Wallin's Muweila-Meshed journeys. Shakespear's was the fourth cross-ing, and easily the most fruitful geographically.

The journey took three and a half months. Shakespear's records of work in these years remained in official archives, but the account of his last journey was brilliantly edited in 1922 by Douglas Carruthers, who sums up the results as follows:

For the whole distance, 1810 miles, Shakespear kept up a continuous route-traverse, checked at intervals by observations for latitude. He also took, as on his previous journey, hypsometric readings for altitude, which give a most useful string of heights between the Gulf and the Hejaz Railway. The initial results of Shakespear's last journey may be summed up as follows: the first complete traverse of the Wadi er Rumma in its lower course—as the Batin—between Hafar and Ajibba, where the great fiumara is blocked by the Dahana sand-bed, and also of the region southwards to Zilfi; the first reliable map of the Tuwaik settlements between Zilfi and Audah, and of a new route onwards to Riyadh; a great deal of new detail between Riyadh and Buraida; a completely new route from Buraida to Jauf, and also between Jauf and the Wadi Araba on the frontiers of Southern Palestine. For the eastern limits of the Great Nafud sand-bed we are indebted to him; also for the true trend of Jebel Tubaik, and for much information on the various sand-belts which seam Kasim and Sudair. But even where he was on old ground his surveys were of much value. . . . Routes which had hitherto been mere conjecture could now be drawn more or less correctly, many errors put right, and many a problem solved.[1]

A full list of all astronomical observations taken by Shakespear was included in a pamphlet dealing with astronomically determined positions in Northern and Western Arabia, compiled for the Geographical Section of the General Staff by Carruthers and E. A. Reeves in 1918. It was largely due to Shakespear that better maps existed in 1922 of the centre of the peninsula than of the districts near Medina and Mecca.

Carruthers himself carried out in 1909 a notable exploration in the Hejaz east of the railway, and described it in his book *Arabian Adventure to the Great Nafud*. He was out in search of the oryx, which is probably the fabled unicorn, left Damascus accompanied by a camel-dealer, and joined the Beni Sakhr tribe. Then with a Sherarat *rafik* he proceeded south-eastward and reached Teima. Unwelcome there, he left by night and returned along the western edge of the Nefud to the Sakhr, having made valuable additions to knowledge. He saw his oryx, game of extreme shyness, and discovered the ruins of a large khan on the old Basra-Egyptian route.[2]

---

[1] *Captain Shakespear's Last Journey*, in *The Geographical Journal*, 1922.

[2] It is interesting to compare his impressions of the colour of the Nefud with those of Palgrave and the Blunts. Carruthers says "pure carmine in a low morning light," white in the midday glare, and at dusk "wine-red and of an intangible velvety texture." At close quarters the sands were "of every shade of yellow and red, blending softly into an amazing mixture for which one can find no name."

An outstanding traveller of the pre-War days was A. J. Wavell, who visited the Haramain, the region of the holy cities, in 1908-9, and left an excellent account of Medina, Mecca, and the ceremonies. Two years later he visited Sana and gave the best description of the city since Manzoni's, a quarter of a century before. The most complete modern account of the holy

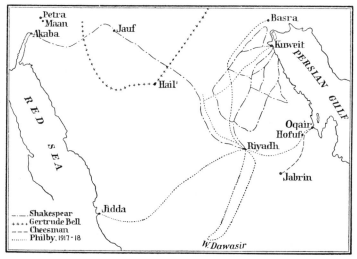

ROUTES OF FOUR MODERN EXPLORERS

cities as seen by a Westerner is that of Eldon Rutter, who visited them in 1925.

Books on Arabian travel had interested him from boyhood, and after serving in the War Rutter studied Arabic, and accepted a position in the Malay States, where he learned to speak the language fluently among emigrants from the peninsula. In Egypt he lived as a native, and at length undertook the pilgrimage. At this time Ibn Saud was at war with Hussein, and Jidda was besieged, so Rutter made his approach from Massawa, sailing by dhow in a mixed company of Moors and Abyssinians to El Gahm, on the coast of Asir. During rough weather the bag containing his compass and aneroid was washed overboard, but it is unlikely that he would have been able to make much use of them in the Holy Province. Moreover, in the hot season during which the pilgrimage was held in 1925 most of his travelling was done at night, so that not much topographical observation was possible, though in the Tihama along the coast he was crossing virgin territory. Two days' march brought him to the Hejaz frontier.

He travelled as Sallah ud Din, a Damascene from Egypt, a character adopted merely to avoid notice, for a true Moslem of any Western nationality, provided that he knows the formulas, prayers, and ordinary usages of Islam, should in theory be as safe as an Easterner. Actually Rutter was recognized in Mecca by a Syrian acquaintance, and was known afterwards as Sallah ud Din el Inglizi. As an English *haji* he had audience with Ibn Saud.

A year's stay in the country, with visits to Medina and Taif, enabled him to give a valuable picture of the Wahhabis and a careful description of Mecca, the inhabitants and their customs, history, theological beliefs, and ceremonies. Medina fell to the Wahhabis at this time, and the pilgrims were allowed to visit the mosque to pray, not to visit the Prophet's tomb, as the Wahhabi creed forbade such veneration. The population of the city, owing to the War and the recent invasion, had shrunk from 80,000 to 6000.

Rutter's journey was not without its exciting moments. Once when he was down with fever his pilgrim-guide, who had stolen his keys, sat waiting for him to die, so that he could search his baggage for anything worth stealing. Rutter left Arabia by mail-steamer from Yenbo to Port Sudan in the summer of 1926. *The Holy Cities of Arabia*, the book in which he describes his experiences, is necessarily in the old tradition of the less scientific travellers, but to the ordinary reader not primarily interested in *wadis*, *harras*, and the exact positions of places it is as desirable as any.

A picture of the Arab in less known scenes has been provided by P. W. Harrison, a medical missionary in Eastern Arabia, who saw the Bedouin of the oases and waste lands, many of them belonging to the poorest classes, including the pearl divers. His description does not avoid the ugliness, filth, and sordid aspects which Doughty shunned in his writing, and it is but a regional study which would apply truly only on the east and parts of the south of the peninsula. But as such it is valuable.

DOUGLAS CARRUTHERS ON A "SHARARI" CAMEL

In Arabia he usually wore an old khaki suit, native sheepskin coat, rope-soled shoes, and a rag
round his head—when not bareheaded.

From "Arabian Adventure," by Douglas Carruthers, by permission of the author

THE MAIN WADI OF HADHRAMAUT NEARING THE SEA
Royal Air Force official photograph. Crown copyright reserved

299

Eldon Rutter's quiet and scholarly manner is in contrast to the shrewd, humorous, and pithy style of one of the great pre-War explorers. G. Wyman Bury, or "Abdulla Mansur," as he was known to the Arabs, began his career in the Royal Warwickshire Regiment, and gained his first experience of Moslems when fighting on the side of Moroccan rebels in 1895. The following year he began a quarter of a century's contact with Arabia, lived with the Arabs on the Indian Ocean littoral, endured all their hardships as one of them, and gained a complete knowledge of their vernacular. He served on the Aden Boundary Commission in 1902, and two years later accompanied the Aden Hinterland Expeditionary Force as Political Officer. An attempt to push north into the Jauf of Yemen greatly excited the Turks, and seems to have done Bury little good with the authorities at Aden and Bombay. At any rate there was some quarrel between Aden and the explorer which was not amicably settled for a number of years. Perhaps it was for this reason that Somaliland was the scene of his preparations for an expedition backed by the Royal Geographical Society in 1908. Bury's aim was no less than to cross Yemen and proceed along the western fringe of the Great South Desert to Southern Nejd. He landed on the coast outside the British controlled area, and within two days was robbed of all his equipment.

South-western Arabia was a home to Bury: his lady went out to be married at Hodeida, and the honeymoon was passed at Sana—surely a unique experience for any European pair. His pre-War travels gave rise to two books, *The Land of Uz* and *Arabia Infelix*, both of which are fascinating, shrewd, and pithy in manner, and those who wish to know Yemen may find them more palatable to modern taste than the more dignified Niebuhr. They show how fully Bury understood the wild tribesmen, whom, like Englishmen generally, he preferred to the townsmen. Describing the way from Hodeida to Sana, 150 miles over plain, followed by mountains rising to 9000 feet and descending to some 7000, he shows a vivid panorama of hot desert, barren scrub, parched mimosa, and then parklike country, ravines, fortresses on sheer precipices, spurs and hillsides planted with coffee, and all the birds, beasts, crops, and variations of climate of the land. Passing out of the coastal plain, the Tihama, he wrote,

> while the morning is still grey you may hear the rapping shots of some tribal *fracas* from the foot-hills, a cheery sound, denoting that the world is once more astir and taking an intelligent interest in its affairs.

Agriculture in the lowlands was exciting, as, owing to widespread blood-feuds, the farmer "never knows when he may be 'potted' while ploughing, in a quarrel he had never heard of." The highland farmer was rather of the opinion that such feuds were a waste of time and energy, and in Bury's opinion this class of agriculturist was the strength of Yemen. But the transit of all agricultural produce was hindered by marauding bands.

Coffee was still, as in Niebuhr's time, the main Yemen product, despite the falling prices due to Brazilian output. The local consumption was enormous, though the Arabs used the husk for their own needs and kept the berry for the market. Bury described the methods of cultivation, the extent and quality of output in the various districts, and noted that Aden was the coffee port for the southern districts since Mocha had ceased to exist commercially, a demise due to heavy taxation in the past, and the proximity of Aden. The only other agricultural product worth more than passing mention was kat.

Katha edulis was first classified by Forskal, of Niebuhr's expedition, and is a standard shrub with alternative, simple serrate leaves and terminal panicles of small white flowers. The tender shoots and leaves which appear after rain are in much demand, and find a good sale in any Yemen market. These leaves and shoots are chewed as an exhilarating drug, but its use was largely confined to the natives, as Europeans did not like it and the Turks never became addicts. At first the kat-chewer experienced a feeling of intellectual ability, and would be quite ready to sit up all night, passing the time in discussion about everything and anything. But in time the addict became incapable of consecutive thought without the stimulus, and its absence induced nervous irritability. In time there resulted constipation, insomnia, impotency, flaccid gums, loose and discoloured teeth, and an incapacity for real thought or efficient work by any temporary deprivation. Slight addiction was marked only by failing memory, and those who could get kat only in small quantities and at long intervals suffered little; a short bout, however, would always induce mental 'fuzziness.' The drug permeated every class that could pay for it, and sometimes a man would starve himself and his family to get it. The shrub was cultivated in limited areas and at about 5000 feet. Along the trade routes of Southern Yemen it reached Lahej, where it had devoted adherents, but at Aden heavy taxes put its price beyond the average native, and it would not stand the voyage for exportation.

Bury's quick eye missed little at Sana or in the country east of Aden, and up to the War he had no rival in his own field. In 1916 the doctors gave him a few months to live, but his wife's care prolonged his life another four years. During the Great War he acted for a time as Intelligence officer in the Canal Zone, was concerned with the preparations for the Hejaz Revolt, and was present at the curtain-raiser, the capture of Jidda. No European of his time knew Yemen like Bury, and his knowledge of Turkish Imperial administration was unrivalled.

Yemen and Asir received special attention from the Arab Bureau in Cairo during the War. Almost the sole 'inside' information on Asir came from the reports of French officers with the Egyptian forces, who had served under Mohammed Ali against the Wahhabis. The map drawn up by Jomard (1839) looked convincing, but was really conjectural. Colonel K. Cornwallis in 1916 adduced much important information by rounding up and questioning natives from those parts in the bazaars. Any wandering trader was interrogated, and a picture of the natural features, products, and tribal organization was built up. This work, carried on and supplemented by Bury, was found to be accurate when checked by Political Officers on the coast.

A short but exciting journey into Asir was made at the end of 1922, when Rosita Forbes landed at Jizan from Port Sudan, and by favour of the Emir visited Sabya. Her account revealed a fanatical population inimical to all strangers, and her progress from village to village was "a succession of minor fights." Farther south Ameen Rihani's journey through Yemen has provided an interesting picture of modern conditions, though his writings suffer from an anti-British bias. It appears that the Jews are still despised, though heavy fines are imposed on those who ill-treat them. There are 6000 in Sana, and even the fairly prosperous jewellers and merchants live in the Ghetto, parts of which Rihani describes as "incredibly clean." The Jews have to pay tribute, have to wear black and dress their hair with side-locks, are allowed to make and sell wine, but not to Moslems, and are exempt from military service. Asked if the Jews were content under these laws, a rabbi answered, "We have security." The number of Jews in Yemen was estimated in 1928, by the German traveller H. von Wissmann, as about 70,000.

When the War began there were great gaps in European knowledge of the peninsula, not only in Yemen and Asir, but along two-thirds of the Red Sea coast, over vast areas of the west and centre, and everywhere inland a few miles on the south coast. In Asir the position of Ibha, the capital, was not known even within a day's journey, and it was still to be learned that the authority of the Idrisi chief, an ally of Britain, ran only in the coastal regions and not in the highlands.

The journeys of H. St J. Philby in Central Arabia, which will be mentioned later, made supremely valuable additions to existing knowledge. The skill and daring of the Red Sea naval patrols solved problems of the Hejaz, Asir, and Yemen coasts, whose triple coral reefs had deterred the curiosity of previous marine surveys. Inland the Western Hejaz was travelled by many officers, notably in the region of the Wadis Hamdh, Jizil, and Ais, the last of which was previously unknown. The first British officer to reach the Hejaz Railway from the coast was Captain Garland, who later made his way from Wadi Ais, behind Jebel Radhwa, to Yenbo by a new route. Major Davenport and Lieutenant N. W. Clayton brought in much information about long stretches of the railway, and much of the Wadi·Hamdh was actually mapped by British officers who were primarily engaged in warfare.

Lawrence's fighting has naturally attracted more interest than his geographical work, which covered great areas of new country. Less known than his ride to Akaba are his journeys from Wejh to the Wadi Ais and his description of the confluence of Hamdh, Jizil, and Ais. It was Lawrence also who contributed a most important piece of information gathered in the first place from a remark of the Emir Feisal's during a conversation on the physical features of the Hejaz. Feisal said that the Wadi Akik, which rises south-west of Taif, passed well east of Mecca and went northward as far as Medina. It was already known that pilgrims on the way to Rabegh had to cross a *wadi* of this name south-west of Medina, but this valley had not been connected with the channel near Taif, three hundred miles away. These data were specially important because they showed that the main divide of the peninsula lay inland of Taif.

The Arab Revolt opened the district behind Wejh to exploration, and advantage was taken of the opportunities as far as active service conditions in a difficult country allowed. The surrender of Medina in January 1919 brought forth a useful Turkish staff map giving the wells, posts, and tracts for thirty miles round and a plan of the city. But it is indicative of our knowledge of interior Hejaz that there were no satisfactory determinations of longitude anywhere along the five hundred miles of the Hejaz Railway from Maan to Medina. A British officer's survey in June 1918 moved Maan four miles to the south-east. Another officer, working only by compass and dead reckoning, pushed one section of the railway about nine miles eastward. On another section, after several traverses and much reckoning, two officers reached the opinion that the line had been mapped twenty miles too far east. Their result was confirmed by a traverse made by Lawrence and by the computations of aeroplane pilots flying from the coast. Two years after the War the longitude of Medina was still unknown!

Lawrence's description of the gallant German retirement in Syria at the end of the Palestine campaign is well known, but fewer people have heard of those Germans who were the first in the War to enter the Holy Province. Early in 1915 a party of fifty men, led by an officer named von Mucke, landed at Lith after entering the Red Sea at a time when the British patrols were not greatly concerned with coastwise craft. They were members of a demolition party left on Cocos Island by the *Emden* when the Australian cruiser *Sydney* appeared on the scene, and were trying to reach Germany by land routes. Hussein had not yet thrown off the Turkish yoke, and partly by his favour they managed to secure camels and began the march north to Jidda. On the way they were ambushed by the Harb, but with four machine-guns and a quantity of small arms they held the tribesmen off for three days and two nights. Their water failed and their dead camels poisoned the air; finally they would have been forced to surrender to the invisible snipers who surrounded them, but Hussein saved them, and eventually they won through.

The second German party, under Captain von Müller, came from the East Indies, landed east of the Aden Protectorate, and reached Jidda after a three months' march. Thence they moved northward, against Turkish advice, and just south of Rabegh were hacked to pieces with savage ferocity by the Harb. A relic of these brave and unfortunate men came into the hands of D. G. Hogarth long afterwards—some torn pages of Bury's *Land of Uz*, clotted with blood.

III

The last months of the War saw the first important journey of this century into the Hadhramaut when Captain W. H. Lee-Warner reached Wadi Duwan by the Wadi Himam, a route previously untravelled, visited Shibam, and made a valuable report on conditions in the country. Brief but informative, this report shows the social organization of the people, from the Seyyids, with their great influence in religion and local politics, through the fighting tribes, which sometimes led a settled existence but still drew tribute from the townsfolk as a guarantee for the latter's safety, down to the slave population. Apart from tribute to the tribesmen, taxation was paid in the main to the Kaiti dynasty as far as Shibam and east of that town to the Kathiri. Slaves formed the lowest class of the community, and included Chinese girls who were smuggled into the country. At the time of Lee-Warner's visit the African source of male slaves had been terminated by the British Red Sea patrols, but the slave trade in past years had been a highly organized and profitable business, and the explorer put forward the interesting suggestion that the marked xeno-phobia of this country was partly due to the knowledge that the foreigner was determined to stamp it out. Slavery in Mohammedan countries, however, does not always connote the misery associated with it in European minds. The slaves of Hadhramaut appeared cheerful, and many of them rose to positions of trust.

Unable to sustain a large population, Hadhramaut sends many of its inhabitants overseas. The three considerable streams, the report says, go to Hyderabad, East Africa, and the Netherlands East Indies, whence the emigrants send back money enabling their relations to sustain life in Hadhramaut and carry on the family tradition.

Regarding the water supply, Captain Lee-Warner noted that from Katan eastward down the main *wadi* water was available, and near Shibam quite plentiful. Here the inhabitants did not depend on local rainfall, whereas in the Wadi Duwan the cultivator prepared his fields and then waited for rain. When it came it was caught in irrigation channels, and was diverted into the fields. Then "without delay the dhurra (barley) and other quick-maturing seeds are planted; and without any further water supply the plant grows, matures, fruits, and is reaped within a period of seven to eight weeks." Among the agricultural products of the Wadi Hadhramaut, he remarked indigo, sesame, millet, durra, wheat, and lucerne, as well as dates, the staple food, and delicious honey which the bees collect from the date flowers. Packed in large round tins, this is one of the few exports from Hadhramaut. The Hamumi tobacco is also grown, a moderate crop which is in much demand on the shore of the Red Sea. It is marketed for the Kaiti Sultan by a group of Bombay Parsees.

To-day most of the 80,000 Arabs in the East Indies are from Hadhramaut. Such an immigration naturally aroused Dutch interest in the country of origin, and gave rise in the spring of 1931 to an expedition lasting six weeks and led by Dr D. van der Meulen, a former Netherlands *chargé d'affaires* at Jidda, and Dr H. von Wissmann, an able German geographer, who had performed notable geological and archæological work in Yemen in 1927–28. The Kaiti Sultan to-day spends most of his time at Hyderabad, but the travellers were supported in his absence by his governor at Mokalla, and were allowed to join a camel caravan returning to the interior. Outside the town Bedouin were lying in wait for members of the caravan with whom they had a blood-feud, so the two Europeans started in one of the governor's motor-cars and joined the main party when it had passed the danger-zone. This manner of beginning a journey was a far cry from the days of von Wrede, Bent, and Hirsch, but later they travelled without mechanical transport, like the men of old, and reaching the Wadi Duwan regarded it as a marvel of beauty after the arid plateau. The old, blind governor of the district, who remembered the visits of Hirsch and Bent, entertained them for a few days in his turreted, battlemented, and loopholed fortress. They passed through Sif, and found the inhabitants unfriendly to strangers, though less actively hostile than in former days. Entering the portals of Wadi Hadhramaut proper through the ruins near Meshed, they first turned aside to visit, in the Wadi Amd, a Seyyid favourably known to the Netherlands Government in Java. His town, Hureida, had never previously seen a European within its walls. The place was waging an unequal war with Nature, groups of slaves drew water from wells thirty feet deep, and only the money sent from Java by emigrants kept the place alive. From Hureida to the main valley the Europeans were taken by motor-car. Cars to-day are brought up in sections from the coast on the backs of camels. A Seyyid of Terim was building a motor road to the coast at his own expense, and had already constructed a rough mountain road for cars.

From the Amd and the Wadi Kasr they motored between the high rock walls, with the hot wind cutting hands and faces like a northern frost, and arrived at Shibam. The high houses built close together made the streets into dark tunnels, for only the top five or six stories and the roofs were whitewashed, the rest being a greyish brown. The travellers were impressed by the beautiful lines achieved by the Hadrami builders, out of no other material than mud and scanty, crooked, and poor wood. "Whether it be the poor man's hut, an imposing fortress, a beautiful villa, or a mosque with its graceful minarets, every edifice here is made of sun-baked mud."[1] The hygienic arrangements, however, were primitive:

> Gutters of hollowed-out palm-stalks jutted out from kitchens, bathrooms, and toilets, and the fluid waste poured down from various levels into the streets below. Running through the middle of the streets are open masonry drains, clogged with garbage, on which chickens, cats, and donkeys feed. We had to walk warily, with our eyes continually uplifted, ready to dodge any rain of filth from above.

Seyun, the capital of the Kathiri rulers, they considered the largest and most beautiful city in Hadhramaut. The houses were low and spread out, and the garden quarter was within the walls. The influence of Java was here so pronounced that Malay was constantly spoken at Court, and dress very similar to that of the Javanese was worn. Hundreds of Arab-Dutch subjects live in Seyun, so that the ruler could say with Eastern politeness, "Here you are Sultan and not I, for your subjects outnumber mine."

Thirty years had brought change to Terim. Where Hirsch's life was demanded by an angry crowd, from which he was saved only by leaving the town immediately, these representatives of the Netherlands were entertained in the palace of the most influential Seyyid. They visited Kabr Hud, von Wrede's old objective, travelling part of the way by car, and continued even farther, to the site of the 'volcano' of which Bent had heard. "Hud was a prophet," writes Dr van der Meulen, "sent by Allah to the Addites, the aboriginal inhabitants of Hadhramaut." Those who turned from his teaching were choked by hot winds or turned into apes. Their descendants, it is said, still live on a hill near Aden.

> As he preached of repentance he called the people to conversion and threatened them with Allah's terrible punishment if they did not obey. His words resounded in the wilderness. He was persecuted, and is said to have fallen into the hands of his enemies on this spot; but Allah intervened and cleft open a rock which received him. His faithful *naqa*, or racing camel, on whose milk he lived, died at his tomb and was turned into stone.

---

[1] Article in *The National Geographic Magazine*, 1932. Also see *Hadhramaut: some of its Mysteries Unveiled*, by D. van der Meulen and H. von Wissmann (Leyden, 1933).

The *naqa* mosque was later built against the petrified camel, and over the split rock a repentant posterity erected the domed tomb of Hud. The body of the prophet, more than thirteen feet long, projects far out beyond the cupola, and is marked by a whitewashed stone railing. Inside the dome we saw the split rock, whose sides were polished smooth by tens of thousands of hands, passed prayerfully over it, and by countless lips which in ecstasy had kissed the holy stone.

Passing down the wild rocky Wadi Barahut, accompanied by Bedouin guides of a remote Hadhramaut tribe living on the borders of the Great Southern Desert, they found the reputed volcano to be only a large cave with gigantic boulders strewn round its wide entrance, behind which was a dark fissure and a low cleft for entrance. The passage they followed had many side corridors, some of which were entered by crawling through small openings. It was intensely hot down this passage, but it was ascertained definitely that Barahut was no volcanic crater.

The aim of this mission was political, but von Wissmann made a map of the country, based on measurements and surveying. The German's knee had been shot away in an aerial duel on the Western Front, and at Terim he was a hero with the younger generation, which had only recently seen the new strange visitants in the skies.

At the end of October 1929 a flight of the Royal Air Force landed at Mokalla from Aden, and proceeded to photograph the surrounding country within a radius of a hundred and fifty miles, mainly along the Wadi Hadhramaut. The difficulty of identifying the many places not marked on any existing maps was overcome by the assistance of Seyyid Abu Bakr, the Sultan's Wazir, who pluckily volunteered as observer, and seems to have been naturally gifted in recognizing things seen from the air, for without any special training he unhesitatingly named the villages in the main Hadhramaut valley.

On such reconnaissances the aeroplanes first climbed to 6000 feet to clear the coastal mountains, reaching the summit in twenty-five minutes, a distance which took the Bents four days. From this point the country sloped gently from the north, down to 2400 feet at Shibam, and was all cut away into intricate formations and patterns, as though, according to Squadron-

SHIBAM

From "The Southern Gates of Arabia," by Freya Stark, by permission of the author

MAJOR R. E. CHEESMAN AT BAHREIN ON HIS RETURN FROM THE
JABRIN EXPEDITION

By permission of Major R. E. Cheesman

Leader the Hon. R. A. Cochrane, A.F.C., it had been rained on by some corrosive liquid which, once it had eaten through the top protective layer, was able to bite deeply into the soft core underneath, the result being a maze of narrow, twisting, winding canyons, some of them 1000 feet or more in depth.

The cliffs of the range lying behind the aeroplane flying north faced east and northward, and their line could be used to fix the position of some of the towns in Eastern Hadhramaut, as with the excellent visibility, especially in the early morning, bearings could be taken from the air above the neighbourhood of the Wadi Hadhramaut.

After thirty-five miles of the rugged plateau scenery the airmen saw the Wadi Duwan, a particularly wide and deep canyon, its floor a mass of date-palms, with villages clustering on the slopes where the cliff walls had fallen. The north end of the *wadi* ended in dried mud and drift sand, and the faint outlines of ruined villages and irrigation ditches could be seen on the ground. At this confluence of Duwan and Hadhramaut the observers estimated the valley to be some four to six miles wide. It was quite barren, but eastward along the main *wadi* numerous villages lay under the cliffs on either side, surrounded by date-palms and bright green cultivation.

After flying over Shibam, Terim, and Seyun the aircraft came to districts less known and unvisited by Europeans. It was seen here that the *wadi* narrowed to about a quarter of a mile, with many windings, and farther along its course villages became scarcer, while drift sand and scrub formed the valley bottom. After passing the white tomb of Hud the *wadi* ran south-east for nearly fifty miles before bending to the east again. On this section it was estimated to be not more than a quarter of a mile wide, with cliffs less than 200 feet high. The surrounding country was barren plateau, cut by small canyons. Suddenly the *wadi* turned south and ran through the mountains to the coast.

From Terim the stream could be seen intermittently, but some miles from the sea, about the fiftieth meridian of east longitude, it vanished completely under the sand. The nearest volcano to Barahut was an extinct one, fifty miles away.

Some of the principal places east of Shibam and elsewhere

had been fixed on previous maps only by distances judged by marching time. This, of course, was a variable, influenced by such things as weather, or even the local tribal situation. The Royal Air Force reconnaissance fixed Kabr Hud some thirty-five miles west of the accepted position and Terim fifteen miles. The photographs taken revealed the character of the land more forcibly and clearly than could the words of an explorer, gaining his impressions while striving to make headway along the rocky plateau, or marching through narrow gullies and valleys under a burning sun. To unveil Hadhramaut under such conditions the explorer has needed in addition to his normal qualities of endurance and courage the more unusual artistry in words. Arabia has had her full share of gifted writers, and among them one of the most brilliant is a recent traveller in Hadhramaut.

It was pointed out by Captain Lee-Warner that no one on reaching the head of the Wadi Duwan had turned westward towards Shabwa. Von Wrede had crossed by a direct route from the Wadi Amd to the site of this old city, finding only collectors of desert salt where once existed a key position on the frankincense route to Marib from Dhofar, and a convergence of roads along which Indian produce was brought from the southern ports, to join the westward and northward stream of merchandise. This age-old city Freya Stark, an explorer with a former Persian journey to her credit, resolved to visit in 1935.

Starting from Mokalla, her way led east to the Wadi Himam, then across the stony plateau, or Jol, to Khuraiba, in Wadi Duwan, Sif, Hajarein, Meshed, Hureida, Katan, Shibam, Seyun, and Terim. Illness prevented the western journey, and she was flown back to the coast by a Royal Air Force aeroplane. *The Southern Gates of Arabia*, in which she told her experiences, showed the Hadhramaut with a beauty and aptness of description achieved by no other traveller. The little towns clinging to the sides of the *wadis*, their backs to the high walls for defence; the feudal atmosphere of the castles, where there was affectionate reverence for a local governor like that paid to a Highland chieftain; Duwan, most luxuriant valley of the Hadhramaut, rich in crops of date and millet by reason of its proximity to the main watershed and the torrent that passes after the summer rains; the unveiled Bedouin shepherdesses with their flocks of goats, and the Arab women of the villages, working the fields, black-veiled and wearing high conical hats; a night ride to Hajarein, and a hundred scenes and reflections made one part of Arabia wholly present and vivid to the reader. Her photographs, intimate and exquisitely balanced, were the perfect complement to the wider aspects of the district recorded by the airmen. Freya Stark's, van der Meulen's, and those of the Royal Air Force, are the most striking photographs yet taken in Arabia.

A journey less colourful than Freya Stark's, but of considerable scientific value, was made by O. H. Little in 1919–20 along the coastal plain and the southern slopes of the Hadhramaut plateau in the neighbourhood of the Wadi Hajar. This expedition provided a complete picture of the geography and geology of one district. Another post-War journey deserves mention. In 1929 Eldon Rutter travelled from Damascus to Hail, passing north and then east of the Wadi Sirhan and Jauf. Parts of his inward route had not been previously used by Europeans. He returned farther to the west, touching the Sirhan on his way to Amman.

In the summer of 1936 Philby travelled from Ashaira to Ibha, in Asir, then to Nejran, the ruins of Shabwa, Shibam, and the Seyun-Terim district. After visiting Sheher and Mokalla he returned to Saudi Arabia.

CHAPTER XVII

THE EMPTY QUARTER

I never found any Arabian who had aught to tell, even by hearsay, of that dreadful country. Haply it is Nefud with quicksands, which might be entered into and even passed with milch dromedaries in the spring weeks.

CHARLES M. DOUGHTY, *Travels in Arabia Deserta*

AT an evening session of the Royal Geographical Society on June 2, 1930, a paper was read for Mr Bertram Thomas by Sir Arnold Wilson, before an audience smaller than one expected from the rare nature of the communication. The Society was, in fact, hearing the most important paper ever received to that date on the subject of the Great Southern Desert of Arabia, the Rub' al Khali, or Empty Quarter of the peninsula, a region as large as Germany, France, and Spain combined, and until that time almost wholly unexplored.

The fringes of the desert had been touched by previous explorers, who had communicated their results to the Society. Mr G. M. Lees had told of journeys in 1925–26 in Oman and along the south coast. Major R. E. Cheesman, under the protection of Ibn Saud through the good offices of Sir Percy Cox, had journeyed in Eastern Arabia and along the northern border lands of the Rub' al Khali, acquiring useful information regarding the drainage of the Nejd uplands and studying the distribution of resident birds and the movement of migrants through the Great Desert. He had travelled from Oqair (which he identified with the ancient Gerra) to the ruins of Salwa, and from Hofuf south to Zarnuga, a Murra centre, and thence by six waterless stages through a country of dunes and bare gravel plains to Jabrin (until that time unvisited, and a place arousing much conjecture). Here he ascertained that the Murra wandered as far as Maqainama, 120 miles farther south, and heard it said that tribesmen had crossed even to Nejran, in Yemen, in a month's journey. Cheesman was the pioneer of exploration in the northern area of the desert. In the south Bertram Thomas had travelled along the south-east desert border lands from Sur to Dhofar, and had described the six-hundred-mile journey through a district little known and almost unvisited since the days of the *Palinurus*. On this march, in 1928, Thomas had obtained information regarding the Rub' al Khali which roused an ambition to penetrate as far as possible into the desert, to enter country untrod by Europeans in all historical times, and, if possible, to cross it from the south to the Persian Gulf. In the discussion following the reading of his paper to the Society Sir Percy Cox recalled a view of the Great Southern Desert from Jebel Akhdar thirty years before, and a scheme, regarding which he made preliminary inquiries, for a crossing from Muscat to Aden.

The Great Southern Desert was almost unknown to European explorers. Palgrave and Burton knew its characteristics but vaguely. Halévy, in the west, and Wellsted, in the east, had perhaps seen it from afar; but the former was probably misinformed by guides anxious to avoid the locality, and it is improbable that Wellsted, at a great distance on the heights of Jebel Akhdar, could have distinguished much of its character. Von Wrede touched the desert on the south, and the Bents may have sighted the approach to it from the Qara range. Now in this paper of June 2 Thomas described a farther South Arabian venture, which penetrated to the edge of the great sands. It was the preliminary to his magnificent dash across the whole vast region.

The party for this journey was assembled at Salala, in Dhofar, and consisted of twenty-eight tribesmen (twenty-five Kathiri, Rashidi, and Imani, two Daru from Oman, and a Karbi from Hadhramaut), Thomas's secretary, Ali Mohammed, and a servant. Thomas was more fully equipped with scientific instruments than his great predecessors in Arabian exploration, for in addition to cameras he carried a prismatic compass, aneroids, hydrometer, sextant, artificial horizon, and chronometers. On January 13, 1930, he left Salala, entered the Dhofar range, and, after crossing the mountains, followed the Wadi Ghudun to the Wadi Umm al Hait. This *wadi* system was then traversed north-east to Al Ain; a short expedition was made into the sands, to the Ramlat al Mugshin, and the explorer then returned by the Wadi Dauka to the plateau, and down to the coast.

It was established by this march that beyond the coastal ranges of tropical vegetation which lay some three days' journey from the coast there was a single dry *wadi* system in a vast sandstone steppe which fell from south to north and from west to east. The trunk *wadi*, Umm al Hait, which had various regional names, possessed six main tributary *wadis* rising at about 3000 feet in the mountains, and running roughly parallel and northward, to be lost in the desert at not more than 400 feet above sea-level. The main *wadi* was lost in the sand at Mugshin; north of this *wadi* the great sands extended to the Persian Gulf and westward to Dawasir and Nejran, sometimes crossing the *wadi*, sometimes falling back from it or running by its side. Like the *wadi* itself, these neighbouring sands were known by various regional names. Towards the Hadhramaut, the edge of the great sands turned west-south-west. In some of the *wadis* there was water near their mountain sources, but for the rest they were "cruelly dry," with steep narrow banks and beds that were pebbly until the valleys widened out towards the Great Desert, where at length they could be traced only by parched scrub. The whole region was arid and desolate, the resort of Bedouin who led a hungry and thirsty life. Even the Bedouin could sustain life only for part of the year in this area, and in the summer were driven back to the perennial water-holes in the highlands. They lived mainly on camels' milk, and raiding was the great excitement of their lives. There was scarcely a man in Thomas's escort who had not forayed into the Northern Hadhramaut or who had not suffered from raids. Among them might was right, life and property were held precariously, and blood-feuds divided the tribes. Of these tribes those of the desert were called Bait Kathir, Mahra, Manahil, Awamir, Sa'ar, Nahad, and Karab. The Mahra numbered many thousands, and the last two only one or two hundred respectively. Among the Mahra and Kathir were some small tribes, non-Arab and non-raiding, like the Balhaf and the Bautahara, a small tribe with a language of its own, and reputed to have possessed at one time the whole region of the Wadi Ghudun.

Out in the steppe, south of the great sands, life for the Bedouin was extremely primitive. Every little hollow in the rocks capable of holding rain-water had a name, and the Bedouin clung to them with their flocks and herds until the drought drove them away. In the mountains they lived in caves, and in the desert under the shade of acacia. The men were illiterate, prayed, but knew nothing of the Koran. In their code petty theft was immoral, but murder and plundering on a raid were honourable, and they had a great respect for shrines. Medical treatment was confined to the use of certain herbs, the gastric juices of animals, the urine of the young cow camel, cautery, and exorcism. The women were allowed to milk only sheep, and "beautified" themselves by smearing their faces and bodies with indigo.

The vegetation of the steppe consisted of various acacias, bushes, and scrub. In the middle and lower courses on the *wadis* there were some antelope, gazelle, hare, and foxes. Many varieties of sand-lizards, some of them edible, were noted, and, on the edge of the sand, hedgehogs and sand-rats. Birds were rare, the crow being the most common; vultures were plentiful in the mountains.

Thomas was able to collect information regarding the eastern quarters of the desert from his two Daru, who had come from Oman by this route, and could add to it the knowledge he had acquired on his previous journey in the south-east. Thus, from Mugshin the edge of the sand, he wrote, ran north-north-east for four days, then turned due north, westward of Ibri, thrust into the Oman peninsula, and then ran westward behind the coast of Trucial Oman on the Persian Gulf. The eastern districts of the sands were used by some of the Bedouin season-ally, while other tribes lived in the sands all the year and used the black camel-hair tents. This desert existence was aided by occasional summer rainfall. Water-holes were very brackish, and in some parts of the desert salt water could be found very near the surface. In the eastern sands water was found at from twelve to thirty-six feet in different localities, and in the western at very great depths. To the Arabs the term Rub' al Khali, he found, meant only the sand and steppe which would not support life.

Such were the main points ascertained on this reconnaissance to the edge of the Rub' al Khali, but Thomas mentions two other matters of general interest which had engaged the attention of former travellers. He questioned Mahri tribesmen about the supposed volcano of Barahut—the sole volcano of Arabia—and all of them denied its existence. They told him, however, of superstitions regarding the *wadi* of Barahut, the chief one being that it was a place for the departed spirits of wicked men. "As a variety of hell," Thomas comments, "it may well be that its supposed volcanic activity has symbolical significance."

The other point of interest lay in the desert quicksands of Umm es Samim, a treacherous area reported to extend a two days' march. In appearance it was a salt plain, and many travellers, it was said, had perished in its wastes. This plain recalled von Wrede's story of the white patches and the experiment with the plumb-line in the "Bahr es Safi," but most of Thomas's Bedouin who had raided north of the Hadhramaut, and moreover the Karbi who hailed from that district, had never heard of "Bahr es Safi," and said that the quicksand existed only at Umm es Samim.

These lines merely summarize Thomas's paper on his preliminary journey, and can give no idea of the vividly clear, balanced, and complete style in which he pictures the main features of the area north of the Qara range. In its clarity and precision the paper strongly recalls the writings of the great French *savants* who made Roman North Africa their field.

On this journey, as on his former march from Sur to Dhofar, Thomas wore the Bedouin dress, spoke the local dialects, and avoided the use of tobacco and alcohol, "to win a reputation for orthodoxy that would ultimately help . . . in the crossing of the Great Desert from sea to sea." He was now physically acclimatized for his great final adventure, and was superbly equipped with scientific knowledge, grasp of Arabic dialects, long experience of Arab peoples, and understanding of their manners and customs. He possessed also in the highest degree a sensibility and tact revealed throughout all his dealings with the primitive Bedouin. Moreover, as Wazir to the Sultan of Muscat, he had become known throughout South-eastern Arabia, and had won a general tolerance, despite his Christianity.

Thomas had never sought British permission for his various journeys, as the official attitude (with which he agreed) was inimical to exploration by reason of the anarchy that usually existed in the desert. Thus, in planning his crossing of the Great Desert he followed his usual practice, and none knew of his intention except the Prince of Oman, son of the Sultan, and a Rashidi tribesman, Sahail, whom he had rewarded after his journey to Mugshin, and who had promised to meet him in Dhofar for an expedition northward across the Great Desert to Doha, near Bahrein.

Now, any man who writes of his travels in Arabia challenges two comparisons, one based upon a standard of courage and the other on that of literature. There must be the moral and physical bravery of a von Wrede, Burckhardt, Burton, or Doughty; and judgment must inevitably be swayed by recollection of the writings of the last two and of Lawrence. Bertram Thomas's account of his journey across the desert from sea to sea, *Arabia Felix: across the Empty Quarter of Arabia*, meets both challenges triumphantly.

II

Landing in Dhofar at the beginning of October 1930, Thomas was delayed for several weeks by Sahail's failure to keep the tryst, but to this delay the reader owes a fascinating description of this tropical enclave of Arabia, a land of coconut, cane, cotton, millet, and wheat; stories of the old wars of Dhofar; a visit to the ruins of Khor Rori, more than thirty years after the Bents; and vivid information on devil dances, slaves, and local customs. One interesting anthropological point arising from head-measurements which he took suggests that the nearest kin to the Southern Arabs of Dhofar are among the tribes on the African side of the Red Sea, rather than among the Semitic group of Northern Arabia.[1]

As curiosity was being aroused by his sojourn near the coast,

[1] Cheesman collected some evidence on this point when exploring Ethiopia in the years after his Arabian journeys. His book *Lake Tana and the Blue Nile* (London, 1936) has all the colour of the older travel books and the accurate, scientific character of the modern work on exploration. Its appearance was delayed by the theft of the manuscript, which had taken six years to compile.

Thomas decided to visit the Qara mountains, where he could wait for two envoys, Mayuf and Khuwaitim, whom he had sent inland to seek Sahail or some other camel party to escort him northward over the sands. Of these hill regions, into which, it seemed, early settlers or aborigines had been driven by more virile peoples, Thomas gives an entrancing account, dealing with the country, its inhabitants, their customs (such as faith cures, sacrifices, taboos, circumcisions), legends, witchcraft, and pagan cults. Only a little may be quoted to show the colour and resilient prose of the first chapters of his book. Here is the picture of a dance, in mourning rites, performed three days after a death. At one end of the large circle of spectators sat a dozen stalwart negro "drum-boys," naked but for their loincloths, with rattles of dried mangoes about their knees, adding a swishing sound to the beat of the drums. A master of ceremonies dashed round the circle, slashing the ground in front of the crowd with his whip when it pressed forward.

> A dozen paces within the ring was the path of the main per-formers—the stream of young negroes and negresses, who came sweeping round and round the circle in grand parade. Young slave girls, singly or in pairs, sturdy, black as ebony, and high of bosom, selected doubtless for their superior graces in the eyes of men. A black muslin veil shrouded each girl's head, and drooped about her shoulders, of so flimsy a material that it did not conceal, but rather accentuated the effect of her flashing eyes, her thick scarlet-painted lips, her nose-ring, earrings, and necklaces of gold.

Each wore a robe of starched indigo that glistened in the sun, and danced with a sinuous, shuffling step, while a youth leaped in front of her with a quivering drawn sword, and seemed spellbound as he danced. The whole dance, the scene, and the atmosphere of barbaric excitement are brilliantly described.

As the afternoon continued more dancers joined the ring, and the great moment arrived when the evil spirit should be driven from the dead body into that of a specially chosen "drum-boy." The excitement grew wilder, the boy developed a frenzy of contortion and slobbering, and rifles were discharged into the air, adding to the din, as Thomas left the place, disgusted with the orgy.

In the Qara mountains illness such as the failure of milk

in animals is easily ascribed to the evil eye, and exorcism is practised, usually at sunrise or sunset, by a frankincense rite. Thomas saw this ceremony performed over a cow, the owner of which brought an incense-burner containing smouldering wood, broke a fragment of incense into three pieces, spat upon these three times, and placed them in the burner. The animal was held by two tribesmen, one seizing the lower jaw and the other twisting its tail and lifting its near hind-leg off the ground. The burning incense was circled three times over the cow's head, while these words were chanted in the Shahari tongue:

BERTRAM THOMAS'S ROUTE IN 1930

" Look at this your sacrifice: frankincense and fire: from eye of the evil spirit: of mankind: from afar: of kindred: near by: and from afar: be redeemed if from me: be redeemed if from another: from the evil spirit: from mankind: I am a man: bringing expiation: for the Evil Eye: of man: of woman: look at this your sacrifice: frankincense and fire! "

Then the animal was allowed to bound off merrily. After cattle were stalled at night women would sometimes go among them carrying burning incense.

At the beginning of December Thomas was back in Dhofar, and it seemed that the expedition might perforce be abandoned for lack of the escort of desert tribesmen. But on December 6, 1930, Mayuf and Khuwaitim returned, when Thomas had almost given up hope, with a party of forty Bedouin, led by Sheikh Salih, a renowned Rashidi of the Great Desert, "a short man, with a rather large head, big of bone. . . . His brow was large, perhaps from his baldness, and his eyes large, his countenance open and frank, his voice slow and measured; he inspired confidence."

After swearing him to secrecy Thomas unfolded his plans for crossing the desert from sea to sea. Salih was difficult to persuade. "Impossible, *sahib*!" "What is possible, then?" "We can take you into our country, the Rashidi *dira* of the Southern Sands, and bring you back, and God deliver us from the Sa'ar, but we cannot take you into the grazing grounds of another tribe." Such a journey would entail traversing Murra country. Furthermore, the Bedouin did not want to travel during Ramadan. They had come thinking that Thomas merely wanted to visit their camp in Dakaka, for they had heard of his generosity to Sahail, in the previous year. "Avarice. That is the Bedouin's burning passion," said Salih.

The sands of Dakaka, in the central Southern Desert, were in truth the key to Thomas's journey. The fact that they had received the previous year's rain had given good pasture, and had enabled the Rashidi to come down to the coast with full milk-skins. The herds were together in these sands, and a relay party could be gathered there for the final advance northward. If the rains had not fallen there, or had come farther north-east, the camels would have been too far off for Thomas to get relays with which to cross the desert quickly, burdened with scientific instruments.

After three days of argument and steady persistence in his object Thomas agreed that Salih's men should be told that the escort was to be only as far as Dakaka; and that when the expedition was fairly started Salih should make ahead, arrange for fresh camels, and try to find a Murra *rabia* to meet Thomas and the main body at Dhahiya. Here, at the edge of the sands, a smaller party was to make the journey north to Shanna and Farajja, and then through Murra territory to Doha. Salih engaged to see to all this, under oath. Thomas agreed to act under his advice, and to reward him at Doha with a rifle, a robe, and a camel.

The journey thus outlined included 550 miles of the Great Desert, north-west for 150 miles to Shanna and then due north to Doha. The main danger on this route lay in the chance of meeting a raiding party of the Sa'ar, a tribe from the far north of Hadhramaut, mustering two thousand rifles, men of terror in the southern sands and at bitter feud with the Rashidi. On one occasion the latter tribe had sent four envoys to try to arrange a truce with them, and Kilthut, one of this embassy, told Thomas the story. They set off hoping to meet a Sa'ar *rabia* who would lead them in safety to the tribe.

One afternoon they dismounted, crept to the edge of a *wadi*, and, looking over the side, saw five Sa'ar Bedouin round a fire and their camels at pasture. It seemed like a gift from Allah! For peace had not yet been made, and at nightfall the Sa'ar would sleep. They could be killed then, and the camels would be plunder. Kilthut and another young man of the party, Musellim, an Imani, urged that full advantage should be taken of the position, but the two older men would not consent, for in their opinion the five men were only part of a larger body in the neighbourhood, a raiding force which would not listen to peace proposals. The right course, therefore, was to retire. Kilthut and Musellim said that they would not leave without the camels, and at length the older men rode away alone.

About midnight, when the Sa'ar fires died down, the two young Arabs crept over the side, loosened the hobbles on the camels, and started homeward. But the Sa'aris discovered the theft before dawn and followed their tracks by moonlight. The next afternoon Kilthut and Musellim, thinking they had a long start, halted to sleep. Suddenly Kilthut awoke, to see an Arab a hundred paces away, covering him with a rifle. He leaped behind a rock with his own rifle as the Arab fired and missed. Then, thinking that his opponent might be a friend, he called out the name of his tribe.

"By my face," came the reply, "I am so-and-so of the Sa'ar, and we (mentioning his section) are at peace with the Ruwashid. You have my camels, and we are stronger than you; thirty men are behind me."

Kilthut shouted, "Deliver me with my life, my camel, and my rifle."

The Sa'ari answered, "By my face," but when they surrendered camels, rifles, and daggers were taken away, though rifle and camel were later restored. This Sa'ar party afterwards met a Mahri with his wife and camel. They slew the man and took the camel, but were themselves caught in Manahil country by a raiding force of Bait Kathir and Mahra, who routed them and killed their sheikh.

In the Sa'ar danger-area Thomas's party was larger, and once with a Murra *rabia* on the northern section of his route there would be little risk from outside attack. But to Thomas risk was in effect a daily condition, as a Christian in the wilderness, surrounded by fanatical Moslems, who, moreover, held life as nothing.

"Bear witness," cried one of Salih's tribesmen on one occasion, inviting Thomas to repeat the Islamic formula.

Taking hold of his beard, which he had let grow, for by his beard a man must swear, Thomas said in Arabic, "God is great."

"There is no god but God," said the Rashidi, and Thomas repeated the words.

"And Mohammed is the Prophet of God," the Arab continued.

"Let me explain," said Thomas. "He is your prophet, a great and good man of your race of Arabs; but we are of another race, also creatures of God, and we say and believe that Jesus is our prophet."

"Jesus, son of whom?" the Arabs asked, for they did not know the Koran, which records that Jesus was the Spirit of God. Then Salih intervened: "True," he said. "To every people their prophet. But, God be praised, this man is no unbeliever, but a confessor of Allah, the One and Indivisible."

III

On December 10, 1930, Thomas's expedition set out, left the foliage and meadows of the Qara range, and moved towards pale sandstone hills, the steppe, and the vast, red, rolling waste beyond. In the desolate *wadi* beds which ran northward across the steppe the wild frankincense-tree flourished. Shisur, south of the Umm al Hait, was a lonely watering-place, the only water for many days, and therefore a likely haunt of raiders. Such places were approached with circumspection, and on arrival the Bedouin scattered and searched the surrounding ground for signs of an enemy. The mere trickle of water at this place made watering the thirsty beasts with small leathern buckets a prolonged business, and the party proceeded in relays as they were finished. There had been rain, and the Umm al Hait was green when they crossed it to skirt the edge of the sands for five days, making for Dhahiya through mountainous sands and patches of gypsum.

After some days of uneventful travel there came a cry which must have thrilled the explorer. The Arabs were pointing to the ground and shouting, "Look, *sahib*, there is the road to Ubar!" It was a great city of old, they said, wealthy with treasure and date gardens and a fort of red silver (gold?). Now it was buried under sand, a few days northward.

On the ground there were well-worn tracks, about a hundred yards wide, graven into the plain. On former journeys Thomas had heard of the fabled city of the desert. Ubar, Wabar, Ophir? Were they the same place? Was Ubar a city on the old trade route, a frankincense route, from ancient Gerra to the Hadhramaut?

That in former times there should have been trade routes over sands now almost impassable was no wild conception. When the higher latitudes of the Northern hemisphere lay beneath an ice cap Southern Arabia, which is held to have had no Ice Age, was under a pluvial period, writes Thomas,

> from which period date the great gorges draining the coastal mountains, and the limestone fossils washed down to the edge of the sands. This very different climate may have long persisted in modified form and made possible a very early civilisation in this region.

But it was impossible for him to turn from his main objective to investigate, for the way to Ubar was arid and pastureless, and his Bedouin were already highly nervous of attack from the Sa'ar.

Shortly after this incident Thomas met the phenomenon of the 'singing sands.' The party was pushing on through heavy dunes when the silence was broken suddenly by a loud, musical droning. "*Hanaina, hanaina*" (bellowing) shouted the Bedouin.

The sound came from a sand-cliff, about a hundred feet high and a hundred yards or so on the right. Thomas was concentrating on the noise, but he noticed that the time was 4.15 P.M. and that a slight wind was blowing from the back of the cliff.

Before this, in similar wind conditions, many such cliffs had been passed but no sound was heard. Of this cliff the leeward side was a fairly steep slant, and Thomas searched vainly for a more funnel-shaped gorge of sand that by the rush of wind might explain so great a volume of noise. For the term 'singing sands' seemed hardly appropriate, as the sound was like the siren of a fair-sized steamship. It continued for about two minutes and, "like a ship's fog signal, ended as abruptly as it had begun."

Salih, who had gone ahead, did not arrive for some time when the party reached the arranged meeting-place at Dhahiya, but his camel tracks and the tracks of twenty others, with the footprints of a Murra tribesman, Hamad bin Hadi, were observed. The Bedouin of the sands could tell at a glance the footprints of every man and camel of Thomas's caravan, and "claimed to know those of his absent tribe, and not a few of his enemies."

When Salih came in with the fresh northern Bedouin it was arranged that Hamad should act as *rabia* for the smaller party making the next stage to Shanna, and then lead a still smaller party for the final dash to Doha. Hamad was a man of medium height, dark complexion, hawk-like face thickly bearded, shifty black eyes, and a curious quick voice. "No better guide in all the sands than Hamad bin Hadi," said Salih, "no doughtier fighter, no more skilful hunter; and loyal . . . none knows the pastures and the water-holes like Hamad; he knows a way across the sands and agrees to be our *rabia*."

The next stage, to Shanna by the sands of Dakaka, was reached, and the Southern Bedouin were paid off, together with the *rabia* of the Southern Awamir and Karab. Then Thomas with twelve picked men well mounted, and five pack-animals, began the dash due north, across an area where *hadh* was the only vegetation, and where loitering on the way meant death. Hamad was on the watch night and day for the Sa'ar.

Even single-handed he had raided into their country, and occupied a prominent place on their black list. Also he had inherited a Manasir blood-feud, and these things caused him many "ghostly fears." He would halt the party and search the horizon with Thomas's telescope, and after the day's journey would slink back over their route, lest they were being tracked by an enemy, coming back at nightfall to say that the camp-fires could be lighted with safety. But when Farajja was reached, about two hundred miles farther on, the dread of raids ceased, for the Sa'ar danger was past and the Wahhabis of the north were quiet during Ramadan. The tension lessened, and Thomas was able to relax.

Conversation, stories, and legends now passed the hours, as they marched through low sandhills and rolling red dunes. The work of collecting specimens in the desert steadily proceeded—a reward of one rupee being allotted to each find brought in. This section of the journey, actually the most crucial, proved uneventful. About half-way to Katar the ground changed to gravelly steppe, and then again to rolling hills of sand. Then, after a night spent under drizzling rain, the last sand-hill was passed, and beyond a stony plain rose the towers of Doha, seen against the waters of the Persian Gulf. "Half an hour later we entered the fort. The Rub' al Khali had been crossed." Such is the modest conclusion to a brilliant story of adventure.

So well organized was the crossing, and so skilfully executed according to plan, that it seems to have been accomplished easily. Yet actually, even at Farajja, it was by no means certain that the journey could be completed. A delay of ten days arising from tribal war or from failure of pastures at the outset of the final stage might well have turned them back to a place where they could find at least sustenance. On the southern half of the journey it was merely a matter of chance that no large raiding party was encountered; all the way Thomas's men were highly nervous, for almost the only men who move between the water-holes of that thirsty land are bent on killing and plunder. Any party met would be presumed to be hostile—yet the Bedouin never made defence dispositions when camping! Reliance is in God! What is written must come to pass!

In the acceptance of destiny is comfort; the doctrine of Free Will a disturbing heresy. Unless the beast became his by the will of God, a man could not enjoy killing the master and riding away upon her. War would become wicked, blood-feuds impious, and the practice of religion impossible.

Even in Thomas's party the peaceful relations between the Murra and Rashidi elements were obviously only temporary. If a Murra in his territory went to inspect the state of a pasture or water-hole it would not have been wise for one of the Rashidi to follow or inquire.

To lead such men swiftly and without friction for almost two months through the wilderness called for the highest courage, faultless organization, unwearying patience, and limitless tact. Thomas, however, accomplished more than the feat of organization and endurance involved in a desert march. Geological and natural history specimens were collected diligently and preserved, to be examined later by experts, whose reports were printed with his narrative. His book contained also erudite anthropological and zoological appendices, lists of flora and fauna, and names and positions of regional sands and water-holes, topographical terms, and even notes and illustrations of camel brands and Arab chants.

For the ordinary reader, and hardly less for the geographer and scientist, Thomas threw a white light over the whole of life in South-eastern Arabia. Scenes of everyday existence, panoramas of the country from sea to sea, conversations in the Arab idiom, stories, legends, codes of Bedouin life, loyalties of the desert, the acceptance of the absolute Allah, the reasons underlying Arab actions and outlook—all were shown with final realism.

Bertram Thomas explored not only a region, but the way of life and the soul of a people.

IV

Bertram Thomas's penetration of the Rub' al Khali from the south was followed a few months later by H. St J. Philby's amazing march from the north. Philby was equipped with vast experience of the Arab lands, beginning in 1917, when he was lent by the Government of India, as a Military Political Officer,

326

to the British Expeditionary Force in Mesopotamia, to assist in organizing the administration of districts won from the Turks.

On the flank of this new territory Ibn Rashid in Arabia was a constant menace, so that in October 1917 Philby was sent on a mission to Ibn Saud to concert measures against him. Arriving at Riyadh by Bahrein and Oqair, he found in the ruler not only an ally for his country but a firm friend for himself. At Ibn Saud's capital there should have been a party from Cairo, consisting of other members of the mission, but it had not arrived and it seemed that the Sherif of Mecca, who controlled the western approaches to Central Arabia, was by no means anxious for it to reach Riyadh. Philby therefore volunteered to visit the Hejaz to bring back the Cairo party, and made an interesting but uneventful journey, noting ranges and the direction of drainage, to Taif, and then to the coast at Jidda.

Thus, for the first time since the days of Captain G. F. Sadlier, a hundred years before, the peninsula was crossed by a European from sea to sea. In view of the Sherif's opposition to relations with Ibn Saud, Philby could only return to Basra. Meanwhile Lieutenant-Colonel F. Cunliffe-Owen, who was a member of the mission to Riyadh, made a brief excursion to Kharj, being the first European, except possibly Palgrave, to visit that district.

Some months later Philby was again with Ibn Saud, but found him too closely occupied with affairs in his own dominions to act with the British. Philby, however, took the opportunity of being in Central Arabia to make an expedition to the Wadi Dawasir. The story of these journeys, which were rich in geographical and political interest, he narrated in his first book, *The Heart of Arabia* (1922). In 1918 he visited the Kasim with Ibn Saud, again in connexion with plans against Hail. This experience of Central Arabia led, in 1928, to his book *Arabia of the Wahhabis*.

One interesting expedition in these years was made into unexplored regions, three hundred miles south of Riyadh to the oasis of Dam, twenty settlements numbering about 9000 people, of the Dawasir tribe, and people of negro origin. The oases of

Nejd he described as consisting usually of a town surrounded by scattered hamlets, with a few square miles in all of cultivated land, and with populations never exceeding 10,000, except at Riyadh, which had 12,000–15,000 inhabitants. In Aflaj and Kharj irrigation was discovered (unexpectedly) to be by subterranean conduits from natural reservoirs or deep wells. Philby also visited what is perhaps the largest permanent lake in Arabia, at Umm al Jabal, south of Laila. It measures three-quarters by one-quarter of a mile. He showed that the Nejd oases were not marked by tropical luxuriance, that no line of oases stretched from Nejd to Asir or Yemen, that no fertile regions existed between Nejd and Oman, and no settlement between Nejd and either Oman or the Hadhramaut. His expeditions, by their positive and negative results, entirely modified the picture of Central Arabia drawn by Palgrave, and proved much of it to be fantastic. Philby became the leading modern authority on Central Arabia, and the great value of his work was recognized by the Royal Geographical Society Founder's Medal, while the results of his travels were incorporated in the War Office map of 1927. It was due to him alone that Southern Nejd became as well known to geographers as any other part of Arabia.

Throughout these years Philby experienced one great longing and ambition—to cross the Rub' al Khali. Between 1917 and 1930 he saw great changes in the peninsula. The Arabia of his early years had been indistinguishable from that of Niebuhr and Doughty, a seemingly immutable land. But the post-War years brought the introduction of motor transport, the fighting between Ibn Saud and the Sherif of Mecca, and the resurrection of Wahhabi power. About this time a plan to cross the Rub' al Khali with Mrs Rosita Forbes, who had recently crossed the Libyan desert to the little-known oasis of Kufra, came to naught, largely through sickness, which attacked Philby at Jidda. Then came a reorientation of Philby's career, for he retired from the Government service in 1925, accepted Islam, and made Mecca his home.

Living in the Hejaz, he was not within comparatively easy reach of the scene of his subsequent explorations, as Bertram Thomas was; he could make no preparatory journeys, and had to wait patiently until Ibn Saud was able to arrange and support the expedition, so keenly desired, into the Empty Quarter.

Burton had hoped to cross that great blank on the map from east to west. In his time and until the Great War a longitudinal crossing from north to south was practically impossible because of the barriers raised by Turk and Wahhabi; from south to north the obstacle to exploration was formed by the fierce desert tribes, as the ruler of Muscat's writ was respected only on the coast. The European War resulted in the disappearance of the Turkish barrier, the rise of Ibn Saud, and other political changes. The longitudinal crossing then became a possibility, and was achieved by Thomas. But it was not until Thomas had made this great pioneer crossing that Ibn Saud gave Philby his opportunity. Even when permission for the journey was received Ibn Jiluwi, the Governor of Hasa, whence the expedition was to start, was too occupied to help him, and Philby had to bear as best he could a further delay.

v

At length all preparations were made, *personnel*, camels, and stores were mobilized, and on January 7, 1932, Sheikh Abdulla Philby marched from Hofuf. He had thirteen companions, and four others were to join two or three stages ahead. Ibn Jiluwi had given this escort full instructions to take the explorer wherever he wanted to go.

"Look you," he said, . . ."this man is dear to the King and dear to us all: see that you have a care of him. See that he wants for nothing within your power to provide. You will take him to Jafura, even to Salwa and Sikak and Anbak, until you come to Jabrin. In all things serve him as you would serve me. Thence you will go to Maqainama, and beyond that is beyond my ken. He speaks of Wabar. You will take him thither—you have guides with you who know the deserts in those parts. You will take him to the Hadhramaut if you can find the people to whom I have addressed these letters . . . see that you avoid danger, but take him whither he would go. For his life you answer with yours. Forget not that. And when you are come thither your return is across the desert, even the Empty Quarter, to Wadi Dawasir. . . .

So in the keeping of God, but see that you do all my bidding, and more." [1]

The party contained six Murra, three Ajman, and two Manasir tribesmen, representing the tribes of the northern desert, but there were none from the southern groups, Sa'ar, Rashid, Manahil, or Kathir, as there were none to be found in the Hasa when the expedition set out. This lack of southern

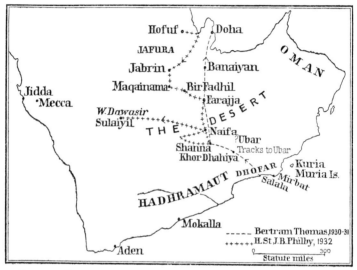

BERTRAM THOMAS'S AND PHILBY'S ROUTES ACROSS THE RUB' AL KHALI

rabias, Philby realized, was very unsatisfactory, but he had at least Ibn Jiluwi's letters to leading men of the south, and he hoped also to pick up suitable *rabias* on his route. In any case, when at last the great opportunity for exploring the Rub' al Khali had been offered, nothing would have held him from the venture.

He had thirty-two camels, all but one female, dune-bred and of the Oman breed, three of them milch-camels. Rations for three months were carried, consisting mainly of dates, rice, coffee, and tea. They took no flour, and missed it later.

From Hofuf Philby arrived at the palms and springs of Salwa on January 10, after a journey over bare, rolling dunes, and

[1] H. St J. Philby, *The Empty Quarter* (London, 1933).

reached Jabrin, travelling over patches of gravel and pebble ridges, a week later. On this section of his journey he was covering virgin territory, for Cheesman, who had fixed the sites of Salwa and Jabrin astronomically, had approached the latter place direct from the north. The salt flats of Salwa, Philby considered, were once an estuary from which the sea had receded, converting Katar from an island to a peninsula. A thorough exploration of the whole oasis of Jabrin led him to the view that it had formerly been an important centre in touch with the sea, reduced to ruins by the process of desiccation. Salwa, he thought, may have been one of its seaward forts, and there was evidence of outpost settlements facing Central Arabia and the south. There was pasturage, water, and food, though no signs of man. "Yet here, many centuries ago," he writes,

> there was something like civilisation and a well-organised society, though human memory retains little of the past beyond the one romantic fact that the poet Farazdaq was born and lived in Jabrin to sing of the chivalry whose champions are forgotten or merged in legends.
> Yet their works live after them in the ruinous remnants of a dozen mansions, solidly though simply built of clay and coarse masonry for protection rather than display, and scattered about the oasis to remind us of a past at least more impressive than the present. . . . We may be certain that the history of Jabrin as a centre of human activity goes back to a very early period in the annals of man, if only we could unearth the necessary material for its reconstruction.

At Jabrin Philby met an Arab called Jabir Ibn Feisal, travelling north from the Hadhramaut, accompanied by his wife, two children, and forty camels. The nomad Arab always acts with circumspection, and Jabir had secreted his family and belongings before investigating Philby's camp. When at length he ventured to approach he produced as a peace-offering a hare which had just been run down by his Saluqi bitch. He told the exploring party of continued drought in the south and a lack of game. He ate with them, "a youngish man of keen, frank visage, and the charming courtesy of the desert-born," but spoke little, and measured them. The next day Jabir pitched his tent near theirs and killed a young camel calf, so that at night they dined well on tender meat. Jabir also presented

Philby with the Saluqi, which shared his wanderings in the Great Desert to the end. It was difficult to give in return without offending such generosity, but Philby endeavoured to recompense the family.

> I slipped the silver (twenty dollars, about one pound) into the fist of the larger of the two naked sons of the house. The boy ran with it to his mother, who invoked charming blessings on my head. And so we parted from our last contact with the world of men, to see no more of humanity till fifty-three days later, when we came up out of the Empty Quarter into the inhabited world at Sulaiyil.

Jabir went off northward carrying a box of natural history specimens, stores, and fossils, which he undertook to deliver into the hands of Ibn Jiluwi in the Hasa.

The route from Jabrin to Maqainama, which was reached on January 24, lay along the eastern side of a broken limestone plateau and over sandy downs with some gypsum, ghada-bushes, and gravel plain. Ostrich shells were seen, and antediluvian shells of some extinct bird of the ostrich genus which lived before the land was desert. At Maqainama only an arrowhead of some ancient bow was found. The well water there was highly polluted with sewage, the albuminoid ammonia content being far in excess of what should be considered the potable proportion, and Philby observes:

> The conflict between European science and Arabian practice is manifest, but *quot homines tot sententiæ*! One can scarcely perhaps expect the West to appreciate the virtues of camel urine tempered by countless generations of seepage through sandstone rock.

The well, however, was 171 feet deep, and suggested the work of a more advanced civilization. Maqainama, Philby thought, might once have been a station for caravans from Gerra to Mecca.

At this point Philby could feel well launched on his enterprise, and he intended next to visit the legendary remains of Wabar, or Ubar. Of this city, which was said to have been destroyed by fire, he had been told that ruined mansions remained, that blackened castle walls could sometimes be seen, and that on the site were a wondrous block of iron "like a camel" and other relics of ancient human occupation.

Before relating the march to Wabar in his book *The Empty Quarter* Philby discusses the use of the term 'Rub' al Khali.' Generally, he writes, it has been the term accepted by geographers and the educated public for the country between Jabrin and the Hadhramaut, Oman and Nejran. The Arabs whom he met used the term in this sense, and also more particularly for the waterless tract west of Naifa. The area of the Great South Desert frequented by nomad tribes and containing countless wells they called "Ar Rimal." The name "Ahkaf" was used only by pedants and pedagogues. (In the experience of Bertram Thomas the Arabs living there did not understand the term 'Rub' al Khali' in its geographical sense, the steppe-lands having various local names and the sandy region of the desert being known as "Ar Rimal.")

Three days eastward from Maqainama, across alternating sandy downs and stretches of gravel, Philby came to the wells of Bir Fadhil, with ancient shafts 126 and 143 feet deep. Here the guides suggested making for the wells of Umm el Hadid— "the Mother of Iron." Could this be fabled Wabar? Philby had not encouraged himself to think in terms of Petra or Tutankhamen, but his dreams were full of "long low barrack buildings whirling round on perpetually radiating gravel rays of a sandy desert." Would a capital of prehistoric Arabia be found?

South from Bir Fadhil, over the rolling valleys of sand, across gravel flats and then eastward, after four days Wabar was sighted.

I looked down not upon the ruins of an ancient city, but into the mouth of a volcano, whose twin craters, half filled with drifted sand, lay side by side, surrounded by slag and lava outpoured from the bowels of the earth. That at any rate was the impression that flashed through my mind at that moment. I knew not whether to laugh or cry, but I was strangely fascinated by a scene that had shattered the dreams of years. So that was Wabar! A volcano in the desert! And on it built the story of a city destroyed by fire from heaven for the sins of its king, who had heeded not the warnings of the prophet Hud—generally identified with the Biblical Heber—and had waxed wanton with his horses and eunuchs and concubines in an earthly paradise until the wrath came upon him with the west wind and reduced the scene of his riotous pleasures to ashes and desolation!

One could scarcely have imagined a more sensational solution of the riddle of the Great Sands. And it must be admitted that the two great sand-filled craters, encircled by lofty walls of slag, did bear an absurd resemblance to the tumbled remnants of man-made castles. Many of my companions were already on the scene, burrowing in the *débris* for treasure. As I descended the slope towards the first crater they came running up to me with lumps of slag, and tiny fragments of rusted iron and small shining black pellets which they took to be the pearls of 'Ad's ladies blackened in the conflagration that had consumed them with their lord. . . . "This may indeed be Wabar," I said, "of which the Badawin speak, but it is a work of God, not man. These are no castles of the ancients, but like the volcanic peaks of the *harra* which you have seen doubtless on the way to Mecca . . . these mouths are as the mouths of the *harra* thrust up by the inner fire from the belly of the earth." "No," replied Ali stoutly, "but they are the castles of 'Ad . . . they are his mansions for sure, and see how the bricks have been burned with fire as they relate!" . . . "Fear not," I replied, "this is certainly the place of which you spoke, and you have led me to it, Ali, as you promised. And these are the castles of Wabar, as you say. I am content, but take it from me, they were not built of men."

Philby gathered specimens of iron, flint, and slag, which on expert examination proved to be not of volcanic, but of meteoric origin. At Wabar there must have been a shower of great masses of iron that excavated the group of craters, two of which, lying exposed, were some 200 and 100 yards across respectively. The slaggy masses which suggested the buildings of a buried city were of nearly pure silica-glass, "the most abundant and remarkable occurrence of silica-glass that has yet been discovered in nature," according to Dr J. L. Spencer, of the British Museum. By such a fall of meteorites as occurred at Wabar, says the expert's report, London would be completely wiped out.

The views of the two famous explorers of the Empty Quarter are divergent on the subject of Wabar, or Ubar, in regard to its spelling, nature, and site. Philby's Wabar is two hundred miles north-west from the position, based on information gathered, marked conjecturally on Thomas's map. However, in a review of Philby's book in *The Geographical Journal* (November 1933) "P.Z.C." points out that it seems doubtful if either of them had seen the article on Wabar in the *Encyclopædia of Islam*, where the name is said to apply to a district and tribe of the earliest period in the southern half of Arabia, and that it was given not only to particular districts, but even to all the central tract between Jabrin and the Hadhramaut.

In the second week of February Philby moved southward on a two-hundred-mile journey towards Shanna, mostly through dunes or bare rolling sands, with occasional desert vegetation, *abal*, *andab*, *hadh*, and *alga*. So far no excessive heat or cold had been experienced, though the Arabs after keeping watch at night in a temperature of 40° F. came into camp in the mornings "tittering with cold."

After five days the party was slowly approaching the crest of a long winding range in the sands, when one of the guides suddenly pointed downward, almost at his feet. "Look! Ain Sala!" he shouted, and Philby saw a great pit two hundred feet below, and a patch of rock.

He dismounted to examine the scene, while the camels made a wide circuit to reach the entrance to the hollow, which was completely surrounded, except towards the south-west, by high steep slopes of sand.

> A high point in the dune range immediately above the pit must have been at least 300 feet above its level, but the ridge in general was from 50 to 100 feet lower . . . about 50 feet above the floor of the depression an intermittent stratum of friable, greyish sandstone appeared from under the heaped-up sands. Downwards it shelved to a rock floor of similar formation, some acres in extent, and curving round the actual wall area in an imposing semi-circular cliff of ten or twelve feet, whose horns penetrated and lost themselves in the steep surrounding sand slopes. . . . The single well is sunk to a depth of seven or eight fathoms, as they say, through the sandstone rock, having a mouth only two feet in diameter and reinforced by a framework of wattle.

Philby had seen many horseshoe formations in the northern Jafura, but thought it astonishing that such a patch of bedrock surrounded by sands should remain always more or less exposed, and suggested that possibly in such deep hollows the wind causes an eddy of the sands which sweeps the floor clean. It was, in fact, difficult to find a suitable camping site there because of the sudden whirlwinds that came without warning, and thrice during the stay here (February 10–15) blew his tent down.

335

The well had not been used for some ten years, was buried and 'dead,' so that water was brought from Naifa, another well in a horseshoe depression some miles distant, where Philby closely investigated the phenomenon of 'singing' or 'booming' sands. He noted that the sand slipping down the sides of a natural amphitheatre began by making a grating noise, followed by a *crescendo* of booming, an organ-like note, as though the sand was passing over a sounding-board. Usually the sound lasted two or three minutes, while the sand moved fifty or seventy feet. The movement and sound ceased together. He took specimens of the sand for scientific examination and experiment.

For some time Philby's men had been restless and unwilling to march farther south. It was now decided that two of them should go ahead to seek the sheikhs for whom Philby had letters of introduction, or at least to find *rabias* for the journey among the southern tribes.

These scouts had no success, and probably spent a considerable part of their week's absence hunting oryx instead of seeking the Kathir and Rashid tribes. Then the Arab escort definitely refused to travel to Dhofar; nor would they make for Kabr Hud, in the Hadhramaut. They desired to return to the Hasa. At many times in the journey most of them had proved childish, mercurial, treacherous, and mercenary. Shanna (February 20) was the farthest point south that Philby could reach.

"For weeks and months," said an Arab, "we have seen nought but the blowing sands. No country is this of the Muslimin, nor yet the country of the infidel—just the Empty Quarter." Argument and wrangling went on; Philby flatly refused to turn back to the Hasa; the Arabs, unwilling to lose their rewards and afraid of the anger of Ibn Saud and Ibn Jiluwi, hesitated or did not dare to leave him. But they preferred being thrown into prison to moving south (one of them had been left for dead by the Sa'ar), and they thought they might persuade Ibn Jiluwi that Philby had demanded their accepting unreasonable dangers. In the absence of southern *rabias* their attitude was not wholly blameworthy!

At length a compromise was reached; they should turn due

westward and make for Mecca *via* Sulaiyil, the farthest point reached by Philby in his exploration of Southern Nejd. This route involved a journey across four hundred miles of waterless and, as it proved, rainless desert.

On February 22 a start was made under favourable conditions, through a region of sand, scattered dunes, and some exposed rock. The night temperature was 45° F. and 85° by day, but the latter, after some days, rose to 93°. The camels were strained, and though the men discussed retreat they wasted their own and their beasts' energy by searching for oryx and gazelle away from the line of march. After five days with nothing to eat but dates they expected Philby to produce food out of the wilderness, like a prophet of old. Finally the party fell back through exhausting heat, wind, and sand, to Naifa.

In these books of exploration we see the Arab through the eyes of the European; it is rarer to learn the Bedouin view of the traveller. "We notice two things in you," said a man of Philby's escort on one occasion. "Firstly, you are hot-tempered and easily get angry if we do not as you please. And, secondly, you are ever ready to disbelieve what the guides say." Then he went on very frankly and confidentially: "Tell me, were you like that from the day God created you? Or what is the reason for it? Surely you know that the guides do not lie deliberately, and this is their own country, where they should know every bush and every hummock. Why then should you suspect them of lying?"

"As for the guides," Philby replied, with equal frankness, "I know that they should know this country, and you say they do not lie deliberately. Do you remember that day marching down to Ain Sala when I wanted to go aside to visit Adraj on the way and Ali told us it was distant a day's journey? Afterwards we went to Adraj, as you know, and when I drew it on my map I found it was but an hour's ride from our route. Tell me, did Ali really not know or was it otherwise?"

"You speak sooth," the Arab replied. "Ali lied, but he was thinking of our need of water."

After a short recuperation at Naifa a few showers of rain elated the Arabs, and they were ready to start again into the desert westward. At the former attempt the party had been too heavily laden, so that Philby now decided to divide his men, some returning to the Hasa, while eleven men, with twenty-four skins of water and fifteen camels, made the dash for Sulaiyil. Of the departure of the Hasa group Philby writes:

> Each of them saluted me with a kiss on the forehead. "Forgiveness for our failings!" said Ali. "There is nothing to forgive," I replied, "but I thank you for your services. In the keeping of God!" And so I parted from eight of the companions of two months' wandering in the wilderness. The farewell of the Arab is manly indeed. With fair words on his lips he strides off into the desert and is gone. He never looks back.

The Sulaiyil march began at night in a gentle drizzle. By day the shade temperature was 90°, but for three days there was grazing for the camels. By the fifth night 170 miles had been covered, and more than 200 more lay ahead. In low dunes and undulating sandy plains the heat was intense, and the conditions were exhausting to man and beast. The Arabs clamoured for halts, but no time could be wasted, and Philby hastened on, for it was now impossible for him to turn back.

They entered a vast gravel plain without fuel or grazing, but clouds appeared and the temperature fell. After a week's march, beyond a steppe of broken rock and patches of gravel, the end came in sight. The droppings of sheep were seen, blossoming sarh-trees twenty and thirty feet high, and yellow-tasselled acacias, a boon to the eyes after the treeless desert. A shepherd's little round watch-tower was the first habitation of man to be seen since they left Jabrin two months before.

Suddenly there was movement in bushes ahead of them. It seemed like men moving in open order, and the escort grasped rifles. But it was only black-smocked, black-veiled women gathering wood for their village fires. Greetings were exchanged, an old woman acting as spokesman.

> "What is the news?" asked Zayid. "All good," replied the old lady, "but welcome to you and whence come ye?" "We come, as ye see," replied Zayid, "from the desert. . . . " "And saw ye tracks of foes?" she asked. "None," said Zayid.

Then they came to Sulaiyil:

> The waterless desert had been crossed probably for the first

338

time in human history, 375 miles between water and water. Yet the camels drank but sparingly. They were too thirsty.

The modern explorer is more fortunate than the men of other days in having on his return the ready services of scientific experts to examine and assess the value of his finds, while their pleasure in a new or interesting discovery adds to the traveller's joy of achievement. As on his former journeys, Philby diligently recorded observations and collected everything likely to be of scientific interest. His dramatic book *The Empty Quarter*, written in sturdy, colourful, pliable English, contains in appendices the results of expert examination of his specimens and comparative notes on other observations. They show, for instance, the birds indigenous to the Rub' al Khali and those that merely cross the desert to their summer breeding quarters, and catalogue the specimens of butterflies, moths, bugs, beetles, and reptiles. The sand specimens of the Rub' al Khali are described as almost entirely quartz, pale yellow or pinkish buff in colour, with some small traces of limestone. The appendix on the 'singing sands' is suggestive as to causation, but nothing unusual mineralogically was discovered in the samples Philby brought back.

No comparison should be drawn between the achievements of Thomas and Philby, for their tasks were essayed under very different conditions. Both succeeded in feats demanding the highest courage, endurance, and knowledge; both recorded their discoveries and adventures in memorable books. It is enough that the figures of these two British travellers in the Empty Quarter dominate all modern exploration.

SUMMARY OF RECORDED ARABIAN EXPLORATION
TO THE YEAR 1893

The following tabulation may help to fix some of the older Arabian journeys in relation to the period in which they occurred:

DATE	AREA	EXPLORER	CONTEMPORARY HISTORY
1503	West coast	Varthema	Reign of Henry VII
1513	Yemen	Alboquerque	Battle of Flodden
1609	Yemen	Jourdain	Reign of James I
1690	Hejaz	Pitts	Battle of the Boyne
1762–63	Yemen	Niebuhr	The Seven Years War
1807	Hejaz	Ali Bey	Napoleonic War
1814	Hejaz	Burckhardt	Napoleon at Elba
1819	Trans-Arabia	Sadlier	Regency Period closing
1835	Oman	Wellsted	First year of the English Poor Law
1843	Hadhramaut	Von Wrede	English income tax 7*d.* in the pound
1845 and 1848	Nejd	Wallin	Great Irish Famine; revolutions in European capitals; Second Republic
1853	Hejaz	Burton	Eve of Crimean War
1863	Nejd	Palgrave	Second Empire period; great Polish rebellion
1864–65	Hasa and Nejd	Pelly and Guarmani	American Civil War
1869–70	Hadhramaut and Yemen	Miles and Halévy	Franco-Prussian War; Suez Canal opened
1876	Oman	Miles	Balkan rising against the Turks
1877	Nejd and Hejaz	Doughty	Russo-Turkish War. "We don't want to fight, yet by Jingo if we do . . ."
1878	Nejd	Blunts	Russo-Turkish War
1878	Midian	Burton	„ „ „
1883	Nejd and Hejaz	Huber and Euting	Gordon in the Sudan
1889	Yemen	Glaser	Kaiser William II's reign beginning
1892–93	Hadhramaut	Hirsch and Bents	Franco - Russian military convention against Triple Alliance
1893	Nejd	Nolde	Second Irish Home Rule Bill rejected

BIBLIOGRAPHY

MANY books and reports have been mentioned in the foregoing pages. The following short list contains only a few of those works for which enthusiasm is felt:

ALBOQUERQUE, AFONSO D': *Commentaries* (Hakluyt Series); translated and edited by W. de Gray Birch (London, 1877).

ALI BEY: *Travels* (London, 1816).

BAKER, J. N. L.: *A History of Geographical Discovery and Exploration* (London, 1931).

BEAZLEY, SIR R.: *The Dawn of Modern Geography* (London, 1897–1906).

BENT, J. T.: *Southern Arabia* (London, 1900).

BERG, L. W. C. VAN DEN: *Le Hadhramaut et les colonies arabes de l'archipel* (Batavia, 1885).

BLUNT, LADY ANNE: *A Pilgrimage to Nejd* (London, 1881).

BRAY, N. N. E.: *A Paladin of Arabia* (Leachman) (London, 1936).

BUNBURY, E. H.: *A History of Ancient Geography* (London, 1879).

BURTON, SIR R. F.: *A Pilgrimage to Al-Madinah and Meccah* (London, 1855).

—— *Gold Mines of Midian* (London, 1878).

—— *The Land of Midian (Revisited)* (London, 1879).

BURY, G. W.: *The Land of Uz* (London, 1911).

—— *Arabia Infelix* (London, 1915).

CARRUTHERS, D.: *Arabian Adventure to the Great Nafud* (London, 1935).

—— *Captain Shakespear's Last Journey* (in *The Geographical Journal*, 1922).

CARY, M., and WARMINGTON, E. H.: *The Ancient Explorers* (London, 1929).

CHEESMAN, R. E.: *In Unknown Arabia* (London, 1926).

DOUGHTY, C. M.: *Travels in Arabia Deserta* (new edition, London, 1926).

ELMGREN, S. G.: *G. A. Wallin's Reseanteckningar från orienten åren 1843–49* (Helsingfors, 1865).

EUTING, J.: *Tagbuch einer Reise in Inner-Arabien*, vol. i (Leyden, 1896).

FINATI, G.: *Travels*; edited by W. J. Bankes (London, 1830).

GIBB, H. A. R.: *The Travels of Ibn Battuta*, 1325-54 (London, 1929).

GUARMANI, C.: *Il Neged settentrionale* (Jerusalem, 1866); translated as *Northern Nejd* (London, 1917).

HARRISON, P. W.: *The Arab at Home* (London, 1925).

HIRSCH, L.: *Reisen in Sud-Arabien* (Leyden, 1897).

HOGARTH, D. G.: *The Penetration of Arabia* (London, 1904).

—— *The Life of Charles M. Doughty* (Oxford, 1928).

HUBER, C.: *Journal d'un voyage en Arabie* (Paris, 1891).

HURGRONJE, J. S.: *Mekka* (The Hague, 1888).

JARVIS, C. S.: *Three Deserts* (London, 1936).

JOURDAIN, J.: *Journal* (Hakluyt Series); edited by William Foster (London, 1905).

KEANE, J. S.: *Six Months in the Hejaz* (London, 1887).

LAWRENCE, T. E.: *Seven Pillars of Wisdom* (London, 1926; new edition, 1935).

MAFFEI, G. P.: *Historiæ indicæ* (Venice, 1592).

MEULEN, D. VAN DER, and WISSMANN, H. VON: *Hadhramaut: some of its Mysteries Unveiled* (Leyden, 1933).

NIEBUHR, K.: *Beschreibung von Arabien* (Copenhagen, 1774); translated by R. Heron as *Travels through Arabia* (Edinburgh, 1792).

PALGRAVE, W. G.: *Narrative of a Year's Journey through Central and Eastern Arabia* (London, 1865).

PHILBY, H. ST J. B.: *The Heart of Arabia* (London, 1922).

—— *Arabia of the Wahhabis* (London, 1928).

—— *The Empty Quarter* (London, 1933).

RIHANI, A.: *Arabian Peak and Desert* (London, 1930).

RUTTER, E.: *The Holy Cities of Arabia* (London, 1930).

SADLIER, G. F.: *Diary of a Journey across Arabia* (Bombay, 1866).

SPRENGER, A.: *Die Alte Geographie Arabiens* (Berne, 1875).

STARK, F.: *The Southern Gate of Arabia* (London, 1936).

SYKES, SIR P.: *A History of Exploration* (London, 1934).

TALLQVIST, K.: *Bref och Dagboksanteckningar af Georg August Wallin* (Helsingfors, 1905).

THOMAS, B.: *Alarms and Excursions in Arabia* (London, 1931).

—— *Arabia Felix* (London, 1932).

TOZER, H. F.: *History of Ancient Geography* (Cambridge, 1897).

TRENEER, A.: *Charles M. Doughty : a Study of his Prose and Verse* (London, 1935).

VARTHEMA, L. DI: *Travels* (Hakluyt Series); translated by J. W. Jones and G. P. Badger (London, 1863).

BIBLIOGRAPHY

WELLSTED, J. R.: *Travels in Arabia* (London, 1838).

WREDE, A. VON: *Reise in Hadhramaut* (Brunswick, 1870); edited by H. Freiherr von Maltzan.

ZWEMER, S. M.: *Arabia, the Cradle of Islam* (Edinburgh, 1900).

Journal of the Royal Geographical Society, 1839, 1845 (Haines), 1871 (Miles), 1864, 1865 (Pelly), 1835, 1837 (Wellsted), vols. xx, xxiv (Wallin), 1844 (von Wrede).

The Geographical Journal, 1894, 1895 (Bent), 1910, 1912 (Leachman), 1896 (Miles).

Handbook of Arabia (Geographical Section, Naval Intelligence Division, Naval Staff, Admiralty).

The best map of the whole of Arabia is that published by the War Office, Geographical Section, General Staff, No. 2957, Sheets 32 and 44, Persian Gulf and Gulf of Aden.

INDEX

ABDUL AZIZ, Wahhabi ruler, wars of, and death, 106
Abdul Aziz Ibn Saud, career of, 289
Abdul Wahhab, and Wahhabism, Niebuhr on, 100; reformation of Islam by, 100, 101, 105, 106
Abdulla, of the Shammar, the Rashid house established by, 286; his mode of rule, 287
Abdulla, son of Feisal, 230; and Palgrave, 253 *et seq.*; and Pelly, 261
Abdulla, Wahhabi ruler, defeat of, and fate, 107, 229
Abdulla Ibn Rashid, and the Emirate of Hail, 230; reign of, 235
Abdulla Mansur—*see* Bury, G.
Abraha, Christian king of Abyssinia, 37; expedition of, against the Koreish, 38
Abu Bakr, Seyyid, as air observer, 308
Abu Shahrein, 30
Abu Zeid, geographer, 44
Abulfeda, geographer, 45–46, 52, 102
"Abyssapolis," 221
Abyssinia, 77; dominance in Yemen of, 35; decline of her dominance, 37; Christianity in, 37; Covilham's stay in, 52–53; and Prester John, 71; vessels of, 86; flora of, 222
Adelard of Bath, 41
Aden, 210; the *Periplus* on, 32; early comments on, 44; Ibn Battuta at, 51; Covilham at, 53; Varthema's misfortunes at, 63–64; as *entrepôt*, 67; Alboquerque's son's description of, 69; Alboquerque's raid on the harbour at, 71–72, 101; the *Ascension* at, 76; described by Jourdain, 78; Middleton made prisoner at, 81; British-Indian annexation of, 206
Aden, Gulf of, sea route from, to Southern India, 28
Adim, Wadi, 211; honey of, 217
Adraj, 337
Aflaj, 12, 271; Palgrave's visit to, 246, 257; irrigation in, 328
Aga Mountains, 235, 237
Ageyl, tribe, Central Arabia, Lawrence and, 150; Burckhardt on, 150

Agyd, the, functions of, 152–153
Ahkaf, use of the term, 333
Ais, Wadi, discovery of, 302; Lawrence's journey to, from Wejh, 302–303
Aisa, Wadi, cultivation in, 214; Himyaritic ruins in, 216
Aja range, 14
Akaba, 149; heat at, 171
Akaba, Gulf of, 186, 188, 295; Lawrence's ride to, 302
Akik, Wadi, course of, learned by Lawrence from Feisal, 303
Al Ain, 313
Al Hamra, 175
Albania, Finati in, 108
Albertus Magnus, 40
Alboquerque, Afonso d', 67; attack of, on Aden, 68 *et seq.*, 101; Indian schemes of, 71
Aleppo, 55; Burckhardt's studies at, 118
Alexander the Great, 21, 22, 23, 26
Alexandria, 26, 55; exports from, 31; port of, 47; Burton's self-training at, 164–165
Algiers, pirates of, 83
Ali Bey el Abbasi (Domingo Badia y Leblich), travels and observations of, in the Hejaz, 108 *et seq.*, 185, 291; death of, 116
Ali Mohammed (Bertram Thomas's secretary), 313
Allenby, Field-Marshal Viscount, 291
Amboyna, the massacre of, 82
Amd, Wadi, 208, 306, 310
American Geographical Society, maps of North Arabia printed by, 266
Amman, 311
Anazeh, tribe, 264; original home of, 17; Burckhardt on, 151 *et seq.*
Androsthenes, 22
Aneiza, 16, 227, 269; conquest of, 107, 230; visit to, of Guarmani, disbelief in, of Doughty, 265; Doughty at, 271
Anglo-Dutch quarrels over Eastern trade, 81–82
Anville, J. B. d', map of Arabia by, 103
Ar Rimal, 333
Arab farewell, the, 338

Arab horses, Burckhardt on, 150–151, 155; Ibn Rashid's stud of, Lady Anne Blunt's notes on, 285–286; Crabbet Park stud of, 286
Arab Revolt, district opened by, 303
Arab trade routes, 42, 43
Araba, Wadi, 232
Arabia, geography, geology, and physiography of, 11 *et seq.*, 33–34; unexplored areas of, 11; temperatures of, 12; produce of, 15–16; area and population of, 16; explorers of, 20 *et seq.*; coastal exploration of, 20 *et seq.*; spice regions of, 21, 22, 204, 205; archæological evidence of early civilization in, 23; caravan trade of, 23, 24, 28; religious war in, 35; overthrow of Christianity in, 36–39; independent districts in, 41; tribal wars in, 24; Covilham's commercial visit to, 52–53; Portuguese coastal settlements in, 72; Danish expedition to, 88 *et seq.*; desert regions of, sandstorms and mirage in, 182, 183; exclusive policy of, 291; regions of, unsurveyed in 1900, 291; crossings of, 295, 327; most striking photographs of, 311; Doughty's and Philby's travels in, contrasted, 328
    Central, after Ptolemy, 33–34; and Eastern, principal states in, 105; largely unknown, 224–225; Ibrahim Pasha's evacuation of, 225; Philby's journeys in, 302
    North Central, exploration of, 230 *et seq.*; described by the Blunts, 277 *et seq.*
    Northern, Christianity in, 36; maps of, 261, 286; area explored in nineteenth century, 264–267; main drainage channels of, 274; Sabæan inscriptions in, 294
    South-west, Roman expedition to, 24 *et seq.*; notable travellers visiting, 101–102
    Southern, Jews of, Tudela on, 44–45; Varthema's account of, 64–66; frankincense-trees of, 204; unexplored areas in, 267
    West and South, coasts of, surveys of, 193
"Arabia Deserta," 15 and *n.*
Arabia Deserta (Doughty), 268, 272, 274, 276, 292; importance of, and style of, 268, 275, 276; reception of, 276, 277
"Arabia Felix," 15 *n.*
"Arabia Petræa," 15 *n.*

Arabian coast, early knowledge of, 20–22; marine surveys of, 302. See also *Palinurus*
Arabian exploration from 1503 to 1893, summary of recorded, 340
Arabian Nights, the, Arab characters seen in, 46; Burton's translation of, 162, 191–192
Arabs, the, Niebuhr on, 101; social life of, Burckhardt on, 151 *et seq.*; and North American Indians, Burton on, 180; of the Hadhramaut, 205
Arafat, Mount, rites at, 59, 62, 85, 142; the rites at, described by Burckhardt, 126, 130, 138 *et seq.*
Arair, in Hasa, 105
Archias, 22
Archimedes, works of, in Arabic, 44
Ared (Riyadh), 16
Ared mountain range, 227
Arethas, and his wife and daughter, fate of, 37
Aristotle, works of, in Arabic, 44
Arnaud, Louis, in Yemen, 101–102; von Wrede supported by, 210
Arrian, 21
Arsinoë, Scylax's expedition to, 20, 21; Ælius Gallus at, 25
Ascension, the, 76–77, 79
Ashaira, 311
Asir, 12, 50, 204, 311; early knowledge of, 291, 302; 'inside' information on, 301; Rosita Forbes's visit to, 301
Aspebætos, sheikh bishop, 36
Astronomical knowledge of Moslems, 44
Ataiba Bedouin, Burckhardt on, 149; wars of, 264–265
Athlula, taken by Rome, 25
Auda, blackmail by, of Captain Shakespear, 295
Augustus, Emperor, Arabian trade under, 23, 24; expedition sent by, to South-west Arabia, 24 *et seq.*
Ayaina, 105, 106

BAB EL MANDEB, Straits of, 20, 70, 71; first Englishman to pass through, 77
Babylon, incense used at, 27
Bacon, Roger, 40
Badger, Dr G. P., 244
Badia y Leblich, Domingo—*see* Ali Bey el Abbasi
Baghdad, 44, 286; observatory built at, 44; Ibn Battuta's journey to, from Mecca, 50; Gertrude Bell's death at, 292
Baghdad Railway, 289; financial possibilities of, 286

Bahr es Safi, 210, 316
Bahrein, 258; pearling industry of, 22; British treaty with, 193
Baida, 25
Baluchistan, 21
Bandar, Emir of Hail, 230
Banyans, at Sana, 79, 96; in Mecca, 148; in the incense trade, 219
Barahut, Wadi, 222; non-volcanic, 307, 308; tribal beliefs on, 316
Barakat ash-Shami (Jurayjuray), 242
Barbary pirates, raids of, extent of, 86
Barbier, Dr, 90
Bartholomew, St, journey of, to Ethiopia, 36
Basra, 74, 224
Batina, plain, 15, 199
Baurenfeind, George William, 88; death of, 97
Bazwa, valley of, 48
"Beat-Allah," at Mecca, 85
Bedia, oasis of, 195
Bedouin, the, home of, 16; migration routes of, 17; tribal organization of, 17; characteristics of, 17–18, 151 *et seq.*, 160, 248; Strabo on, 30; and pilgrims, 50, 85, 134; fighting and raiding habits of, 56, 151–156, 235–236; Varthema's account of, 56; Niebuhr on, 98–99; Burckhardt on, 148 *et seq.*, 160; religion of, 156, 241, 325–326; marriage customs of, 156 *et seq.*; of East Midian, unfriendly to Burton, 189–190; of the Hadhramaut, 205; of Qara, 218; cave-dwelling among, 219; Wallin on, 241; attitude of, to Doughty, 270; Southern, Leachman on, 293–294; his journey with, 293; political importance of Leachman's journeys with, 294; treachery and rapacity among chiefs of, 295; fatalism of, 325–326
Beit el Fakih, coffee depot at, 92; local irrigation at, 96–97
Bell, Gertrude, career of, and books by, 292
Beneyton, A. J., mapping and survey work of, for a Hodeida-Sana railway, 102
Beni Abu Ali, the, of Oman, piracy of, and punitive expeditions against, 193 *et seq.*
Benjamin of Tudela, *Records* of, 44–45
Bent, James Theodore, exploration of, in Hadhramaut, 211 *et seq.*, 306, 307, 308, 313; work of, at Zimbabwe, 222

Bent, Mrs James Theodore, 212, 214, 222, 313
Berber, Burckhardt at, 119
Bereida, 16, 269, 295; conquest of, 107, 230; Doughty in danger at, 271; discourtesy to Leachman at, 293
Berenice, port, 23, 45
Berg, L. W. C. van den, description by, of the Hadhramaut, 223
Berggren, servant with Niebuhr's party, 88; death of, 97
Betha, Wadi, settlements along, 195
Beyrout, 55
Bibliothèque orientale, of d'Herbelot, Arab writers made known by, 52
Bir Abbas, 175
Bir Ali, Wadi, 211, 217, 227
Bir Fadhil, wells of, 333
Bireima, Wellsted's efforts to reach, 196 *et seq.*
Bishr, tribe, the, raid by, 270
Black Stone, the, at Mecca, 38, 110, 111, 127, 146
Blunt, Lady Anne, 266; account by, of the journey to Nejd, 277 *et seq.*
Blunt, Wilfrid Scawen, 276; on Palgrave, 245, 246; travels of, in Nejd, and the results, 277 *et seq.*, 286; political views and foresight of, 288; Lawrence on, 288
Bombay, Moslems in, about A.D. 900, 43
Bosra, 47
Bridges, Robert, 276
Bruce, James, at Jidda, observations of, 104–105, 182
Bunbury, Sir E. H., on Ptolemy's world map, 33
Bundar Abbas, 258
Burckhardt, Johann Ludwig, 18, 185, 193, 224, 231; Varthema's narrative known to, 65; travels of, in Asia and Africa, 118 *et seq.*; Petra discovered by, 118; prophecy of, on Turkish power in the Hejaz, 122; interview of, with Mohammed Ali, 123 *et seq.*; at Mecca, his account of the temple and of the city, 119, 126 *et seq.*, 144 *et seq.*; books by, 161; death of, wild story on, 161; road taken by, to Mecca, 181; on the Shammar, 231; books by, nowadays neglected, 268
Burne-Jones, Sir Edward, 276
Burton, Sir R. F., 161, 241, 273, 317; on the medieval Arab as seen in the *Arabian Nights*, 46; Varthema's narrative quoted by, 65–66; cited,

confirming Pitts, 86 n., 87; biographical notes on, 162 et seq.; pilgrimage of, to Mecca, and translation by, of the Arabian Nights, 162, 191–192; languages acquired by, 163; books by, now neglected, 164, 185, 186, 187, 191–192, 268; party with, from Suez, 169; Burckhardt confirmed by, 185; other expeditions of, 186; search of, for gold in Midian, 187 et seq.; on Palgrave, 244; on Arabia Deserta, 276; and the Rub' al Khali, 329

Bury, G. Wyman, cited, 26 and n.; journey of, through Yemen, 96; life and explorations of, in Arabia, 299; book by, 304

Byssel, battle of, 151, 152

CAIRO, 47, 55, 118, 161; Burton at, 165 et seq.

Calicut, 52

Camels, best present-day breed of, 151; Doughty's descriptions of, 275 and n.

Canary Islands, 33

Canton, Moslems in, about A.D. 900, 43

Carruthers, Douglas, on maps of Arabia, 291–292; on Shakespear's trans-Arabia journey and its results, 295–296; exploration of, in the Hejaz, and book by, 296 and n.

Carter, Assistant-Surgeon H. T., interested in the incense trade, 203–204

Cave-dwellers, 205

Cheesman, Major R. E., pioneer of exploration of the Rub' al Khali, 312–313, 330; on Palgrave, 245, 258; book by, 317 n.

Christianity in Arabia, 35 et seq.

Cinnamon-harvesting, 21

Clayton, Lieutenant N. W., 302

Cleopatra, Nabathæan defeat of, 27

Cochrane, Hon. R. A., 309

Coffee, Jourdain's error on, 80

Congo river reached, 52

Coptos, 26

Cornwallis, Colonel K., and the map of Southern Arabia, 301

Cotton, wild, in Southern Arabia, 222

Coutenho, Garcia da, 75

Covilham, Pedro da, commercial mission of, to the spice lands, and stay of, in Abyssinia, 52–53

Cox, Sir Percy, and coal in Oman, 195 n.; British treaty concluded through, with Ibn Saud, 290; and the Rub' al Khali explorations, 312, 313

Cramer, Christian, 88, 91; death of, 97

Crusades, effect of, on Levant trade, 41

Cruttenden, Lieutenant, I.N., in Hadhramaut, 204

Cunliffe-Owen, Lieutenant-Colonel F., excursion of, to Kharj, 327

DAHNA, the sands of, 15

Dakaka, the sands of, and the Rashidi tribesmen, 320

Dam, oasis of, Philby's visit to, 327

Dama, Wadi, 188

Damascus, 47, 55, 118, 188; pilgrim caravan from, arrival of, 228; Doughty's journey with caravan from, 269

Danish expedition to Arabia, personnel of, and progress of, 88 et seq.

Dar Mahass, 118, 123

Darb el Sharki road, Burton the first European to use, 182–183

Darius Hystaspis, exploration party sent by, to Arsinoë, 20

Dariya, 224, 225, 260; siege and fall of, 107; ruins of, 227; rebirth of, 229

Darwaysh—see Dervishes

Dauka, Wadi, 314

Davenport, Major, and the Hejaz Railway, 302

Dawasir, oasis, 224

Dawasir, tribe, 327

Dawasir, Wadi, 16, 271; Philby's expedition to, 327

Dawes, Dr, I.N., 260

Decline and Fall of the Roman Empire, by Gibbon, sources used for, 103

Dena, Wadi, barrage across, 24

Dervishes, characteristics of, 165

Dhahiya, 320, 324

Dhofar, spices from, 16, 205; Hatshepsut's expedition to, 20; cultivation at, Ibn Battuta on, 51; second visit to, of the Palinurus, Bedouin unfriendliness at, 203–204; Qara country of, incense trade of, 213; Bent's journey to and beyond, 217 et seq.; unmapped, 291; description of, by Bertram Thomas, 317; head measurements in, 317

Dhofar range, 313; examination of, and report on, 201–203

Dhu Nuwas, Himyaritic ruler, persecution by, 37

Diu, 70

Doctoring the Arab, Palgrave on, 250 et seq.

Doha, Bertram Thomas's journey to, 317, 324, 325

Doheym, Palgrave's companion, 248

INDEX

Doughty, Charles Montagu (Khalil), 18, 241, 317, 328; on Palgrave, 245, 259; Arabian travels of, book on (see *Arabia Deserta*), extent and character of his journeys and geographical results, 268, 269 *et seq.*, 274; religion of, 270, 272 *et seq.*; attack on, by a sherif, 271–272; compared with Burton, 273–274; at Hail, 289; still remembered as Khalil, 295

Dutch East Indies, Hadrami emigration to, 223, 305–306

Dutch struggle for monopoly of the Eastern trade, 82

Duwan, Wadi, 99, 211, 304, 306, 310; ruins in, 204; von Wrede's arrival at, 207; irrigation in, 305; confluence of, with Wadi Hadhramaut, 309

EAST AFRICA, Ibn Battuta's visits to, 50, 51

East India Company, English, 104, 193; attempt of, to secure Indian trade, 76; and piracy in the Persian Gulf, 225; military expedition of, to Katif, 228

Edom, wilderness of, 26

Egypt, 52; and Alboquerque's scheme, 71; the Wahhabi state subject to, 229

Egyptian army, the, Mohammed Ali on, 125–126

Egyptian expeditions against the Wahhabis, Europeans with, 107 *et seq.*

Egyptian trade with Arabia, 20

El Ahkaf, desert of, 208

El Makranah, Varthema's account of, 65

El Ula, oasis of, 48

Elesbaan, Abyssinian king, invades Yemen, 37

Englishmen in Arabia, the first, 76 *et seq.*

Equator, the, crossed, 52

Equatorial Africa and the Burton-Speke controversy, 186

Eratosthenes, 33

Eritrea, plants of, Schweinfurth on, 202

Euclid, works of, in Arabic, 44

Euphrates, the, 23, 29, 44, 286

Euting, Julius, with Huber, 265, 266

FALKENER, SIR WILLIAM, 84

Farajja, 320, 325

Farazdaq, poet, birthplace of, 330

Feid, 50

Feisal, Wahhabi Emir, sons of, quarrels between, 230; and Palgrave, 253; breaks off relations with Indian Government, 259; and Pelly, 261; death of, 261

Fezzan, 118, 161

Finati, Giovanni, of Ferrara, story of, 107–108

Forbes, Rosita, journey of, to Asir, 301; to Kufra, 328

Forskal, Peter, botanist, in Yemen, 88 *et seq.*, 222, 300; death of, 97; work of, on Yemen flora, 101

Fort Muweila, 187, 188, 190

"Fortunate Isles," the, 33

Frankincense, Herodotus and, 21; imposts on, 31; Carter and the trade in, 203–204

Frankincense country, the, ports of, 32, 213

Frankincense route, the, 310

Frankincense-tree, Ibn Battuta on, 51; yield of, 213; character and collection of, 213, 219; wild, 322

Frederick V of Denmark and an Arabian expedition, 88

Fresnel, Fulgence, and the Wadi Duwan, 205; von Wrede supported by, 210

Frumentius, Christian missionary, 36

Fukara, tribe, 270, 272

Fuljes (horseshoe-shaped hollows), the, 282–283

GADES (Cadiz), Eastern trade of, 31

Gallus, Ælius, Arabian campaign of, 25–26, 28, 29, 32

Gama, Estavão da, attack on Suez by, 72

Gama, Vasco da, 67, 72

Garland, Captain, travels of, 302

Gaza, 26, 47, 243, 257

Gaza-Katif journey of Palgrave, 257, 295

Germans in the Hejaz in 1915, 303–304

Gerra, 23, 323; Strabo on, 29; decay of, 41. *See also* Oqair

Ghassan, kingdom of, 35

Ghersid, Wadi, beauties of, 219

Ghrazzu, the; 18

Ghudun, Wadi, 313, 314

Gibbon, Edward, 87; sources of, for Islam and Arabia in *Decline and Fall*, 102–103

Glascock, Philip, 77

Glaser, E., in Yemen, 102 and *n.*

Goa, 68, 70

Good Hope, Cape of, rounded by Portuguese, 52; results, 67

Great Southern Desert—*see* Rub' al Khali

Great War, the, and Arabia, 11, 290, 291, 301 *et seq.*, 327, 328, 329

Greek expedition to Arsinoë, 20 *et seq.*

Grelaudière, Major de la, 90

Guarmani, Carlo, mission of, to buy Arab horses in the Nejd, 264–265; maps by, 265; Doughty and, 265

Gubbe—*see* Jubba

Guinea coast, slaves and gold from, 52

Gulashkird, 22

Gurandel, Wadi, 232

HABBAN, 211

Habbash (Taif), 84 and *n.*

Hadhramaut, produce of, 16, 305; Niebuhr on, 99; inland trade from, 203, 305; variants of the name, 204; the Seyyids of, 205, 211, 304; physical features and incense-trees of, 206, 213; incense trade of, 206, 213; East Central, von Wrede's report of, 210; ruins in, 211; Hirsch's travels in, 211, 306, 307; Addite ruins in, 212; Bedouin of, 214; Bent prevented from visiting, 221; Eastern, tomb, ruins, and volcano in, 221–222; wealth in, source of, 222–223; emigration from, 223, 305–306; knowledge of, in 1900, 291; first journey of this century into, 304; slaves and the slave trade of, 304–305, 306; conditions in, Lee-Warner on, 304–305; water supply in, 305; motor vehicles in, 306; O. H. Little in, 311

Hadhramaut, Wadi, 12, 102, 212, 213; country at its reaching the sea, Haines on, 203; towns in, 210, 214 *et seq.*; the first European to reach, 211; collateral *wadis* of, features noticed in, 213–214

Hadjy, title of, the essential qualification for, 140

Hafa, 218, 219

Hafar, wells of, 295

Haibalgabrain, 212

Hail, 16, 327; emirate of, 230; struggles affecting, 230; visited by Wallin, 232, 239; described by Wallin, 237, 239; house of Abdulla Ibn Rashid at, 237–238; visited by Palgrave, the city centre of his ideal state, 247 *et seq.*; the Emir's stud at, Lady Anne Blunt's notes on, 285; ruler of, and Guarmani, 265; visited by Huber, 265, 266; visited by Doughty,

269, 271, 289; visited by the Blunts, 283 *et seq.*; new altitude measurements of, 286; Gertrude Bell at, 292

Haines, Captain S. B., I.N., South Arabian coastal survey by, 193, 199–200, 210; observations of, quoted, 200–201, 202–203

Haj, the, and the prosperity of Mecca, Burckhardt on, 132–133; the great routes travelled by, 134–135

Hajar, Wadi, 208, 311

Hajarein, 216, 310, 311

Halévy, Joseph, 102, 313

Hamad desert, 15 and *n.*; crossed by Wallin, 232

Hamad bin Hadi, guide, fear of, for the Sa'ar, 324–325

'Hamail,' the, Burton's use of, 173–174

Hamdh, Jizil, and Ais, Wadis, confluence of, 303

Hamdh, Wadi, 274; mapping of, 302

Hanifa, Wadi, 16, 227; column at, 260

Haramain, the, the first Englishman to visit—*see* Pitts, Joseph

Haran, Selaib of, place of pilgrimage, 263

Harb, tribe, 104, 174, 230, 304

Harid, Wadi, battle at, 25

Haroun al Raschid, 50

Harra, the, 16, 109, 274; Burton on, 186; Lady Anne Blunt on, 277–278

Harris, W. B., Sana described by, 102

Harrison, P. W., on the Bedouin of the oases, etc., 298

Hasa, 12, 105, 224, 257, 291, 329; Sadlier on, 226; Turkish occupation of, and interest in, 230, 289; Palgrave's alleged crossing of, 258; Philby on, 246; Philby's trouble concerning, 336, 338

Hasa coast lands, 14

Hatshepsut, Queen, expedition sent by, to Dhofar, 20

Hauta, 211

Haven, Frederick von, 88; death of, 94

Hejaz, the, richest tribe in, 38; Christians in, 39; Niebuhr on, 99; European sources of knowledge of, 104, 193; travellers in, useful observations of, 108 *et seq.*; Burckhardt's travels in, 119 *et seq.*; night attacks in, 154; Ibrahim's return into, 226; British activities in the Great War based on, 290; Ali Bey's observations in, 291; knowledge of, in 1900, 291; Western, travellers in, 302; unsurveyed area of, 291, 303

Hejaz Railway, 11, 47, 296, 302

Hejaz Revolt, the, 301
Henry the Navigator, 52
Herbelot, B. d', book by, on Arab writers, 52, 103
Herod, 25
Herodotus, 20, 21
Hieron, expedition of, 22
Himam, Wadi, 304, 310
Himyar the Red, 19
Himyarites, the, 23; language of, inscriptions of, 102 and *n.*, 204, 208, 210; ruins of, found by the Bents, 216, 217
Hippalus, 28
Hipparchus, founder of trigonometry, 32; world-map idea of, 33
Hira, kingdom of, 35; heretical Christians in, 36
Hirsch, Leo, travels of, in the Hadhramaut, 211, 306, 307
Hodeida, town of, 92, 299; Danish expedition sails to, 91; route from, to Sana, Bury on, 299–300
Hofuf, 15, 224, 226; Palgrave's description of, 258; geographical position of, 261 and *n.*; attack on, Turks removed from, 289–290; Cheesman's journey from, to Zarnuga, 312; Philby's start from, 329
Hogarth, Dr D. G., 11, 239, 304; on Wallin, 231 *n.*; on Palgrave, 245, 257; book by, 245; on the *fulj*, 282–283; on Gertrude Bell, 292
Holy cities of Arabia, the first Englishman in, 83 *et seq. See also* Mecca *and* Medina
Holy Land, the, pilgrims to, 41
Howeitat, tribe, 149, 232, 295
Huber, Charles, journeys of, from Jauf to Hail, and inscriptions seen by, 265; murder of, 266; notes of, for mapping Northern Arabia, 266
Hud, the prophet, and his shrine, Kabr Hud, 209, 217, 307–308, 309, 310, 323; shrine visited by von Wrede, 209; miracles attributed to, 217
Hulayfa, mosque of, donning the *ihram* at, 48
Humboldt, Baron F. G. von, 210
Hureida, 306, 310
Hurgronje, J. Snouck, visit of, to Mecca, 186
Hussein, Sherif of Mecca, 320, 327; support of, to Britain, and conquest of, by Ibn Saud, 290; and the Germans, 304; and Philby's mission, 327
Huteym, group of Bedouin, 190

Huwera, Wadi, 212
Hyderabad, 305, 306

IBHA, capital of Asir, position of, unknown, 302; visited by Philby, 311
Ibn Battuta, travels of, 46 *et seq.*; works of, first appearance of, 52
Ibn Daas, at Manfuha, 105
Ibn Haukal, book by, 44
Ibn Jiluwi and Philby, 329–330, 336
Ibn Khurdadbih, geographer, 44
Ibn Muammar, at Ayaina, 105
Ibn Saud, Wahhabi ruler, capital of, 16; territory of, 193; and the revival of Wahhabism, 290; campaign of, against Ibn Rashid, 290; British treaty of friendship with, 290; Hussein conquered by, 290–291, 328; and Shakespear, 290, 295; and Rutter, 298; and Philby, 327, 329
Ibra, oasis town, architecture of, 195–196
Ibrahim Pasha, campaign of, against the Wahhabis, 107, 225, 227, 259; rule of, in Upper Egypt, 125; Sadlier's mission to, 225 *et seq.*
"Ideal State" of Palgrave, 248, 283–284
Idrisi, early geographer, 45, 102, 104; work of, printed, 52
Idrisi, ruler, authority of, 302
Ihram, the, 48 *n.*
Ikhwan movement, meaning of, 290
Imam Sherif, Khan Bahadur, Bent's companion, 212
Incense, plants, trade, and trees, 21, 22, 23, 24, 27, 29, 30, 31, 32, 213; decline of the trade, 35. *See also* Frankincense
India, way to, opening of, 52; Alboquerque's scheme concerning, 71; Burton in, 163; Hadrami commercial property in, 222–223
Indus, the, 20, 21, 23, 28
Iraq (Mesopotamia), 239, 292
Irwin, Eyles, coastal travels of, 104
Isaac and the devil, 62
Islam, 39; effect of, on the incense trade, 35; a forced conversion to, 83; Sunnite sect and, Niebuhr on, 100
"Isle of the West," 204
Ismail Pasha, Khedive, and Burton's Midian expedition, 187 *et seq.*, 190
Istakhri, 44

JABIR IBN FEISAL, and Philby, 331–332
Jabrin, 224, 293, 329; Cheesman, at 312; route to, and Philby's views on, 330–331

Jaffa, storm damage at, 41

Janszoon, Hendrik, 82

Jauf, 240, 267, 290, 299, 311; wells of, 15; Southern, 23; drainage problem of, 102; Wallin at, 232; compared with Jubba, 233; Palgrave's objective, and description of, 243, 246; Guarmani at, 264

Jawasimi pirates, crushing of, 225

Jebel Akhdar, 99, 196, 199, 313

Jebel Garrah, 200

Jebel Kora, 122

Jebel Radhwa, 171, 302

Jebel Shammar, visited by Wallin, 235; visited by Guarmani, 265; visited by Doughty, 269; new altitude measurements of, 286

Jebel Shera, 283

Jebel Zahura, 207

Jedayda, Tussun defeated at, 175

Jerusalem, 266

Jesus, tomb space for, at Medina, 178

Jewish geographers, the first of the, 44–45

Jewish-Arabian persecutions of Christians, 36–37

Jews, 35 et seq., 56–57; medieval, as middlemen of Oriental trade and as explorers, 44; cities of the, 45; persecution of, at Sana, 95–96; in Yemen, 302

Jidda, 47, 76, 89, 90, 109, 228, 266, 269, 305; merchandise from, 45; Varthema's life at, and observations on, 62–63; Danish expedition at, 90–91; Burckhardt's account of, 119–122; mixed population of, 120; Indian trade at, 120–121; trades pursued at, 121; pilgrims at, 135; beggars and menially employed pilgrims at, 135–136; capture of, 301

Jizan, 193; produce at, 63

Jizil, Wadi, 302

John II of Portugal, 52

Jomard, E. F., on Ptolemy's mapping, 33; use made by, of Sadlier's work on Nejd, 229

Jourdain, John, 76, 77; Aden described by, 78; journey of, to Sana, 76, 78; description of Sana by, 79–80; stay of, at Taizz, 80; death of, at Patani, 82

Jubba, Wallin's account of, 232 et seq.

Juheina, tribe, Burckhardt on, 149

Jurayjuray, Palgrave's companion, 242

KAABA, the, as pagan shrine, 37–38, 130, 185; the Black Stone fetish in,

38; Varthema on, 60–61; Ali Bey on, 110 et seq.; Burckhardt's account of, 119, 126 et seq.

Kabr Salih, the Bents at, 217

Kahtan Bedouin, the, and Doughty, 271

Kaiti rulers of Mokalla, 211; in the Hadhramaut, wealth and xenophobia of, 223

Kasim, 16, 224; Guarmani arrested in, 265; Turks driven from, 289; visited by Philby, 327

Kasr, Wadi, 306

Katabanu, Arabian kingdom, 23

Katan, 310; Bent at, 214

Katar, 330; sandhills of, 325

Katha edulis, effects of eating, 300–301

Katif, 15, 193, 224; military expedition to, of the East India Company, 228; Palgrave at, 257; Turks evacuated from, 290

Keane, John F., visit of, to Medina and Mecca, and book by, 190–191

Kefyl, the, functions of, 154

Keith, Thomas, Agha of Mamelukes and Governor of Medina, 107

Kenne, patronal festival at, 128

Kerak, castle at, 48

Kerbela, 286

Khalfah, Hajji, book by, on Nejd, 224

"Khalil" (Doughty), still remembered on the Hejaz frontiers, 272; well spoken of at Aneiza, 295

Khalil Agha (Carlo Guarmani), 264

Khar, Wadi, Leachman's notes on, 293

Kharj, 12, 328; Cunliffe-Owen at, 327

Khatiya, ruins, 220

Kheibar, 274; the harra of, 16; "Mountain of the Jews," 56–57; population of, 264; Guarmani's visit to, discredited by Doughty, 265; Doughty's visit to, 269, 271; volcanic areas between Tebuk and, 274

Khor Rori, ruins at, visited by the Bents, Carter, and Thomas, 203, 220, 317

Khuraiba, 209, 310

Khurshid Pasha, 125

Kilthut and Musellim, 321

Kinda, tribe, supremacy of, 35

Kiryat, 72

Kishm Island, 22

Koran, the, Burckhardt's knowledge of, 118, 122; Burton's memorizing of, 163

Koreish, tribe, 35, 138; Abraha's expedition against, failure of, 38

Kuba, 176; mosque of, Burton at, 178

Kuntilla, 295

INDEX

Kurdistan, Anatolia, and Syria, Leachman's travels in, 293
Kuweit, British treaty with, 193; country beyond, 260; Turkish interest in, 289

LAHEJ, 301; Varthema's account of, 65
Lauka, Gertrude Bell at, 292
Lawrence, T. E., 151, 295, 317; on the heat at Jidda, 119–120; Arab tribes mentioned by, 149; on the land near Yenbo, 174; famous book by, 242; discipleship of, to Doughty, 276, 292; on Blunt in old age, 288; geographical work of, 302–303
Leachman, Captain G. E., on the Selaib, 263–264; Arabian journeys of, political value of, 292–294; murder of, 294
Lebanon, the, 118
Ledanum, 21
Lee-Warner, Captain W. H., journey of, to Wadi Duwan and Shibam, 304, 310
Lees, G. M., journeys of, in Oman, 312
Leina, 293
Leuke Kome, 24, 25, 27
Levant trade and the Crusades, 41
Lisbon, Venice supplanted by, in spice trade, 67
Little, O. H., journey of, in Hadhramaut, 311
Lith, 303
Loheia, 91–92
Lunt, William, 212

MAAN, 232; described by Palgrave, 243; visited by Doughty, 268; position of, rectified, 303
Maazeh, tribe, 189
Madeira, 33
Maffei (*Historiæ indicæ*), G. P., 73
Maghair ("Madiama" of Ptolemy), 188
Maghrabis on Burton's vessel, 169–170
Mahbub, Wazir, and Pelly, 261
Mahra country closed to the Bents, 221
Mahra Desert, 204
Ma'in, city, 23, 102
Ma'in, kingdom, 23
Makalla—*see* Mokalla
Malta, 121, 126
Maltzan, Baron von, von Wrede's journal published by, 210
Mamelukes, the, 123; privileges of, 55; Varthema enrolled among, 55 *et seq.*;

Varthema deserts, 62; Mohammed Ali's struggle with, 106
Manfuha, cultivation near, 226
Manzoni, Alessandro, 102
Manzoni, Renzo, at Sana, 102, 297
Maqainama, 312; well at, 332
Marib (Mariaba), capital of Saba, 23, 24, 25, 26 and *n.*
Marib dam, 24, 102 and *n.*
Marib–Dhofar incense route, 310
Marinus of Tyre, world map of, 33; works of, in Arabic, 44
Marsyaba, or Maryama, Roman siege of, 25
Mashonaland, Bent's work in, 222
Masudi, travels of, 44, 45
Matrah, 72
Maude, General, 291
Mayuf and Khuwaitim, 318, 319
Mecca, 17, 262, 269; Christians near, 39, 41; fair women of, 40 *n.*; pilgrimages to, 41, 73, 83, 134; geographical knowledge gained from pilgrims to, 43; Ibn Battuta, journey of, to, 46–49, 50; Ibn Battuta's account of the inhabitants of, 49–50; journey of Ibn Battuta from, to Baghdad, 50; Varthema at, 53, 59–60; Varthema's account of "the pardoning" at, 60 *et seq.*; trade and traders of, 60, 147–148; the first Englishman to visit, 83; his account of, 84–85; interest centred in, 104; Wahhabi conquest of, 106; Wahhabism unpopular at, 109; position of, attempt to fix astronomically, 109 and *n.*; the Sherif of, 109; his methods, 109; "the Chief of the Well" at, 109–110; the temple at, described by Ali Bey, 110 *et seq.*; Burckhardt's visit to, and description of, 119, 126 *et seq.*, 144 *et seq.*; the Kadi at, surprised by Burckhardt, 122; water-carriers of, and their song, 134; Burton at, 162, 184–185; Huber at, 266; two twentieth-century accounts of, 297; the Sherif of (Hussein), 327; Philby retires to, 328
Medain Salih, banned water at, 48; rock-cut houses of, 241; inscribed cliffs at, Doughty's visit to, 268, 269
Medina, 48, 50, 227, 228, 271; ignorance concerning, 11; pagan pilgrim route from, to Mecca, 26 *n.*; a relic of Mohammed at, 48; Varthema's account of, 57 *et seq.*; mosque at, and Mohammed's tomb, 57 *et seq.*,

85–86, 99, 177–178; Alboquerque's scheme as to, 71; first Englishman to visit, his account of the place, 83, 85, 86; Burckhardt at, 119, 148, 186; arrival and life at, Burton on, 176 *et seq.*; and the Medani, described by Burton, 178–180; Wallin at, 238; and Mecca, region between, unsurveyed, 291–292; two twentieth-century accounts of, 297; longitude of, unknown in 1920, 303; Turkish staff map of, 303

Meifa, Wadi, 211

Mekkawys, the, 131; Burckhardt on, 132–133

Mengin, Félix, on Ptolemy's mapping, 33; book by, on Egypt, 228

Mermaids' island, a, 21

Meroua, ritual walk between, and Szafa, 127, 128–129

Meshed, 310; Himyaritic ruins near, 216, 306

Meshed Ali, Wallin at, 239, 240

Mesopotamia, 327. *See also* Iraq

Meulen, Dr D. van der, expedition of, in the Hadhramaut, 305–306; on Hud, 307–308; photographs by, 311

Michaelis of Göttingen, 88

Middleton, Sir Henry, 90; imprisoned at Aden, and his revenge, 81

Midian, 239; Burton's search for gold in, 187 *et seq.*

Miles, Colonel S. B., explorations of, in Oman, Bireima reached by, 199; travels of, in Arabia, 210–211; on Palgrave, 258

Minæan power, the, chief towns of, 23; language of, 102

Minna, cultivation at, 196

Mirbat, 213; and Ras Risut, country between, 218

Misenat, 200

Moahib, tribe, 270, 272

Mocha, in the *Periplus*, 32; as *entrepôt*, 76, 77; shipping at, 78; and its trade system, described by Revett, 80–81; Niebuhr voyaging to, 90, 91; trouble at, of the Danish expedition, 93–94; English trade advantages at, 97; French bombardment of, 97

Mohammed, the Prophet, 104; tribe of, 35; attitude of, to Jews, heathen Arabs, and Christians, 39; and the water of Medain Salih, 48; tomb of, at Medina, 57 *et seq.*, 85–86, 99, 177–179; body of, Alboquerque's plan to seize, 71; rule of, 130–131

Mohammed Abdulla, companion of the Blunts, 279–280

Mohammed Ali, Pasha, 225, 228; expeditions of, against the Wahhabis, 101, 106–107; Finati with, 108; and Suez, 121; at Taif, interviews of, with Burckhardt, 122 *et seq.*; and the English, 124; gains of, from pilgrims to Jidda, 135; at the Arafat ceremony, 139; and the battle of Byssel, 151, 152; and Wallin, Hogarth on, 231 *n.*

Mohammed el Basyuni, Burton's companion-servant, 168

Mohammed Ibn Rashid, Emir of Hail, 230; and Doughty, 270–271; and the Kahtan Bedouin, 271; manner of speaking of, 275; Lady Anne Blunt on, 284; victory of, 230, 289; and Philby, 327

Mohammed Ibn Saud, of Dariya, and the Wahhabis, 106

Mohammedanism, in Niebuhr's view, 99

Mokalla (Makalla), 210; British treaty with, 193; Haines on, 200–201; slave trade at, 200–201; Kaiti governors of, 211; the Bents' journey from, 212; Philby at, 311

Monsoon, the, 19, 22, 67, 81; utilization of, 28

Moresby, Captain, 188, 193

Morris, William, 276

"Moscha," 221

Moslem trade ships harried by the Portuguese, 67

Moslem travellers, defects in accounts given by, 42

Moslem views, Western habits offensive to, 89, 189

Mucke, — von, landing of, at Lith in 1915, 303

Muhanna, battle of, 289

Mulaida, battle of, 230, 289

Müller, Captain von, at Jidda, fate of, near Rabegh, 304

Muna, Wadi, rites at, 85; described by Burckhardt, 126, 136, 142 *et seq.*

Murra, tribe, 320; wanderings of, 312

Murshadi, Sheikh el, 47

Muscat, 72, 198, 199, 217; Niebuhr at, 99; trans-desert journey from, to Mecca never attempted, 185; Wellsted on, 194; Sadlier at, 225; Palgrave's error as to, 258; crossing from, to Aden projected, 313

Musil, Alois, maps by, 266, 291

Musliman, Mount, 233, 234–235

INDEX

Muweila, 238
Muzdalifa, mosque of, 62, 142
Myos Hormos, 23, 26, 45

NABATHÆANS, of Petra, 23; and Augustus, 25 *et seq.*; wars of, 35
Nahiz, Wadi, 220
Naifa, 333, 337; singing sands at, 336
Najaf, Gertrude Bell at, 292
Najil, Wadi, 188
Nakab el Hajar, ruins of, 204; von Wrede's attempt to reach, 208
Napier, Sir Charles, 163
Napoleon I, 30; and Ali Bey, 109; at Elba, 124, 126
Napoleon III, Palgrave financed by, 242–243, 245; and Guarmani, 264
Nasca (now Baida), taken by Rome, 25
Nazareth, Lady Hester Stanhope at, 118
Nearchus, exploration of, 21, 32
Neckham, Alexander, knowledge of, of the magnet, 40
Nefud, the, 15, 104; width of, 224; Wallin's crossings of, 232, 235, 240, 246; Palgrave's crossing of, 246–247; Nolde's crossing of, 266; colour and charm of, 278, 280 *et seq.*, 296 *n.*; origin of, Hogarth on, 283; horses bred in, 285; Shakespear's crossing of, 295
Negrana, taken by Rome, 25
Negro pilgrims, Saud's respect for, 136
Nejd, 176; Western, geology of, 14; a Turkish work on, 224; Northern, Burckhardt's knowledge of, 224; soil of, 236; horses of, Guarmani's mission to buy, 264; Southern, unexplored at end of nineteenth century, 267; the first Europeans openly visiting, 277; the Blunts in an exciting incident in, 279; horses of, rarity of, 285; oases in, Philby on, 327–328; Philby's knowledge of, 328
Nejd al Ared, 224.
Nejd al Yemen, 224
Nejran, 26 and *n.*, 224, 267, 312; Christianity in, and its end, 39; massacre at, 37; Jews in, 102; Philby in, 311
Nejran, Wadi, 25
"Nesca," site of, 102
Nezwa, 196
Niebuhr, Karsten, 92–93, 97, 104, 193, 224, 231, 299; confirming Varthema, 65; and the Danish Arabian expedition, 88 *et seq.*; on Sana, and on the Jews there, 94–96; book by, 97

et seq., 101; on Wahhabism, 99–100, 106; work of, value of, for Arabia as well as Yemen, 102; value of, to Gibbon, 103; area explored by, 119
Niger, the, 162; sources of, Burckhardt's intended exploration of, 118
Nile, the, 23, 26, 55, 71, 118
Nile Delta, as a trade clearing-house, 45
Nisab, Wadi, 211
Nizam Djedyd, the, 125
Nolde, Baron E., on Palgrave, 245; visit of, to Hail, route followed, 266
Nomads, tribal organization of, 17. *See also* Bedouin
Numan Ibn Mundir, protector of Christians, 36

OASES, 16
Obri, 197, 198
Ohod, Mount, 176
Oman, 12, 72, 217; mountains of, 15; Mesopotamians at, 20; Arabian coast beyond, 23; Ibn Battuta at, 51; history of, 193 *et seq.*; rulers of, British co-operation with, 225; Palgrave on, 258; knowledge of, in 1900, 291; Lees' journey in, 312
Omar, and the end of Arabian Christianity, 39
Omra, the, the visit to, 127, 129, 131
Omran, tribe, 149
Ophir, 323; Phœnician voyage to, 20
Oqair, 312; Turks evacuated from, 290. *See also* Gerra
Orma, wells at, 260
Ormuz, 68, 70, 75; barrenness of, 51; the Jesuit missionary at, 72–73
Oryx, from the Nefud, 284–285, 286, 296

PALESTINE, pipe-line between Iraq and, 291
Palgrave, W. G., 18, 228, 241; opinions on, 202, 244–246, 257–259, 268, 328; Arabian journey of, 248 *et seq.*, 277, 295; books by, 243, 259 *n.*
Palinurus, Indian Navy survey ship, Red Sea and other surveys of, 188, 193, 199, 203, 206, 210, 313
Palmyra, 118
Pantenæus, Christian missionary, 36
Parthia, 23, 32
Paul, martyr bishop, 37
Pelly, Colonel Lewis, journey of, to Riyadh, 259 *et seq.*; maps by, 291
Perim, 71, 78
Periplus maris erythræi, the, on Arabian coasts and ports, 31–32

355

Persian Gulf, the, 19, 29, 257; heat in, 12; highlands of, 12; Nearchus in, 21–22; Christian traders in, 41; Ibn Battuta in, 51; Covilham in, 52; pirates of, 107, 225, 259; British influence in, 193; Royal Geographical Society's desire for information on country between, and Riyadh, 259; unsurveyed areas beside, 291; reached by Thomas, 325

Persian pilgrims, returning, the Blunts journey with, 286

Petra, 24, 27; under Roman rule, 23; trade of, 26; described by Strabo, 29; decay of, 41; site of, discovered by Burckhardt, 118, 161; visited by Doughty, 268

Philby, H. St J. B., journeys of, knowledge gained by, of Central Arabia, 302, 327; journey of, in 1936, 311; penetration of the Rub' al Khali by, 326, 327 et seq.; book by, 327, 333, 339; Palgrave discredited by, 328; award to, by the Royal Geographical Society, 328; adoption by, of Islam, and home of, at Mecca, 328; an Arab view of, 337

Phœnician trade with Ophir, 20

Pilgrim caravans, Wahhabi and other raids on, 106, 231, 236

"Pilgrimage Pass," the, dangers of, 176

Pilgrimages, to Mecca, 17; to the Holy Land, 41; geographical knowledge gleaned from Meccan, 43

Piracy, in the Red Sea, 22; at Algiers, 83; on the Oman coast, 193; in the Persian Gulf, 107, 225, 259

Pitts, Joseph, of Exeter, first Englishman to visit the Haramain, 83 et seq., 104; book by, cited, 84 et seq.

Pliny, 102, 216, 217; and his knowledge of Arabia, 30–31

Portuguese, the, in Arabia, 52–53, 67 et seq.; use by, of the Cape route, 67; overthrow of, 81

Prester John, 71

Ptolemaic astronomical system, the, 32–33

Ptolemy, Claudius, 45, 102; honesty of, impugned by Bunbury, 33; geography of, and map by, 33–34, 40, 44

Ptolemy I, expedition to the Red Sea sent by, 22

Ptolemy II, trade between Egypt and Yemen begun by, 22

Ptolemy III, piracy in the Red Sea suppressed by, 22

Punt, reached by Egyptian ships, 20

QARA MOUNTAINS, 218, 219, 313, 316, 318, 322

Qara, tribe, 218, 219, 220, 318

Quadras, Gregorio da, Arabian journey of, 73 et seq.

RABEGH, 266

Rakiyut, 213

Ramadan, 320, 325; at Cairo, Burton on, 167, 168

Ramlat al Mugshin, 314

Ras el Hadd, 200

Ras el Kheima, pirates of, harried by Ibrahim Pasha, 225

Ras Fartak, 28, 221; Haines on, 201

Ras Musendam, 21

Ras Risut, 218, 219

Rasha, Wadi, 208

Rashid, house of, rise of, 286–288

Rass, 227; Egyptian conquest of, 107

Raunkiaer, B., journey of, from Kuweit to Oqair, 295

Red Sea, the, 11, 52, 228; heat in, 12; features of, 19; origin of the name, 19; expedition of Philo down, 22; piracy in, 22; commerce in, 23–24, 41, 45; coast of, Strabo on, 29; gaps in knowledge of coast of, in 1914, 302; navigation in, dangers of, 44, 51, 63; Alboquerque's scheme to close, to Moslem commerce, 67, 68; Alboquerque's voyage in, 71–72; Burton on his voyage in, 168 et seq.; British naval patrols in, 302, 303

Reeves, E. A., 296

Reinaud, —, mission of, to the Wahhabi Emir, 224

Religion, Arabian, Niebuhr's views on, 99–100

Rema, wells of, 226

Renegade, a, Pitts' tale of, 86–87

Revett, William, on the Straits of Bab el Mandeb, 77–78

Rihani, Ameen, travels of, in Yemen, 96, 301–302

Ristoro of Arezzo, 40

Risut, 213

Ritter, Karl, map of Arabia by, 241; on von Wrede, 210

Riyadh, 224, 227, 327; conquest of, 230; unvisited by Wallin, 238, 239; Palgrave's route to, stay at, and account of, 252 et seq.; a dramatic incident at, 254–256; Pelly's observations at, and map of, 261 and n., 291; power regained by, over Central Arabia, 289; meeting at, of Leachman

INDEX

and Ibn Saud, 293; Shakespear at, 295; population of, 328

Rizat, 220

Roberts, R. E., on Doughty and Burton, 273–274

Roger II of Sicily, 45

Roman Empire, Strabo's panorama of, 32

Roman expedition to Saba, 24 *et seq.*

Romans, the, and Egypt and Arabia, 23 *et seq.*

Rome, trade of, with East, 30–31; interest of, in Arabia lost, 35

Royal Air Force, Arabia revealed by, 291, 308 *et seq.*

Royal Geographical Society, 210, 240, 241, 312; and Palgrave, 245; and Pelly's Arabian journey, 259; and positions of Riyadh and Hofuf, 261 and *n.*; Huber's last journey plotted by, 266; award by, to Philby, 328

Rualla Bedouin, 151, 232, 264, 293

Rub' al Khali, the, 15, 16, 204; camels of, 151; crossing of, suggested by Burton, 164; South-western, Bedouin fears of, 208–209; unexplored before 1930, 267, 292, 312, 313; Leachman's plan to explore, 293; crossings of, effected by Thomas and by Philby, 313, 317 *et seq.*, 328, 329 *et seq.*; fringes of, explorers of, 312; sands of, 314, 315; tribes of, habits of, 314–315; steppe of, 315; vegetation and animal life of, 315; the "singing sands" of, 323–324, 339; use of the term, 333; natural history and geology of, Philby on, 339

Rubruck, William of, travels of, 40

Rumma, Wadi, 14, 274, 296

Rüppell, Edward, map by, 188

Rutter, Eldon, account of and pilgrimage to the holy cities by, 297–298; book by, 298; journey of, from Damascus to Hail, 311

SA'AR, tribe, danger among, 320, 321–322, 323

Saba, kingdom of, 23; Himyarite kings of, Abyssinian strife with, 35

Sabæans, the, kingdom of, 23; Romans' regard for country of, 24; language of, 102; temples of, ruins of, 218; inscriptions of, 294

Sabya, visited by Rosita Forbes, 301

Sadlier, Captain G. F., 268; embassy of, to Ibrahim Pasha, 225–228, 259; first Englishman to explore and first to cross Arabia, 226, 295, 327

Sæwulf of Worcester, cited, 11; travels and perils of, 41

Sahail, a Rashidi, 317, 318, 320

Saihut, trade at, 203

Sakaka, oasis, wells of, 15

Salala, 213; Bertram Thomas's starting-point, 313

Salih, Sheikh, and Bertram Thomas's journey in the Rub' al Khali, 319–320, 322, 324

Salim Abu Mahmud al-Ays (Palgrave), 242

Sallah ud Din (Rutter), 298

Salma, identification of, with Selma, 231

Salwa, ruins of, 312; salt flats of, Philby on, 330

Sana, 92, 99, 101; cathedral at, 37, 38, 39; daily rainfall at, 51; expedition against, 64; walls of, 65; the Pasha of, and Sharpeigh, 76–77; Jourdain's account of, 79–80; Barbier's journey to, 90; Danish expedition at, notes made by, 94–95; Jewish colony at, 95–96, 302; travellers describing, 102, 297; a honeymoon at, 299

Sands, areas of, 13; horseshoe pits in, 247, 281–282, 335; "singing," 323–324, 336, 339

Saud, 230; Abdulla's design against, 253 *et seq.*

Saud (the great), death of, 107

Saunders, Captain J. P., I.N., surveys by, off Dhofar, 203

Schweinfurth, G. A., on the plants of Yemen and Eritrea, 222

Scott, Francis, of Mocha, 94

Scott, Sir Walter, 248

Scylax, and the Arsinoë expedition, 20

Sedeir, 224

Sedus, 260

Seetzen, Ulrich Jaspar, 185, 231; travels of, in the Hejaz, visit to Mecca, and murder of, 116–117

Selaib nomads, Pelly on, 261 *et seq.*; Leachman on, 263–264; Philby on, 264

Seleucid monarchs, trade of, 23

Selma mountains, 235, 237

Semmed, oasis of, 196

Senaar, 123

Ser, Wadi, 216, 217

Serapis, temple of, at Canopus, 32

Seyun, 16, 205, 210, 211, 309, 310; Javanese influence at, 307

Seyyids, the, of the Hadhramaut, 205, 217, 304; castles of, 211

Shabwa, 310; von Wrede at, 208; Philby at, 311

Shakespear, Captain W. H. I., explorations of, and trans-Arabia journey, 16, 294 *et seq.*; and Ibn Saud, 290; death of, 290; astronomical observations taken by, 296
Shakik, wells at, 232
Shakra oasis, 227
Shammar region, settled and nomadic life in, 233, 237; power of popular feeling in, 287
Shammar, tribe, 230; Burckhardt on, 150–151; and the pilgrims, 231, 236; Wahhabism of, 232; area occupied by, 233–234; the people, town, and ruler of, 235 *et seq.*; methods of warfare of, 235–236; Leachman detained by, 293
Shanna, 320; Philby's journey to, and difficulties at, 335–336
Sharma, Wadi, 188
Sharpeigh, Alexander, at Aden, 76–77; at Mocha, 80; in India, 81
Sheher, Hirsch at, 211; Bent at, 221; Philby at, 311
Shendi, Burckhardt at, 119
Sheraa mountains, 243
Sherarat tribe, 232
Shibam, 16, 99, 210, 305, 310; fanatical Seyyids east of, 217; visited by Lee-Warner, 304; houses at, 306–307; country near, 308–309; places near, 309; Philby at, 311
Shinas, 198
Shisur, 322
Sib, 196, 199
Sidara, Mount, hills seen from, by von Wrede, 207
Sif, von Wrede at, 209–210; von Wissmann at, 306; Freya Stark at, 310
Silveira, Jorge da, 69
Simeon Stylites, St, 36
Simoon wind, Palgrave on, 244
Sinai–Alexandria trade route, 45
Sinai visited by Burckhardt, 161
Sindbad the Sailor, 46
Sirah, island of, captured by Alboquerque, 70; fort on, 78
Sirhan, Wadi, 15, 232, 246, 311; described by Lady Anne Blunt, 280
Sirra, Wadi, 16
Sirwa, capital of Saba, 23
Slave trade, Mokalla, 200–201; Hadhramaut, 304–305
Smith, General Sir Lionel, 194
Smith, officer of the *Palinurus*, as Ahmed, travels of, in the Subhan mountains, 202–203

Soares, Lopo, and Aden, 72
Socotra, plant life of, 203
Sofala, 52
Sohar, 72
Solomon and the Queen of Saba, 23
Somaliland, flora of, 222; Bury's expedition prepared in, 299
Sousa, Garcia da, 70
Spencer, Dr J. L., cited, 334
Spice regions, Arabian, 21, 22, 204, 205
Sprenger, A., Ptolemy's credit restored by, 33–34, 231
Stanhope, Lady Hester, 116, 118
Stark, Freya, journey of, in the Hadhramaut, book and photographs of, 310–311
Strabo, *Geography* of, 28, 33, 102; on Petra, etc., 29–30
Suakin, 50; Burckhardt at, 119
Subhan mountains, Haines on, 202–203
Suez, 168; E. da Gama's attack on, 72; Mohammed Ali's action as to, 121
Suez Canal, the, opening of, and Yemen, 101; Burton's forecast on, 167–168; project for, 243
Sulaiyil, 337; the end at, of Philby's journey, 332, 338–339
Suleiman Pasha, at Arafat, 139
Suleiman, Wali, ruler of Dhofar, 217–218
Sur, country of, Ibn Battuta on, 51
Sykes, Sir P., cited, 17, 252
Syllæus, Nabathæan Vizier, 26, 27; fate of, 28
Syria, Frankish conquest of, effect on trade routes of, 45; and Palestine, travels of Ibn Battuta in, 47; Burckhardt in, 118; Burckhardt's judgment of 'Arab' horses in, 150
Syrian pilgrim caravans, route taken by, 134, 135
Syro-Arabian desert, hermits in, 36
Szafa and Meroua, ritual walk between, 127, 128–129

TAIF, 303; Egyptian defeat near, 107; Burckhardt at, 119; and Jidda, country between, 122; Doughty at, 269, 272; visited by Rutter, 298; and Wadi Akik, 303; Philby at, 327
Taizz, 92, 117; Ibn Battuta on the inhabitants of, 31; Jourdain and the renegade at, 80
Taka, 213, 220
Tallal, Emir of Hail, 230, 235; and Palgrave, 250, 252

Tebuk, 48; Wallin on, 239
Teima, Wallin on, 240–241; Guar-
mani at, 264; Doughty's visits to,
269, 270
Teima Stone, the, 265, 266, 270
Terim, 16, 210, 217, 307, 308, 310;
Seyyid of, road-builder, 306
Tewfik Pasha, Khedive, 190
Thomas, Bertram, travels of, 16, 221;
cited, 189; on Palgrave, 258; ex-
ploration of, in the Rub' al Khali,
312, 313, 317 et seq.; book by, 317
Tiberius, Emperor, and Arabian
trade, 28
Tihama, 92
"Toani," Bent's theory on, 216
Tob el Kaaba, the, 112–113
Tor, 171
Towaf, the, 127–128, 129
Towns and settlements, 15
Trade routes, medieval, via Arabia, 43
Traders, Western, distant journeys of,
in Middle Ages, 41
Trajan, Emperor, 35
Travellers and traders in Arabia in the
Middle Ages, 40 et seq.
Travellers' tales, why unreliable, 34–35
Tripoli, 47
Trucial Coast, the, 193. See also Oman
Turkey and the Wahhabis, 106
Turki, restorer of the Wahhabi State,
229
Turks and Arabs, contrasted by
Niebuhr, 98
Tussun Pasha, defeat of, by the
Wahhabis, 106–107; a European
with, 107–108

Ubar, or Wabar, fabled city of, 323,
332 et seq.; silica-glass at, 334
Ubne, Wadi, 208
Umm al Hait, Wadi, 313, 314, 322, 323
Umm al Jabal, lake at, 328
Umm el Hadid, wells of, 333
Umm es Samim, quicksands of, 316
Umm Lej, 35

Vaissière, —, 107
"Valley of Hell, the," 48
Varthema, Ludovico di, travels of, in
Arabia, book by, and description of
Mecca and the Hejaz by, 54 et seq.,
64–65, 90, 104
Verde, Cape, passed in 1445, 52
Vincent of Beauvais, 40

Wabar—see Ubar
Wabra, 260

Wadis, 14
Wahhabis, the, Ibrahim Pasha's operations in dominion of, 107, 225,
227, 259; raids of, 106; extent of
domination of, 106, 289; rule of,
effect of, on commerce, 120, 122;
with Baghdad caravan, 182, 184;
plan to reduce power of, 225; vicissi-
tudes of, 229–230; revival of power
of, 328; and the pilgrims of the haj,
134, 135; characteristics of, noted
by Burckhardt, 149; invasion by, of
Oman, 193, 197–198; obstructive-
ness of, 224; country of, Wallin's
journey in, 231 et seq.; history of, 286;
Rutter's picture of, 298; Philby's
book on, 327
Wahhabism, Niebuhr on, 99, 100, 105;
renounced by Bedouin, 156; birthplace of, 224
Wakisa, 50
Wallin, G. A., 268, 277, 287; travels
of, in the Muweila region, 188, 295;
in the Wahhabi country, 231; on
Jubba, 232–233; at Mount Musliman, 234–235; on the people of Jebel
Shammar, 235 et seq.; book and
papers by, 238–239; biographies of,
241
Wavell, A. J., journey of, to the Haramain, holy cities, and Sana, 297
Weisit, 232
Wejh, 171, 193, 266; Lawrence's
journey from, to the Wadi Ais,
302–303
Wellsted, Lieutenant J., reconnaissance
by, in Oman, 194 et seq., 313;
estimates of, and fate of, 198–199;
at Nakab el Hajar, 204
Wild, J., book by, on Mecca and
Medina, 104
Wilson, Sir Arnold, 312
Wissmann, Dr H. von, on the Jews in
Yemen, 302; work of, in Yemen, etc.,
305–306, 308
Wrede, Adolf von, exploration by, to
the edge of the Great Desert, 206 et
seq., 306, 310

Xavier, St Francis, precepts of, 72

Yemama, Egyptian march through,
226; Palgrave's travels through, from
Riyadh, 257
Yemen, 12, 15, 17, 22, 24, 27, 32, 77,
78, 90, 99, 104, 106; coast of, 20,
25, 73; trade of, 30, 45, 92; Abyssinian dominion in, 35; Jews of, 36,
302; Christianity in, 36, 37; pilgrim-

ages to, 38; 'deserts' of, 44; governors and government of, 50, 78, 101; Ibn Battuta in, and its learned ruler, 50–51; the first European account of, 55; troops of apes in, 65; accounts of, by Varthema and by Niebuhr, 65; Turkish rule over, relaxation of, 78; shipping lanes to, plundered by Middleton, 81; Danish explorations across, 90, 92 *et seq.*; coffee of, 93; flora of, 101, 222; rock inscriptions in, 102; early information on, 104; West Indian trade competition with, 120; Sabæan ruins in, 210; the Jauf of, route to, from Nisab and Harib, 211; independence maintained by, 291; agriculture and coffee-growing in, 300; von Wissmann's work in, 305–306

Yenbo al Bahr, port, 71, 90, 104, 228; Burckhardt at, 119, 148; "the fountain of the sea," 171; Burton's description of, 172 *et seq.*; Garland's new route to, 302

ZAHLEH, Jesuit college at, 242
Zambei, Emir, wealth and raids of, 56
Zamil, Emir of Aneiza, 230; and Guarmani, 265
Zarnuga, Cheesman at, 312
Zebid, 73; Ibn Battuta on, 51; Varthema on, 65
Zemzem, well of, 38; Ali Bey on, 110, 115, 116; Burckhardton, 128, 130, 146
Zeyd, Sheikh, and Doughty, 270
Zilfi, 295
Zimbabwe, ruins at, 222
Zobeida, reservoirs provided by, 50